D0936126

MANAGEMENT:
AN
EXECUTIVE
PERSPECTIVE

Sigmund G. Ginsburg

University of Cincinnati

Robert F. Dame, Inc.
1905 Huguenot Road
Richmond, Virginia 23235

© Robert F. Dame, Inc. 1982

ISBN 0-936-328-07-X
Library of Congress Catalog No. 81-66815

PRINTED IN THE UNITED STATES OF AMERICA

Designed and typeset by Publications Development Co. of
Crockett, Texas, Developmental Editor: Nancy Marcus Land,
Production Editor: Bessie Graham

DEDICATION

For all my family and especially . . .

My parents, Rose and Saul, who came to this country with great hopes and dreams for themselves and their children and have provided a warm and wonderful heritage including a concern for high aspirations and achievement.

My wife, Judith, who shares and gives meaning to my life and who enriches, encourages and expands my aspirations while at the same time pursuing high aspirations of her own.

My children, Beth and David, who help make it all worthwhile and to whom I pass on the heritage with the hope that they will build on it, form their own visions and goals, strive with all their strength and achieve their aspirations, and in turn, pass this on to their children.

In memory of my best friend, Jay Galatan, who was a profile in courage.

For my role models and mentors, oustanding executives whom I am privileged to call my friends . . .

Harvey Sherman, who as my boss at the beginning of my career, encouraged me by precept and practice, and has remained an inspiration, a valued counselor and a resource.

Timothy W. Costello, my boss for twelve years who personifies a wise, successful, caring executive and supervisor, who encouraged and permitted me to fly as high and as fast as I could and whose friendship and wisdom is a constant source of strength and support.

For my readers . . .

In the hope that this effort will be of some value in encouraging and assisting them to excel in the challenge and joy of management.

INTRODUCTION

Successful, imaginative management is both a stimulating challenge and an invigorating joy. This book attempts to provide information, concepts, and ideas that will encourage and help the executive to be more successful in meeting the challenge. It also strives to encourage and increase the satisfaction that comes from performing executive functions and activities at a high level of competence and creativity.

Management can be fun! Managerial tasks can and should be approached with zest and enthusiasm. All too often, we, as professionals, have become calm, cool, and collected problem solvers, decision-makers . . . rational managers. This is valuable and indeed professional, but we need more heat and fire, more caring, passion, emotion, and concern as we strive to achieve the significant, to do better, to *be* better.

In our view, the successful executive applies both the art and science of management. There are management theories, concepts, processes, practices, techniques, and technology that can be applied, with modifications as necessary, to practically all management situations. These constitute the *science of management*. There are also elements of art in successful management—sensitivity, empathy, creativity, leadership, a concern for environment, culture, feelings. The successful executive combines some of the skills of the scientist, artist, salesman, dreamer, planner, counselor, preacher, warrior, diplomat, operator, and philosopher. He is a boss, colleague, peer, subordinate, teacher, student, mentor and role model. Let me point out here that executives, once were predominately male, but now are both male and female. Because the English language does not have a pronoun that adequately reflects both male and female and he/she is distracting, I have used the customary masculine words in a broad way to include both males and females.

The 1980s will be the decade of the manager. The United States as a nation faces critical needs to: maintain a viable and vibrant economy and a reasonably high standard of living; maintain reasonable and responsible levels of national defense and public services; increase productivity, job satisfaction, and dedication to the work ethic at all levels while being concerned about quality of life issues; increase the number and quality of jobs available and decrease unemployment and underemployment; increase access to jobs and advancement for women, minorities, and the handicapped; improve the balance of trade and our ability to compete with foreign nations; increase our energy independence; reindustrialize our nation; reduce regulations that hamper productivity, efficiency and increase costs and prices; increase basic and applied research and technology; increase innovation and entrepreneurship. Our success as a nation in meeting these needs depends, to one degree or another, upon increasing the effectiveness and competence of management within all organizations and institutions.

To an alarming degree we have become as managers and organizations, fat and sassy, lazy and sloppy, tolerant of mediocrity and merely getting by. In our concern for leading the good life and having a life style that stresses that there is much more to life than one's job, we have deemphasized the need for excellence in what we do. This watering down of standards, of cheapening the value of praise and recognition, permeates not only companies and organizations but also our educational systems. We are too much of a permissive, "laid back," mediocre level of aspiration society, and it affects each individual from kindergarten to graduate school through the upper rungs of management.

We need to be concerned about talent, enthusiasm, hard work, and striving for true distinction. Whatever one's position or job, we must develop the organization structure, environment, style, and executive leadership that encourages, demands, rewards full effort to the best of one's ability. We must strive to continually improve and expand each individual's ability and satisfaction and the ways in which the organization is able to maximize the talent and energy of employees at all levels.

There need not be a dichotomy between a concern for productivity and a concern for people. The good executive can focus on and excel at both, and in so doing derive great personal and professional satisfaction for himself. Beyond technical knowledge, techniques, and technology, the executive of today and tomorrow, needs the power and influence of interpersonal skills, personality, drive, empathy, and zest.

Executive management is a continuous learning and experimental process, tuned to new knowledge, situations, and growth and maturity of the individual. The challenge for the executive is to reach beyond one's grasp, to strive for excellence, to set ambitious and hard goals for himself, his unit, and organization. Complacency and acceptance must give way to challenge and a healthy dissatisfaction with the status quo. How we manage in the 1980s and the future decade will determine not only each individual person's or organization's success, but to a large measure the success of the United States as a world power and as a nation whose inhabitants enjoy a good, productive, and rewarding life.

This book is in three parts—management concepts and activities, essays on a variety of topics, and questions that people have raised in regard to management with responses. In the final chapter, we present a prognosis and prescription for the future. In Part I, concepts and activities of the executive are highlighted. We have specified particular activities in order to highlight what we believe are the most important elements of successful management. Another way of looking at management activities is to view a manager as fulfilling certain roles, such as leader, decision-maker, coordinator, collaborator, negotiator, linking pin, figure-head, spokesman, problem solver, etc. In the discussion of activities, the different roles played by a manager will be readily apparent.

This book is a personal statement. It draws upon the works of various management writers but it is largely based upon my own experience as an executive, consultant, observer of executives, teacher, and also upon discussions with other executives.

We will have met our aspirations if the reader is stimulated to believe he can apply some of what is written or if it provides some useful knowledge and pathways. We will have succeeded if the reader is sufficiently incensed to say, "this won't work," "it's better to do it that way," or, "the author didn't consider . . ." and then goes on to plan an original course of action.

The Appendix suggests a way of applying the thoughts in the book and the reader's own thoughts. There is also a listing of important books to use as references for continued growth and learning in management.

Management: An Executive Perspective is written for managers at all levels and those who aspire to management positions. It has been shaped by my experience and thus, I am indebted and grateful to the many people who over the past twenty years I have worked for and with, those I have supervised, colleagues in other organizations and industries who have shared their thoughts and experiences with me and my students who have stimulated and challenged me to think through issues and situations.

I am very grateful to my publisher, Robert F. Dame, for his enthusiasm, encouragement, support and assistance in turning my dream of this kind of approach in writing about management into a reality and to those who worked on the production of the book, particularly the Production Editor, Nancy Land. My administrative assistant, Betty Edington, and secretary, Julie Flammer, performed the difficult task of deciphering my handwriting and typing my class materials which became the foundation of the book and I wish to express my appreciation to them.

CONTENTS

I

MANAGEMENT CONCEPTS, ACTIVITIES, FUNCTIONS

one

Planning

All too often when post mortems are conducted on a project, program, or business that failed or fell short of expectations, the lack of sophisticated, careful, good, or sometimes even rudimentary planning is cited as the basic culprit. Cited equally often is the failure to implement a plan. Chapter One focuses on planning and the planning process. By *planning* we mean conscious analysis, development, and determination of courses of action in order to accomplish specific purposes, goals, and objectives.

Fundamental to successful planning is the need for the organization and its executives at all levels to assess where it is, how it got there, where it wants to be short and long term, and how to get there. In reaching an understanding of the here and now as well as the there and then, there should be a full analysis of the various internal and external factors that influence action, decision making and results.

FACTORS INVOLVED IN PLANNING

Internal factors within an organization include:

- The organization's history, tradition, prior decisions, commitments, and relationships.

3

- The capabilities of present staff—their age, experience, morale, motivation, aspirations, skills, concerns, weaknesses, strengths, growth potential, productivity, accomplishments.
- The ability to recruit staff to fill the gaps in present staff, to meet present and future needs.
- The present managerial and operating style, the reward and motivational structure, system and style, how the company deals with individual, division, and company success and failure.
- How the organization responds to dangers, risks, and opportunities.
- The manner and pace at which it is able to plan, assess, decide, implement, monitor, evaluate, and change course.
- The mood, momentum, psychology of the company, now and in the future.
- The adequacy of technology, physical plant and productive capacity for present and future needs and the ability to expand, repair, replace, and substitute new technology.
- The company's products or services and production processes.
- The research and development capability and the ability to install new products, services, and technology.
- The marketing and public relations capabilities of the company.
- The company's various assets—financial, human, material.
- The past and projected performance patterns in terms of net earnings, profits, return on investment, various types of ratio analysis—the bottom line.

External organizational factors include:

- Reputation within the industry, among customers, clients and suppliers, within the community, geographic area, state, nation, and among foreign countries.
- Reputation with stockholders, investment firms and counselors, governmental agencies, and the public in general.
- Susceptibility to changes in the economy of the industry, related industries, community, region, state, nation, and world.
- Susceptibility to consumer taste changes (and its ability to influence these changes).
- The impact of past, present, and probable governmental regulations, laws and administrative actions and interpretations.
- The impact of changes in political philosophy, values, policies, practices, parties in the community, state, nation, or world.

- The impact of world political conditions and climate and of change in governments or governmental systems in other countries and regions, including national emergencies, wars.
- The impact of actions—both domestic and foreign—by present competitors and those who might become competitors as other firms expand, change their markets, and products.
- The impact of current and future levels, dependability and reliability of governmental and other services—mail, telephone, telegraph, utilities, railroads, trucking, air and sea travel, and shipping.
- Reliance on (and the dependability of) availability and price of natural resources, raw and manufactured materials.
- Demographic trends—locally, regionally, nationally, and worldwide—in terms of labor force, consumers, customers, societies in general.
- The availability and cost of money and capital goods.
- The impact of present and future technology on the company, the industry, on the region or nation or world, on changing customer preferences.
- The impact of psychological factors—the definition of the good life by those in the company at all levels, in the industry, community, region, nation, and world—individuals' expectations, fears, aspirations, pessimism, optimism about the present and future.
- Structural components of society—the ways in which goods are produced, knowledge and technology organized and shared, society reproduces itself and maintains order.
- How the system changes in terms of social welfare.
- How the products of a society—goods, services, knowledge, values, order, people—are allocated among and across the several sectors.

The past and present does not necessarily pre-ordain or predict the future, but they can be helpful guides or benchmarks. There will, of course, be events for the organization, industry, or the nation that are difficult to predict, whether major economic or political upheavals, natural disasters, technological breakthroughs, or competitive factors. Nevertheless, one needs a firm basis to begin planning for the future.

The analysis of the past, present, and future can be done by a planning group in the firm, an ad hoc task force, and/or by special consulting assistance. However it is decided to perform the effort, the planning premises and data base should be reviewed by top management who should be committed through words, actions and time to heavy involvement in the planning process, in the review, in the discussion of alternatives, and of course, in the final decision making. Planning by planners for planners has little utility unless top management is committed and involved.

After developing a base describing where we have been and where we are, the issue becomes where do we want to go. A vision of the future is required. Data abound: various governmental and industry reports and projections, statistical analysis and projections, census data, polling, or Delphi techniques—what is essential is management commitment to the "future view" developed.

It is easy and natural to be overwhelmed and to be tied to incremental changes from the present. Here is where vision and creativity are needed. A pinch of abandon, of dreaming things that never were, of attempting the improbable if not the impossible is necessary to break away from the shackles of the safe and conventional.

A variety of techniques can be used in planning and these techniques should be applied to all elements of the enterprise—production, marketing, sales, staffing, capital formation and spending, new products or services, risk management, money management, customer, governmental and public relations. Strategic and tactical planning, management by objectives, sophisticated mathematical and computer simulations, test marketing and a host of other approaches can be utilized to reach the end product of a specific plan of action for each area tied in to an overall plan for the organization as a whole.

FORECASTING

Basic to any planning is forecasting. Generally, one extrapolates the future from the past and present, but modifies the extrapolation by economic forecasts, technological forecasts, social forecasts, and forecasts of public taste.

Forecasting is not new to the planner and decision maker in business and government. However, current forecasting called *futuristics* is different from previous forecasting approaches because of its explicitness and established methodology. Some of the forecasting methods currently in use in addition to the traditional methods are:

- *trend forecasting*—extension of the past to the future, based upon explicit parameters. One must carefully establish which parameters .to use because mere extension of historical trends can result in unbelievable forecasts.
- *consensus methods*—an example is the Delphi method which is a systematic approach for obtaining and evaluating informed judgment of experts, usually by means of written questionnaires sent through the mail, using sequenced interrogation and feedback. The participants are not known to each other and particular responses are never attributed to an individual.
- *simulation*—the approximation of complex systems by dynamic models. Computer technology has greatly enhanced this method.
- *cross-impact studies*—produce lists of potential future events and their likely dates of occurrence and then, by a matrix analysis which assumes that a particular prediction did occur, attempts to evaluate its impact on the probability and timing of other predicted events.
- *scenarios*—a projection of some aspect of the future by showing how a present situation might change over time or it may take a point in the future and indicate how we reached that point.

Whatever the methodology or combination of techniques used, the forecast provides the basic assumptions for realistic planning. Accuracy and quality are extremely important in forecasting. Some guidelines for evaluating a forecast are:

- Specificity—the forecast should be specific so that one can clearly determine whether or not it occurred.
- Probability—it should be stated in a range of probability of occurrence or a range of dates.
- Reflect necessary changes in current conditions.
- Reflect impact of competitive and complementing developments on the forecast.
- Reflect cost/benefits—social and economic—of the particular development.

Forecasts are sometimes not used because decision makers may lack confidence in the judgment, competence and tools of the person or unit making the forecast. Some decision makers shy away from uncertainty and tend to disregard those events, even those with potential major impact, that have a low probability of occurrence. They tend to focus on events with high probability of occurrences. Another reason for lack of maximum utilization of forecasts is that both the decision maker and the forecaster may miss or underestimate the linkage between the forecast information and the decision to be made.

PLANNING CONCEPTS

Once broad goals and objectives are determined, specific policies and approaches should then be developed down to the lowest units in the organization. The plan, broad to specific, must be understood, communicated, and accepted to insure that all units are working in harmony to meet the organizational objectives.

In developing a master plan for the company or unit, or even an annual operating plan, those involved in the planning process should be aware of some basic planning concepts.

1. Every plan should contribute in one way or another to the accomplishment of particular or general objectives.
2. Planning is basic to every critical management function and is a function of every manager at every level.
3. One must be concerned about the negative consequences and cost/benefits of each proposed plan, the plan may indeed be effective, but at much greater cost than other alternatives or have considerable negative consequences. Thus, the efficiency of plans must be analyzed.
4. The premises of planning, the base line data chosen, must be accepted and consistent throughout the organization.

Other important aspects of a solid planning effort involve: adequate communication about planning; exploring alternatives before settling on a specific plan; monitoring progress against plan so that if conditions change, the plan can be modified; flexibility should be a major consideration in deciding upon a particular course of action; there must be adequate commitment of time and resources to accomplish the objectives; there must be coordination and integration

among and between specific and general plans within the broad objectives and policies of the organization; timing is critical in terms of
the introduction of change, the implementation of plans, and the
planning process itself.

SOME PLANNING TOOLS

Companies seek through the planning process to set realistic goals
for the future, the next year, two, three, five and beyond and to provide methods for successful implementation of developed plans. A
number of useful tools in measuring progress toward goals will be
mentioned briefly here; detailed discussion of some of them will
follow in other chapters.

For many companies a paramount concern is estimating probable
sales volume, the revenue brought in and the net profit. The break-
even chart (Figure 1-1) is a helpful method of determining profit
at given sales levels.

A *short-* and *long-term capital budget* is essential to meet competitive expansion, new product development, repair and replacement needs. An *expense* or *operating budget* allocates money for various activities, some fixed costs, others discretionary. A *cash flow*

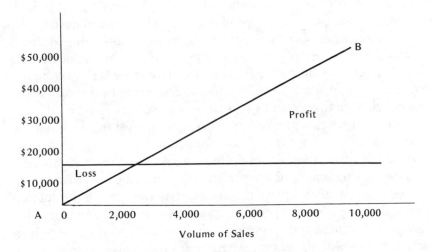

Figure 1-1   Break-Even Chart

budget indicates money available for financing current operations. A *manpower budget* indicates level and number of individuals needed in various units, when they will be hired, and steps and costs involved in their training and development. A *facilities and equipment budget* indicates type and number of facilities necessary.

Various scheduling techniques are helpful for new or improved facility construction, development, testing, production and marketing of new products, sales and production of products or services, etc. *Critical path scheduling* is a useful technique in that it indicates what has to be accomplished prior to starting each phase, which actions can be performed during the same period, what follows each phase. PERT (*Program Evaluation Review Technique*) is also an example of networking or arrow diagramming and indicates all the steps required before a project is completed, the sequence of events, and the time involved.

Aside from developing and introducing new products or acquiring companies that produce other products, thus leading, hopefully, to increased profits, the company may seek to increase its profit margins through use of several techniques which would provide a better return on assets. One approach would focus on increasing sales through product improvements, better marketing, increased sales training, improving production capacity and distribution. Another method is increasing profit margins on sales basically through reducing cost. This can be accomplished by dropping less profitable product lines, services or stores, by reducing inventory, or by instituting a cost reduction program. Another method is employing value analysis which analyzes each component of a product, the materials that go into it and each operation performed in its production. The goal is to reduce the cost of producing the product without decreasing its marketability. Cheaper materials, a different design, new equipment, a change in work flow, are all expense reduction possibilities.

Although a company seeks to plan in each of its functional areas (with much of what is planned at departmental level incorporated into overall plans), two areas stand out for detailed planning, production planning and marketing planning. In *production planning*, which depends on sales forecasts, particular attention must be paid to components necessary, availability at the appropriate time in the production process, insuring a well scheduled flow of work from one work area to another. In *marketing planning*, the firm seeks to determine how much will be sold, to whom, where and how. Various projections, scenarios, sampling data, test market data, questionnaires, motivation research, review of distribution channels, advertising tests, national and local statistical material, sales analysis from the company's records, can be utilized as a means of suggesting immediate, short and long range marketing plans.

SETTING OBJECTIVES

Although there are many sophisticated and valuable approaches in carrying out the planning effort, a basic approach would first involve setting objectives. This would involve determining basic objectives for the organization, such as, percent profit or return on investment, or growth per year, or share of the market. Objectives might be based on the competitive advantages the company has, such as new methods, quality of products, experience, lower costs, reputation, recognition of existing or new markets that are not being adequately satisfied.

In determining objectives, the planners must focus on what business are we really in now and for the future, what products and services are to be provided, to whom, how will we market and sell them, what resources do we need (plant, equipment, raw materials, personnel, capital); what constraints and competitive factors must we consider; what rate of growth can we strive for; what is the optimum size for our plants. In setting objectives, it should be recognized that some may intend conflict and some may, in effect, outrank others.

Based upon these objectives, specific goals can be set, year by year and if necessary, month by month, with particular resources and costs assigned.

The basic plan of the organization, aside from the five-year plan, or annual planning document, is also expressed by the annual and three, five, or ten-year operating and capital budget.

In setting those objectives and focusing not only on today, but what is likely to occur in the future and how the company might take advantage of future events, the long range aspects of planning must not be put aside. All too often because of uncertainties about the future, shortage of resources, the tyranny of the crisis of the moment, month or year, thinking about more than three or five years ahead is put on a very low burner. Business history, however, is filled with the failures of those who, while riding high for the moment, three or five or ten years later were out of business because they failed to assess the future and position themselves to deal with it. Thus, a focus on long-range planning allows one to have a better understanding of the future impact of present day decisions; anticipate issues and areas for future decision making; structure an information flow system and the speed of information flow necessary; implement future decisions in a more careful and rapid manner.

Planning is not simply a master plan, five-year plan or annual plan. It is a comprehensive endeavor involving not only the basic objectives or goals of the enterprise, but also specific decisions, policies, practices, and actions.

Objectives may be set in a variety of areas with as much specificity as would be helpful in making decisions, taking actions, setting policies and practices. Of course, one might start with a basic objective of avoiding bankruptcy! Some areas where one can categorize specific objectives, both short and long range, are: profitability; productivity; competitive standing; social commitments and public relations responsibilities; financial resources and strength; plant and equipment resources; technological resources and strength; human resources—performance, development, motivation.

Too often we focus only on broad objectives which provide the goals or ultimates for the enterprise and its leaders. But we need the same degree of concern for policies which are specific guides to action and which make the action of members of the organization more predictable to others and more consistent with others. Policies and the specific precedents they set and the detailed practices that flow have several valuable benefits for the organization. They help decentralize decision making, encourage consistency yet allow for flexibility, speed decision making, provide a take-off point for future plans or modified actions and can encourage change and initiative.

Given the formulation of plans, objectives, policies, and aspects of planning such as strategic planning, the manager is finally able to achieve results through making decisions and taking action.

After the plans are formulated, communicated, coordinated and agreed to, careful implementation is necessary with concern always for Murphy's Law—"What can go wrong, will go wrong." A good plan will anticipate problems and have some contingency plans available. Once the plan is installed careful monitoring, analysis and evaluation of reality against plan is necessary with modification of approach and plan as necessary. As each new planning cycle begins, top management must assess the results of previous planning, why and where reality reasonably matched plans and projects, why and where it did not. (Figure 1-2)

LIMITS TO PLANNING

We have indicated the critical importance of planning, but it should be recognized that there are limits to planning. There is considerable difficulty in formulating accurate premises. Often change is more rapid and far reaching than anticipated. There may be considerable inflexibilities within the organization involving: human psychology; particular personalities; goals and aspirations of individuals at various levels; the resistance to new concepts, approaches, outsiders. Other problems involve the rigidity of the organization and the difficulties involved in changing policies, procedures and fundamental concepts and approaches; the heavy investment that may have already been made in capital goods and machinery, technology, advertising, product development and research; the expense and time involved.

In addition to the internal environment, there may be external factors such as political, economic and social climate, technological changes, labor relations and organizations.

A commitment to planning—effectiveness, creativity and efficiency in the process, thorough implementation and monitoring—permits an organization to become something of a master of its own fate. Otherwise it must fall prey to the vicissitudes of time, circumstances, and the planning abilities of competitors and other organizations.

The Executive Planning Summary Sheet in Figure 1-3 may be helpful as a planning tool.

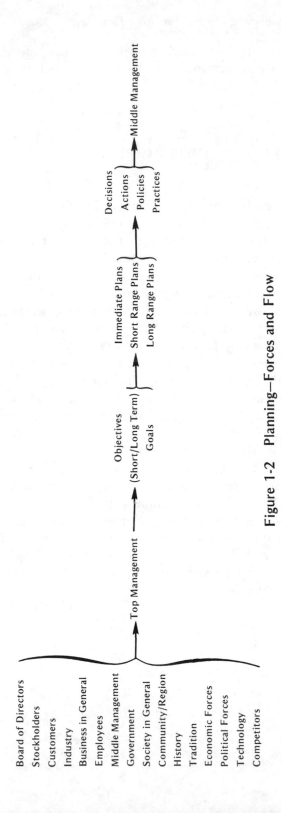

Figure 1-2 Planning—Forces and Flow

Figure 1-3   Executive Planning Summary Sheet

Date Approved _____
Dates of Review_____

I. Area
_____

Target Dates for
Implementation_____

II. Objectives: Overall
_____
  1.

  2.

  3.

  4.

  5.

III. Resources to be Committed   Year 1   Year 2   Year 3   Year 4   Year 5
  Units (% of effort)—Cost

  Individuals (% of effort)—Cost

  Plant (what, where, when)—Cost

  Equipment (what, where, when)—Cost

  Money (what, where, when)—Cost

  Other Resources

    Total Value of Resources

IV. Specific Decisions to be Made, Actions, Policies   Year 1   Year 2   Year 3   Year 4   Year 5
  Units

  Individuals

  Plant

  Equipment

  Money

  Other

V. Method of Progress Evaluation for Each Objective
_____
  Objective 1:
  Objective 2:
  Objective 3:
  Objective 4:
  Objective 5:

VI. Evalution Results for Each Objective—Date(s)
_____
  Objective 1:
  Objective 2:
  Objective 3:
  Objective 4:
  Objective 5:

VII. Milestones—Checkpoints
   Objective 1:
   Objective 2:
   Objective 3:
   Objective 4:
   Objective 5:

VIII. Early Warning Signals
   Objective 1:
   Objective 2:
   Objective 3:
   Objective 4:
   Objective 5:

IX. Major Modifications Made (Date)

   (For Each Objective)

X. Implementation Dates of Each Objective	Planned	Actual

   (For Each Objective)

Evaluation of Each Objective as Implemented	6 months	12 months	24 months	36 months

(For Each Objective)

two

Organizing

There are as many definitions of organizing as there are writers on management. I have found the following definition by Harvey Sherman in *It All Depends* (University of Alabama Press, University, Alabama, 1966) useful, but true to the management writers' credo of not totally accepting anyone else's work I have added "efficiently" to the definition. Organizing—"The process of grouping activities and responsibilities, and establishing relationships (formal and informal) that will enable people to work together most effectively and efficiently in determining and accomplishing the objectives of an enterprise."

We deal in this chapter with how to organize a company or unit stressing organizational approaches. In so doing, it must be noted that the human side of organization is critical, but often overlooked in discussions of organizing. Whether or not the reader accepts or knows about Maslow' hierarchy of needs and the self-actualization, ego, and self-esteem needs of individuals, McGregor's Theory X and Theory Y formulation, Herzberg's satisfiers and dissatisfiers and the other writings of behavioralists and human relations experts, clearly the organization designer must be well aware of the impact of organizations on individuals and vice versa. Chris Argyris made an important contribution by contrasting the growth pattern of a child to an adult and noted that many organizations seek to put mature individuals in the position of being a child. The adult in maturing has grown to independence from dependency, to activity from passivity, to many types of behavioral responses from few, to deep interests from shallow or erratic interests, to a longer time perspective with a sense of past, present, and future from a short time perspective (present), to an equal or higher status position from a subordinate position in family and society, to awareness and control over oneself from a lack of self awareness. However, today, many organizations by their design, structure and style, still encourage and reward the person who exhibits child-like behavior rather than adult behavior. There are many organizations who reward the individual for being dependent, passive, predictable, willing to shift interests as the organization demands, willing to meet variations in organizational needs and not have his own agenda and to view himself as a subordinate. We shall discuss in this chapter and elsewhere the human organization, but turn now to getting organized.

PATTERNS OF ORGANIZATION

There are many approaches to grouping functions, activities, and units. The usual approach would group units depending upon:

1. major purpose of product (all activities necessary to accomplish a given purpose or produced product are grouped under one person),
2. major process or function (activities grouped on the basis of specialized, technical skills),
3. geographical area to be served,
4. client to be served.

Each approach has certain advantages. The latter two focus on the needs of a particular group or region, but it may be difficult to get coordination and consistency in an organization and there may be excess costs due to duplication of staff and equipment. In general the purpose or product grouping appears to be more popular because responsibility is more clearly fixed, coordination is easier, there is broader experience for executives, employees can more readily see the end product. However, the process or function approach does allow for better and more economical use of specialized skills, equipment and machines, brings about loyalty to the enterprise as a whole, and fosters professional development. In Figure 2-1, each approach is shown for the same company illustrating the different options for organizing the company.

To go from this very simple formulation of ways or organization to a complex one, consider Exxon, an 85 billion dollar corporation. The corporation's resources are primarily concentrated in 13 autonomous operating companies or affiliates. Most of these affiliates are oil-related and are organized on a geographic basis. However, there are 17 staff departments at company headquarters who deal with general corporate matters such as legal affairs and corporate planning, but who also advise the affiliates on matters such as marketing. Both groups report to a management committee consisting of 8 executives who serve on the Board of Directors together with 11 outside directors.

No matter which pattern is chosen, and whether one introduces the group executive concept, profit decentralization or other structural devices, there will always be tension and competition among and between various line and staff departments for resources, "power," and prestige. Top management hopes the tension and competition will be creative—at times it can be destructive.

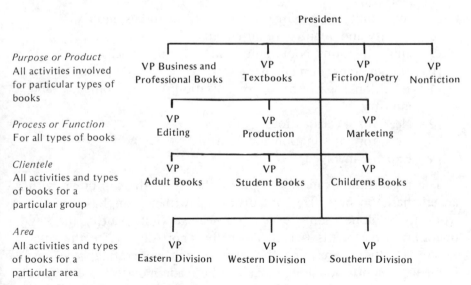

Figure 2-1   Snapshot of Highest Level Organization for a Publishing House.
(Excludes Staff Departments)

It is not unusual to see a new chief executive shift the basic approach in whole or in part from one method of organizing to another. Overall, purpose/product and process/function are the two most common approaches. Further, an approach used at the corporate level may not be used at a division or regional level. It is rare that throughout the organization there is a single organizing theory being applied. Organizations devise structures and logics to fit their particular needs.

Whatever the pattern to be selected—pure, modified, original— there are important considerations which affect the decision:

1. Goals, objectives, policies, and programs of the organization.
2. The type of work in the organization and the amount of work to be done—this involves numbers and types of people, matters and problems to be dealt with, skills required.
3. Complexity of the organization—number and types of products and services, scope of activities, dispersion of plants, offices, customers.
4. Size of the organization—growth potential.
5. Dynamic nature of the enterprise—how quickly must decisions and changes be made and at what levels.
6. The capability and motivation of executive staff and of the workforce.
7. Availability of resources (manpower, materials, money).
8. Quality and quantity requirements.
9. Public relations, community and political implications.
10. Morale, impact on company staff.
11. Traditional patterns of organization in the company and industry.
12. Need for specialization.
13. Need for coordination and control.
14. Expense involved.

The organization can be designed either from the top down with an emphasis on objectives or bottom up with an emphasis on the work to be done. Some executives seek to first identify the key operating departments (which normally report directly to the chief executive), then determine the level at which operating decisions, immediate, short- and long-range can be made most effectively and efficiently, and finally consider the type and location of staff and service units. The answers to these decision factors, which involve questions of centralization versus decentralization, become building blocks of the final organization structure.

We have made an assumption that overall structural planning is based on departments or units. However, how to go about putting activities into particular units and then grouping units into departments or divisions also takes careful planning.

There are several common factors around which departments may be formed—function; territory; customer; method of marketing; homogeneity of work; extent to which work is routine, repetitive, dynamic, or static; shifts or time of work; product; equipment or process; matrix; availability of supervisory time, attention, and talent; caliber of staff; span of control. The factor used may differ for each level of the organization. Whatever pattern or combination of patterns is chosen, the goal is to develop an overall structure that reflects the tasks and activities necessary to achieve objectives and meet and match the capabilities of the individuals involved in an effective, efficient, and economical structure.

Activities, in turn, are grouped together and assigned to managers and departments based upon similarity of work effort or skills and/or on the basis of close relationship to achievement of the unit's objectives. Ways assignments of units are made include: the interest of the executive; who uses it most; who has the most control over policy implementation and interpretation; competition—either to encourage competition or conversely to suppress previous competition; the need for coordination; separating activities that serve as a control on a unit from the head of the unit; related interest—assigning units that are related to the activities of a particular department to that department.

PRINCIPLES OF ORGANIZING

In management literature, "principles of organization" are frequently stated, however, these should be taken with several grains of salt. Herbert Simon, a major management thinker and recent recipient of the Nobel Prize in Economics, thirty-five years ago pointed out that many of the priniciples are much like proverbs, for every principle (or proverb) you can have one that sounds just as "right" that says exactly the opposite. For example, the *short span of control* concept conflicts with the idea of keeping organizational levels at a minimum. It is important to see these principles as, at the most, guides. To illustrate Simon's point, I have asked management classes

to contrast proverbs. Over the years I have received many contrasts—
"look before you leap—he who hesitates is lost," "two heads are better than one—too many cooks spoil the broth," "absence makes the
heart grow fonder—out of sight, out of mind." The most creative
contrast came from a clergyman student who suggested, "Thou shalt
not steal—God helps those who help themselves."

The principles have some validity, or, at least one should recognize
that indeed the principle is being violated, and for good reason—the
needs of the organization, cost, personalities, flexibility, quick decision making, and so forth. Some of the basic principles that have
value are:

Specification of Duties: duties should be clearly defined.

Fixing Responsibility: every individual and unit should have fixed
    duties and responsibilities for which he or it can be held responsible.

Authority Commensurate with Responsibility: an employee or unit
    receiving an assignment must be given sufficient authority to ac-
    complish the task. This principle is often found to have been vio-
    lated and thus the taskforce, project or matrix organization
    approach has been developed.

Delegation of Authority: authority to act can be delegated to a sub-
    ordinate, but ultimate responsibility cannot be delegated. Or, as
    is said in the Army, "The commanding officer is responsible for all
    that his unit does or fails to do."

Accountability for Use of Authority: the subordinate to whom
    authority has been delegated must be held responsible to his super-
    ior for its proper use.

Unity of Purpose: all units must work together toward common
    organizational goals.

Group of Similar Functions: functions that are similar should be
    grouped together under the direction of the same individual.

Chain of Command: communications upward and downward should
    pass through appropriate lines of authority, each succeeding and
    intervening level.

Unity of Command: each subordinate situation and condition should
    be under the control of one and only one immediate superior. This
    "one man-one boss" concept is often violated in order to achieve
    maximum staff utilization or because of workload requirements.
    Those of you who share a secretary should now recognize that
    your secretary is the victim of this violation.

Hierarchy/Number of Levels—Scalar Chain: each unit or individual
    is ultimately responsible through succeeding levels to the chief
    administrative officer at the apex of the hierarchy—the number of

levels should be kept as small as possible to facilitate communication and control.

Span of Control: the number of individuals reporting directly to a supervisor is limited by the level of supervision and the abilities of the superior and the subordinate.

To illustrate the "grain of salt" approach to the principles, I will discuss briefly the span of control. This principle is subject to what I call the "numbers racket," Many writers and practitioners believe that 4-7, 5-8, or 5-10 are absolutely the right number and should not be exceeded, particularly at the higher levels of an organization. I suggest that there is indeed a limit, but it will depend upon a number of factors at work in the organization at a particular time. There must be a balance between added expense, communications and control elements and levels of hierarchy involved in too short a span of control versus questions of effectiveness and efficiency in too wide a span of control. The factors that will help determine the number of departments and/or individuals reporting to a person (and the "standard" pattern in a particular organization may not be "standard" for all levels or for a long period of time) are:

1. Skill, training, motivation, stamina, time availability and style of the superior—some like to have, and are capable of having, more direct command, "hands-on" authority, others are not—some delegate more and better than others.
2. Subordinate skill, training, motivation and ambition.
3. Rate of change in and on the organization—complexity of issues, speed of decision making required.
4. Communication and delegation techniques used.
5. Type, size, and complexity of organization and industry.
6. Public or governmental relations requirements, either external or internal.
7. Frequency of contact needed with subordinates.
8. Need for personal contact with subordinates.
9. The use of standards of performance and evaluation and measurement systems.
10. The quality and detail of existing plans, policies, and procedures.

The amount and kind of delegation or decentralization of authority practiced in the organization will effect the span of control as well as the operating style of the company. In deciding upon the breadth, depth, and style of delegation, each delegator must be aware of several of the management principles noted before—hierarchy, delegation of authority, chain of command, unity of command, authority commensurate with responsibility. Some of the considerations involved in determining the degree of delegation include:

- Superior's attitude toward delegation; his experience as a delegator and as one to whom responsibilities were delegated; his own self confidence; willingness to let others make decisions and share and perhaps steal the limelight; willingness to let others make mistakes, yet still have to share the blame with them and in fact probably take most of the blame; willingness to trust others and to establish broad controls.
- History and dynamics of the organization.
- Management philosophy within the organization.
- Cost considerations involved in major decisions.
- Size, location, and diversity of the organization.
- Availability, abilities, and desires of subordinates.
- Control techniques available.
- Outside influences on the organization.

CENTRALIZATION-DECENTRALIZATION

The issue of delegation is part of a broader issue of centralization versus decentralization. By decentralization we mean the allocation of managerial work by moving decision making responsibility to lower levels in the organization. Decisions can be decentralized geographically and/or within central administration. A further type of decentralization is profit decentralization as applied by large, complex organizations such as General Electric and General Motors. The company is divided into regional or product divisions and the activities and operations necessary to make a profit are organized and grouped under the head of a self-sufficient unit. These units are managed to such a high degree of decentralization that they appear to be at least semi-autonomous. There are some definite advantages to profit decentralization in that operating units of more manageable size are created. There is an appropriate locus for administrative decisions and managerial responsibility, there may be improved coordination, morale, and control. However, there are some drawbacks—technology may make it impossible to divide large operations into smaller ones, there may be duplication of effort and expense of auxiliary and service units, profits may not be the only valid measure or performance and there may be difficult demands placed on the decentralized managers to be creative, independent, and entrepreneurial and on central administrators to avoid over-controlling. And, in effect, the parts may become more important or too independent from the whole.

There can be various combinations of centralization and decentralization of management controls and physical facilities with one being centralized and the other decentralized. In general, the potential advantages of total or a great degree of centralization are: administration is easier; top executives are all near each other; decision making is faster; there may be a higher degree of communication and economies in service and auxiliary departments, greater technical specialization; more standardization. The advantages of decentralization (and the advantages of one in effect are the disadvantages of the other approach) include: prompt action based on first-hand knowledge of the situation; development of managers; less chance of overcontrol, more innovation, flexibility, delegation of authority.

Like delegation, centralization versus decentralization is not a black and white choice. There are various degrees of decentralization and the amount and type of decentralization will vary over time based on circumstances, needs, and personalities. The wise manager will not simply accept the status quo or copy a competitor's approach, but rather assess the situation in terms of: the skills, workload and motivation present at headquarters and in divisions; the complexity, significance, coordination and speed required in making decisions, the impact and use of technology; the effect of centralization—decentralization—recentralization on morale, productivity, esprit de corps, retention of top executives.

LINE AND STAFF

A continuing concern in organizing and in the operation of any company is the issue of line and staff functions, personnel and departments. Unless understood and explicitly worked at, this can be an ongoing problem despite some executives' view that "we're all professionals and are contributing to the good of the company and therefore, we should all be able to work well together."

Line functions very simply are those activities that contribute directly to the achievements of the fundamental goals of the organization. Staff functions, by contrast, are those activities that contribute indirectly to the fundamental objectives by assisting, advising, auditing, or providing other services. This approach of defining line and staff based upon contribution to the enterprise leads to some basic difficulties. How do you measure the contribution of a management consultant, an inventory specialist, a tax counsel, acquisitions expert, etc? Their contributions to the bottom line can be greater than an operating division's vice president. Another approach to line and staff relationships is to look at staff as being in an advisory relationship which complements rather than contrasts with the line concept in which command authority down the scalar chain is delegated to the subordinate.

In complex organizations or in meeting specific problems, the definition between line and staff authority may become blurred through instituting compulsory staff consultation, concurring authority or functional authority. Compulsory staff consultation demands that a staff person be consulted before a manager takes action. The staff person or function does not have veto or override power, but he does have the right to advise. A further strengthening of the staff view is concurring authority which prevents any action being taken until a designated staff person agrees. This is veto power and can slow down or perhaps even water down decisions, but it is hoped that it will improve decisions. Under functional authority, the staff person can give direct orders, in his own name, to operating personnel (this authority can also be conferred upon line operating managers). It should be noted that this type of overlapping authority can bring about some difficult problems (aside from difficulties for the staff person who on some problems or in one time period interacts with a line manager as an adviser and at other times as a superior) such as undermining the status of operating executives, overburdening them with possible conflicting orders and making accountability unclear. Thus, such authority should be conferred carefully and usually if specialized skills not held by operating managers is necessary, or if consistency in several operating areas is critical, or if relatively narrow areas or specific projects within a total operating responsibility is covered.

Whether we discuss an executive's personal staff (e.g. executive secretary), specialized staff (e.g. industrial engineering, auditing, research and development) or general staff (e.g. assistant to), the staff person must be aware of potential pitfalls in his assignment and the way he operates. These are perceptions by others that he: undermines line authority; tends to be unrealistic in terms of the "real" operating world; lacks responsibility for his poor advice; and tends to think if only he had the authority he could do things better, faster and more creatively.

The top manager who seeks to optimize the use of staff must seek to define as clearly as possible the responsibilities, duties, and authority of line and staff functions and personnel. He must be aware of the need to choose and develop good staff people who have a blend of technical and interpersonal skills and who can gain the confidence and respect of operating personnel. He must avoid mixing staff and operating duties (which can happen due to the lack of capable executives or the difficulty in separating functions or because of the pressures of the moment).

A staff person can be successful if he does not misrepresent his authority or the authority or views of his boss, when he relies on thoroughness, in-depth knowledge, persuasion, clarity of presentation, and seeks to understand the other person's views, constraints, and problems. The successful staff man must have the rather unusual capacity of being willing to submerge to some degree his drive for recognition and power. Of course, a staff person's views are more likely to be accepted by operating personnel if, in addition to the above, he has high status or reports to those with very high status, has the strong backing of top executives, has an outstanding track record and has a role in determining salary increases, assignments, and promotions of operating personnel.

NEW APPROACHES TO ORGANIZATIONAL DESIGN

Organizations are dynamic and in recent years there have been several new approaches to organizational design. There is a new field of organizational development which, while dealing with structure, puts significant emphasis on the individual within the organization, change mechanisms, and adaptability. In this section, we deal with some of the new approaches with greatest emphasis on the group executive concept.

Matrix Organization is designed to deal with highly technical, complex, major significance, unconventional, unique, or extreme urgency projects. It's distinctive features involve the appointment of a project manager to supervise a specific objective or mission and specialists from functional and operational areas to perform the tasks. After the project, each specialist, and indeed often, the project manager, returns to his home department for assignment to usual duties. Matrix organization provides the company with the coordination and the specialized capabilities necessary to accomplish certain goals. There are significant hurdles to overcome in this type of organization. The career aspirations of the project team members are rooted in their functional departments. Several project managers may be competing for the time, priority, and resources of functional departments. Functional department heads' goals and rewards may be different from project managers. This form of organization involves heavy emphasis on interpersonal skills, cooperation, communication and commitment and should generally be employed when the more traditional approaches will not suffice.

External Staffs or independent staffs are used by large organizations to evaluate and monitor very substantial commitments of resources. When this approach works well, care is exercised to insure that the external staff is not a substitute for operating staff. The external staff should be judged by the results achieved by the operating unit. They serve to insure that consequences and opportunities have been thoroughly reviewed and planned. At times there will be sharp differences between the external staff and the operating staff and a top executive will have to decide between the alternative approaches offered.

Interest Group demands for representation has been another relatively new force on organizations. Various types of interest groups have asked for membership on Boards of Directors and on its committees and/or to be apprised of major decisions that may affect them as consumers, workers, community members, environmentalists, or advocates of particular points of view. The usual focal point for interest representation has been school boards, universities, public utilities and various governmental projects, but companies are not immune. From a university perspective, one notes the problems involved in having students as voting members on a Board of Trustees, where the students would be naturally opposed to tuition increases or cutbacks in student services. Faculty members on the Board would be personally concerned in voting on salaries, fringe benefits, workload, cutbacks or collective bargaining representation or strategy. (It is possible to draw a fine line by having certain members ineligible to vote on certain issues or by having interest representatives serve without a vote or only as observers. The Board could go into Executive Session when sensitive issues are discussed. However, these fine line attempts may be quite awkward.) The desire for communications, information and opportunity to express their views prior to final or semi-final decisions being reached can be met without undue strain on most companies, except perhaps for negative publicity, premature disclosure to the press (and competitors) or various types of demonstrations or actions. However, placing advocates of a particular view on a Board may create difficulties for the Board to operate successfully. The European approach of union representation on the Board is relatively unknown in the United States, but it may come about. The recent Chrysler example of the union president on the board is worthy of careful evaluation.

Outside Directors increasing the number of outside Directors on the Board has received increasing attention and appears to be gaining momentum. There is also interest in providing the Board with independent staff and a special auditing team or the company's internal or operating auditors reporting to them.

Office of the President—this concept is designed to reduce the burden on the Chief Executive Officer beyond the assistance offered by profit decentralization, general staff and a very active Board of Directors. Generally, a team of two to five or six senior executives, at the level of senior or executive vice presidents, divide and share the executive management responsibilities. The success of this approach depends very largely on the capabilities of the president and the senior officials and their capacity to work as a team.

GROUP EXECUTIVE CONCEPT

The Group Executive Concept has become a major thrust in large organizations. In 1971 only about 40 percent of Fortune 500 industrial companies had the group executive practice in operation; today

over 70 percent use this structure. The concept involves several operating divisions under one executive who in turn reports to top corporation management.

Generally, Chief Executive Officers change to a group structure in
order to achieve improved organizational control, effectiveness, communication and reduction in number of executives reporting to the
Chief Executive Officer. Other reasons sometimes cited are for financial control, cost effectiveness, and establishing an executive training
ground.

There are various approaches in establishing a group structure
with varying degrees of satisfaction for those involved. In general, the
approach that meets with the highest satisfaction is where the individuals feel they are, in effect, presidents of their own company. They
tend to report to the Chief Executive Officer infrequently and spend
a small percentage of their time on corporate activities. They spend
their time basically on group management with major emphasis on
decision making and planning. Their incentive compensation comes
from the group and increased profit and growth is regarded as their
accomplishments.

Another approach or style for group executives is guiding, advising
and team building in regard to the divisions under their control. They
serve as representatives to and from corporate management and tend
to spend one-fifth to one-third of their time on corporate matters.
Their incentive compensation tends to be split in some way between
divisional and corporate.

The least satisfactory approach for these individuals is the liaison
function between corporate and division levels with rather little authority in either area. They spend a significant portion of their time
on corporate activities and their incentive compensation tends to
come totally from that area.

There are some drawbacks to the group executive concept. From
the perspective of the Chief Executive Officer there may be confusion over authority and mission and disputes between group executives and division managers over resource allocation. Group executives
on the other hand may feel a lack of operating authority, confused
mission and authority definitions, interpersonal and authority conflicts with division heads and being held responsible for activities not
totally under one's control.

Clearly, the group structure is here to stay. To make it more effective or to decide whether to put the concept into effect, the following questions should be answered:

- What is the most appropriate management philosophy and style for the company?
- Is the group concept needed or can other approaches be as effective?
- If it is needed, which areas should be grouped together and how many groups should there be?
- What role should the group executives play?
- How will the role and responsibilities of the Chief Executive Officer and division heads be affected if the group concept is implemented with what probable results?

In deciding upon the most appropriate role for Group Executives, some questions are: the ability and style of the Chief Executive Officer, those who will become group executives, those who are division heads; the short and long term growth strategy, complexity and challenges faced by the company; what the future seems to hold for the company internally and externally; the consequences, negative and positive, of various styles for the group executive function.

In addition to the above, to give the group structure a reasonable chance of success, the Chief Executive Officer must carefully think through what he hopes to achieve through the concept and how this might change his operating style, decision making, authority, and status; carefully choose the right individuals to be group executives with a stress on those who are team players and have a broad top management perspective; and focus on the appropriate performance evaluation and reward system for the group executives concept.

We are all accustomed to organization charts, whether the traditional, functional or a new approach is used. It is popular to attack the chart and indicate its shortcomings. However, it does have value in portraying the organization, and as a tool for organizational analysis in highlighting possible structural faults—unbalanced organization, duplication, overlaps, dual reporting relationships, span of control problems, too many levels. It also can be useful in orienting new staff to the organization and in communication both internally and externally. Despite its positive aspects, one should be aware of the weaknesses of inadequacies in any organization chart. Normally it has a short span of usefulness, by the time it's printed and distributed it may be out of date. It certainly does not (nor is it intended to) show informal relationships and often does not show precise functions or responsibilities. Often, in an attempt for clarity and accuracy various trimmings are introduced which serve to confuse.

Dotted lines, circles, dotted boxes often abound. My advice to someone in a dotted box in a dotted line relationship to one or more top
officials is—solidify the line(s) or else look for another job since a
dotted relationship is one step away from an erased or nonexistent
relationship. In many cases the chart shows things the way they are
supposed to be, used to be, or how the Chief Executive or chart
drawer thinks they are, rather than how they really are.

INFORMAL ORGANIZATION

The theme throughout this discussion has been on general and
technical aspects of organizing. Sometimes what is more important
than anything else in the actual results of organizing is the use, reactions and influence of the informal organization.

Any company is in fact a social institution. Individuals tend to
form small groups among their co-workers, often of individuals at
roughly the same level or occupation, but sometimes joining together
a number of levels or occupations. They may come together because
of one or more shared conveniences (car pool), beliefs, attitudes, interests, fears, values, goals or sentiments. They may come about
because of proximity or frequent contact between and among individuals, because of a shared work effort or commonality in work, because of special or common interests.

The informal group, large or small, serves to satisfy one or more
needs or concerns of the members, provides some social satisfaction
in terms of companionship, recognition or status, provides an information, communication or gossip source and may indeed provide
control, consistency and conformity through peer pressures. The
group gives the individual a sense of belonging, a relief from the hum-
drum aspects of his work.

Management cannot stop the formation of informal organizations
and the preceding discussion indicates the values to the individual
and hints at some of the values to the organization of informal
groups. However, there are some dangers to management. Informal
groups tend to buttress normal human reactions of resistance to
change. They encourage rumors and grapevine gossip. They tend,
through peer pressures, to bring about conformity which may hurt
the organization. They may put the members in a difficult choice po-

sition when the formal goals and attitudes of the organization conflict with those of the group. It is difficult for a loyal member of a lunch time group of co-workers to produce the company goal of "x" widgets a day when the group regards "y" as a fair day's work.

The successful manager will indicate by his communications and actions that he accepts the informal organization and understands its concerns. Prior to taking action, he will consider the impact on the group, i.e. he won't quickly decide to switch a job assignment or shift one of the members or leaders of the group. He will make every attempt to harmonize the interests of the informal organization with the formal organization or at least attempt to keep formal actions from unnecessarily disturbing the informal group. He will try to identify and communicate with informal group leaders. At times he will have to take action that will go against the values, happiness and practices of the informal organization, but he should do so with recognition of the problems involved and how he might soften the blow.

In the best of worlds, not often achieved, but certainly worth striving for, through active concern and involvement of management, the informal organization will adopt (perhaps after modifying) the goals and attitudes of the formal organization, thus providing a strengthened system for getting things done. In addition, such an informal organization can help lighten the style and indeed workload of the manager. It can also provide a useful channel of communication and testing site for ideas. In providing cohesiveness and satisfaction for those who belong, the informal organization can be a factor in reducing turnover and absenteeism. At the very least, the fact that it is there will encourage management to think through the implications of their plans and actions and this may indeed result in better actions.

At one point or another, the organization may be subjected to an organization study by outside consultants, by internal management consultants, or by an internal task force. This is a healthy development for an organization (if not done overly often) because if performed correctly it can raise some tough questions and propose answers for immediate, short and long run problems and opportunities. A well planned, well communicated and carefully conducted study will assess relationships, controls, work flow, decision making, delegation of responsibility and authority, caliber of people, morale, reasons for turnover, operating style, division of work, channels of communication, flexibility, resistance to change, capacity for innovation, effectiveness and efficiency, profitability, productivity, resource acquisition, absence of strain, organizational and individual development, growth integration, communications, capacity for growth and survival, control over environment.

Whether or not frequent organization studies are conducted, each complex organization must focus on a continuing organization planning or organizational development function. This can be carried out by formation of a special unit serving the company as a whole and in a staff reporting to a major officer, by each major division having one or more individuals concerned with the problem, and/or through a continuing relationship with consultants or through the use of committees or task forces.

Organizational planning involves planning for the needs of the future with particular emphasis on human, financial, equipment, space, research and development, and organization structure needs. The organization planner should seek, through analysis and discussion, to anticipate new company objectives or changes in approach or emphasis and weigh the strength of existing traditions, policies and practices. He must attempt to relate organizational planning to growth planning which involves the competitive position of each product line, profit responsibility, review of growth and expansion plans, etc. Often, however, the organization planner is fine tuning or suggesting incremental changes. The dynamic organization is always subject to continuous refinement, whether major or minor. The astute planner and manager should be alert to opportunities and need for organizational changes and their effects on other aspects of the company's activities. Timing of changes will always be important both in terms of reactions to external events and to internal needs in the company. The planner should be alert to a variety of factors that might trigger the need for organizational modification. These include the internal and external factors discussed in the chapter on planning, changes in the economic or political situation, mergers and acquisitions, changes in community relations or competitive climate, changes in emphasis on product lines or services and in the means of producing or delivering them, changes in the staff, and availability of capable staff. A valuable information source to managers and planners concerned about organizational planning is budgetary analysis. The budget planning process indicates needs, problems, and opportunities which may be aided through organizational change or may indeed force organizational change. Reviews of requests for new units, groups or categories of positions, service activities, new positions or job classifications will also yield valuable information and early warning signals.

Once the organization or reorganization is decided upon, top management must be prepared to carefully plan for implementation. Change is difficult for organizations and for people. Changing a person's title, place on a chart, reporting relationship, functional unit, are all bound to create significant problems.

Some companies plan organizational changes secretly and implement them suddenly in a surprise attack fashion. Others encourage a great deal of involvement at many levels and from the onset of the planning process, not only in the hope of gaining important information, ideas, and recommendations, but also to encourage the individuals to feel that they are involved and are partners in the change process. In general, when deciding upon a new organizational structure a company must weigh the values, comfort, positives and negatives of stability versus the same factors concerning change. Resistance to change is usually great and may come from surprising quarters. But if management, with thorough analysis and discussion, decides change is necessary, resistance can be overcome or at least neutralized by marshalling facts, figures, analysis, and persuasion. Rumors and tremors will abound, so communication at the appropriate time is important. At times management may want to use the grapevine to reassure, or to float trial balloons.

Whatever the approach toward implementation, management must plan and prepare carefully and thoroughly to put the new organization into effect. Personnel, budgets, space, equipment, records, working relationships, and many other aspects of the organization will be effected and each must be dealt with in the detailed implementation plan and schedule. Forming or changing the chart is the easiest and least important aspect of the whole process of organizing.

Despite studies, planning, good theory, good leadership, and good people, organizations still go wrong and conflict still exists. Conflict within organizations can come about because of: poor organizational design or lack of clarity regarding responsibilities which encourages conflict; competition for scarce resources; deviance in operating style or pressures on one unit as opposed to others; different goals and styles of individuals in different departments.

Some typical signs of poor organization are: difficulty in arriving at sound and timely decisions; friction, poor morale, high turnover rates; poor communications; imbalance in workload; lack of effective controls; attitude of protecting oneself and discrediting others; difficulty in determining accountability, where the buck stops, who decided what, when; and inadequate development of people.

The executive should be aware that frequent causes of poor organization include:

1. Failure to plan properly.
2. Failure to recognize that there's a problem, that various forces—time, growth, competition, external factors, changes in services or products, changes in key personnel and the needs and aspirations of junior and middle level personnel, changes in organizational balance—necessitate change in the organizational structure.
3. Disinterest or lack of support on the part of top management.
4. Over or under emphasis on organization structure.
5. Weakness in relating organization structure to basic objectives.
6. Failure to develop or provide sufficient resources or authority for organizational planning.
7. Failure to distinguish between the short and long range.
8. Lack of clarity in relationships and in authority.
9. Failure to properly delegate authority.
10. Mixing up lines of authority and lines of communication—they are not the same.
11. Accepting authority or power and neglecting the obligations that go with it.
12. Delegating responsibility without providing the necessary authority to accomplish the tasks.
13. Lack of clarity in use of functional authority.
14. Misuse of service departments.
15. Lack of attention to the staff function and to staff-line relationships.
16. Inadequacies in theory and practice.
17. Inertia.
18. Copying the other fellow's chart.
19. A belief that organizing is basically a matter of people—their abilities, motivation, and interrelationships.
20. A view that organizing has nothing to do with people.

IN SUMMARY

The human needs in organizational design will be discussed in Chapter 0. What we have tried to indicate, in brief fashion, is the breadth and depth of the various aspects of the complex matter called "organizing." It involves both an art and a science, technical aspects, techniques, tuning in to problems and people and, of course, the presence of good people. A well-organized enterprise does not guarantee that good people will be successful or that the organization will accomplish its goals. It merely increases the chances of success. It allows good people to function at a greater level of effectiveness and efficiency and in combination with others in the organization to reach, with a greater probability of success, the goals of the company. Mediocre or poor organization just makes things harder. Managing is difficult enough as it is, the organization structure itself should not be one of the major problems, but should rather be an efficient vehicle for accomplishing results.

three

Staffing

How the executive selects, develops, motivates and leads others and how he gets people to work together effectively and harmoniously is a critical factor in the success of any organization. Fundamental to effective use of human resources are issues involved with the function of staffing the organization—finding and keeping the right people for the right jobs.

This chapter deals with staffing—recruitment, selection, training/ development, compensation, promotion and appraisal. In addition, we will focus on special concerns in regard to women and minorities. In the following chapter, as a natural link to staffing, we will deal with motivation, leadership and other aspects of directing.

RECRUITMENT

Each organization seeks to attract the largest pool possible of the best and brightest people available to fill positions at various levels. Depending upon the level of the position, different approaches can be utilized to encourage individuals to apply for positions. These include ads, posters, radio announcements, posting notices in company offices, contacting schools and governmental, civic and community organizations, contacting employment agencies, encouraging present employees to apply for positions as well as getting their relatives and good friends to apply. In some cases, because of a shortage of capable individuals, e.g., in the computer field or engineering, companies pay "bounties" to the employee who brings someone in and a "bonus" to the old and the new employee, if the new employee stays a certain period of time.

Aside from direct recruiting, an organization should be concerned about good professional, industry, public, community and employee relations, and relations with colleges, departments within colleges, and college placement officers. Efforts in these areas will bring about a flow of people who have heard good things about the company and look to the company as a logical choice for employment.

College recruitment is a usual source of attracting entry level technical or managerial talent. Companies have become more sophisticated in college recruitment and the follow-up interviews while colleges have become more professional in assisting both the student and the company. Depending upon the economy and long-term projections, companies vary the intensity of their efforts in regard to college recruiting, summer jobs, training opportunities, and internship experiences. Colleges and universities, in competition with each other, strive to provide better job placement services to students as a means of attracting students. Colleges actively seek to have companies recruit on campus and provide better facilities and information to company representatives. At the same time, they provide informational materials to students about the company and often material and instruction in regard to resume writing and interview techniques. In recruiting college students and graduates, it would be in the best interests of the company, student and college if various types of internship, summer job, and cooperative education opportunities were made available.

For higher executive positions, word-of-mouth, professional contacts, professional organization contacts, are a frequent recruitment source, although ads or specialized employment agencies are still used. There has been an increasing use of executive recruitment firms called "head hunters." Such firms can provide very valuable services, but one must carefully evaluate the qualifications of a particular firm, their performance record and professionalism. Use of executive search firms can be rather expensive because the usual charge is 30 percent of the individual's first year salary, plus expenses. Some firms charge somewhat less, some a bit more. The recruiters locate potential candidates through the resumes they have on file, through their contacts in particular industries and through their information and resource materials on the leaders and up and coming people in various firms and industries. A frequent technique is to call someone they know personally, by reputation or by status, in a company or position they are searching for and ask for names of individuals the recruiter might talk with about the position. At times, the individual they called might express interest. A call from an executive recruiter is flattering, not only in terms of possibilities for oneself, but also because it gives you a sense of power. You can recommend your acquaintances, friends, or even competitors.

To maximize the services of the headhunter, the company must be entirely candid with him. A listing of magnificent accomplishments and traits desired in a potential executive may be quite unrealistic and unattainable. The good headhunter will work with the company in developing an accurate and complete position description. He will talk with a number of individuals in the company to learn: more about the company; the job he is recruiting for; the problems and opportunities in the job and the company; the managerial style and climate; the personal and professional characteristics that would be required for success. The executive search firm would normally recommend a number of candidates, with material provided about the individual's background and the assessment of strengths and weaknesses as an individual and in comparison with others. The company would select a number of individuals for interviews. It is often important for the company to calibrate the efforts of the search firm by seeing a number of individuals.

In regard to recruitment and selection, it should be noted that companies and executive search firms tend to identify candidates who have experience and achievements in positions and in the same or related industry that are similar or reasonably close to the vacancy for which the search is being made. This is a wise and safe practice. However, at times it may pay to cast the net wider, to take a "chance" on those in dissimilar industries or in a different sector of the economy that have outstanding performance records. Such an individual may bring fresh insights and great skills and may be highly motivated to excel in a new industry or sector. But, of course, there are greater risks involving specific knowledge of the industry and adaptability in management style. In my view, executive skills are largely transferable from the private to the public sector and vice versa and from one industry to another, but one should proceed with greater caution in recruiting such individuals.

In most companies, the stress will be on developing and promoting existing staff, but there are times even in these companies that outside candidates will be recruited. For executive first entry positions and lower executive levels, effective outside recruitment is critical.

SELECTION

Given a pool of candidates, the issue is how to select the best individual for the particular position. There are a number of techniques that can be helpful in making a choice or at least reducing the likelihood of error. An important first step is knowing exactly what the position responsibilities are. The more the recruiter or decision maker knows about the problems, opportunities and demands of the job, the better able he or she is to fill the job with the best person. (In fact, this first step is also necessary for determining the recruitment strategy to be followed.) A well-developed application form or personal questionnaire can be helpful. Personality, intelligence, and psychological tests are frequently employed with somewhat mixed results as to their ability to predict performance. At still lower levels, performance and aptitude tests or oral trade tests can be used. These are helpful in indicating who cannot do the work, but less helpful in indicating which of several qualified people would perform best. Sometimes rather unusual techniques have been used such as handwriting analysis.

It is common that past employers are consulted either in writing or by telephone. Frequently, it is difficult to get a former boss to say something candid about the individual if it is negative, because of concern about lawsuits or because he does not wish to hurt the individual. A person could have been in the wrong job in a particular company or he and the managerial style or personalities of others might not have meshed well. Or, he could have grown in ability since leaving the company. In some cases, a present employer will say inaccurate or misleading things in order to get rid of an unwanted employee or in order to try to keep a very valuable employee. A previous employer may be unfair to a former employee because of unhappiness about the individual leaving or how he left. A telephone check (assuming you have the right person on the telephone) rather than asking for written comments is frequently more effective. Some individuals don't want to put negative statements in writing. But from the reference checkers point of view, a telephone conversation permits one to follow up on responses, note difference in tone, hesitations, etc. Although one expects that reference and present employer checking is performed, it is somewhat startling to note how often no check is made. The savvy selector will try to prepare probing questions for those listed as references since one normally expects that they will tend to use a string of very positive adjectives in describing the individual. It would also be important to check with others in the company, and in the industry, if possible, in addition to those listed as references. The goal in reference and previous or present employer checking is to learn as much as possible about what the individual really accomplished, his strengths, weaknesses, style and personality.

The foregoing are helpful and sometimes decisive for lower levels. The interview is also a valuable technique. For middle or upper level management, the interview is of considerable importance, although some interviewers place unwarranted emphasis on their ability as interviewers. The interviewer strives to supplement the information already compiled. He seeks to get a sense of the ability of the individual to respond and think on his feet, to ask the interviewer insightful questions. The interviewer wants to get to know the applicant as an individual and how well he might work with others and in the particular company's managerial and physical environment.

The interviewee will normally seek to establish a relationship with the individual he will work for and to learn as much as possible about the individual's thoughts, goals, style, strengths and weaknesses. He also desires to learn as much as possible about the present, short and long term opportunities, challenges and problems of the position, unit and company. The management climate should certainly be of concern.

There can be a series of one-on-one interviews or various types of group interviews. Stress interview techniques can also be used as a means of seeing how individuals react to tension. Generally, the higher the position the less likely that the Personnel Department will be a primary decision maker in the selection.

As a result of the various selection techniques utilized (and the executive search firm, company executives and psychologists, probable peers can be involved and interviews with the spouse can also be part of the process) the choices are narrowed down. To one degree or another, the usual company desires an individual who has considerable strength in most or all of the areas listed here. The number of areas of above satisfactory and outstanding performance and/or potential required, will depend upon the level of the position and the needs of the company, immediate, short and long range.

1. Thinking ability—intelligence, conceptual ability, integrates data, ability to abstract, creativity
2. Judgment/decisiveness—has the ability to decide and act at the appropriate time in the appropriate way
3. Commitment to the organization's goals and to high standards of excellence
4. Leadership—able to influence, inspire, motivate, get people to work together to achieve organizational as well as personal goals
5. Communications abilities—articulate, forceful, good writer and speaker, listens well
6. Management style—action and achievement oriented, careful planner, directly involved with others and with problems, accessable, concerned with implementation and follow through, forceful without being pushy
7. Interpersonal relations—sensitive to others feelings and takes them seriously, able to empathize, able to relate well to various levels of staff, able to recognize the interdependence on others and by others on him, cares about others
8. Frustration level—can tolerate ambiguity, confusion, stress, is adaptable
9. Self-confidence—enjoys being in a demanding, powerful role; enjoys authority, feels confident that he will do well, wants to do well
10. Stamina—physical, emotional, and mental energy, approaches life with vigor, able to handle a wide variety of problems
11. Maturity—able to work smoothly with higher levels or those temporarily in charge of a function, able to share the power or receive little glory
12. Personal traits—integrity, courage, sense of social responsibility, sense of humor, takes tasks, not himself, seriously, clear personal goals which are consistent with organization's need, optimism, perseverance, uses his own time and time of others well, content but with a healthy dissatisfaction with the status quo, calm, flexible, stable, open to new ideas

COMPENSATION

We will argue elsewhere in the book that compensation is only one of a number of factors in attracting those with outstanding records or potential. However, it is an important issue for those seeking to recruit newcomers and adequately reward present staff.

Executive compensation is a complicated business. There are a number of consulting firms that specialize in divising compensation systems based on sophisticated approaches involving external and internal salaries, position responsibility evaluations, and comparisons. Compensation units have been developed within companies that perform the same function. In developing a job evaluation system leading to a compensation system, the basic step is a job analysis. This is done by one of four general methods:

1. Ranking positions—activities and factors involved in each job are analyzed and the positions are then arranged in descending order. Frequently key or *benchmark positions* are selected and the others slotted in relation to them.

2. Assigning points—the factors in the position for which a wage is being paid are selected and a certain number of points allowed for each. The number of points determines the salary grade in which each job falls. The factors can also be weighted in terms of importance. Factors might include education, responsibility, skill, experience required, physical effort, supervisory responsibility and many others. For blue collar jobs, unavoidable hazards, unpleasant working conditions, mandatory overtime, unusual type of work may also warrant the assigning of points.

3. Factor comparisons—makes use of job factors but each job is ranked by each factor and then the percentage of the total salary paid for each factor is determined. This leads to a determination of the weight of each factor in a final ranking. Depending upon the position, the factors and the percentages will vary. Factors considered range from such things as physical effort and work surroundings to skill level, education, confidential information, contact with others in and out of the organization, experience, supervisory requirement, "bottom line" responsibility, scope of job, complexity, impact on other jobs and units, accountability for errors, etc.

4. Classification system—frequently used in public organizations
   but also for private organizations in which jobs are placed in
   categories or grades according to qualifications and/or skills
   required.

A company must strive to remain competitive with the industry
and the geographic area. In the fight to obtain the best of new business school graduates what is sometimes overlooked is the effect on
those already employed. Hiring a new group of graduates at substantially higher salaries than those hired last year or at rates higher than
for experienced staff will cause severe morale problems. The company, in paying $3,000 more to some new individuals, may have to
raise the salaries of a number of others already employed thus costing a considerable sum. At times, it may have to risk being outbid because of the internal ripple effect throughout the company or in selected areas.

However the pay range is determined, either through job evaluation, negotiating ability of the particular individual or reaction to
market conditions, a compensation figure is established. Compensation involves both salary and fringe benefits.

Salary

For executive levels, tax considerations are often very important
in determining the way salary will be paid. In fact, at higher levels,
one may trade off salary dollars for nontaxable fringe benefits or various types of deferred compensation. The total compensation package for an individual will often depend on the size of the company
(the larger the company, normally, the higher the salary) and the nature of the industry (some industries pay more because of the demands on executives). There is no set formula for the relationship of
the salary paid the highest paid individual and the next levels of executives. However, surveys indicate that the second highest paid individual tends to get 70-80% of the top individual's salary and third highest paid gets about 55-70%, the fourth highest, 45-55% and the fifth
highest 40-50%.

Although studies show that one's compensation doesn't necessarily increase by switching jobs and that companies like to promote
from within, in today's competitive market employers, on occasion,
attempt to lure people to give up good positions elsewhere. The new
and greater challenge may be primary but the money helps. The
"front-end" bonus has become a frequent technique for interesting
people in switching jobs. It is the business equivalent of the free agent

draft in baseball. The bonus offers a no strings payment in addition to salary and performance incentives. While modest bonuses may be paid to middle managers, it is the chief executive officers who reap the seven figure bonuses. The bonus is often geared not only to match but exceed (or sweeten) the value of the accumulated bonuses, stock options, performance incentives and fringe benefits the executive is giving up. Thus, in 1974, Revlon, Inc. paid $1.5 million to lure Michel C. Bererac from ITT, and Archie R. McCardell was given $1.5 million to come to the International Harvester Company in 1977 from Xerox. In 1979, Lee A. Iacocca got $1 million to come to Chrysler and CBS paid $1 million in 1980 to get Thomas Wyman to leave the Pillsbury Company. In addition to upfront money (either cash or deferred compensation), sought after chief executives working with lawyers and accountants can arrange for significant supplemental pension agreements, long-term performance bonuses, sizable annual incentive bonuses, stock grants and options, performance shares and units, guaranteed pensions, choice of car and club membership, fully paid financial counseling services, fully paid health insurance, large group life, long-term disability and travel insurance policies, large termination agreements, all relocation expenses, and various types of mortgage provisions.

For the talented and sought after, agreements can be negotiated that test the imagination and creative impulses of the person being sought, his attorney and accountant. The company, of course, wishes to attract the person, but also to structure a compensation agreement that while providing satisfaction and security also serves to motivate. Thus bonuses and incentives tied to specific performance criteria are of increasing importance.

There is a reverse side to the salary figure. Sometimes market conditions may be such that companies are more likely to recruit, for entry level positions, Bachelor's degree holders rather than MBA's. In a College Placement Council survey of average salaries offered 1980 graduates the following range of starting salaries were indicated.

Bachelor's Degree
Humanities $12,888
General Business 14,616
Economics 15,024
Accounting 15,516
Math 17,700
Computer Science 18,696
Electrical Engineering 20,280

MBA Degree
   Nontechnical   undergraduate $21,540
   Technical undergraduate   23,652

   Some companies are beginning to recruit fewer MBA's and more
BA's because of the cost differentials involved. The average MBA will
earn from about $21,000 to $24,000 but good students at top institutions can get $30,000 and more. In fact, if they join management
consulting firms, their salaries are likely to be in the mid to high $30's.
In addition to the salary differential between BA's and MBA's, starting salaries for MBA graduates of prestigeous institutions are climbing so fast that the new hires may be earning more than someone
hired a year before from the same institution who has had a year's
experience and an increase. Also the "care and feeding" of MBA's
may pose some difficult problems for some companies in terms of
the aspirations of these graduates to be on a "very fast track." The
MBA graduate has, in recent years, been a very sought after person,
and business schools have been besieged by both recruiters and young
college graduates and those already in the work force clamoring to
get in. But it may be that in some instances they may price themselves out of the market or become a glut on the market. Companies
may tend to become more selective as to which jobs should go to
MBA holders and which can go to BA holders and thus have fewer
jobs available for MBA's. It is also likely, given the growth in the
number of MBA programs being developed to meet student demand
(and the demand for universities to generate income—MBA programs
are normally highly profitable to universities) that companies will be
more interested in the quality of specific MBA programs. Thus, graduates from the prestigious programs will always be in demand but
mediocre graduates of mediocre programs may soon overwhelm the
market. The MBA may find that he is not paid more than the BA
holders. In short, all MBA programs and graduates are not equal, and
the differences are likely to show up in job offers, starting salaries,
and nature of the work assigned. (It is interesting to note some techniques companies use to attract MBA graduates of prestige schools.
Although often forbidden by a school's recruiting code, some companies seek to offer "exploding bonuses," which are intended to reward those who quickly accept a job offer. A student might be offered $1,000-$2,000 for accepting the job the day it was offered or
within twenty-four hours of when it was offered and $100-$200 a
day less for each day the student held off making a decision.)

What may happen to MBA's has already happened to attorneys. There appears to be something of a glut on the market. In addition, the Wall Street law firms in New York and the big firms throughout the country have been in an expensive competition for the top graduates from the top schools. But the price of a starting attorney has become so high that a firm is forced to evaluate a young attorney in a tougher and quicker fashion than before. And, to save money, the big firms rely more on paralegal personnel to do lower level work thus freeing the time of the higher cost attorneys. The salary levels, the use of para-legals, greater reliance on word processing equipment may all result in fewer opportunities at very high salaries for young attorneys. The picture is not all that bleak however. Given the pattern of recent years of more and more lawsuits and governmental legislation and regulation and the growth in the size of legal staffs within companies, law school is still not a bad place to spend three years of one's life.

FRINGE BENEFITS

In attracting as well as retaining good staff, fringe benefits are of considerable importance. Pension programs with vesting as required by ERISA and even earlier than required, vacation time improvements, health care and life insurance coverage are all generally standard benefits throughout the United States, with, of course, some companies providing better benefits than others. Fringe benefits as a percentage of payroll costs have been rising significantly over the past decade, 25%-40% of direct payroll is a common range. The issue now for many large companies is to try to get control of these expensive benefit programs, particularly in light of increasing health costs and the demand for new and expensive commitments.

Before discussing particular fringe benefits, it should be noted that a company must decide which programs it will pay for entirely and which in part. It is, of course, to the employees advantage to have the employer pick up the entire cost of all fringe benefits. The problem for the employer is that for fully funded programs he pays more as costs rise, but he doesn't get much credit for it from unions and employees. The cost of fully funded programs is regarded as "old money" in collective bargaining and generally employees ask, "what

have you added," or "what have you done for me lately?" Many employers would like to pay a set dollar amount for health, dental, life
insurance or vision coverage, for example, and anything above that is
paid for by employees. This encourages concern about use or abuse
of the fringe benefits. Further, deductibles are also helpful in reducing abuse for the program. However, under collective bargaining and
because of competitive pressures and wage guidelines, it may be
tempting or necessary for employers to pick up all or most of the
cost of various fringe benefits. In the public sector, it is common to
give rich pension, vacation, work time and other fringe benefit packages in order to hold down the salary increase. This allows the political executive to seem to be agreeing to "moderate" settlements and
thus enhance his political career. But, in fact, the fringe benefits, particularly pensions, will come back to haunt his successors.

Dental care benefits are the fastest growing health care benefit in
the United States. Currently, about sixty million individuals have
such coverage compared to about five million in 1967. Insurance
companies provide most of the coverage. Dental service corporations,
union self-insurance trusts and prepayment plans provide the rest of
the coverage. In 1967, insurance companies alone paid $42 million,
in 1978 they paid $1.8 billion. A recent survey indicated that about
60% of the responding companies provide dental coverage with about
15% of those responding indicating they were considering such coverage. Clearly, dental coverage is becoming the rule rather than the
exception.

Vision care programs are also on the rise though lagging far behind
dental care programs. As a benefit, but also to increase productivity
and reduce health care and lost time costs, alcohol and drug abuse
programs are being offered with more frequency, and physical exami-
nation programs are commonplace for entering employees. Annual or
biennial exams are common for executives and less common for other categories of employees. Some companies now offer smoking and
weight control programs and a good many encourage and provide
facilities for various types of exercise programs.

CAFETERIA BENEFIT PLANS

The huge increase in cost of employee benefits has brought about
increased interest in the concept of flexible benefit plans for employ-

ees, frequently referred to as "cafeteria" benefit plans. We shall describe the concept but wish to indicate from the outset that very few companies have as yet adopted such approaches. Plans exist at American Can, TRW, Educational Testing Service and a few others. There are some real difficulties in the concept:

1. Administrative costs will be significantly higher, at least at the outset.
2. There may be significant collective bargaining implications: (a) that which in effect the employees "purchase" by exercising choice, may eventually become part of the core package and is theirs without purchase; (b) conversely, unions may be unhappy that it undercuts their ability to show exciting bargaining gains—"we got a new vision plan."
3. Planning is necessary—questionnaires are necessary to survey needs and desires of employees (this can help narrow options to be offered and also avoid "adverse selection" which results in employees with great needs choosing an option which then results in great cost increases). "Adverse selection" need not occur. There are a few ways one can reduce the probabilities or effect of adverse selection: (1) subsidizing some coverages, (2) pricing according to probabilities of claim occurrences, (3) grouping of coverages to attract more employees.
4. Good communications, information and counseling are necessary—employees must receive information about the program, what they have chosen, etc.
5. The program should be tested on a small scale first.
6. The employer may have an obligation to insure that the employee doesn't make poor selections.
7. A good computerized payroll and personnel records system is necessary or must be developed to make the plan work.

A cafeteria benefit plan allows employees to select from a range of benefit alternatives available—thus the analogy to a cafeteria's range of selections. Management tends to favor the concept in the hope that it will save money through not paying for things employees really don't want and still meet the ever increasing demands for better and more benefits by creating flexible plans that can be tailored to individual needs. It can also help alleviate dissatisfaction by some employees who feel that the company is spending more money on the fringe benefits of others. For example, an unmarried employee may feel that he or she is entitled to extra compensation of some kind to make up for the fact that the company pays for some of all of the health or life insurance coverage for another employee's spouse and children. Another advantage is that in choosing options employees get a better understanding of the benefits available and their real cost to them and the company. This may lead to greater satisfaction in terms of understanding that their total compensation is a great deal more than their salary. Before discussing a full approach to cafeteria benefits, it should be noted that a number of companies provide some flexibility in allowing a choice between a group medical plan or a health maintenance organization, a choice of deferred profit sharing or cash, a choice of additional cash payment in lieu of vacations.

Full blown cafeteria plans owe their existence to the 1978 Tax Revenue Act which contained provisions which made this approach attractive to both employees and employers. The Act permits offering benefits in areas of welfare benefits/cash, profit sharing/cash; welfare benefits/profit sharing.

Basically, there is a core package and then options. A core program is the fundamental security obligation a company owes its employees—medical coverage, disability coverage, pension, vacation, group term life insurance. The basic coverage cannot be reduced. It can be added to by exercising one's choices. Employees then select additional benefits available based on the credits allocated to them. The credits are based on the cash value of the benefits available to be "purchased." Basically, the credits (or dollars) represent what the value of the package was to the individual prior to the cafeteria approach and the value of the core package under the cafeteria approach.

In each area of the core, there can be options. For health coverage the options might include: the amount of deductible paid by employees; the percentage of cost paid by the plan; an extended or enriched medical coverage plan; choice of plans; vision coverage; health examinations; hearing examinations and coverage; dental plan (with variations as to coverage, payment, percentage and deductible); prescription drugs.

In the life insurance area, options can be purchased for up to four times an individual's salary thus enriching a basic core coverage. Other alternatives might include survivor insurance benefits, life insurance for spouse and dependents, travel insurance, accidental death and dismemberment insurance.

Extra vacation time might be purchased up to a set limit. Improved disability coverage can also be purchased and special retirement plans and other means of capital accumulation for savings or retirement can be offered.

American Can Company has one of the best developed programs. It is interesting to note that in terms of the approximately 9,000 salaried employees involved in the program, the employees' choices of benefits were as predicted. Young single employees and married women tend to opt for more time off, older employees are more concerned with income, saving for their children's education and retirement. Those with young families are most concerned with life insurance and medical coverage.

We have discussed cafeteria plans because they will loom large in the future. However, it is possible to have a middle ground between expensive and wasteful standardized plans and even more expensive and difficult to administer cafeteria plans. A company might develop patterned benefit plans for all employees, perhaps 3, 4, or 5 standard packages to fit the needs of various groupings based on age, family conditions or life style.

Fringe benefits will continue to be a very important area in terms of cost implications, attracting and retaining employees, and staff satisfaction. In addition to the fringe benefits cited in this section there are a number of others that are attracting attention: prepaid legal services, car insurance, mortgage assistance and insurance, increased tuition remission for employees and tuition scholarships or special loans to cover employees, spouses and children, lay-off insurance. In the past quarter of a century, there has been a geometric growth in the cost, breadth and depth of employee benefits. This growth may slow down a bit, but it will certainly continue. In fact, after human imagination just about reaches the limit as to what it can conceive as a new fringe benefit, I expect to see proposals for veterinary cost insurance!

OTHER THOUGHTS ABOUT COMPENSATION

Frequently insufficient attention is paid to middle level executive compensation. The Board of Directors and top management normally focus on compensation for those in the highest levels of management, the unions focus on their constituents but, at times, the middle managers do not receive sufficient attention and may find their percentage increases falling behind both the upper levels and the lower levels.

For middle and upper managers and if possible for all levels of employees, compensation should be tied into performance not only in terms of bonuses and merit aspects of salary increases, but also in terms of considering the "cost of living" increase or the "across-the-board" increase. Satisfactory performance should be expected even to "stay even" in the face of a rising cost of living.

Indexing has become very widespread, particularly in union agreements, as a means of providing salary increases or increases prior to taking into account merit considerations. It is easy and convenient to tie increases for blue collar and some or many levels of white collar workers to the cost of living consumer price index. The problem is that the company may not be able to afford it. Also, one must define which index for which region. There are serious concerns about the appropriate components within the consumer price index, and the more we as a nation become tied to indexing the more likely this will fuel the fires of increased cost of living. Also, employees may tend to regard the cost of living increase as automatic and not related to performance and thus be looking for more (whether related to performance or not) in order to keep ahead or gain on the cost of living.

EXECUTIVE COMPENSATION

Although we have mentioned various aspects of executive compensation previously, we now deal with a conceptual approach. Boards of Directors are taking an increasingly active role in executive compensation through Board Compensation Committees. These committees are likely to be composed of a majority of outside directors. But in determining compensation, it is rare to find a committee with the technical expertise in compensation or the detailed knowledge to evaluate objectives and particular executives' performance against objectives. The issue for the compensation committee is what is the appropriate pay level for top executives and the relationship of performance to pay.

The salary survey is an appropriate starting point for committee consideration, because practically all companies wish to be competitive. Some, in fact, wish to be well above the competition. In using the survey instrument, one must carefully choose the right survey based on which are the right companies as a standard of comparison. Size, performance, type of industry, location, risks involved, complexity are all factors that should be considered. Job titles in one company may not connote the same responsibilities as in other companies. Their functions must be analyzed as well as factors influencing the job.

Aside from the raw data as indicated above, judgment is involved. Weak performing companies will normally pay less than strong performers though these companies may have to pay a good deal to attract individuals or to keep excellent people in order to improve company performance. The value of the total compensation package must be considered as well as the psychic and other non-financial rewards available. The committee should analyze the advantages and disadvantages of paying above or below the appropriate competitive average and the techniques used in developing ranges and salaries within ranges.

Having established some base data and the outlines of a system, the key element becomes relating pay to performance, both short range and long range. Generally, an annual cash bonus is used for short term performance and various types of capital accumulation techniques based on stock acquisition are used for long term performance. It is difficult to judge short term performance, but one approach is to have a reasonable but demanding profit target based on considerable specificity as to what has to be accomplished to meet the objective. There may also be some non-financial objectives that should be considered as part of a bonus plan evaluation, e.g., systems or recruiting improvements. In developing a long term performance plan, the directors should be concerned as to who is in the plan; how and what performance targets are set; how are measurements made; how much will the plan cost and what the size of the awards will be; how often will awards be made; how will the plan and awards be communicated to executives and in corporate reports.

Basic to the above steps is the integration of executive compensation programs into the company's long range financial and business planning. Executive compensation is a reward and motivating mechanism, but it also is a critical tool of the directors and top management in directing the enterprise and in planning and control. Also basic, is the need to define criteria of performance, short and long term. For long term performance, for example, dividends, book value, stock price, return on investment ratios are reasonable measures in addition to net profit. Pearl Meyer in an article in *Management Review*, August 1980, indicated that the executive compensation program for the 1980s must decide:

- The balance of annual versus long term compensation.

- The balance of fixed versus variable income and costs.
- The proper balancing of payment forms—stock, cash and non-cash.
- The timing of compensation—current vs. deferred, midcareer vs. deferred to retirement.
- Appropriate levels of risk.
- The balance of compensation differentials within the organization between levels, units, and job types.

TRAINING AND DEVELOPMENT

Training and development is the big growth area within the staffing and human resources function. By management development we include (based on Peter Drucker's views) a stress on developing management (concerned with organization's health, growth, and survival) and developing managers (health, growth and accomplishments of the individual as a person and as a member of the organization). We also believe that true development is based on job performance and responsibilities but it is aided by a variety of techniques that are relevant to one's present responsibilities or the techniques lay the groundwork for future growth and accomplishment.

Top management in most companies recognize the need to recruit the best people they can and to enhance and update their knowledge through a variety of techniques. Much of the technical knowledge an individual brings to a job will be slightly to greatly outdated within five to ten years depending upon the particular job and industry. Further, an individual's job or job requirements may change and he may now require greater knowledge of supervisory techniques, planning, control systems, computer technology, international operations, marketing, governmental relations, etc. To enrich and expand one's knowledge, to introduce the latest thoughts and techniques, to provide hands on experience as well as new knowledge and skills, to enhance conceptual, technical and human skills, companies spend billions of dollars a year in training. The more progressive companies have an executive development plan involving every executive or potential executive. The development plan involves training of various types through job experience and formal training as well as development in the sense of a progression and variety of task and job assignments. It is wise each year (or semi-annually) to have a training and development interview with each executive or subordinate. One should discuss needs and desires in regard to training and development for the individual by the next year and in the future and to see how progress is being made toward short and long term training and development goals.

This career review meeting might include discussion concerning:

1. Where the organization and unit is heading in the next few years.
2. The employees' goals, aspirations, expectations, activities within and outside the company.
3. Possible job opportunities, growth, development on the job.
4. How the employees' goals, performance, opportunities in the organization mesh together.
5. Ways of developing a specific development plan and how to implement through specific training opportunities, opportunities for experience and exposure, job enrichment.
6. Drawing upon a specific plan including people the employee might contact as resources, how you as a manager might help him, what actions the employee must take.
7. Follow up with a memo to the employee outlining the plan of action, target dates, etc.

American businesses spend an estimated $10 billion a year to provide post high school education and training to 12.7 million people according to one study. Other studies reach figures of $100 billion a year and 16 million students. In comparison, in 1980 federal spending for post secondary education is about $11 billion and in 1979 college and universities spent about $50 billion from all sources to educate an estimated 11.7 million students. In addition to job related training normally conducted by company personnel, companies spend an estimated $500 million a year on tuition assistance plans helping to finance employees taking courses at colleges and universities. Labor unions have negotiated clauses calling for an additional $20 million a year for education benefits for blue and white collar workers.

Tuition assistance programs are the most widely offered employer education plans. Surveys by the Conference Board and others indicate that only about 4% of the eligible employees utilize the program.

Some companies could claim that this shows lack of interest. However, another explanation may be that the low rate is due to difficulties in taking time off, scheduling problems, poor communications and information about programs, lack of encouragement or discerned payoff to the employees, restrictions as to eligibility or poorly designed plans which cost the employees too much.

Although some colleges and universities try to tailor their courses, schedules time and location of courses to the needs of working people or a particular company, many do not. It is difficult in many instances to provide the specific detailed training that a company wishes in a course geared to the general student. The company may find the course too "academic" and not suitable. The educational institution may find that it is asked to be training and not educating, and giving academic credits where these are not warranted. A middle ground can be found that meets company and employee needs without lowering academic standards and integrity, but much more has to be done by the company and institutions in understanding each others needs and traditions. For some levels of training, community colleges can be helpful and attuned to the needs of the local company.

Some companies have established their own training programs using their own staff or outside consultants and organizations. Many large firms have established their own facilities—American Telephone and Telegraph, General Motors, General Electric, International Business Machines, Xerox Corporation.

A formal management education program can consist of specialized training programs performed by in-house or consultant staff to a 26 week, or 6 month, or 1 year course of full-time study at a prestigious business school. At various stages of an individual's career the method and type of training, the training medium and course content will vary. Some universities have set up specialized programs for executives either with or without academic credit. Others offer regular management courses at convenient times.

A well conceived management development program will assess the organization's short and long term managerial and technical needs, the capabilities and background of present staff, the likely progression of specific individuals, the job and special assignments that should be made over time, and the formal education needs and ways to meet the needs. Training needs can be met by:

1. in-house training
2. consultants
3. educational institutions

4. courses available from specific organizations
5. professional programs and courses by associations
6. conferences/conventions/seminars
7. self-study/books/tapes
8. public speaking
9. degree programs/extension programs/MBA and Executive MBA and programs/management, executive and supervisory courses
10. rotational assignments

Some of the common executive development programs include courses dealing with:

- speed reading
- oral and written communications
- sensitivity training
- time management
- management of stress
- problem solving and decision making
- supervisory skills
- developing one's own management style
- labor relations
- quantitative analysis techniques
- control techniques
- computer applications
- business and government
- business and society
- human relations techniques
- affirmative action
- occupational safety and health
- managerial grid
- management theories and concepts
- financial management
- holding effective meetings
- management by objectives
- team building
- evaluating and appraising employees, setting objectives and priorities
- budgeting
- dealing with government regulations
- international business
- administrative and organizational skills

- motivating yourself and others

There are, of course, a wide variety of specialized courses that are given or can be developed in regard to production, marketing, accounting, etc. The numbers and types of courses would depend upon the company's needs and the individual's level and needs. Some companies would also regard physical fitness and health programs, wilderness experience, community and industry service experience, as part of training and development.

Increasing attention is being paid to the training and development needs of new or prospective managers and of first line supervisors. Whether through college courses, company courses or specialized approaches such as American Management Association courses, emphasis should be placed on such things as:

- your role as a supervisor/manager
- establishing yourself as a supervisor/manager
- basic management principles
- communication
- interpersonal relations
- motivating employees
- building team spirit
- planning
- organizing
- focusing on productivity, efficiency and quality
- decision making and problem solving
- legal responsibilities of a supervisor/manager
- managing work and workers
- time management
- conflict resolution
- appraising performance
- developing a results orientation for employees and the unit
- controlling
- evaluating results

We have stressed formal courses, but it should be noted that there are other important ways of developing an executive. These include: planning and progression of different assignments; assignments to committees, task forces, as assistant to, as project team member or leader, junior board of director; and jobs and experience in and out of the company. Further, the training courses and job assignments should be tied together to enhance the ability to perform current or new assignments.

A quality and successful management development program:

- Involves a commitment of significant attention and resources by top management.
- Stresses the primary importance of the job as the foremost development vehicle aided and abetted by the other techniques. Formal training is used to improve or prepare for on the job development. Job assignments are made to build upon new skills developed.
- Stresses a development plan for each individual involving the techniques indicated above.
- Management development for the individual is linked with his performance and the assessment of his potential.
- Development of subordinates is considered an important managerial task and an important component of the executive's appraisal.
- Self-development efforts are encouraged.
- Development programs are evaluated on a cost effectiveness basis.
- A variety of approaches are used geared to the needs of the company and the individuals.

Much money is invested in training and like all other expenditures, the effect should be evaluated. Is the company getting its money's worth? Before that question can be answered in a factual way the company must be very clear as to what it wants to achieve, short and long run, and how it will measure results (including student's views). Training can, indeed, be very expensive and wasteful, but if done creatively and correctly it is critical in assuring the short and long run success of the company.

APPRAISAL

We recruit, select and compensate as best we can, we develop and train and then we want to see the results. Performance appraisal is a vital aspect of good management. However, it is often a much criticized function.

Performance appraisal systems can be used to achieve several goals. Part of their problem in regard to effectiveness and acceptance may well be that in trying to accomplish more than one goal they confuse, raise doubts and prove ineffective. Although one form (probably a very long one) can be used for the four broad purposes listed below, generally it is best to have a specific form for each of the following purposes:

- Determining salary increases based on the degree to which established objectives are met (either below, at, or above the levels set), and as compared with other employees performing similar organizational levels. This is the most frequent use of performance appraisals. When used in this way they can be tied in to management by objectives systems.

- Determining incentive or bonus awards which may be based on specific tasks or year-end results.

- Determining potential and suitability for promotion—through assessment centers and use of management inventories a determination can be made as to how well the individual meets the company's present and future needs.

- Determining employee development needs.

Many companies have stumbled in developing appraisal programs or lifting one "off the shelf" from a consultant or another organization, based on: difficulties in defining performance (is it results as management believes, or effort as employees believe?), defining the factors relevant to the job, defining the way in which ratings will be conducted—the scale to be used, standards of comparison, "hard graders" vs. "soft graders." A major difficulty is training raters in using the forms. Some very sophisticated (and at times expensive) techniques can be used. Other times, simpler methods will do. At the end of this section, one simple approach is outlined.

Depending upon the company and its needs, appraisal techniques can be applied annually, semi-annually, quarterly, on the employee's anniversary date, upon completion of the project or some other pertinent benchmark. Experts group appraisal techniques into the following categories: (1) trait evaluation, (2) management by objectives, (3) responsibility rating and (4) free form—essay. We will discuss each category briefly.

Trait Evaluation

For a group of employees a standardized form is used which involves a check list of qualities, attributes or "traits" of performance. The rating scale can be 0-10, 0-100, letter grades from F or D to A, or words such as outstanding, above average, average, below average, unsatisfactory. Depending upon the gradations desired, instead of a five-point scale, one might have seven or ten. Traits generally used involve quality of work, quantity of work, cooperation, job knowledge, creativity, initiative, dependability, effort, timeliness, planning ability, supervisory ability (if appropriate) and a host of other characteristics.

This method is simple to install and administer, but the traits are general, don't relate to performance standards and can vary widely as used by different raters.

Management By Objectives

Employee suggests and supervisor agrees on employee's performance objectives for the rating period. The objectives are stated as specifically as possible in terms of results or standards to be achieved. Periodically, progress is monitored and at the end of rating period it is assessed.

This method is performance based and valuable as a planning and appraisal technique. However, each employee is rated on different factors and sometimes on different scales. There can be a difference in standards applied to setting objectives and the negotiations between employee and supervisor may result in easy or too hard objectives for one individual as compared with others. A good deal of training is necessary in goal setting and the administration and installation of the system may be very time consuming.

Responsibility Rating

Requires the development of position descriptions or a list of job responsibilities in order of importance with indications, where and when appropriate, of specific standards of performance for each criteria or responsibility. Job responsibilities are reviewed each year and standards set. Results and expectations are reviewed periodically and at the end of the rating period an assessment is made usually on a three-point scale, Outstanding—Superior—Satisfactory. A fourth point—Unsatisfactory—can be added.

This system has the advantages of a common rating scale with rating factors specifically tailored to the position and the necessity for a review of position responsibilities. Two problems associated with it are: many job descriptions may be needed and the need to communicate objectives at the beginning of a rating period.

Free Form

As the name implies, there is little or no format set for rating the subordinates. It could involve an essay about the employee; it could involve answering very general questions such as "what are his major contributions," "significant strengths," "significant weaknesses," "areas to be developed or improved." There may be a forced choice method among generalized descriptions of performance. Another approach is evaluation at critical incidents, benchmarks or milestones.

This system focuses on exact performance, not traits, objective or generally assumed responsibilities. But, widely fluctuating standards and methods may be used and the system depends very much on the writing ability of the rater.

To Summarize

In looking at all four approaches, one has to determine which goal or goals he wishes the appraisal system to fulfill and then evaluate the system.

In general, the trait checklist is good for salary administration, but very weak in terms of incentive awards, promotability evaluation or employee development. MBO is excellent for incentive awards and good for promotability evaluation, but weak for salary administration or employee development. Responsibility rating is excellent for salary administration, good for incentive awards and employee development, and weak for evaluating promotability. The free form method is excellent for employee development and promotability evaluation, weak for incentive awards and very weak for salary administration. Of course, other considerations should also be used in evaluating a technique: cost; ease of installation; ease of administration; training required; objectivity; "halo-effect," relationship to job.

Another way of looking at performance evaluation is that one attempts to evaluate the effort the individual is putting forth, the skills and abilities he brings to the job, and the understanding he has of what he is supposed to do (his role). The appraisal then, is a means of evaluating all three aspects and improving all three aspects. One can judge traits, abilities, skills, efforts, role understanding, as well as behavior and outputs.

A few general points should be made. It is natural, especially if it's an annual rating, to go over the appraisal form and then immediately mention the salary increase. Although the employee and the supervisor both expect the reward system to be very much related to the performance appraisal, it is better to keep salary increases separate from the appraisal meeting. Further, when talking about salary, it is wise to indicate that the appraisal was only one determinant (although a major one). Economic status of the company may be another factor. This allows full discussion and a sharper focus on the immediate topics at hand. It is also helpful if the employee had the opportunity to comment on the rating orally and in writing before the rating is cast in concrete, and some means of airing any grievance about biases or judgment of the supervisor.

There is often a tendency to either rank everyone as satisfactory in order to escape justifying high or low ratings, or to rank everyone high. The ranking style may also be associated with what the supervisor wants to do in terms of merit awards or bonuses, or a plea to higher authority for more money for merit awards. It is important for top management to stress the importance of fair but discerning evaluations, based on reasonably high standards of performance, communicated well in advance of the rating discussion to those affected. Individuals affected as evaluated or as evaluators should be encouraged to be involved in developing or refining systems. The goal is that the subordinate believes that the system as applied to him and others is fair and that while judgments, often subjective, are involved, that there are reasonable criteria reasonably applied to all. Management must look to the system(s) to fulfill its goal(s) in a manner which can be, in fact, appraised. Appraising the appraisal is necessary in order to determine the need for modifications in order to meet company objectives.

Appraisal systems and philosophies currently in use are undergoing critical analysis. Most experts want to develop systems that do more than determine salaries. But the issue is—are the appraisals judging results, behavior or both. Further, shouldn't the appraisal highlight managerial behavior that should be rewarded and reinforced or discontinued, serve as a development tool, indicate future potential, and in time of litigation or potential litigation, stand up in the face of court challenges in regard to discrimination. Current trends include: some greater use of the critical incident method; a review of the appraisal by the rater's superior; a concern for the costliness of evaluation systems; training in the use of performance appraisals; involving subordinates, peers as well as superiors in an individual's appraisal; evaluating the appraiser as well as the appraisee by requiring appraisers to indicate the most important tasks performed by the subordinate, how well he does them, his assets, liabilities, strengths and weaknesses, supervisor's plans for helping employee improve his current position and prepare for promotion; hybrid systems that combine an emphasis on goal setting, results achieved, evaluating behaviour. There is also increasing concern for the often conflicting goals in a performance appraisal system—salary increases vs. employee development; being a mentor vs. being a judge; promotion decisions vs. career planning or succession planning.

Some observations regarding appraisal systems include:

1. Perhaps the most important effect of performance appraisal is in role negotiation and goal setting. Setting goals improves role understanding, but not necessarily motivation.
2. The performance appraisal form and system you use is as much a matter of philosophy and trust as it is a matter of science. You need to reach agreement among raters and ratees that the system is right for the organization at this moment in its history. Legitimacy has to be created for the system and the form, but don't get overly fixated on a particular form or system.
3. It is valuable to have those being rated prepare or compile information to be used in the appraisal interview. Future performance goals tend to be discussed more thoroughly and subordinates perceive this as a means for more discussion of personal and career goals. They perceive significantly higher participation, ownership, contribution and tend to be more pleased and committed. Managers are also more satisfied about the interview. Even if the employee doesn't actually participate in developing the appraisal system or contribute to the interview, the invitation to participate results in increased motivation and better role understanding. (Be careful about a backlash effect. Some higher executives may feel that a manager has given in to subordinates if he invites their full partici-

pation. There may also be polarization of views about the job between the evaluator and the person being evaluated.)

4. Appraisal is an extension of work climate—if there is openness, great trust and support—there will be great support of the appraisal system.

5. If jobs are well specified in terms of descriptions and understanding of objectives, role, etc. there tends to be significantly higher positive results from performance appraisal—increased motivation, learning, information exchange, a sense of supervisory assistance, setting future performance goals.

6. The evaluator should consider talking about career goals in a context separate from the performance appraisal interview. It appears that discussions of such goals have no real effect on the performance appraisal and just takes time away from the interview. (As discussed earlier, salary increases should not be discussed during performance appraisal sessions.)

7. Despite the various problems and costs involved, performance appraisal systems force something important to be done on an individual and organizational basis that would not be done without a system.

8. Sound implementation is critical to success of a performance appraisal system.

   (a) Get appropriate persons involved early in the discussions; include those who will be evaluated under the system, will evaluate others, will administer the system.

   (b) In designing a system, be clear as to your philosophy and purposes in regard to performance appraisal and have the philosophy and purpose widely disseminated and clearly stated in all descriptions of the system. Any system must be consistent with management philosophy and practice.

   (c) Be sure you have thought through the mechanics of the system—what unit and individuals will administer the system, how, what resources and capabilities are available or must be obtained.

   (d) How is performance appraisal to be linked to other personnel systems—promotion, training, salary, transfers.

   (e) Any system must recognize the nature of work at various levels. Management work, for example, is very varied.

   (f) Be concerned about your compliance with legal requirements. By creating appraisal data you can be creating legal problems for yourself. Thus, the appraisal system needs to be validated and documented in the sense that the system and instruments used are reasonably related to the jobs being appraised.

(g) Above all, as indicated previously, one needs top management support and use of the system. Employees at all levels should perceive that appraisals are taken seriously at all levels and the results effect both the individual and the company.

An Example

The following describes a simple appraisal system in one area of an organization. Although the forms are used in helping to determine the merit component of salary increases, their primary function is evaluation, appraisal and planning for improvement within a context of full discussion between staff members and supervisors. The categories and descriptive terms for all levels were shared among all staff and were intended to communicate what top management expected, what was important to them as well as to staff being reviewed.

In describing the evaluation process, it was made clear to all supervisors that they were expected to set reasonably high standards of performance and not be overly harsh or lenient in the ratings. The goal for the meeting between the supervisor and the subordinate to discuss the evaluation was that in the event improvements or further training were necessary each should understand what is to be done, why, how it should be accomplished, how it will be evaluated and how the supervisor can be helpful. Even if no specific improvements are necessary, it is expected that the evaluation meeting would result in setting performance objectives and goals for the next year.

The forms were developed by several top officials and commented upon and modified by those who would be involved in their use both as evaluators and as evaluated.

The system deals with four levels of professional staff:

Professional Staff Member
Unit Head (Manager or Supervisor of a Section or Unit)
Assistant Administrator (Assistant Controller(s))
Administrator, Associate Administrator (Budget Director, Controller, Associate Controller, Directors)

The goal was to keep the criteria and forms as simple as possible. Most of the evaluation categories that were established are applicable for all four levels. As the level became higher, additional categories were added and, in some cases, some categories were eliminated. Exhibit I illustrates the form that is used for the Professional Staff Member. The same format holds for all levels, namely:

- Specific categories and descriptive material, guide for rating in one of three columns; ample space on the form to indicate: (1) particular skills, ability, demands of the position, significant contribution to the Office and the University not covered in the criteria and columns; (2) areas where further effort, concentration or training are necessary; (3) suggestions by Supervisor (Rater) for how improvements can and should be made.
- Additional comments to explain a rating.
- Overall evaluation.
- Additional justification for determining that the individual is in the highest or lowest overall category.
- Signatures by rater, person rated, and the rater's supervisor.
- An opportunity for the person evaluated to attach comments.
- A description of each category, as well as a "Guide to Ratings."

The basic categories as indicated in Exhibit I are: "Dependability, Adaptability, Attendance, Cooperation, Quality of Work, Quantity of Work, Job Knowledge, Reasoning, Potential, Public Relations and Communication Skills."

For the next level, Unit Head, an additional category was added, "Managerial/Supervisory Ability." This category, which also applies to the next two levels, is outlined in Exhibit IIA.

For the Assistant Administrator level, "Attendance" and "Quality of Work do not appear, but "Administering Work Programs" is added as a new category as indicated in Exhibit IIB.

For the highest level of the Division, Controller, Budget Director, Investment Administrator, Associate Controller and Directors, "Attendance, Quantity of Work, Job Knowledge, and Potential" do not appear. However, "Administering Work Programs" (as noted above) and "Professional Development, Planning and Perspective" are added as indicated in Exhibit IIC.

SUMMARY

Performance Planning and Progress Evaluation Appraisal, by whatever name or approach, is just a tool. The critical aspects are the

Exhibit I

Exhibit I

PERFORMANCE PLANNING AND PROGRESS EVALUATION ANALYSIS

Name of Individual: Unit:

Period of Evaluation: From   To

Professional Staff

RATER: Very carefully analyze employee performance in each work factor area indicated. Be certain you rate each factor separately, based solely on the performance during the evaluation period. Keep in mind that the concept behind this performance planning and progress evaluation analysis is that the supervisor and each employee should discuss jointly what work is being done in relation to departmental goals and how well that work is being done. Please check the most appropriate box based on the material in the guide to ratings and the category description.

Category Description	O E	Guide to Ratings M I	P
Dependability: Degree of supervision needed to carry out tasks to completion to meet job goals; keeps supervisor informed of new issues, potential problems, progress.	Self-starter; rarely needs supervision; always keeps supervisor informed on new issues, potential problems, progress.	Needs some supervision; dependable on routine work; usually keeps supervisor informed of new issues, potential problems, progress.	Needs frequent supervision and reorientation on job goals; sometimes or often doesn't keep supervisor informed of new issues, potential problems, progress.
Adaptability: Ability to learn quickly; ability to adjust to changes in job assignment, methods, personnel or surroundings.	Quick to catch on; welcomes new assignments; undisturbed by changes.	Learns well and willingly; accepts change.	Learns with difficulty; tends to resist change.
Attendance: Consider number of absences, times arriving late, length of lunch periods and number and length of refreshment breaks.	Outstanding record of attendance, punctuality and use of time.	Rarely absent, late or misuses time.	Some problems with attendance; punctuality or misuse of time.
Cooperation: Willingness to respond to supervision, ability to get along with co-workers, recognizes value of establishing objectives	Responds with enthusiasm to challenge, responsibility, supervisors and co-workers.	Usually responds well to supervision and co-workers; sometimes takes initiative.	Needs prodding; some problem with co-workers; difficulty setting objectives.
Quantity of Work: Ability to meet or surpass established goals; consider frequency of need for personal overtime and use of time during normal workday.	Rarely misses deadlines; sometimes ahead of schedule; sets new goals upon task completion.	Produces all assigned work; usually makes good use of time.	Rarely behind in work but does not seek other tasks when job goals are met.
Quality of Work: Consider accuracy, attention to detail and neatness of work, need to re-do work; orderliness of work place, thoroughness, creativity and innovation.	Exceptional accuracy, constant attention to detail; very well organized.	Few errors; usually thorough and attentive; generally neat.	Does acceptable work but needs more attention to accuracy; sometimes lacks neatness; sometimes work is unacceptable.

Category Description	O	E	Guide to Ratings M	I	P

Job Knowledge: Degree of familiarity with job procedures and skills essential to the job, ability to take timely action.

O: Has completely mastered all phases of job; can adapt knowledge, methods and procedures to new tasks.

E: Thorough knowledge of most phases of work; uses skills well.

P: Insufficient knowledge of some phases of job; does not use skills well.

Reasoning: Ability to use good judgment to arrive at sound conclusions and the ability to take timely action.

O: Always takes decisive, timely action using sound judgment.

E: Uses good judgment most of the time.

P: Makes frequent errors in judgment; slow to take action.

Potential: Expresses interest in professional/career development and seeks out additional responsibilities; interested in self-initiating work or ideas.

O: Has mapped out goals which support departmental objectives; expanding knowledge of work.

E: Obvious career interest and dedication, but needs more careful planning; taking action on development.

P: Speaks of advancement but takes limited action toward career goals and development.

Public Relations: Ability to communicate effectively with the public; degree to which a positive image of unit is projected and sustained within the unit, within the University and with the public.

O: Always gives courteous service; is a very effective representative of the unit.

E: Usually is positive and supportive of mission; gives unit good image.

P: Tends to be impersonal and perfunctory in dealings with the public.

Communication Skills: Ability to communicate clearly and persuasively in written and oral communications.

O: Able to write and speak effectively.

E: Able to write and speak in a satisfactory manner—sometimes better in one.

P: Tends to be weak in either or both written or oral presentations.

Particular skills, ability, demands of the position, significant contribution to the Office and the University not covered above or as an illustration of the above

Areas where further effort, concentration or training are necessary

Suggestions by Supervisor (Rater) as to why and how improvements can or should be made

(1) *Evaluation Measurement*
P—Performance is consistently below standards
I—Improvement necessary for performance to meet expected standards
M—Performance meets expected standards
E—Performance exceeds expected standards
O—Performance consistently superior or outstanding

Overall Evaluation_____(I)

_____
Name, Title and Signature of Rater

Note: Attach additional pages to further explain a particular rating if you believe this is necessary. (It may be that an individual rates higher in one aspect of a category and lower in another.) Additional information should be provided to indicate why an overall Evaluation of "P" or "O" has been given.

Exhibit IIA

Category Description	O	E	Guide to Ratings M	I	P
Managerial/Supervisory Ability: Ability to motivate; set high standards; recognize internal and external constraints, completes units assignments in an economical, effective, efficient and timely manner; able to deal effectively with personal and subordinates work stress and tension; concern for Affirmative Action, encourage thoroughness, creativity and innovation.	Consistently sets high standard of performance and motivates subordinates to meet these standards; units assignments always met in a timely manner; consistently performs well as a supervisor or manager.	Usually sets high standard of performance and sometimes motivates subordinates to meet these standards; assignments usually met in a timely manner; usually performs well as a supervisor or manager.	Does not pay enough attention to setting high standards of performance; seldom motivates subordinates to meet these standards; assignments frequently or at times not met in a timely manner; frequently or at times does not perform well as a supervisor or manager.		

Exhibit IIB

Category Description	O	E	Guide to Ratings M	I	P
Administering Work Programs: Ability to develop short-term goals and standards, methods of implementation and assists in developing long-term plans and goals; delegates responsibility and makes decisions.	Develops realistic goals and standards; makes timely decisions and is effective in delegating more routine responsibilities; consistently performs executive duties in a superior manner.	Usually develops realistic goals and standards; usually makes timely decisions and delegates some routine responsibilities; usually performs executive duties in an acceptable manner.	Is sometimes lax in developing goals and standards; finds it difficult to delegate responsibility and is prone to procrastination; at times does not perform executive duties in an acceptable manner.		

Category Description	O	E	Guide to Ratings M	I	P
Professional Development: Ability to keep current in specialized field and expand knowledge of college and university administration; potential to undertake new or expanded assignments and responsibilities.	Consistently reviews pertinent professional literature and analyzes for possible internal application; seeks to attend selected professional seminars and workshops.		Usually reviews pertinent professional literature and analyzes for possible internal application; occasionally seeks to attend selected professional seminars and workshops.		Pays little attention to pertinent professional literature and analysis for possible internal application; does not seek to attend seminars and workshops.
Planning: Ability to evaluate short and long range proposals and alternative solutions, formulate action plans and implement.	Places major emphasis on initiation and encourages ideas for operational and system improvements.		Initiates and encourages ideas for operational and system improvements.		Tends to emphasize crisis management.
Perspective: Outlook on University issues; serves on University or University related committees; able to represent supervisor to internal and external units, officials and public; concern for meeting University goals in affirmative action and other areas.	Consistently evaluates issues from a University-wide perspective.		Usually evaluates issues from a University-wide perspective.		Tends to view issues from an internal unit standpoint only.

planning that goes into setting departmental, unit and individual goals; and the challenge, training, motivation, recognition, satisfaction, accomplishments, communications and style of supervision that exist during the rating period. The appraisal form is a compilation and indication of the degree of success achieved during the period by both the staff member and the supervisor.

PROMOTION

If the assessment centers, management inventory of needs and people, and the appraisal systems work right, decisions about promotion should be relatively easy. But the promotion decision is seldom easy. The problem for the decision maker is that often the new job involves at least some different skills and responsibilities. The issue is then how well does past performance predict future performance in some areas new to the individual. Of course, the question can also apply (but be answered more easily) for those tasks similar to the old ones. The promotion decision maker may also not be directly familiar with the individual candidates and may have to rely on advice and ratings of others. To overcome this, the decision maker may want to interview the final candidates if the decision is a very close one. The danger of this is that he may be undercutting the role of the person making the recommendations. At times, a company may be in the embarrassing position of not knowing what talent it already has.

In deciding among candidates for a promotion, previous performance, potential assessment, training and experience, recommendations of those who have worked with the individual are all important. The decision maker must seek to gain a clear idea of the responsibilities of the position and how the individual matches up. The promotion decision bears some similarity to an initial selection decision, but this time the individual has a track record in the company. (Most companies stress promotion from within, but on occasion it is necessary to go outside.) Depending upon the position and circumstances, as noted before, a formal interview procedure might be helpful.

A survey of 1708 senior managers in Fortune 500 companies indicates some pathways to the top.[1] In terms of the most frequently mentioned traits that enhance success the following were mentioned (noted in order of frequency):

1. concern for results
2. integrity
3. desire for responsibility
4. concern for people
5. creativity
6. ambition
7. aggressiveness
8. loyalty
9. exceptional intelligence
10. social adaptability
11. appearance
12. others

The author of the article noted that it was a bit surprising that the traits often sought by corporations—creativity, ambition and aggressiveness (in addition to a concern for results) were not among the top three traits.

The top three reasons cited in the survey as the biggest single factor in the individual's success were:

[1] As reported in *Management Review*, July 1979, the survey was conducted by Korn/ Ferry International.

1. hard work
2. ambition, drive, desire to achieve
3. getting along with others, human relations

An article in the Harvard Business Review in September-October 1980, "Who Gets Promoted" based on a ten-year study of 11,000 top executives promoted from 1967 through 1976 indicated:

1. New top executives are better educated than their predecessors and their non-business peers.
2. The largest percentage of advanced degrees is in business administration (and there has been a marked rise in such degrees), engineering and law come next.
3. Newly promoted executives are about at the same age as those promoted before them, but there are variations on the basis of particular positions. For example, Presidents who were also CEOs had a median age of 47, but those who were not CEOs had a median age of 49.
4. The most frequent path to a presidency is from a group vice president position (rather than from executive or senion vice president positions) within the company and the individual will generally not have spent more than four years in his previous position.
5. Top executives are more mobile because of differences in their own opportunities and promotional patterns.

It is interesting to note that in regard to undergraduate and graduate education or business executives a relatively small number of educational institutions have provided a significant proportion of degrees to leaders in business.

The Top 12 In Undergraduate Degrees

1.	Yale University	1,827
2.	Harvard University	1,494
3.	City University of New York	1,339
4.	Princeton University	1,313
5.	New York University	1,250
6.	University of Pennsylvania	1,171
7.	University of Michigan	1,125
8.	University of Illinois	1,072
9.	University of Wisconsin	1,017

10.	Northwestern University	932
11.	Cornell University	904
12.	Dartmouth College	882

The Top 12 In Graduate Degrees

1.	Harvard University	3,920
2.	New York University	1,365
3.	Columbia University	1,210
4.	University of Michigan	811
5.	University of Pennsylvania	726
6.	University of Chicago	696
7.	Northwestern University	659
8.	Massachusetts Institute of Technology	568
9.	Rutgers University	556
10.	Stanford University	516
11.	University of Wisconsin	479
12.	Yale University	428

Based on a Standard & Poor's Corporation survey of 56,000 executives, the lists above indicate the top dozen institutions granting undergraduate and graduate degrees. Six institutions were among the top dozen in both areas, they are:

> Harvard University
> New York University
> Yale University
> University of Michigan
> University of Pennsylvania
> University of Wisconsin

The Harvard Business Review article dealing with those who get promoted indicated that the top 10 universities for those receiving various degrees were:

Bachelor Degree

Yale	University of Illinois
Harvard	University of Minnesota
Michigan	Dartmouth
Princeton	M.I.T.
Cornell	University of Wisconsin

Masters Degree	Law Degree
Harvard	Harvard
New York University	Michigan
Columbia	Columbia
M.I.T.	Yale
Stanford	New York University
University of Chicago	Fordham
Michigan	University of Virginia
University of Pennsylvania	Cornell
Northwestern	George Washington
Dartmouth	University of Chicago

Highest Degree

Harvard	Yale
New York University	University of Pennsylvania
University of Michigan	University of Illinois
Columbia	Stanford
M.I.T.	Cornell

In considering candidates for promotion (as is also true in selection) one should be concerned as to whether the individual is a "shooting star" or "flash in the pan." Some people do extremely well the first few months or year or two on the job or in a new position. But then when the excitement of something new wears out or the techniques that were successful elsewhere have been tried on the new job, their enthusiasm, effectiveness or personal relations may cease improving or actually decline. In promotion, selection and appraisal, a factor that should be more often discussed is how well does the individual handle routine or non-crisis situations. In effect, how well does the individual wear over time, not just during the period of great challenge.

SOME OTHER CONCERNS IN THE AREA OF STAFFING

Career Planning

A recent development in human resource management is the concept of career planning. This involves the commitment of organizations to assist employees in analyzing their interests, abilities and objectives and to help plan and implement activities that will develop their careers and lead to the attainment of their objectives. It has long been standard in most companies to have informal counseling by superiors or by the personnel department staff. Generally, there have also been newsletters, booklets and other communications in regard to job requirements, salary and promotion systems, affirmative action policies and programs, and the company's financial condition. Many companies are building on the standard approach to bring about individualized career planning programs geared to the needs of a particular individual or group. The new approaches include individual self-analysis, career planning workshops and workbooks, life planning workshops and some special programs for minorities, women and career employees, those approaching retirement age, handicapped individuals. Career planning is important both for the company and the individual. Many organizations are concerned about a shortage of management talent and wish to develop and promote from within rather than recruiting outside the company. Other management concerns that are closely linked to establishing career planning programs involve concerns about productivity and turnover, a desire by management to be responsive to employees' interest in career planning and affirmative action programs. Career planning can enhance job performance, talent utilization and the value of personnel systems to the company and the individual. But in order to be effective, top management commitment is necessary to the idea of implementing specific career planning actions to meet specific needs of particular employees and groups. Personnel Department staff support and commitment is necessary with integration of career planning into the personnel system.

Different Work Weeks

Four-day work week, flex time, job sharing, are approaches to the problem of meeting needs of both the company and the individual. The four-day work week is used by a small minority of firms. In times of unemployment one can see this as a way of keeping more people employed. Generally, it has been used as a means of increasing productivity, meeting employees' desires, being helpful in recruitment, lateness, turnover and absenteeism problems. The record is mixed as to its effectiveness. For certain companies or activities within companies, it may indeed accomplish the goals sought. In other cases, the cost benefits will indicate no improvement or even losses due to strain on supervision or poor supervision.

Flex time originated in Europe in the 1960s and spread to the United States, and now involves about 2.5 to 3.5 million U.S. workers. Generally, it allows employees to set their own starting and ending times provided they work a "core" period. It may be 9:30 a.m to 12:00 noon and 2:00 to 4:00 p.m. The goal of flex time is increased morale and job satisfaction which would lead to increased productivity and reduced absenteeism, turnover and lateness. Flex time enables one to arrange one's schedule each day and each week to suit one's lifestyle and family needs. The individual might come in early and leave early, come in late and leave late, come early and work late so that they only work 4½ days or even 4 days per week. The results so far seem reasonably encouraging, but good planning as to the company's work flow is necessary as is good supervision and scheduling.

Job sharing can be described as a permanent full-time job shared by two people who generally split working hours, job responsibilities, salary and fringe benefits. This is a new trend that has not caught on greatly as yet, but it does appear to have some potential for the future. It meets the needs of individuals who don't want full-time employment because of family responsibilities, easing in to retirement, those who want time for education, hobbies, leisure or other pursuits. It can bring to the company those who are more qualified or dedicated than traditional part-time workers and can offer these people a sense of achievement in terms of their job duties and compensation.

Relocation

Resistance to moving is increasing throughout the country. (Moves outside of the country have been sharply curtailed because of the enormous expense involved in terms of the extra allowances, the shrinking value of the dollar, etc.) The resistance is both personal and monetary. In a personal sense, many executives are concerned whether the promotion that is usual with a relocation is worth the strain on their families. Prior to the 1970s executives, generally willingly, relocated their families and regarded this as necessary to corporate success. A 45-year-old manager could have 4-10 moves in his career to-date. The Employee Relocation Council, a Washington consulting firm, found in one survey that 96% of transferred employees are men, about half are in their 30s, about one third have school age children 6-18, and about 40% have moved at least four times. Although moves represent value to the company in developing executives and thereby value to the individual, the strain on the family can be great. It is difficult for the wife to adjust to a new community. Increasingly, with women working, a move may disrupt her own career development. Firms may have to pay more attention to finding jobs for spouses in the new area and increasingly it may be the male rather than the female spouse. The children also find frequent relocations difficult especially in the high school years. Differences in atmosphere, style, tradition, reactions to newcomers, finding new friends, all create problems. The nomadic existence common to corporate success results in a high price paid by wives and children. The executive of today is far more likely than his predecessors to conclude that upsetting his family and cutting off the roots and lifestyle he has established is just not worth one more step up the ladder. In the past, if you didn't accept a relocation, you were likely to be dismissed or be kept from future opportunities. Although this still may occur, companies are tending to be more understanding of the reason for turning down a relocation or asking that it be delayed until the children are out of school.

Another important factor in relocations is the expense involved. From the employee's point of view even a 35 to 40 percent promotion increase or an offer from another company may result in less disposable income due to high mortgage rates and housing costs, differences in state income and real estate taxes, the need for private rather than public schooling, costs in fixing up a new home, possible loss of spouse's income if she/he is not able to find a good job. Firms must place more emphasis than in past years on recruiting locally, particularly in high cost areas such as California or New York City. To meet the challenge of much greater amounts in mortgage debt at higher interest rates and higher state and local taxes, companies must offer large relocation packages. For middle level executives, the package may not be enough to maintain the current standard of living. For the highest level of executives, the package may be large indeed. The package could include guaranteeing the selling price of the individual's current home, payment of the difference between the old mortgage rate and the new one for three to five years, all moving and relocation expenses, all selling and buying costs, perhaps making up in some way the difference between the costs in buying a new home and the price received on the old one. Up front bonuses as discussed earlier are also in vogue. Some or many of these would apply to middle or upper-middle executives. Some other possibilities include tuition for private schools for children if this seems necessary, and paying for house hunting and job hunting trips for one's spouse.

Two Career Family

The last decade has seen an increasing number of two career families. This has very significant implications not only for the individuals and families involved and for the economy, but also for the companies employing the individuals. Our concern here is not the spouse who has a part-time job but rather one who has a position which he or she regards as providing career opportunities. (Even those who are just filling time or doing something interesting, but not career oriented, may not want to leave their job). The company requiring an individual to travel more, work unusual hours, relocate and entertain more involving his spouse, may find this in direct conflict with another company's similar or usual demands on the other individual in the marriage. The juggling of two careers, a marriage, family and community responsibilities is a formidable task. The company may find that its executive, because of the needs of the spouse's career and family responsibilities which are more likely to be shared since both individuals are working, is not able to comply with the company's desires in terms of relocation or travel. Or, there may be the very difficult requirement for the company to help find a comparable job opportunity for the spouse in the new area. Given the changes in the last decade and the projections for the future in the numbers of working wives and those embarked on full fledged careers, the problem of the two career family is very likely to become more difficult.

Another aspect of this is the growth in the number of two career families when both partners are employed by the same firm. These duos and the company face the problem of jealousy over pay, promotion and the possible competition inherent in the situation. On the other hand, it has value in understanding each other's job responsibilities, may build greater togetherness and may be a means of staying together because of relative ease in meeting relocation needs of one or the other. Most firms shy away from hiring duos and seek to solve the issue by hiring one and helping the other find a job elsewhere. But the problem may still crop up at a time of transfer and relocation.

TWO SPECIAL CONCERNS: WOMEN
AND EXECUTIVES

Women

Companies of all types and sizes are paying more attention to the selection and recruitment of minorities and women in order to meet their own needs, governmental regulation and community and societal pressures. Skilled and motivated people are needed, perhaps as never before. Firms must recognize that they will be in tough competition for the very able women and minorities and possibly face internal problems if they are forced by competition to pay higher starting salaries or greater salary increases in order to attract or retain the very talented. They will also face problems of reverse discrimination charges and morale factors. In order to meet governmental requirements, a firm may have to reach out to individuals with adequate or less than adequate credentials or experience and high or ordinary potential and seek through special training programs and assignments to develop them. This, too, carries implications for the rest of the workforce.

In this section we wish to discuss women in particular as the group that in terms of large numbers, represents a force with major impact on the business life in America. Women are joining the labor force in large numbers and are a major factor in industry. Some statistics are revealing:

1. Women represent close to 43 percent of the American workforce. In 1958 they represented 33 percent. By the end of the 1980s, the figure will be close to 50 percent.
2. Two-thirds of the working women work to support or help support their families.
3. 50 percent of the working women are in low paying jobs such as clerical workers, sales—retail goods, nondurable goods and manufacturing.
4. Women earn 59 cents for every $1.00 earned by men.

In terms of data about women and how they view the workplace, a study conducted by the Roper Organization, Inc. in 1980, entitled "The 1980 Virginia Slims American Women's Opinion Poll" indicates:

1. **The Workforce**—twice as many women, one out of three, are working today in full-time jobs as were similarly employed in

1970. Within this group, the greatest increase is among women 30-39 years old; nearly three times as many (42%) hold full-time jobs, as opposed to ten years ago (15%). Among women in their 40s, 43 percent have full-time jobs, almost double the number in 1970(23%). Among college educated women, 45 percent now have full-time jobs, slightly less than double the number of those who worked full-time in 1970 (24%).

2. **Future Plans**—Nearly three-fourths (73%) of non-working women under 30 years of age plan to work in the future. More than three-fifths (62%) of the non-working women now in their 30s intend to get full-time jobs eventually. Among those in their 40s, nearly two-fifths (37%) of those not currently working plan to get jobs in the future. Nearly one-half (46%) of the women with college degrees who are not working now plan to enter the workforce.

3. **Part-time Employment**—In 1980 only 12 percent of women work part-time, in 1970, 11 percent held part-time jobs.

4. **Careers**—More working women today (45%) plan to make their jobs full-time careers than planned to do so in 1970 (39%) Particularly inclined toward full-time careers are employed women who have college degrees (56%).

5. **Why They Are Working**—43 percent say they work to bring in extra money, 27 percent to support themselves, 19 percent to support their families, 14 percent for something interesting to do.

6. **Discrimination**—57 percent believe that there is discrimination against them in attempting to reach a leadership position in business. The percentages are higher for those currently working full-time (65%) and those working in cities with a population of one million or more (73%). For top positions in government employment, the figures are roughly similar, 55% believe there is sex discrimination, 63 percent of those working full-time and 69 percent of those living in large cities believe that such discrimination exists. For positions in the professions, 52 percent of the women interviewed believed that discrimination existed, 62 percent of full-time job holders expressed that view as did 67 percent of those living in large cities.

7. **Equality in the Work Situation**
   (a) Responsibility—68 percent believe they have an equal chance with their male colleagues.
   (b) Salary—55 percent indicate that their salary treatment is equal to male co-workers.

     (c) Promotions—52 percent felt they had an equal chance with male co-workers.

College educated women score higher in each of the categories—72 percent in regard to responsibility, 63 percent in regard to salary, and 59 percent in regard to promotion.

8. **Working for a Woman Superior**—About two-thirds of all working women indicate that it does not matter to them whether their boss is male or female.

9. **Career and Family Life**—

    (a) There was an increase from 35 percent in 1974 to 45 percent in 1980 of women who want to work rather than stay home. About 55 percent of college educated women make this choice versus about 40 percent of those who were not college educated.

    (b) 77 percent of those interviewed stated that a woman should seriously consider giving up her job if her husband had to relocate.

    (c) 87 percent say that their spouses approve of their working (89 percent of men say they are in favor of their wives working).

    (d) 57 percent believe they are equally as good wives as compared with what they would have been if they were not working.

    (e) 47 percent believe they are just as good mothers while 16 percent believe they are not as a result of their working.

    (f) 43 percent claim they make up for lost time with their children by improving the quality of time spent with them, 14 percent claim they do not.

    (g) 49 percent believe that holding jobs make them more interesting to their husbands, 18 percent do not.

    (h) 57 percent believe that their family would have difficulties financially if they did not work, 31 percent do not.

Finally, in regard to statistics, we might note that future business leaders are more likely than in the past to be women. Currently, nationwide, one in five students working toward an MBA degree is a woman and at some very prestigeous schools the percentages are higher ranging in the high 20s to low 30s. And, the new incoming classes at some institutions show that one-third to more than two-fifths of the class are women. In accounting, as another example, that traditional male profession has changed so that recently about one out of three graduates is a woman.

Though the statistics certainly show progress, there are significant problems still ahead in regard to equality for women in the workplace. There is, of course, the issue of the relationship with one's husband as indicated by Maryanne Vandewelde's classification of the corporate husband as one of four types: (1) non-achiever, facilitator, (2) achiever, obstructionist, (3) achiever, facilitator, (4) non-achiever, obstructionist. But, increasingly, we must regard the monetary importance of a job to a woman not as secondary family income, but as support for herself and/or her children as we see more women remaining unmarried or becoming divorced and heading single parent households. Further, even if married, the income may be a vital component of family income and/or of great importance to the woman's need for self-esteem and self-actualization.

Beyond the relationship to family, there is the relationship at the workplace. Sexism still prevails despite laws and regulations. Learning to deal with the opposite sex in a superior-subordinate or peer relationship presents difficulties for male and female superiors, subordinates and colleagues. Sexual harrassment, subtle or overt, exists as does a feeling of isolation. These problems should be lessened as companies become more sensitive to and concerned about sexual harrassment issues and as more women are hired and advance, thereby providing colleagues, role models, "old boy"-"new girl" networks. The age old prejudices still abound. Witness the considerable media coverage in September 1980, of the promotion of a 29-year-old, attractive, female (separated from her husband) to a major vice-presidency in the Bendix Corporation. The Chairman, 42-years-old, recently divorced, had to deal with rumors that the promotion was the result of a personal relationship. The vice president had joined the company with a Harvard MBA and good experience 15 months earlier as Executive Assistant to the Chairman. She then became a vice president after about a year and all the publicity developed about the move to another vice presidency for strategic planning in September. The Chairman, in discussing personnel changes before a large group of employees, had to deny the rumors. The result of all the publicity was that the vice president requested a leave of absence from her position though she was going to remain as a consultant. To the credit of the Bendix Corporation, the Board turned down her request and she was to remain as vice president. Both the male and female in this situation regarded the problem as caused by gender and not age (a 28-year-old male moved into the Treasurer's slot at Bendix about a year earlier) and as an indication of basic views held by some people as to how women achieve positions of influence. However, about a week later, the individual resigned her position with the Bendix Corporation. It appears clear after a survey conducted by a Board subcommittee that the top employees thought her promotion was warranted and that she had good judgment. They also thought the publicity would jeopardize her effectiveness.[1]

The Bendix case, as it may come to be called, raises some interesting questions. Aside from questions of judgment as to how the Chairman handled the issue, there is the question of the role of women in the executive suites in business. Mary Cunningham, the former Bendix Vice President, is an example of the outstanding women now being graduated in larger number from the nation's business schools. (In the last ten years Harvard Business School graduates more than 10 times the number of women than they had graduated in all the years before') They are young, very capable, and very ambitious. Gail Sheeley has said about this case "All it takes to start the fires of sexual envy are a woman, too bright, and a man, too progressive—surrounded in an organization by more ordinary mortals." Ms. Sheeley also states, "Eventually, the presence of many high performance women in high places will make ambushes on their private lives appear ridiculous, if not irrelevant."

In recent years there have been hundreds of cases in which organizations and governmental agencies have been forced by lawsuits to pay back wages to women, raise their salaries and make arrangements to overcome the effects of past discrimination. In recent years, Western Electric agreed to pay $7 million in back wages to 2,200 women in two plants and another $1.5 million to women in nine other plants. The American Telephone and Telegraph Company settled for $40 million, General Electric for $32 million, Northwest Airlines for $25 million, Uniroyal, Inc. for $5.2 million, and Merrill Lynch, Pierce, Fenner & Smith for $4 million. Individual awards have surpassed $250,000. Between October 1979 and April 1980, the Office of Federal Contract Compliance Programs obtained $13 million in settlements with 120 contractors in sex and race discrimination cases and the Equal Employment Opportunity Commission collected $20-30 million. Government itself is not immune. In May 1980 a federal district judge in Washington awarded more than $16 million to 324 women in the Government Printing Office. The Printing Office had two classifications of workers who performed basically the same job.

---

[1] The story has a "happy ending." The individual received numerous job offers and became Vice President for Strategic Planning of a major corporation.

However, the men were classified as bookbinders at an average of $25,000 and the women as bindery workers at an average of $15,000.

The academic profession is not immune to charges of discrimination against women in terms of hiring, promotion and tenure. There have been a number of recent cases in favor of claimants and the cases and class action suits filed are growing. Brown University and the University of Minnesota in recent years, as a basis of settlement, have had to create special panels of faculty members to review tenure and promotion. At Minnesota, a court representative must be included on the panel. The Brown settlement in September 1977 has already cost the University over $1 million. The Minnesota settlement called for payment of $100,000 to an individual.

Various government agencies and lawsuits have fought for "equal pay for equal work." A trend may be a concept of equal pay for comparable work, which will have significant implications if successfully upheld in court.

Turning back to the business sector, a 1979 survey by Spencer Stuart & Associates, an executive search firm, indicates that fewer than 5 percent of the executives earning $40,000 or more in the top 50 industrial companies in the United States are women, and no woman heads any of these companies. Bureau of the Census figures showed that in 1978 5.6 percent of full-time working males earned more than $25,000 but only .4 percent of all full-time working women earned a similar salary. A Columbia University study tracked 40 pairs of young individuals who graduated with MBAs from the Columbia Business School between 1969 and 1972. Half of each pair was male, the other female. The pairs were basically evenly matched in regard to academic and socio-economic backgrounds and career goals. Each member of the pair started working at relatively minor differences in salary—$13,692 for men and $12,414 for women—a 9.3 percent difference. But by 1979 the men's average annual salary was $48,900 and the females' $34,036—a difference of 30.4 percent. As women move up the executive ladder there will be more hirings, more progression and more firings without the great amount of media discussion and analysis as exemplified in Jane Cahill Pfeiffer's ouster from the NBC chairmanship.

There are significant gains in the executive ranks for women, but they get paid far less than males. A Heidrick Inc. survey of women officers of the nation's 1,000 largest industrial companies and 50 leading financial and retailing concerns, indicated that in 1980 the proportion of women officers who have reached vice presidential levels or above is 28 percent compared to 25.5 percent in 1979 and 25.2

percent in 1977. But the typical women executive earns less than $50,000 annually in cash compensation. Six of every ten women officers earn less than $50,000 a year. Three in ten earn less than $30,000. One in five receive $70,000 or more, and one in about twelve receive $100,000 or more.

The "soft" industries such as retailing, banking, advertising and computers are easier for women to enter and be promoted because of their emphasis on managerial skills rather than technical know-how. (Only recently have women earned a significant number of degrees in areas which have traditionally enabled men to move upward—business, engineering and accounting or finance. The engineering change, for example, is indicated by the growth in engineering degrees awarded to women from .7 percent in 1970 to 7.0 percent in 1980.) As indicated in the Columbia University study, however, degrees may help a women enter the corporate world, but do not insure keeping pace with male counterparts. Even in an industry which is actively seeking women, banking, very few women have made it to the upper echelons. Citicorp, a major United States bank, is proud of the fact that in just two years, comparing 1977 to 1979, the percentage of its officers who are female jumped appreciably from 15.8 percent to 22 percent. However, only 6 percent of the bank's vice presidents are women and just one senior vice president is a woman.

Increasingly, there are consulting firms, colleges, individuals, department stores and organizations who provide services for women in aiding them to enter and succeed in the corporate world or in other organizations. These enterprises should be approached with a "caveat emptor" philosophy. Some can indeed help, others are filled with gimmicks. The services that are provided include career counseling, resume writing, networking, assertiveness training, skills assessment, dressing for success, learning corporate gamesmanship, etc.

A number of organizations attempt to upgrade the knowledge and experience of newly hired women or those who have been with the firm only a short time to provide them with managerial and technical skills necessary for success. Career development is given extra emphasis for these women.

The growth of women in the labor force has profound implications for society. It also has implications as to what is full employment and the fact that a higher level of joblessness may be tolerable since if one family member loses his job, there's an even chance or better that some income will still be coming in through the spouse's paycheck. This may moderate the depth and length of recession. The growth of productivity may have temporarily slowed down or been flat because of, to a small degree, large numbers of women holding first time jobs who are not as well trained as men. But this will quickly be corrected as women (and minorities) gain experience.

Beyond the statistics is the essential fairness necessary of providing equality of opportunity to women, who constitute a majority of the United States population and a majority of those now in college. The fairness issue is not just a moral, legal and democratic imperative, it is an economic and organizational imperative. We need to tap the talent and energy of the best, brightest and most motivated among us and that certainly demands much greater opportunity and access at all levels of organizations for women and minorities.

Executives

We have touched upon top executives in various sections of this chapter. We note here some of the particular problems the highest executives face. (Many of these problems are also faced by other executive levels.) The demans, risks, responsibilities, and changing nature of their positions are well-known. It appears from a recent survey that the factors most decisive in top executives seeking to change positions are a desire for increased responsibility and increased challenge. Other factors in decreasing order are: better compensation package, faster advancement, increased creativity, a more desirable location and increased status. The top person is more likely, as seems natural, to get fired when things go wrong, but can gain some comfort in the large settlements and/or consulting agreement (termination agreements) that are usually negotiated as part of the compensation package to begin with or at the time of leaving. The financial security (at least short term) of the settlement can provide the cushion for fulfilling ambitions one has had to do something new and different; however, the shock of no longer being very powerful can be great indeed. "Out placement" is a growing field where those who are let go receive expert assistance, as part of their leaving, in how to market themselves and obtain new employment. Out placement is used at many levels in the company for those "de-hired" as well as those laid off because of economic conditions. (Of course, an "unfair" firing, e.g., because of age, can be fought in a lawsuit.)

Recent economic strains in the United States have resulted in great turnover in executive suites, particularly for those at the top or in number two positions. The number two spot can be a particularly vulnerable one. The turnover in number two executives can be traced to the growth in the number of corporate mergers and the increased rate of outside recruiting of chief executives where boards of directors look for those with great track records in other companies to improve the company. Another factor is the personal chemistry between the No. 1 and No. 2 man. As one executive put it, "the No. 1 man has the power, the No. 2 man has the ambition." Given the above, there is less certainty than in the past that No. 2 will become No. 1 and thus the increased risk and the desire for No. 2 people to jump at a chance in another company for the top slot.

In an August 1980 story of a Wall Street Journal/Gallup survey of chief executive officers of a large number of United States corporations including chief executives of 306 of the largest United States corporations, the following points were made:

- The executives typically work 60-70 hours a week.
- They travel 6-10 days a month and often give up their weekends for work.
- Many have relocated 6 or more times in their career.
- Most put their jobs before their families.

A survey of a cross section of 60 presidents of Fortune's top 1,000 companies indicated that the most anxiety producing problems they faced in order of most frequently cited were:

1. Failure by subordinates to accept or carry out responsibilities.
2. Failure to get critical information.
3. Firing someone.

The survey also indicated that while the job of chief executive is indeed prone to great anxiety and stress, little or no training is given to top executives in regard to dealing with stress, anger, confrontation or conflict resolution. Further, the survey indicated that the skills upper level managers thought vital for the 1980s were headed by leadership skills and interpersonal communications skills.

Executive development at all stages of an individual's career, including when one has reached the top or very near to it, will continue to be a major need of every organization.

SUMMARY

We have touched just the tip of the iceberg of the variety of issues and concerns involved in staffing. In the chapters on Directing and Management In the 80s and 90s we shall discuss other aspects that relate to managing human resources. The more top management understands, plans, organizes, innovates, implements and evaluates in regard to improving the organization's management of its human resources, the greater the chances for success.

four

Deciding

In each aspect of the managerial function and challenge, the executive earns his reputation and his salary by the decisions he makes, how he makes them and how he follows up. Whether it is planning, controlling, representing, organizing, innovating or the other activities highlighted in this book, the executive/manager must make choices and determine whether or not to take action. The executive may delay for some specified or unspecified time taking any action or take some type of deferring or delaying action. A conscious decision not to decide *is* a decision. Sometimes, however, the individual or the organization delays a decision in an unconscious way and that is not a decision, it is a weakness in the individual or organization.

Decision making or deciding is sometimes emphasized as the basic function of the upper level executive. However, it is linked to and part of all the other activities. Strength as a decision maker, but with significant weakness in another area often results in failure for the individual just as skill in the other aspects and an inability to perform well at decision making may spell even faster failure. We all know of good managers who could not make a decision (or a "right" decision) if their lives depended on it. This may be due to a lack of self-confidence or that in the face of the magnitude and complexity of the problem, the reactions and power of the opposition, the strain and pressures of the moment or of years of being in the hot seat, the individual just cannot bring himself to make a decision. He then tries to compromise, delay, refer to a committee, study the issue to death through use of committees, task forces, consultants, etc. Another cause for avoidance of clear decision making is a lack of confidence in the ability, knowledge and judgment of subordinates or of staff units, the organization's information gathering and analytical processes, the equipment and technology being utilized or planned.

We describe in this chapter the decision making process, techniques that aid in decision making, group and individual decision making, the human side of decision making and why decision making breaks down.

THE DECISION MAKING PROCESS

There are eight basic steps in decision making:

1. Recognizing that a problem or need for a decision exists.
2. Defining the problem or need as clearly and specifically as possible.
3. Analyzing the reasons for and results of the problem or decision situation.
4. Developing and finding the most promising alternative solutions or courses of action.
5. Analyzing and evaluating the feasible alternatives including a concern for probable and possible positive and negative consequences.
6. Selecting the best solution or course of action.
7. Implementing the solution chosen.
8. Monitoring and evaluating the results.

1. Recognizing a Problem or Need for a Decision

The decision maker must first become aware of a problem or need for a decision. This may come from personal observation or symptoms of a problem, various control reports, audits, conversations or other internal sources, and from external sources such as customers, government agencies, competitors, suppliers, auditors, the media.

2. Defining the Problem or Need

This involves specifying what the situation is, where the problem is located, how great it is or how important it is, the present or potential impact, what the trend seems to indicate, when is the problem occurring and for how long has it been occurring. It is also helpful to contrast what the problem "is" versus what it "is not" as means of indicating what is distinctive about the problem or decision to be made.

3. Analyzing Reasons and Results

The decision maker is attempting to understand the reason for a gap between planned for (desired) results and what is actually happening. The relationship between expected and actual (and actual may be better than expected, but this too deserves analysis) is the basis for diagnosis. We must avoid jumping at the symptoms rather than looking for basic causes. In seeking to identify the causes of the problem or need, it is helpful to focus on the "is" and "is not" suggested above and look at situations where a goal is being realized and where it is not. This will lead to exploration of the differences between the situations and the changes that have occurred. This may involve several changed conditions, or ones that affect each other or ones that combined with differences that do not show change. Each possible cause should then be identified and tested to see if we can disprove them or shoot them down or if they do not explain the problem situation completely (at times the explanation may be a combination of causes).

4. Developing and Finding Alternatives

We may rely on past experience and past approaches and solutions to the same or similar problems or we may seek creative approaches (see discussion on Innovation). Clearly our ability to generate alternatives for review will depend upon the time, cost, priorities, and resources available. All alternatives should meet the test of being consistent with broad objectives and policies of the enterprise (unless the solution is so unusual and excellent that it forces changes in objectives and policies). In addition to analytical techniques, one technique in developing alternatives is to ask knowledgeable people about possible approaches.

5. Analyzing and Evaluating

Once we understand the problem, the deviation from plan, in decision making, we are seeking to determine what action should be taken to correct the deviation. We must be clear as to whether we want one or more of the following types of action: immediate correction; a short term or interim solution which patches things up pending further detailed study; or establishing new objectives and directions. In seeking to choose among alternative decisions it is helpful to list what the decision *must* accomplish (the constraints it must meet and additional considerations that would be of importance but are not musts and are rather "desirable." Each alternative would be evaluated against the "must" list. All other things being equal on the must list evaluation, the alternative chosen would score better in regard to the "desirables." In developing "must" criteria, we must be specific and careful that they are indeed "musts." Failure to meet even one "must" should immediately disqualify the alternative from further consideration. Some useful ways of comparing alternatives involve disregarding the common aspects of all approaches and highlighting immediate, short and long term results. Using dollar terms is a useful way of doing this, but other measures should also be used—staffing, equipment needs, space, etc. In looking at dollar costs, we should analyze both sunk and incremental costs, fixed and variable costs, operating and capital costs. Consideration should also be given to which solutions require more up front or immediate expenditures versus longer term or spread out commitments and the effect on cash flow. The effect on the organization, policies, procedures, practices, need for skilled manpower, technology and equipment requirement, ease and cost of administrative implementation including communication should also be among the criteria used in evaluating alternatives.

6. Selecting the Best Solution

By applying our "musts" and "desirables" we are able to narrow the range of choices. We must judge the probabilities of expected results and adjust for uncertainty. In the final countdown toward making a decision we must not overlook evaluating possible adverse consequences. It is human nature to focus on the good things that will happen if choice A, B, C, or D is agreed upon, but what about negative consequences? In many cases, we might choose the alternative which has fewer desirable, positive consequences because it has fewer probable or possible negative consequences as compared to other choices. The positives are generally apparent, but the negatives may be found in terms of the demands of the alternative on:

Organization—relationships among people, functions and units, coordination, formal and informal organization and relationships, control, communication, delegation, authority.

Money—return on investment, profit, operating and capital costs, costs and expenses, cash flow.

Duration of the Decision—length of time period during which the effect of the decision will be felt and the costs in money, manpower, equipment, etc.

People—performance, productivity, skills and abilities, motivation, advancement, status, turnover, growth, safety, health, loyalty, goals.

External forces—competition, regulation, legal, governmental, reputation and image of the enterprise, economic forces.

Materials needed—availability and security of source, immediate, short and long range price, quality and quantity needed, storage and transportation requirements.

Product or Service—quality and quantity.

Facilities, Equipment, Technology—needed facilities, equipment, technology and cost involved, type, amount and location of space, compatiability, flexibility and adaptability.

7. Implementation

Once having decided, one must plan carefully for a successful implementation of the decision. This involves: communication to those involved; anticipating potential problems and setting up contingency plans to deal with likely occurrences; scheduling and phasing the various steps involved including milestones and early warning checkpoints; providing the necessary resources, manpower, money, material, time, facilities,to accomplish the tasks.

8. Evaluating the Decision

At appropriate time intervals, through operational reports, inspections, and audits by those without vested interest in the decision, the effect of the decision should be evaluated. Fine tuning, major modifications, and even reversal of the decision might be necessary based upon the results.

TOOLS AND TECHNIQUES FOR DECISION MAKING

Mathematical Techniques

Mathematical techniques are helpful in making decisions in which there is a good deal of uncertainty and there are factors over which the decision maker has no or very little control. Some of these techniques include:

- *Payoff Tables*—are based upon an estimate of the probabilities of certain acts occurring and display the results. For example, in deciding whether to maintain a certain price, reduce it by various different amounts or increase it by certain amounts, one would attempt to estimate probable sales for each price and the profits that would result.

- *Decision Trees*—goes a step beyond the payoff table by allowing the decision maker to see the effect of decisions on possible future alternatives that will have to be faced. As in payoff tables, the estimate of probability of occurrence is most important.

- *Matrix Summaries*—converts the major intangible considerations into a quantitative index with an overall index developed by weighting each intangible factor in proportion to its estimated importance in the decision.

- *Marginal Analysis*—enables the user to evaluate additional costs and revenues or additional output from input, while highlighting variables in a situation.

- *Venture Analysis*—used for deciding how large a new plant should be based on assumptions as to demand for the product, price involved, risk and potential foregone returns.

- *Cost Benefit Analysis*—attempts to identify not only monetary costs and benefits, but other effects of a particular decision. This technique is usually applied to public sector actions which involve social costs and values, but it can also have value for the private sector firm by forcing it to look at areas not usually evaluated. Cost effectiveness analysis is related to cost benefit analysis in that it seeks to determine the most economical means of achieving a desired outcome or of achieving the greatest return from a given level of expenditure.

Operations Research Techniques

Operations research has been defined in various ways. It provides a quantitative basis for decisions, it ends up in bad answers to problems which, if the techniques were not used, would result in worse answers, it is applied decision theory using mathematical, scientific, or logical means.

Operations research (OR) stresses the idea of "system"—a set of interacting variables with each system part of a larger one. "Systems analysis" can be considered as just analysis of the controllable and uncontrollable variables in a system to determine how the system operates and thus is a component of OR. A broader definition of systems analysis would involve presentation of a range of alternatives with varying aspects of effectiveness and cost and emphasis on questioning objectives. OR stresses the optimum solution, the best possible, in which the advantages outweigh the disadvantages by the greatest amount, as differentiated from the ideal.

Operations research has a systems orientation, relies on an interdisciplinary approach and stresses the scientific method. In following an OR approach, the analysts formulate alternatives through construction of mathematical models, calculate or devise a solution from the model including prediction of payoffs, test the models, provide controls, and implement the solution. This is reasonably similar to the previous discussion of decision making steps. OR techniques can be applied to the following types of problems:

- *Inventory Control*—to achieve a balance between dangers of being out of stock and the costs of excessive inventory.
- *Allocation of Resources*—to produce the best possible returns.
- *Routing*—insure that goods arrive at the quickest possible time or at the least possible cost or an optimal mix between the two objectives.
- *Queuing*—to reduce waiting time without excessive costs as applied, for example, to customers waiting to be served or craftsmen waiting for supplies or equipment waiting for servicing.
- *Replacement*—to determine when equipment should be replaced.
- *Scheduling*—involves sequencing and coordinating activities to produce the best possible returns and limit negative consequences.
- *Search*—determining how much information is required.

OR techniques include: probability theory, linear programming, nonlinear programming, game theory, queuing theory, servo theory, information theory, symbolic logic, value theory, Monte Carlo techniques, networking techniques, decomposition, and simulation. We mention simulation in a bit more detail because it is being employed to a greater degree than in the past due to the increased power and sophistication of computer technology.

Simulation is a technique of determining what might happen if certain steps were taken. By use of a model we can depict the real world without running the risks and costs of experimentation in the real world (although simulation can be expensive). We are used to using the architects' model of a building. Role playing and business games are also simulations. In foreign affairs, defense policy analysis and business analysis, simulations and "scenarios" are increasingly being used. The mathematical model makes possible penalty free trial and error.

In using the powerful tools of operations research it must be recognized that it does not substitute, except in routine instances, for managerial judgment. The reactions of people and outside forces can never be exactly quantified and even by quantifying we are often discussing probabilities. Further, top management (particularly those not familiar with OR techniques) have difficulty understanding OR approaches which rely on sophisticated mathematics normally not easily comprehensible to a majority of executives. Thus, there is a need for OR people to be good communicators of their approaches while at the same time tuned in to the real world the executive faces. The successful OR team stresses the applied role of its mathematical techniques and does not rely on the "overwhelming" truth and precision of the mathematical formulas to gain acceptance of proposed solutions.

Other Techniques

We can attempt to test a choice through means other than simulation and the mathematical approaches indicated. Ways of testing include:

1. The devil's advocate approach—an individual or group searches to find weaknesses in the proposed action and if significant weaknesses are found, review the other alternatives that were discarded. The devil's advocate would question fundamental assumptions made in defining the problem and in all other steps in the decision making process.
2. Seeking to gain acceptance or consensus through discussion or polling devices- this method can be used in regard to a choice made or in terms of developing alternatives.
3. Using a pilot or small scale operation as a test. This, in effect, converts a simulation to a small portion of reality.
4. By formulating detailed plans, policies and practices based upon the decision we can evaluate its administrative and operational practicality and cost.
5. Decisions can be structured to flow sequentially thus providing a test of a current decision before proceeding to the next one.

Various processes, procedures and forms have been developed by organizations to meet their particular decision making needs. One approach that can be helpful to organizations is to divide a decision in regard to a major problem or issue that may have multiple causes into three parts:

1. A perspective on the matter,
2. Analysis, and
3. Final decision making and implementation.

The perspective would offer concise analysis as to the problem as it exists today; past history on it and future projections as to how bad it might get; its magnitude and cost; how it has been handled previously; how it is related (in fact or potentially) to other activities or problems. In the analysis portion, various causes of the problem would be identified and alternative ways of dealing with each cause would be described. Each alternative would be evaluated against criteria with a numerical score assigned as well as a weighting factor for each criterion. The selection of specific criteria dealing with direct positive and negative consequences, as well as the effects on other issues, is most important, as is the weighting factor used. Criteria could include effectiveness, cost (short/long range, operating/capital), efficiency, effect on individuals, effect on plant, etc. Although a staff unit could provide most of the analysis and perspective, the top decision makers must be involved in regard to approving the criteria, weighting factors, scores assigned, etc. Finally, the decision makers would approve the suggested action and the implementation plans. In some cases the analysis would stop short of suggested decisions and leave that final step for the decision makers.

INFORMATION NEEDS FOR DECISION MAKERS

In recent years the buzz word for any progressive management has been Management Information System (MIS). It is true that in today's complex world, management needs as good an information system as it can afford in order to make decisions and to control. But in some cases MIS's have failed. They may have been oversold by internal or external consultants or staff or not adequately understood by top management in regard to what will be available, how soon, at what development, implementation and operational cost, how will it be used, who will use it, when, how can it be modified.

We tend, at times, to overbuild or overdesign what we need. If a pistol will provide what is needed, one has to be concerned as to why the design or purchase order calls for, in effect, a rifle, automatic rifle, machine gun, or cannon. Certainly, one wants to leave areas for growth in both hardware and software and project future needs. But technology and needs change rapidly and a careful analysis must be made as to what is needed now in the short term, in long term, and the state of information technology before committing significant resources. Whatever computerized system is developed, for reporting, control and decision making, as well as in manual reporting systems, one must recognize that all data is not information, all information is not knowledge, all knowledge doesn't necessarily lead to correct analysis or decisions. In designing an information system for decision making which will be different from control needs, stress should be placed on who has to know what, in what level of detail, in what time frame(s), in which method of presentation. There are critical data elements and other aspects of decision making information that have to be identified, how they will be collected, by whom, delivered in what time frame, in which method of presentation to whom, what analysis and research must be conducted, how, etc.

Many companies have long suffered from a lack of timely, relevant, accurate and detailed information on which to make decisions. Now a number of organizations suffer from being snowed under by computerized reports that either don't assist in decision making or clog up the channels of communications flow and thought so that while the data is there, it is overlooked because of the sheer volume of information available. Experts can help top management in terms of analyzing needs, developing and implementing management information systems geared both to control and to decision making. But top management must tune in closely and finally decide what it wants and needs.

GROUP VERSUS INDIVIDUAL DECISION MAKING

As we become more participative in our management style, we tend to involve a greater number of people in the decision making process. We hope to gain more knowledge and insight through participation of others and thus end up with better decisions. Involving others also gives individuals the opportunity to feel part of the decision process and committed to the successful implementation and operation of the particular decision. Ultimately the chief executive officer bears responsibility for decisions made even though there may be an office of the president or group executive organizational design. Increasingly we tend to reach a decision through consensus, consultation and committees.

There is great value, both direct and indirect, in the use of group problem solving or decision making techniques, but there may also be increased monetary costs due to the total hours of involvement of each decision maker in the group. There may be time delays in reaching consensus (although pulling a group together to work on a problem can save time). In short, there is no absolute answer valid for all organizations for all times as to the degree of participation in decision making and using group problem solving versus individual problem solving. It depends on the nature of the problems, the organization, the groups, and the individuals.

THE HUMAN AND ORGANIZATIONAL ASPECTS
OF DECISION MAKING

We have discussed various techniques in regard to problem solving and decision making. The technology is becoming more sophisticated and we now can receive huge amounts of data (information?), very quickly, in several modes and formats and we can interact with the computer and change figures, ask "what if" questions, simulate, etc. But beyond technology and techniques, there is still the fundamental question of the human role in decision making. The characteristics of the decision makers are important, for example, their personality, style, intelligence, experience, emotional balance, self-confidence, communications and articulation abilities, concern for others, knowledge, stamina, frustration level. They may have all the information and analyses they need, but their human characteristics may well determine what decision is made, how, and when. (External forces may also play a vital role in decision making.) The characteristics of their staff and those who develop and transmit information and carry out decisions and operations are also of great importance.

In making a decision, one of the criteria for choosing among alternatives should be the effect on individuals. This would involve whether their careers, working conditions, levels, compensation, status, power, morale, influence, individual goals and needs, working relationships, productivity, space, etc. are affected and, if so, how. Who gains, who loses, who is disrupted to what degree? Depending upon the answers to these and related questions, one alternative cause of action may be chosen over another because it has a less disruptive effect on individuals. In gaining acceptance for the decision and cooperation necessary for successful action, those effected must not only be considered, but should also be talked with and involved as far as possible.

In making major decisions, those involved must also look at the effect on the organization structure and the organization as a going concern. (Of course, other considerations will involve short and long range monetary impact, facilities impact, impact on competitors, customers, suppliers, impact on raw material needs, governmental regulations and relations, community impact, etc.) What is the relationship of the decisions and their effective implementation to the broad and specific objectives, goals, plan, policies and procedures of the organization? What stress do they place on the existing structure, relationships, hierarchy, decentralization/centralization style? What changes in structure may be called for? How do they effect prestige, power and working relationships of various units and top officials and their outside relationships? How consistent are the decisions with previous organizational history, philosophy, methods of operation and, if inconsistent, can the problems be overcome?

As part of both human and organizational consideration, the question of delegation of decision making arises. Again, this may well depend upon the characteristics of the problems, of the decision maker, and of those to whom they might delegate certain types and levels of decision making authority. It may also depend upon organizational history, style, competitive pressures, external forces, organization structure, degree of centralization or decentralization, technology and control systems available, rate of change or need for quick action, etc.

One can characterize styles of delegation as complete delegation, veto authority delegation, very limited delegation. In complete delegation, the individual to whom you have delegated authority can take action without contacting you. He may either not inform you at all, after the fact, or inform you in informal or formal methods. Veto authority provides the individual the authority to advise you in advance of the action he plans to take unless you tell him not to do so. An alternative form of this is that the individual cannot go ahead until he receives your approval. Practically no delegation allows the individual to pose alternatives and either to recommend one with supporting data or to leave the choice entirely up to his superior. In either case, the individual does not have effective authority in regard to actual decision making.

Most ambitious, competent subordinates prefer the maximum amount of delegation possible, consistent with their knowledge, experience, and status within the organization. However, depending upon the risks involved in the decision in terms of cost, priorities, binding the corporation over long periods of time, effect on various aspects of the organization, the top officials may be very careful about what is delegated. It will also depend upon their own style, ego and other needs.

BARRIERS TO EFFECTIVE PROBLEM SOLVING AND DECISION MAKING

What was stated in the previous section are some practical ways for dealing with choices. But despite concern for the importance of good decisions and good decision processes, there are poor and at times terrible decisions made. Some of the barriers faced are:

1. Wrong attitudes, approaches, emotional states, expectations on the part of decision makers.
2. Unavailability of accurate, timely, relevant, clear information (and sometimes there may be deliberate omissions or falsifications of figures).
3. Ineffective use of the information.
4. Poor analysis of the problem, alternatives and consequences of action, implementation and followup, unwillingness to modify plans.
5. Handicapping characteristics of the decision maker—less than adequate intelligence, confidence, decisiveness, thoroughness, analytical ability, memory, experience, intestinal fortitude, frustration level, communications and persuasive abilities, leadership of others, etc. The decision maker may be rigid, unable to win confidence or respect, have prejudices and biases. He may be thrown off by wisecracks and other put downs, personal attacks or inappropriate analogies and generalizations or he may grasp at the simple or easy solutions or those that don't rock the boat too much.

CONCLUSION

Decision making is both an art and a science calling for qualities of mind, character, personality, maturity, stability and judgment. Techniques and approaches can be studied and applied to: reduce the risks of uncertainty, but they can never be entirely eliminated; gain an understanding of how others are likely to decide issues on a given set of circumstances; understand how wrong decisions can be made based on poor analysis and emotional biases, including one's own; understand rational processes and techniques for reaching better decisions. But beyond technique and knowledge of the decision making process, the company will still have to rely on the information generated and the knowledge and judgment decision makers up and down the line bring to bear on the information and problems before them. We'll never have *all* the information and insight necessary. And even if we have very little, a good process for deciding and the development of knowledge, judgment and a willingness to decide, will determine the success of the firm and the individual. We need bold though not foolhardy decision makers who are willing to stick their necks out and take reasonable risks. The timid, the doubting, those who want to wait for 100% of the facts, will be left behind in today's competitive climate.

five

Budgeting

Budgeting can be considered both as part of planning and as part of controlling. Because of its importance and its dual role, it is treated as a distinct function of executive management. We shall place greatest emphasis on the financial aspects of budgeting. However, if we regard budgeting as allocating resources, we also budget for (allocate) other resources in addition to financial resources—manpower, time, space, facilities, equipment, etc.

BUDGETING: THE PLANNING DIMENSION

A budget can be described as a set of objectives with costs attached. It is clearly linked to planning in that the organization must determine through the planning process what its objectives are for the coming year, short term, and long term. For some managers, setting objectives may appear to be an academic exercise. But the reality of the "exercise" becomes apparent when price tags are attached and when decisions are made as to who will receive what proportion of new or continuing resources and who will take cuts in their proposed budgets. A budget reflects aspirations, commitments, and priorities and has, therefore, major ramifications not only for the company as a whole, but for its component units and for managers and workers within those units. In the public sector, the budget is also a political document indicating priorities, trade-offs, and potential for political gain for the administration.

It is, therefore, no surprise that the periodic battle of the budget and preparing for the battle is a major event for every manager. Many, in fact, view it as a "battle" and a variety of offensive and defensive strategies and tactics are employed in order to "win." Analyses of past, present, future, and of competitors within and outside the company, psychology, strategy, tactics, charts, slides, models, oral and written presentations, assessment (intelligence missions) of the other's style, intelligence, power, performance—are just a few of the weapons employed. There are games played by the budget requesters, reviewers and decision makers in order to achieve results. The requesters wish to gain sufficient funds to carry out the objectives they see as vital for continued or potential success, or for the turnaround to a profitable status of their units as well as for items of lesser criticality, but still regarded as very important. And, as a hedge, if possible, they seek to have some margin for error, for incentive, for taking advantage of opportunities that may arise. The reviewers seek to remove the fat, to as far as possible come up with a reasonably bare bones budget for each unit so that funds not allocated to one operation can be used for other units or for corporate needs, both short and long range. The top executives seek to balance competing needs of units as well as providing for unforseen circumstances or broader and/or longer range objectives.

There is much more to budget formulation than putting together numbers. Analysis, technology, information, emotion, power, status, ego, risk, reward, incentive, personalities, psychology, negotiating skills, credibility, biases, predictions as to the present and future, assessment of the market—all these and more enter into the formulation of a budget. Those charged with company budget review and the development of the corporate budget must be aware of the various factors and currents at work. They must also attempt to be aware of their own biases and credibility. The top executive decision makers must be aware of the psychological effects of their fiscal decisions.

TYPES OF FINANCIAL BUDGETS

There are two major types of financial budgets—a capital budget and an expense or operations budget. A third type of budget linked to the other two, a cash flow budget, is of increasing importance.

Capital Budget

In essence, the capital budget depicts the company's investment in land, equipment, facilities, and technology. It is a transfer of assets from one form to another. Its goal, by investing, is to plan for increased sales share of the market, and/or profits, generally through new or improved products, manufacturing facilities, or technology. Capital budgeting, since it involves large dollars, time commitments, and future commitments, must be very carefully done and place great concern on priorities and projections as to internal and external forces (see Chapter on Planning) operating now and in the future. At times, some capital items must be budgeted because of legal requirements (e. g., safety, pollution controls), others need replacement or repair, new capital items may be needed to match innovations or capabilities of competitors, or pressure by unions for improved work facilities.

Expense Budget

The funds allocated to be spent on day-to-day business activities are called the expense budget. These budget allocations cover:

(a) fixed expenditures such as interest payments on outstanding debt, and a variety of overhead expenditures;
(b) variable expenditures based on the level of activity anticipated and planned for in regard to production, sales, marketing, research, and development, improvements in different aspects of management, compliance with regulations, etc. Although most of the expense budget can be exactly planned because of knowledge of labor costs, cost of supplies, there are always a fair number of "guestimates" that must be made. This leads to adding a "cushion" to the various budgets allocated to

organizational units and/or to a division, group or company-wide contingency fund or reserve. The cushion or reserve is used for unforseen occurrences such as a larger than expected rise in cost of supplies or labor, necessity for expert assistance in regard to new regulations or lawsuits, repairs, and replacement or machinery, higher interest rates on money borrowed, and the many other costs that may go up or sales that may be less than planned.

Cash Flow Budget

In practically all organizations there is a flow of cash needs related to peak and slack periods of sales and expenditures. Anticipating the peaks and valleys of cash flow needs, the lag of receipts from sales based on credit arrangements, the relationship of cash flow to production costs and inventory size, is of great importance. Poor budgeting results in the expenditure of unnecessary interest costs because of the need to borrow money to meet immediate or short term requirements. It also could lead to a loss of the opportunity to invest temporarily idle cash, thus earning interest income.

For each type of budget, there is a need to develop long range budgets which are related to long range plans. Each long range objective should have attached to it, as part of the analysis, a projected budget. The budget allows the decision maker to gain a quantitative sense of the commitments necessary and the impact on the entire organization. The budget would then be one means to choose among alternatives for the short and long range and to compile objectives into an overall plan. What is "long range" to one firm may be "short range" to another. Some firms can project three, five, ten years, or more. Certainly in capital budgeting one needs to have a longer time perspective than for operating budgets. The answer to the question of what is a reasonable length of time depends upon the nature of the particular company and industry, and external and internal forces. In developing long range budgets, careful analysis must be made as to financial projections for future years, the inflationary rate, the value of the dollar, etc.

WAYS OF BUDGETING

Basically there are six broad methods that can be used in budgeting with variations possible for each method:

1. Lump sum budgeting
2. Line item budgeting
3. Incremental budgeting
4. Program budgeting
5. Performance budgeting
6. Zero base budgeting

We shall spend more time discussing the two newer approaches, program budgeting and zero base budgeting.

1. Lump Sum Budgeting

Provides funding to organizational units rather than focusing on expenditure objects or categories of items. The unit receives a lump sum and normally it can transfer funds from one expenditure category to another.

2. Line Item Budgeting

Every object of expenditure has to be justified and particular expenditure categories are approved, e.g., salaries, travel, office supplies. Normally, it is difficult to transfer funds from one expenditure category to another. Managers criticize this method as constraining their ability to manage and be flexible.

3. Incremental Budgeting

Assumes the same budget as in the past and expects budget submissions to indicate need for changes from previous levels, based upon inflation rate, changed objectives or needs, increased or decreased productivity, etc. This method does not lead to analysis of choices or effectiveness.

4. Program Budgeting

This approach was made famous because of the use of PPBS (Planning, Programming and Budgetary System) in the United States

Department of Defense in 1961 and then elsewhere in government. Actually, earlier versions of it were used in General Motors in the 1920s and in World War II by the War Production Board. It is based on establishing programs and program goals. The idea was to alter processes and results of governmental budgeting in important ways, and to improve the planning process and program development prior to budgetary decision making. A program is a group of activities which can be considered as an entity for purposes of organization, management, budgeting, and controlling, e.g., limited warfare cap- ability, street patrol (police). Programs rather than units are the cen- tral focus and the programs need not be confined to within one agency. PPBS hoped to relate budgetary decisions to broad goals; evaluate which programs would most probably achieve their ob- jectives by use of new types of information systems; present a com- plete picture on all funds used for a particular program; provide an objective basis for reaching funding decisions; indicate clearly budget- ary inputs (dollars, facilities, manpower, supplies, equipment) needed to deliver program outputs.

Program budgeting was not generally successful beyond the De- fense Department and it has had a minor lasting effect on govern- mental budgeting. Reasons for its demise as a formal budgeting tech- nique include:

a. Lack of advance preparation for a new technique and a lack of understanding by advocates of budgetary traditions, loyal- ties, relationships,

b. Lack of top management support and an inadequate commit- ment of resources,

c. Short supply of skilled analysts and good data,

d. Conflict with traditional political values in budget making in terms of representation of political interests and decentral- izing the budgetary decision making process,

e. Resistance of those who were leaders in budget making to im- plementing such a major change. One might note that the general reasons for the failure of any attempt at change or innovation apply in this instance.

The concept does have value for both public and non-public or- ganizations if it helps to focus on assessing the relationship of pro- grams or activities to objectives and the funding decisions that must be made to permit programs to operate. It can help management understand: the interrelationship of many factors (and the costs involved) in achieving a particular objective; the need for information; the impact of programs; and the need for defining objectives.

5. Performance Budgeting

This budgeting method uses budgeting as a means to measure efficiency. The performance budget is basically concerned with output or results. Program budgeting would compare the effectiveness of alternative programs and seek improved results. Performance budgeting focuses on control, efficiency, lowest possible cost, highest possible productivity. Activities, not programs, would be the major concern with various workload indicators used to measure performance, e.g., number of tons of garbage collected per sanitation vehicle, arrests made per police officer, miles of road repaired by a repair crew. Performance budgeting has considerable value, but there is a tendency to overlook the issue of whether what is being done is necessary, desirable or preferable to other alternatives. There is also a question as to whether the appropriate workload indicators are being used. For example, "number of arrests made" is a reasonable indicator of performance for a detective, police officer or unit, but a better indicator is the number of "good" arrests made (those that result in convictions or guilty pleas).

6. Zero Base Budgeting (ZBB)

This method was launched at Texas Instruments, Inc. in the 1960s, introduced in Georgia under Governor Jimmy Carter in 1971-75, and in numerous industries. It was also introduced on a selective basis into the Federal Government in 1977 under President Carter. The four basic aspects of ZBB are:

1. Identification of "decision units"—the lowest level entities for which budgets are prepared, e.g., programs.
2. Analysis of these units and formulation of "decision packages" by the manager responsible for establishing priorities and preparing budgets within the administrative unit. The decision package represents alternative levels of cost and service and often alternative ways of performing the function. Each pack-

age is, in effect, an incremental budget request as well as an alternative to another budget request for the same or a different activity. The analysis involves questioning the consequences of giving the "decision unit" zero dollars, in effect, eliminating it. This involves cost effectiveness and efficiency studies, and finally the preparation of the decision packages. Each manager prepares several decision packages pertaining to the same set of activities to allow higher level reviewers to choose among alternatives at different funding levels for delivering the same functions.

3. Ranking of decision packages according to priority from highest to lowest.
4. Higher level officials establish priorities among all packages from all units based on funding available.

Theoretically a department manager assumes he has zero dollars available. He must identify the activities or programs under his supervision, evaluate the benefits of each and the cost/benefits, and then list them in priority order with detailed costs. In practice, it may be too cumbersome and impractical to begin, in fact, at zero, or to look at every item every year. Thus, ZBB is often used as a form of marginal analysis and of forcing attention not only on the usual requests for additions to the budget, but on deletions or subtractions from the budget. As in all new approaches to budgeting, there are problems of gaining acceptance, concern about too much paperwork, concern about its effectiveness in improving resource allocation. So far, it appears that ZBB has resulted in better management information and more detailed planning prior to budget preparation. Further, there is considerable more involvement by lower level management personnel in the budget process. There is some evidence that it has, in fact, been helpful in evaluating competitive requests for new funds, evaluating current level funding and for deciding upon the most appropriate program levels and expenditures. If one does not get unnecessarily tied to a rigid set of procedures, ZBB can be helpful in facilitating choices among broad and specific policy alternatives.

LET THE BUDGET SUIT THE SITUATION

Each approach to budgeting must be tailored to the needs of the individual firm and the capabilities and concerns of top management.

One approach can be used for the corporate budget, but a unit manager may wish to use a different approach for managing his own budget. Changing times and personalities may result in different approaches, a modification or combination of several of the approaches.

The climate may not be right to introduce something that could seem threatening and might have been oversold as the answer to management's problem. On occasion, this has happened to ZBB and PPBS. A wise financial officer will carefully assess the situation and environment before introducing any new concepts, procedures or forms. We should be greatly concerned about problems with the present system, goals of the new system, discussion, briefing, training, explaining, testing, modifying any new system before changing ways of doing things. For example, one may accomplish some of the goals of ZBB without some of the problems associated with it by using the method outlined below. It is not as good as a straight ZBB approach and it may eventually be considered a step toward ZBB. It does establish the groundwork for a ZBB approach and may end up being sufficiently effective without going further.

A Sample Budget Process

Step   1.   Establish general planning variables and constraints.

This might include price increases, production and sales increases, salary increases, costs of supplies, equipment, raw materials, advertising, utilities, manpower increases.

Step   2.   Analyze unit base budget.

Each unit prepares a base budget analysis and alternative base budget analysis based upon specific assumptions included in the general planning variables. For example, if sales are expected to decline, what is the specific impact on the particular unit?

Each unit then identifies the potential for savings from increased efficiency or productivity. Basic workload indicators are examined for internal trends and comparison with appropriate internal and external performance standards.

Finally, programs and activities are ranked in order of priority.

Step 3. Develop requests for new or expanded programs and activities and quality improvements in programs.

For each new program or activity, a form is submitted detailing: description of the program/activity, discussion of the contribution of the proposed program to the unit's mission or goals and the relationship of the proposal to existing programs. The funding request should be supported by a detailed analysis of the staffing, capital, start-up and operational costs and income (including break-even points where appropriate) for the first year and for several years beyone (2-10 years and sometimes more—the number of years depends upon the company and the particular program).

The Expanded Program Request Form would indicate description, contribution to unit's objectives, and funding and income needs and expectations for several years as outlined above.

The Quality Improvement Form would follow the same format as the two forms just described. The basic reasons for improvements must be detailed along with a detailed resource requirement analysis and projected benefits.

In all three forms, these should also be an indication of possible negative or adverse consequences.

Step 4. Review by the next higher authority.

Step 5. Review by the next higher authority.

Step 6. Review by the budget planning staff and response through the appropriate chain of command.

This may involve requests by the budget staff for clarification, additional reasons and data, refinement of costs, etc. Formal "hearings" may also be involved.

Step 7. Preparation of proposed budget and presentation of overall company budget to top management by budget planning staff, including methods of implementing, monitoring and controlling budget.

Step 8. Requests for additional clarifications, data, change in assumptions resulting in budget changes as decided by top management with follow-up to units by budget planning staff.

Step 9. Preparation and presentation of revised budget by planning staff to top management.

Step 10. Discussion and decision by top management.

Step 11. Communication of budget decisions.

Step 12. Development of budget and methods of monitoring and controlling the budget by budget planning staff and units.

DEVELOPING A BUDGET

In developing a budget, the bottom up, top down or a combination approach can be used. In the bottom up approach, each unit may be asked to state its needs, either in a program, performance, line item or other method. Depending upon the type of system used, the budget forms might call for indicating results achieved from last year 's allocations and what results are predicted if certain funding levels are granted. The budget request would include manpower, salary increases, equipment, facilities, etc., with costs involved. Priorities might be set, desired satisfactory and minimal levels might be indicated. A modification of this approach would have the budget drawn up under general guidelines set by top management, such as total income will increase by X%, net profits will increase by Y%, total spending will decrease by Z%, etc. A top down method would set basic parameters, but could also be quite specific in terms of objectives to be accomplished, various income/expense/profit ratios to be achieved, specific activities to be funded. In a top down approach, the central budget unit plays a very powerful role, some would say, too powerful.

CUTTING AN APPROVED BUDGET

From time to time, it is necessary to cut a budget after it has been approved. This is a very difficult and often emotional experience.

Commitments made have to be modified or rescinded, staff may have to be laid off, promotions and reclassifications held up, plans for new products and services shelved, current service levels or improvements cut back or out.

There are several ways of facing up to this difficult task. One approach is an across-the-board percentage cut for all units. Although many would agree that different units have different needs and are "more important" to the company as a whole, the across-the-board approach is used because it appears to be fair and is the easiest to sell to all units. Each unit appears to be taking its fair share of the problem.

We would argue that the company as a whole has to establish priority concerns and in applying these it may have to protect certain units, functions and activities more than others. It is indeed more troublesome and time consuming to take this approach, but in both the short and long run it simply makes more sense. Analyses have to be made as to where do we hurt the most or least if we reduce expenditures, then appropriate cuts geared to the analysis should be made.

In general, it is best to have top management set general guidelines and ground rules for the cuts and to have them monitor results. It is wise to have operating units pick and choose what cuts they will make within the general guidelines. In most cases, companies have shaken the fat out of budgets. Therefore, when cuts must be made, there are real risks involved. One of the risks is that services, whether to customers or employees, will have to be diminished or eliminated, and that various types of standards of performance will be diminished. The decision makers must choose where they cannot hurt production, services or planning and where, reluctantly, they can. Often, cuts are made in staff, planning, research and development areas first in order to save the line activities. This is understandable, but often shortsighted.

As budgets become tighter, the frills will long ago have been eliminated. The issue really becomes how efficient, effective, creative can we become in terms of increased income and decreased expenses. But along with that is the need to take actions that are necessary even though they change the things we do and how we do them. Delaying taking distasteful actions that hurt units, individuals, products or services, often result in even more massive cuts at a later time. The decision makers must seek to use a scalpel rather than a hatchet, but he who delays deftly using the former, ends up swinging the latter.

NEGOTIATING THE BUDGET

Budgetary discussions often involve strategies and tactics similar to labor negotiations. We shall describe some approaches used by requesters and some used by reviewers. The tactics used, of course, depend upon the company, the situation, the personalities involved, past history of negotiations, the availability of funds, power of internal competitors for funds, external forces, etc.

It should be recognized that for many, the size of the budget administered determines power, prestige, title, bonus, compensation and potential. The dollars, people, equipment, facilities involved are not trivial issues. They may very well determine how fast and how high the individual climbs in the organization and his attractiveness to other companies. His ability to negotiate things of value for himself and his staff, salary increases, additional personnel, new ventures, equipment, space, are important in terms of his own self-perception, the perception of others, the morale of his unit. For many subordinates, the test of their boss' leadership is that he is able to deliver personal and professional things they desire. What he delivers is measured both in an absolute sense and relative to other units and past performance. Often, the arena in which he battles for them and ultimately for himself, is the battle of the budget.

Tactics of Those Seeking Funding

1. The Honest Guy Approach.

This calls for being perceived as playing the game very straight. To achieve that perception, one seeks to be completely accurate and relatively low key in describing past accomplishments, potential gains, current needs, failures in the past and risks in the future. The requests submitted indicate no or very little cushions in the numbers and requests. If one is successful, the budgetary process is relatively easy and quick and filled with little tension for both submitter and reviewer. The unit head, in time, earns the confidence of the reviewer and may be required to produce fewer analyses and justifications than others. The unit would tend to get all or a very high percentage of its requests. The danger of the approach may be that the reviewers do not believe the individual is being that honest, that, in fact, there is a substantial cushion in his requests. Thus, when they cut the requests, or are forced to cut even the honest guy's request because of across-the-board cuts, the unit may be hurt more than others because it, in fact, has very little or no "fudge factor" in the request.

2.   The Decoy Approach.

In submitting the budget one may build a beautiful case for an expensive new idea or for an apparently unrealistic improvement or expansion of an existing product or service. The idea or improvement would be fought for in a very hard and tough fashion. But deep down, it is a decoy. One hopes the budgeteers will focus on that and knock a good part or all of it out, and feel satisfied that they have done a good job of reducing the requests for new funding. Meanwhile, it is hoped the other programs and requests, with sufficient cushion, will emerge relatively unnoticed, unanalyzed and unscathed. Another tactic would be to sacrifice one's pet project (but really the decoy) in order to guarantee the level of funding requested for the other programs. If the strategy doesn't work, the decoy is quickly knocked out and the other programs get a tough review.

3.   The Savior Approach.

In this role, the requester builds the case that with the appropriate funding based upon the unit's past achievements and projections for the future, they will more than return the investment. They will, in fact, generate enough profits to carry several other units, divisions, or the company itself. The savior trys to put the burden on the budgeters and the onus on them for risking the financial well being of the company. Offshoots of this basic tactic, for those who don't quite have the outstanding track record or solid projections for the future, is the "Trust Me" Tactic or "This Is the Big One I've Been Waiting For or the Company Needs."

4.   The Opportunity Cost or Venture Capital Approach.

This calls for making an appeal to the budget's financial planning concerns by indicating that there are "opportunity costs," "targets of opportunity" or "venture capital" needs that the unit must meet.

"If successful, and the probabilities are high," the unit manager would say, "we have a chance to make a bundle. . . establish a new position in the industry. . . leave our competitors far behind. . ."

5.   The Drowning Man Approach.

This calls for stating that the unit has historically (one's definition of historical may be the past year or two) been underfunded and because of this has been unable to meet its objectives. The plea is to save the drowning man, provide the necessary funds. One would present documentation as to underfunding and, if possible, compare it to the other units.

6.   I've Done So Much With the Little I've Had, Think How Much More I Could Do With More.

The title of the approach says it all. The tactic should be backed up with performance results, ratio analysis, comparative data, if possible. The purpose simply is to project what would have happened if more funds would have been available. This also ties in to the "Savior" tactic.

7.   This Is My Chance to Make My Mark or This Is My Last Big Chance or I Retire Soon, I Want to Go Out Riding High

This approach is based on analysis, past performance, future projections, or an attempt to capture the emotions of the reviewer.

8.   Cut at Your Own Risk, This Is What I Need.

This approach is a tougher stand than the "Honest Guy." It may also be straight and factual, but a more aggressive defense. On the other hand, it may be a negotiating stance to protect everything one has put in the request. The requester might go into combat by indicating that he will carefully document any failure to meet objectives by attributing it to unwarranted budget cuts.

9.   The Fairness Approach.

This would stress that all we want is equitable treatment and then demonstrate how others have received more in the past and delivered less. Thus, we want our fair share based on our performance.

10.   Correct Past Injustices or Let's Play Catch Up Approach.

This is related to the "Drowning Man," but stresses the past underfunding or inequitable treatment and asks for partial or full restitution.

11.   Cut Me and You'll Kill the Unit, the Company, My Future, My Job.

The title says it all, but aside from appeal to emotion, it can be used to lay the onus of poor performance on the budgeters or on top decision makers.

12.   Cut (or Don't Give Me What I Request) and I May Have to Consider Whether I Stay with the Company (or I'll Resign).

This is a clear threat to leave. It may indeed work, if the individual is really that valuable. On the other hand, if he overestimates his value, his "bluff" may be called.

13.   If I Disagree With You I'm Going Straight to the Chief Executive Officer.

Only the strong and powerful can get away with this approach.

14.   The Good Soldier Approach.

This indicates that the unit head has come up with the minimal budget he needs, he can't cut anymore, he leaves it for the budgeter to decide and he'll carry on as best he can.

15. **This is Rock Bottom, Bare Bones Budget But Tell Me What I Have to Sacrifice and Let's Work Together to Lessen the Damage.**

This tactic is useful after some preliminary pruning has taken place.

16. **The Surgeon Approach.**

The requester indicates that he's cut everything to the bare bones, in fact he's cut into some bone. Any more cutting would damage or destroy vital organs. The requester might show the requests that came to him and how substantial have been the cuts he has made prior to his presentation to the budget unit.

17. **The Garderner Approach.**

The requester sprinkles some, or a lot of water into each component of his budget, with a good deal of backup material, fancy slides and graphs and a well rehearsed presentation by several of his colleagues. He expects that the budgeters will shake out some or most of the fat or non-vital requests, but that he will emerge with practically all that he really wants.

18. **The Martyr.**

At the final moments, the requester may suggest that for the few thousand dollars at stake he's willing to give up part of all of his salary increase, or meeting a need for additional secretary or assistant for him. This may be dangerous, the budget maker may take the challenge.

There are variations on and combinations of the above approaches. Depending upon the circumstances, different ones will be tried by different people at different times. Success of one approach over another will also vary based upon conditions, who were the presenters, who were the reviewers. Facts are important but so are personalities, trust relationship, reputation, strategy, tactics and style.

Tactics of Those Reviewing Requests

In listing the tactics employed by reviewers, I risk making life more difficult for myself and my colleagues on the same side of the table, but fairness demands informing the reader of what he might prepare for.

It should be noted that the outstanding budget professional is concerned with what is best both for the company (immediate, short and long range) and the individual groups or units. At times the budgetary objectives conflict among units and between a unit (or combination of units) and the company as a whole. It is the task of the chief budget officer to present to the highest decisions makers his recommendations based on solid, impartial, accurate analysis. The analysis should indicate the risks and opportunities involved in certain funding decisions. It is very difficult to screen out reaction to personalities, reputation, presentation dynamics and dramatics. The reviewer is human and has his likes and dislikes, susceptibility to certain approaches and distaste for others. But the goal must be, as far as can be humanly achieved, to be objective, thorough and fair, to try to get all the facts, to assess them thoroughly, to probe for opportunities or weaknesses not fully developed.

There can be an important creative side of budget making and budget review, if there is trust, confidence and competence on both sides. By raising tough questions and by jointly working on them, the requester and reviewers can forge better ideas, solutions, cost effective approaches. The budget reviewer can, in fact, become an objective consultant and colleague rather than the detective or cop. This may indeed be difficult, because after having come up with the optimal solution to the problem, he may appear to "double cross" the requester by turning down the request because of later budget constraints.

What I am appealing for is a broader scope and perception by and of those who review and recommend budgets. The system that merely puts the budget analysts in the enforcement, cut down on water role, and rewards them on the basis of the amount and percentage of their cuts, is not maximizing the effectiveness available through proper use of the budget review function. It is indeed true that the satisfaction many budget people receive is in cutting, eliminating, combining, saying "no." This lends credence to the penny pinching, green eye shade, narrow minded, negative outlook stereotype many have. But, though some aspects of this may be necessary for their job success, budget reviewing can be broader. In being broader, in working for better answers and ways to meet legitimate budgetary needs, an even greater contribution can be made to the organization.

SOME TACTICS USED BY REVIEWERS

1. *The Inquisition Technique.* This involves detailed scrutiny of every document submitted, developing their own data, sharp, somewhat nasty questioning, memos and oral requests for more data and analyses. The goal is to get the individual requesters so defensive that they regard it as a victory if they are only cut X%.

2. *I Really Want to Help You, But I Need Your Help.* This offers to give on some things if only the requester will reduce his figures or needs. The budgeter may exaggerate how much he needs back from the individual so that if he gets it he has a cushion for his dealings with others. If he doesn't, he may seem like the good guy when he says, "You came close, let's split the difference."

3. *The Honest Guy.* He sets out the bottom line and dollars goals he hopes to achieve and plays it straight. He is willing to reduce or elinimate his set goals in the face of facts presented to him. The same advantages and disadvantages apply here as in the "Honest Guy" approach by the requester.

4. *The Time Saver.* This appeals to the presenter's concern about dragging out the review process and what might happen if early agreement is not reached. The reviewer says "let's save time and anguish, what's your absolute bottom line and I'll see if I can sign off now."

5. *The Spy.* The budgeter suggests that if the presenter can give him information helpful in cutting other units, he'll be able to meet most or all of the requester's needs.

6. *I'll Be the Heavy.* The budget official indicates that he'll play the role of the bad guy who slashed mercilessly, thus getting the requester off the hook with his subordinates and peers. The budgeter says "what do you really, really want and let's get rid of the other things."

7. *Do Me a Favor.*   The budgeter tries to get the requester to understand the time constraints and pressures he is under and the goals he must reach. He indicates that he'll try to pay the requester back during the year or in future years, but he really needs a big cut now.

8. *Let's Make a Deal.*   This approach suggests that the reviewer will drop his objections to some things if the requester drops various other things.

9. *Split the Difference.*   (This can also be a technique used by the requester.) As the title implies, the differences are split in half. However, the wise budget analyst will first get as many things knocked out as possible before splitting the difference.

10. *Wait Till Next Year.*   The budget maker indicates he understands the validity of the requests, but it is impossible to meet all, some or any of them, or that a cut is necessary from base budget. However, he assures the requester that he will take the facts and the requester's cooperation very much into consideration next year and the requests will be high on the priority list.

11. *Changes Bring Loose Change.*   This approach suggests that there's a small amount of dollars available if the requester can show that he is making changes in work methods, organization, evaluation techniques, productivity standards, etc. The budget maker is attempting to force improvements in the requester's operations and seeks to reward it by extra funding or limiting the cuts.

12. *The Salesman.*   The budgeter suggests that he can reshape and improve the submission and sell the most important parts of it to higher echelons, but he needs to have trade-offs so that the bottom line is lower.

We have discussed strategies, tactics, ploys. In one form or another, with more or less documentation, sincerity and vehemence, they will be utilized by one or both of the parties involved in negotiating the budget. The point is that despite the game playing suggested above, we must strive to build budgetary processes that are rational, responsive to needs of all involved, and based on credibility and integrity. In my own experience, as both requester and reviewer, I have found that one form or another of the Honest Guy approach pays off, certainly in the long run, but frequently in the short run. This calls for integrity and a lack of gamesmanship on both sides of the table.

THE BUDGET AS A CONTROL TOOL

By comparing actual performance against the budget, the company is able to determine whether it is spending and earning more or less than planned, identify the explanations for deviance from plan (budget), either up or down, and then seek to make necessary changes and corrections.

To be effective as a control tool, the actual expenditures must be reported in a timely fashion to those responsible. The reporting format must be such that it provides the necessary level of detail. For example, a report that indicates only that the unit is $50,000 or 15% above budget is not as useful as one that indicates the specific areas in which there are overruns and perhaps even the dates in which the overruns occurred. The latter report provides the means to identify problems and make corrections. The level of detail provided will depend on the level of review. The lower the echelon, the more detail is necessary. Top management may be interested in a cost overrun on a capital project, or how expenditures compare with budget. The project manager will be concerned about actual and projected material and labor costs in relation to the planned and actual percentage of completion of the project.

Whatever budgetary process is adopted, top management must have a way of comparing actual performance to budget and of pinpointing the areas, individuals or factors that have caused variances. One way of doing this is by budget performance and variance reports that go from the highest level down through group, division, plant, department and unit. The variance report and the analysis involved may highlight poor management, planning, control, supervision. It may also indicate conditions beyond a manager's control, e.g., poor facilities, equipment, understaffing. This would necessitate corrective action and funding beyond the budget for the particular area.

An off-shoot of the budget variance report is the budget variance projection report. This would indicate that based upon expenditures and trends to-date, by the end of the quarter, half year or year,

what expenditures would be in each area or for each object of expenditure. This allows management to anticipate potential problems
and take timely corrective action.

The budget variance and budget variance projection reports not
only indicate problems or opportunities in one area, but can be
refined to indicate potential problems/opportunities in areas that
are linked closely to the area showing a significant variance. A 10%
variance in one area can have a decided impact on allied areas.

The control function of the budget is usually seen as a whip and
as a means of evaluating a manager's performance. We would urge
at least equal concern for the use of the control aspect as a way of
highlighting potential problems or opportunities and providing the
information and detail necessary for management to step in quickly
and effectively.

As was noted in the discussion of control, we must walk a fine
line in using the budget performance and budget variance reports
so that we neither over or under control.

PUTTING BUDGETING IN CONTEXT

It is clear from the foregoing discussion that budgeting is of major
significance for planning, controlling and decision making. The process, plans, procedures and reports associated with budgeting are
powerful assets to management. But in using the budgeting techniques available, we must also recognize some inherent weaknesses
in budgeting. There is a reliance on past history and historical trends
that may not apply in the future. The personal and status factor is
important. Top management influences the budget greatly and in
their zest for greater profits, unrealistic budgets might be built.
The same holds true for lower level managers. They may seek to have
safety factors or cushions built into the budget while their superiors
may shave things too closely in the hope of motivating or forcing
better performance. If the budget is unrealistic in terms of performance or profit expectations, managers may be forced to resort to
poor short or long run practices in order to avoid blame for budget
overruns, i.e., attempting to save on necessary maintenance, begin
expansion too soon to force management support, sell in advance
in order to meet this year's targets, but risk next year's results,
maximize short term cash flow results risking long term results.

Above all, those involved in budgeting as requesters, reviewers, and decision makers must be tuned in to the effect of the budgetary process and system on individuals, as well as the company. The needs of planning, control and effectiveness of the budget for the company as a whole versus the needs of individuals for flexibility and a sense of mastery of their own fate often produce a conflict situation or undercurrents of conflict and dissatisfaction. There is no easy answer to resolving the conflict, but deeper awareness of the problem and greater discussion of better ways of solving it, tailor-made to each company, is necessary.

six

Innovating

The successful executive and company, over the long run, is able to do the usual better and to devise new, unusual, creative ways and activities involving products, services, markets and marketing, productivity, money management, etc. The innovative or creative act may be something that can be patented or copyrighted, wins international acclaim, earns $500 million, or just is a simple twist on what was done before and helps do things better without earning much praise or money.

Trying to innovate, trying to be creative and create a climate and environment for innovation is a difficult task. One cannot sit down on a particular sunny afternoon and say "today I'll be creative." But however one arrives at creative climates and creative acts, in the face of competition the race belongs to those who "dare to dream things that never were and say, why not."

The executive should seek to sharpen his own creative abilities and the abilities of others in the organization. He should strive to encourage ideas, blue sky and otherwise, and to create a process in which ideas receive serious consideration. It is true that many ideas will not be fruitful and in evaluating them the company will lose time, energy, money. It is also probably true that most expenditures in research and development departments do not end up in usable results. But

major breakthroughs and small modifications come from repeated attempts to do things better or come up with something different
or better.

A concern for innovation need not be only on the truly new or existing product, invention, process. It can also entail major or minor
fine tuning of what is already done. Managers who innovate tend to
go about asking, what am I doing, why, is there a way to save time,
energy, motion, money, to simplify, to eliminate, replace, combine,
merge. The why, what, where, who, when, how, in regard to everything that is done should be raised and analyzed to see if there is a
better or new approach.

To have an innovative atmosphere, throughout the organization
there must be encouragement of change and change agents, evolu-
tionists as well as revolutionists. A climate and environment should
be created where people feel comfortable thinking about new and
better ways of doing the current and anticipating future needs (see
chapter on Planning).

Prior to embarking on various ways to encourage innovation, the
company may wish to get people thinking about breaking out of the
usual constraints that hamper creative thought. People interested in
developing this atmosphere sometimes begin by setting up "exercises"
or "games" ranging from detective mysteries, to identifying causes of
problems based on various clues, or some pencil and paper exercises.
For instance: (For those who must have the answers, see the end of
this chapter).

1. With four straight lines, touch all of the points in a cluster of
    nine without lifting your pencil from the paper. Time limit:
    one minute.

    0   0   0
    0   0   0
    0   0   0

2. Pick five common tools, utensils or objects around a house.
    Re-design them for greater effectiveness and ease or safety in
    use.

3. You are being held hostage in a small cabin in a remote loca-
    tion, guarded by two vicious dogs who patrol the outside of
    the cabin and three armed, very tough and not too bright crim-
    inals. What do you do?

4. You are a newspaper reporter and want to get the views of a very important person. But he has refused to meet with anyone and his staff has been successful in keeping everyone away from him despite calls, letters, people waiting near his home and office. How do you get to see him?

5. What is the general rule that governs the series: 18, 11, 15, 14, 9, 6, 13, 12, 20 (Hint: the solution may not lie in mathematical manipulation of the numbers).

6. Give as many plausible explanations as you can for the following statement: "May is the month of the greatest number of suicides."

7. You have found out that your best friend's son, age 15, is drinking hard liquor heavily. What various approaches and appeals might you make to get him to stop?

Coming up with creative thoughts would be much simpler if we could readily identify creative or innovative individuals. Although high intelligence seems to be a reasonable prerequisite, there are problems in defining intelligence and then applying intelligence to situations. The most intelligent person, if we define intelligence as the quality measured by intelligence tests, is not necessarily the most creative person. Possessing a great amount of knowledge or a Ph.D degree is no sure sign of creativity. Nor, is the common assumption that creativity people are nonconformists. It is true that we "tolerate" nonconformity by some people in organizations because of their supposed or real creativity but there are numerous examples of non-conformists who are merely acting out various attitudes, personal beliefs, style and possible psychological reactions. There will continue to be approaches to identify creativity through psychological tests and problem solving exercises. In my own experience, the best indicators have been the person's previous record, analysis of the record by persons very knowledgeable about the individual's field and performance, and interviews by these individuals and by skilled interviewers.

ENCOURAGING INNOVATION

Analysis of Current Work Methods

The Group Executive or Division Head or Unit Manager might wish to analyze the major processes under his supervision and seek to improve effectiveness and efficiency. He should identify the task(s) or function(s) to be improved. In order to use his own time and the time of the internal and external consultants more efficiently, the selection of activities to be improved is important. There is normally not sufficient time to look at everything and the costs may not justify a full scale review of certain processes. Therefore, one should identify:

(a) activities that take a good deal of time, effort and money and are of considerable importance to the unit and company;

(b) areas or tasks that involve excessive overtime;

(c) areas that involve excessive delays in the unit or that result in delays for other units or for other steps in producing a product or service;

(d) areas where there are considerable backlogs;

(e) bottlenecks in the work of the unit;

(f) areas of poor quality or high rate of returns or recalls or internal or external dissatisfaction;

(g) work that involves unpleasant tasks or that create physical or mental strain;

(h) units or activities that have a high degree of absenteeism or turnover;

(i) activities that require a good deal of coordination, multiple clearances;

(j) activities that are very complicated; and

(k) methods that have not been reviewed for a number of years.

Once having identified targets of opportunity with potentially high payoff, the next step is to carefully analyze what is currently being done. This would involve such things as: what is done, why is it done, when is it done, where is it done, who does it, how is it done, how much is done, how much time does it take, how much does it cost, what have the trends been in each of the foregoing categories in the past year, three years, five years and what are the projections for the future? Useful tools in the analysis include a work distribution chart and the preliminary steps involved the task list and activity list, the flow process chart, work count studies and layout studies.

The Work Distribution Chart is particularly helpful in depicting the activities that take the most time, whether there is a poor allocation of effort, whether skills are being used properly, are employees performing too many unrelated tasks, are too many employees involved in the same task thereby leading to delays, buckpassing, etc., is work distributed evenly? (See Exhibits I, II, and III.)

The flow process chart can help in the analysis of procedures and therefore lead to change when: (1) there are major changes in volume of work, processes or personnel taking place; (2) there is a procedural problem or current practices are too costly; (3) when conducting a periodic review of a unit; and (4) when establishing a new unit or merging units.

Layout Studies pinpoint the relationship between the physical location of work area facilities and space and the optimal work methods and flow. Such studies can improve: utilization of space and equipment, working conditions, flow of work and physical movement.

The Work Count determines the effect of volume of effort on the procedures and methods under review. Total count can be performed or various sampling techniques used. The work count can result in improvements in regard to: scheduling; evaluating effectiveness and efficiency; relating activities; allocating work; spotting bottlenecks; and evaluating personnel needs.

Other methods that can be employed to pinpoint possible improvements are: management analysis studies, organization studies, forms analysis, sampling for quality control, work measurement and productivity measurement.

In conducting these types of analyses, one must continue to ask, "why." Nothing can be taken for granted. One's natural curiosity, detective instincts and investigative reporter tendencies must come to the fore. Every detail must be challenged. Why do we do this to begin with, is it really necessary, must it be done by this person or unit in this location, in this sequence, in this way?

Through questions, observations, analysis of reports and data, developing alternatives, we can seek to eliminate unnecessary functions and steps within functions, merge or combine activities and steps, change the location and sequence of tasks and the persons or units who perform them and end up simplifying the whole process.

In the process of finding the better way, remember that all wisdom is not in the minds of the reviewers. Those who work in the present system if encouraged and not threatened by change, can be valuable sources of information and ideas. It is often said that a consultant gets paid for presenting orally, on paper, slides and film, with

EXHIBIT 1

ORG. UNIT						NAME				
DATE						TITLE				

TIME	TASK	QUAN.	INTER. LETTER	INTER. QUANT.		DESCRIPTION	TOTAL TIME	TOTAL UNITS	UNIT TIME	POSTED TO ACT. NO.	HOURS PER WEEK
:00					1						
:15											
:30					2						
:45											
:00					3						
:15											
:30					4						
:45											
:00					5						
:15											
:30					6						
:45											
:00					7						
:15											
:30					8						
:45											
:00					9						
:15											
:30					10						
:45											
:00					11						
:15											
:30					12						
:45											
:00					13						
:15											
:30					14						
:45											
:00					15						
:15											
:30											
:45											
:00					LETTER A	INTERRUPTIONS					
:15											
:30					B						
:45											
:00					C						
:15											
:45					D						
:30											
:00						TOTALS					

EXHIBIT II

ACTIVITY LIST
FOR WORK DISTRIBUTION CHART

DEPARTMENT:	ORG. UNIT:	SUPERVISOR:	DATE:

ACTIVITY NO.	ACTIVITY (FUNCTIONS)

EXHIBIT III

WORK DISTRIBUTION CHART

ORGANIZATION UNIT CHARTED

PRESENT ☐ PROPOSED ☐ DATE

CHARTED BY APPROVED BY

ACTIVITY NUMBER	ACTIVITY	ACTIVITY NUMBER	NAME POSITION TASKS	ACTIVITY NUMBER	NAME POSITION TASKS	ACTIVITY NUMBER	NAME POSITION TASKS	ACTIVITY NUMBER	NAME POSITION TASKS	ACTIVITY NUMBER	NAME POSITON TASKS	ACTIVITY NUMBER	NAME POSITION TASKS	ACTIVITY NUMBER
	TOTAL													

bells, whistles and many colors, the ideas of others. Consult those who have lived and live with a system. Their participation is important not only as a source of information and ideas but also because their sense of participation in actions that affect them will lead to greater acceptance of change. Rely as much as possible on observable facts rather than judgments. Seek fundamental causes and the cure for them rather than attacking the symptoms.

Once you have developed reasonable alternatives, consider the costs and benefits involved, short and long range. This should include not only the monetary aspects but also the effect on other processes and units. (You may improve one activity but hurt others in your areas or in other areas.) Consider installation, new equipment and start up costs and costs of dismantling or throwing away old equipment or forms. Consider the effect on morale, status of people, the need for layoffs, job changes, reclassification of jobs (and the costs that may be involved). You should consult with a wide range of people who will be affected.

Finally, after choosing the "best" approach you are ready to install the improvement. This will involve planning, preparation, discussion, briefings, training and, of course, the necessary approvals and commitments of resources. After installation, there should be monitoring of results to determine whether fine tuning or changes are necessary.

Brainstorming

Whether in a two-hour meeting at company headquarters or two days in a retreat location, top management may seek to encourage creative thinking through brainstorming. Either with or without an agenda, without regard to the status of the individual discussant or the status of the existing service, product, organization or way of doing things, a free flow of discussion is encouraged with nothing ruled out, no matter how zany. The group can be together all the time, divided into teams, or individuals may come up with their own "solutions." Through dialogue, debate, cooperation and conflict, some new ideas may come to the fore or long buried suggestions may see the light of day.

A Review and Innovation Retreat

Similar to brainstorming, the idea is to get away from usual surroundings, interruptions, dress and status symbols and to take a fresh look at what's happening in the company. Brainstorming may be used or there may be a formal agenda and position papers distributed in advance.

Alternative/Junior Executive Board

Choose junior or middle level individuals who have demonstrated creativity and a flair for non-traditional thinking and place them on an Alternative Executive Board. The selection should be considered a high honor. Encourage them to review plans, programs and to give their views on what should be done and how. Or, ask them as a group to come up with specific suggestions.

Task Force Approach

A number of your best and brightest staff drawn from various levels and units might be appointed to a task force to review, create, comment in regard to new approaches.

Operations Research Team

An aspect of the previous approach is the building of an operations research team approach to problem solving drawing upon the tools and processes and the wide range of talents tapped for an effective operations research approach.

Team Approaches

Several teams of capable individuals might be appointed to tackle the same problem. A competitive approach might be encouraged, without letting this get out of hand.

Use of Outside Consultants

Consultants can be hired to tackle a particular problem or several problems or for an over-all approach to coming up with innovative ideas or for encouraging innovation in the organization. It might be helpful to have staff members work directly with the consultants to provide information and entry for the consultants but also to learn from the consultants.

Suggestion System

This is the traditional approach to innovation and often gets bogged down in administrative processes and trivial ideas. However, stress can be placed for a period of time, or a special contest can be held, to focus on specific types of innovation.

Extra or Standard Compensation Based on Innovation

Either as one component in determining an individual's annual increase or as a major factor in determining bonuses or special merit awards, innovations introduced and/or implemented by the individual might be stressed.

Analyzing What Others Do

A company need not attempt to re-invent the wheel. A search through the literature or looking at other organizations will indicate various ways to encourage innovation. Beyond process, one can look at what competitors are doing in terms of new or improved products or services and determine whether to copy what is being done and in so doing go one or more steps beyond and thus offer a better product or service than the competition. The first company up and running with a new approach may not, in the long run, be the most successful. Others may take more time to plan, develop or implement, or may learn from the first company's weaknesses or errors.

Using "The Return From Bankruptcy" Approach

Assume that you have just filed for bankruptcy and were now attempting to start over. What would your goals be, what business would you be in, what products and services would you offer, how would you plan, organize, staff, control, etc.? In preparing this type of blueprint you are really stating what you would do if you had to or were able to do it all over again. The point is how many of those things are you willing to do now before you really are in bankruptcy.

Using "The Explain to a 17-year-old" Approach

Imagine that you are explaining all aspects of your organization— past, present and future—to a very bright, inquisitive high school senior who knows nothing about management. The point is that though the questions will be naive, uninformed and simplistic, one can imagine the questioner asking again and again, "why," "how," "why not." This can help you evaluate where you are and where you are going.

Using "The Deathbed Approach"

Assume you are dying and were instructing your next in command what he should do to grant your deathbed wishes or what you would have liked to tell your superior or the President of the company. After you have listed these things, why not see what you can do about them now.

Often, the ideas or dreams are there but the timing for introduction of innovative approaches just doesn't seem quite right. So we wait for the "right" time or opportunity and it never seems to come or comes too late to be of help to us since time, momentum or competition may have passed us by.

THE RIGHT TIME FOR INTRODUCING INNOVATIONS

There are various events that present the possibility of being the "right" time for introducing one or more innovations, whether of major or minor significance. These are when:

1. Opening or creating a new division, plant, office, store, service or product.
2. Merging with or acquiring another organization.
3. Facing the need to introduce or complete a new and/or complex task, activity, product, service much more quickly or at significantly lower cost than is the normal practice.

4. Expanding or contracting staff.
5. Facing new or increased competition.
6. Seeking to meet the problems of (a) increasing income or sales; (b) increasing expense; (c) decreasing income or sales or decreasing profits or return on investments.
7. Meeting new or stricter enforcement of regulations or laws.
8. Meeting changed societal, political, economic conditions and trends.
9. Facing a change of leadership at one or several levels due to impending retirement or sudden departures.
10. Confronted with declining productivity, quality and morale and increasing turnover and absenteeism.
11. Introducing a new system in one or more of the following areas: accounting, budgeting, planning, personnel, personnel evaluation or compensation, marketing.
12. Introducing new technology, production methods or procedures.
13. Providing more emphasis on research and development.
14. Receiving reports and studies in regard to improvements and innovations.

THE RESEARCH AND DEVELOPMENT UNIT

Frequently we look to the research and development unit as the major source of new product ideas (while we look to the planning unit, organizational development unit, and other units for ideas in other areas). The organization of the research and development unit is important. Where it is located in the organization structure, the receptivity, status and power of the person to whom it reports, and the qualities of the director of the department are critical to the effectiveness of the unit. The director must combine an ability to win the respect of the scientists, engineers and others in the department while also being a skillful administrator of the unit and representative to higher echelons and other units in the organization. Within the unit, one can organize by putting all individuals of a single discipline in one group and thus have groups of the various disciplines. Another approach is the multi-disciplinary team. Many research and development organizations adapt their structure to particular needs and projects and therefore both approaches can be found in the same unit. Of major concern in conducting research is the need for balance between freedom for the researchers to pursue their interests and hunches, while at the same time attempting to select projects that are suited to the short and long range concerns of the company, and thus lessen the risk of unproductive efforts. The Director and perhaps a research committee drawn from the heads of various departments and ultimately top management play a vital role in maintaining this very difficult balance.

At appropriate intervals a careful evaluation must be made of the results achieved by the research and development unit as well as of particular individuals in the unit. Research and development units must be managed and held accountable like all other units. However, there must be greater sensitivity to the nature, difficulties, fixed costs, experimentation, exploration and opportunity costs associated with research and development and the goals, interests, operating style and motivation of researchers. The management techniques used in managing and evaluating a research and development unit is indeed significantly different than a production or sales unit but it is not as completely different as some researchers and research unit directors believe.

IMPLEMENTING INNOVATION

One executive said, "Great ideas are a relatively rare commodity, but successful great ideas are truly rare." The point is that there are considerable roadblocks to translating the conceptual to the actual. Well planned and executed conceptual design and plans can come to naught if equally great emphasis is not placed on planning for and executing the idea.

Communication, involvement, and sensitivity are critical to successful implementation. Those involved, in both a primary and secondary sense, have to know the what, why and how in regard to the idea. They may be able to offer valuable suggestions and fine tuning in regard to implementation. (This also assumes that they have been involved, where appropriate, in the development of the idea itself.) Individuals affected should have an important role in the design of the implementation plan and the schedule. They can help identify possible ramifications and adverse consequences in implementing innovations. Care must be taken to understand and plan for the effects on: the formal and informal organization; the security and status of units and individuals, the natural resistance to substituting the new and untried for the familiar and safe; the need for consultation, consideration, briefings, training sessions, training manuals, at times running the new parallel with the old until the bugs shake out—all can help in reducing the disruption and disorientation that frequently result when changes are introduced.

The creative act itself is difficult to describe. For some, it is a flash of insight. For some, it is the culmination of painstaking trial and error or building on one's own achievements or the achievements of others. In other cases, it is the result of team efforts, a combination of insight, hard work and good fortune, or a combination of all the ways mentioned. An executive is accustomed to achieving goals and supervising and doing things well. But, creating something new out of one's own mind and with one's own hands is indeed similar to the feeling of accomplishment of work of the great artist upon completion of a work or the conqueror of a high mountain peak.*

Innovation is difficult, time consuming, costly; however, it ultimately determines the degree of success of the organization. Innovating is energizing, status quoism is enervating, debilitating and sentences the organization to a slow (sometimes not so slow) decline and death.

---

*The New York City Urban Fellowship Program provided that feeling for me. Nothing quite like it has existed before. It received Foundation funding and then New York City funding. In essence, I created the program based upon my knowledge of the White House Fellows Program, the New York City Urban Corps, and the Summer Internship Program I had created earlier in the Office of the Mayor. The program conducted a nationwide competition to select twenty individuals who would spend their senior year of college or one of the graduate work years, working full-time in New York City government for an academic year. They would serve in challenging positions as Assistant to Commissioners and other top level officials or on specific projects. In addition to a stipend from the City, the universities and colleges were expected to contribute a small sum, and the educational institutions were asked to provide academic credit for the experience, a full year's credit if possible. In addition to their work experience, there were weekly seminars with top governmental officers and other prominent individuals. Each Fellow wrote an evaluation report at the end of the year. Many stayed in government after completing their fellowship year or upon completion of graduate work. One became the youngest College President in America, one a Deputy City Administrator, etc.

SUGGESTED ANSWERS TO EXERCISES
ON PAGE 134

1. The secret is to extend the lines beyond the clusters of points.

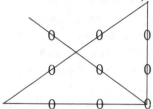

2. (a) Design the handle of a shovel to reduce the strain on the wrist. Have the handle point the other way.
    (b) Change a four leg step ladder into a three leg step ladder to provide greater stability and balance.
    (c) Change the bottom hinged oven door to one that opens laterally like a refrigerator to reduce back strain.
    (d) Change the trigger pull on many tools by replacing it through use of the thumb on a button or pull. The thumb is much stronger than the individual finger.
    (e) Have the controls on the electic skillet further away from the head and set the controls with a lever rather than a dial.
3. Some suggestions—Try to talk the guards into a big reward and have them lead you past the dogs. Try to frighten the guards so that they leave the cabin—because you have set a fire—the dogs will chase the guards and you slip out the back. Overpower the guards; use their guns to kill the dogs.
4. Follow the person and find out where he is heading so that you can deliver a message to his table or pose as a waiter. Find out his favorite candy, tobacco or gift item. Dress up in appropriate costume and say you are delivering a special gift from a friend. Pose as one who is delivering a singing telegram or flowers from a friend.
5. If you spell the numbers out, you will find that they are listed in alphabetical order.
6. There is no "correct" answer, but some of the following may have some validity:
    (a) There is great anxiety in May over cheating done on tax returns in April.
    (b) Since May is the last full month of school, more students commit suicide in May.

    (c) The sunny days and good weather of spring make those who are depressed feel more depressed, thus, leading to more suicides.

    (d) Many businesses have a fiscal year closing in June and, thus, in May, major fiscal problems will become apparent.

7. Here are some actions you might take:

    (a) Provide literature about the problem.

    (b) Propose various kinds of rewards if he stops drinking.

    (c) Have him seek help or counseling or go to Alcoholics Anonymous meetings.

    (d) Show him skid row or the alcoholics treatment facilities in a hospital.

    (e) Have a heart-to-heart talk with him.
       hospital.

    (e) Have a heart-to-heart talk with him.

    (f) Indicate the money that can be saved by not drinking.

    (g) Indicate various kinds of punishment if he doesn't stop drinking.

    (h) Have him list and discuss with you advantages and disadvantages of drinking.

    (i) Arrange for him to meet various and/or ex-alcoholics.

seven

Communicating

Much of what an executive does involves communicating to those in the organization and those outside (see Chapter on Representing). He is reaching his various audiences, whether large numbers of individuals or a single individual by memo, position paper, policy, plan, letter, article in company newsletter, a short comment on a letter or note, or even by his signature on a line. He is also communicating orally in speeches, informal remarks, meetings, conferences, discussions, one-on-one conversations. And, in fact, he is communicating by body language, expression on his face, physical appearance, signs, symbols, pictures, posture, gait, sprightliness (or lack thereof), style and neatness of dress. His tone, vibrancy of voice, clarity, richness of expression and even silence all have an impact on his audience and organization and indeed on his career.

The executive, in essence, seeks to convey, clearly, persuasively, sensitively, his views, comments and reactions, and to explain decisions he has made, what they are and why he chose a certain course of action.

In this chapter, we shall discuss the communication process, upward and downward communication and improving communication.

THE COMMUNICATION PROCESS

In a non-technical way the communication process can be simply described as:

Creation of Communication → Coding the communication →
Transmitting → Receiving → Decoding/understanding →
Acting upon/storing the information.

Creation —The communicator has a message he wants others to know and/or act upon. It may be factual information, an idea, an order, a referral, a reaction to previous communications, an opinion, or a suggestion.

Coding —The communicator puts his message (ideas, facts, etc.) in a form that can be utilized by others—words, graphs, numbers, sounds, physical model, pictures.

Transmission —The message is sent through some type of channel (assuming timing is right and those who are to receive the message are able to tune in to the transmitting channel)—it could be letter, memo, brochure, radio or TV program, disc, cassette, tape, newsletter.

Receiving —The audience receives the message, hears it, sees it, feels it.

Decoding/Understanding—The receiver is able to understand the message and translate its content into ideas of meaning to him.

Action Upon/Storing the Communication —The receiver, assuming he understands and accepts the message, takes some type of action based upon it or uses and stores it for general information or for referral or action at some later date.

The point of all this is that through communicating we hope to achieve some type of action or reaction, to influence behavior or thought processes. The actions can be those that are measurable or discernable directly or those that are internalized by the individual, attitudinal, psychological. The action may not take place immediately (e.g., the effect of a clergyman's sermon or a course in college) or even ever, but the goal is that the communication have some type of influence or impact in some way at some time.

ORAL AND WRITTEN COMMUNICATION

Although the words of a communication can be carried in different ways and forms, basically we communicate by words (leaving aside the truth of the statement that actions speak louder than words!). Some individuals and companies prefer to place great stress on oral communication. Oral communication has the obvious advantages of being more personal, and if necessary informal, provides faster feedback, reaction, participation, ability to judge very quickly whether message is being understood or has to be repeated and clarified. It also allows one to use and react to nuances, tone, expressions, mood, body language. It can be an immediate two-way street. Written communication has advantages in terms of the complexity of the subject matter and the backup material that must be used in understanding the message, the ease of duplication for others to review, its repeated use at various times, its long term and historical significance, its easy and permanent access to large numbers of people, its common nature as a document, as an official act.

All communications suffer from: some degree of distortion because of the inadequacy of language to convey ideas with 100 percent precision; some amount of unconscious or conscious filtering by transmitters and receivers of messages whereby "facts" are interpreted or manipulated to favor one or the other; semantic problems—words mean different things at different times to different people; overkill—too many words or ideas to be digested at one time, or saying in ten words what can be said in two; time and space distances between people; the unwillingness of some to listen to or accept either the message itself or the person presenting the message.

THE COMMUNICATIONS LADDER—
DOWN AND UP

Executives are most familiar with downward communications. We are accustomed to sending messages to our subordinates, in turn we get downward communications from our superiors. We have become more and more skilled in technical and visual improvements in downward communications, but we still often miss the human impact element in its overall effectiveness.

The effective downward communicator will seek to develop several skills and follow eight commandments. *First*, develop a commitment toward communication and an attitude of accuracy and openness in communication. *Second*, plan your style and format of communication—what will you generally communicate (of course, exceptions and emergencies will arise), how, in what format and style, with what frequency, to whom. *Third*, become well informed about issues and events in the company and about the matter to be communicated. Before transmitting information received from higher sources, make sure you understand it and, if possible, have some additional in-depth information so that, if questions arise, you can put the communication in context or provide further detail. *Fourth*, attempt to communicate about your communications approach so that others understand what you hope to accomplish, what to expect, what is in it for them and what is expected of them. *Fifth*, recognize that individuals are most interested in things that effect them directly or come close enough to have some potential impact, rather than general information or information about matters not connected with them. *Sixth*, get information and communications out as quickly as possible, stale news is not really news and weakens the credibility of the communication. *Seventh*, be concerned about what is appropriate to communicate. "Secrets" clearly should not be communicated and mistakes rarely happen in this area. Where mistakes sometimes occur is a perception by receivers of messages that their political, social, economic, religious or other non-business related views are the subject of the communications and that attempts are being made to influence their views. Another appropriateness aspect is over-communication. At times we feel inundated by the number of messages reaching us that seem to have little or nothing to do with our positions. Memos, referrals to publications, articles, copies of letters and memos, etc., that have nothing to do with our jobs other than taking time to transmit, sort, read and file, have a negative impact for individuals and the company. People can miss the important communication when buried under unnecessary paper. *Eighth*, be honest and accurate, fair and credible.

EMPLOYEE COMMUNICATION—THE HOUSE ORGAN

The formal downward communications device is the house organ (although attempts can be made to have it be something of an employee/management communications channel). Often top management sees the role of the company's chief communications person as the individual who produces various types of publications to recognize and motivate the employees and to include major items of interest. A more sophisticated view of employee communications would involve concern that the communications: explain in a reasonably enthisiastic way (without overselling) company changes, plans, programs and activities as new ones are being put into effect (or standard ones are being carried out if there is a need to describe ongoing activities); respond to criticisms, concerns or complaints by discussing the reassons for the program, but also giving due credence to problems and, if possible, reporting on attempts to resolve the problems. In addition, the communication should give a sense of a steady hand at the helm and the contributions of a wide range of people to the success of the organization and the meaningfulness of their work to the unit, the company and to themselves.

UPWARD COMMUNICATION

Upward communication has major, and hopefully, obvious importance to the success of the executive and the organization. On one hand it is the way in which management can learn whether what is created, coded and transmitted has been received, understood and acted upon. On the other hand, it is the way in which subordinates can convey their reactions, actions, concerns, views and attitudes about the wide range of matters that effect the effectiveness, efficiency, economy and future of any organization.

For top management, upward communication provides a test of the clarity, persuasiveness, believability and acceptability of downward communication and presents early warning signals of potential problems and failure. It provides the opportunity for subordinates to be involved in formulating, shaping or at least commenting upon proposed and implemented actions. It encourages subordinates to offer suggestions and ideas that may be of considerable importance.

For subordinates, a credible upward communications system helps satisfy a need to feel that to some extent one is master of his own fate, that he is being recognized, listened to, valued as an individual, that he has personal worth in a complex organization. It provides an outlet for expression, for creativity, for impact and for release of emotional or work pressures and tensions.

What supervisors need from an upward communication system is information, comments, reactions about:

1. Subordinates' progress, achievements, activities, future planned efforts.
2. Identification and description of present or potential problem areas affecting the work of the unit.
3. Identification and description of present or potential conflicts or controversies within the units under their supervision, between and among units under their supervision, and with other units in the organization.
4. Recommended changes or modifications of existing plans, programs, policies, practices.
5. Suggestions for improvements within the unit or company.
6. Subordinates' feelings and concerns about their work, their unit, their colleagues and supervisors, the company as a whole, their outlook about the future.
7. Unusual conditions or deviations from plans—unusual absenteeism, overtime, backlogs, turnover, etc.
8. Other aspects of their responsibilities for which the supervisors might be held accountable to those above them.

COMMUNICATIONS BARRIERS

Despite the commitment that progressive managers presumably have there are rather formidable obstacles to overcome in bringing about successful upward communications. The obstacles involve the organization itself, superiors and subordinates.

The organization may be very large, complex and widely separated geographically, with a large and complex hierarchy and bureaucracy. Trying to breach the barricade may take a good deal of time and effort, seem to violate protocol and run into the problem that a good number of supervisors do not like to have bright ideas come from below which would lessen their glory. Superiors might shelve such ideas, delay them or steal them. The mere movement of an idea through many layers and with intervening time tends to delay, dilute, compromise or destroy the original idea, although at times, it will be improved as a result of various reviews.

Another example of an organizational barrier is inter-departmental conflict which is causing problems for one or more of the units involved in the conflict. One unit's efforts may be held up by its dependency on another unit that because of managerial weaknesses fails to meet its responsibilities. The unit that fails to accomplish its goals or that is forced to hire more staff or work overtime because of the failures of the other, may still be reluctant to hurt the other manager by "squealing." Of course, if the "good" manager's performance begins to be seriously questioned because of added costs or delays, he will have no choice but to point the finger at the other unit. The issue here is to encourage a system that provides accurate information on a timely basis to top management before additional costs, complaints or delays come about.

Despite their positive pronouncements about upward communication, supervisors may constitute a significant hurdle. Like all human beings they tend to be defensive about what they do and how they act. Their attitude may convey a feeling of "don't bother me, I'm too busy," or "let me know just the really important things, the rest you should be able to handle yourself." They may have failed to do anything about previously communicated ideas, views, problems or have taken credit for others' ideas without sharing the glory. They may not have (or think they don't have) the time to be a good listener or to read lengthy memos. They may find it uncomfortable and perhaps beyond their knowledge and responsibility to become involved in personal problems of subordinates (on occasion we all face the unpleasant and difficult task of not promoting or firing someone; it becomes even more difficult if we know a good deal about a person's family life and problems).

(A Vice President I know had a style of soothing anyone's complaints by saying, "Write me a detailed memo and offer suggestions on how to solve the problem." That made the staff member feel good, except the vice president used to wait months to take any action. His hope was that in sitting down to write the memo, the complaintant would get tired and not bother, or that in waiting months to respond, the problem or concern would go away.)

For the subordinates, attempting to communicate upward may present some formidable problems. They don't have the same status and freedom to interrupt or make demands on their boss' time. Generally, organizations and bosses strongly discourage going over your superior's head or questioning his actions, attitude, style or judgment. The subordinate does not have the same staff support and assistance for upward communications as is available downward, nor is the reward system and obligations the same. Frequently, the subordinate's response must meet some type of time deadline and thus may not be prepared with sufficient analysis or care. Often subordinates do not (as is also true of superiors) recognize their biases and this will affect the receptivity to what they communicate. Finally, subordinates generally seek to tell only the good news (straight or slightly exaggerated) and withhold or tone down bad news, negative results or trends, mistakes or failures.

The challenges for improving upward communication are substantial, but they can be met. It will involve an honest and realistic commitment by management at all levels with the impetus from the top. If those at the level just below top management find that they are being encouraged, listened to and rewarded for communicating upward they are likely to do the same in regard to the level below them. This attitude would then have a snowballing effect throughout the organization. To be effective, the upward communications flow or system should be clear to all, should be handled on a timely basis (some companies require responses within a certain number of days) and the listeners or receivers of upward communication must be empathetic, sympathetic and unbiased. There is a danger to all this. You had better not embark on an all-out effort to encourage such communication unless you are strongly committed toward a reasonable degree of responsiveness and action.

The methods or ideas for improving upward communications have been around for a long time; it's the commitment and implementation that have been problems. Some approaches are:

1. There should be an attitude of reasonable access and an open mind and ear. (These are more important than an "opendoor." One prominent government official removed the door to his office, thereby, literally having an open door. There is no evidence as to the effect of this action.)
2. Suggestion systems that are objective, do not create an administrative nightmare and are real rather than just going through the motions.
3. Availability of counseling (both job and personal) and grievance systems.
4. Encourage employee letters.
5. An informative house organ.

6. Participation in social activities which provide an opportunity for informal conversation.
7. Communicating with employees' families.
8. Including staff specialists and those lower down in discussions.
9. Providing opportunities for subordinates to make presentations.
10. Utilizing employee attitude surveys and exit interview data. In addition, the usual techniques of monthly or other timed reports to indicate progress and problems and the management or operations audit can provide valuable information.

One matter that sometimes is of concern to some managements is what role the union should play in communications. Normally, the union has its own downward and upward communications system and its own communications problems. Some managements try to utilize the union, either overtly or covertly, in communicating with employees since the employees normally accept and believe the word of the union newsletter, steward or official at least equally, if not more so, than the word of the company. A further positive aspect is that if the union supports the communication, the chances of acceptance are greater; conversely, if left out of the information flow it may hurt the employer by making its own and different interpretation. There are inherent dangers in using the union as a communications channel. Management is not able to control what is said and how it is presented, but will have to bear the responsibility. The union may have its own objectives and needs and, therefore, not be willing to help or be seen as co-opted by management.

A wise management will certainly communicate information to the union in a timely fashion, but should not, in my view, normally rely on the union to do management's communicating to employees. Each has a role in communication. It is helpful if they can agree on the facts and interpretation so that employees do not receive cross messages and thus have to decide on who is more credible. A wise management, while keeping the union informed early in some cases, without delay in others, will want to make sure that on most matters the employees get the word first from management. Supervisors should get the word before the rank and file and preferably before the union or at least concurrently with the union. There will, of course, be a few occasions when it would be helpful if there were joint announcements by management and union and even rare occasions when it is helpful if the union is out front in providing information.

INFORMAL COMMUNICATIONS

Our discussion has centered on formal communications, but just as there is informal organization, there is informal communication. Word of mouth, unofficial, hot tip communication can help spread the word and buttress formal communications and, in turn, receive unofficial, informal oral responses. However, there is the very real danger of rumor, distorted or false information being spread very rapidly through the grapevine. One can dignify the grapevine by calling it the communications system of the informal organization, and in fact, that is what it is. Management would be wise to understand the grapevine, recognize that it will always exist, tune in to it, occasionally feed it accurate information through its leaders (getting caught feeding inaccurate information is very dangerous to the organization and to the individual's career). One of the tough decisions a manager faces in regard to communications is how to deal with rumors, distortions, personal gossip and outright falsehoods carried through the grapevine. It's tempting to fire all one's guns to destroy a false statement being carried, but then some employees will wonder why are they making such a fuss, maybe there's something to the rumor—"where there's smoke, there's fire." Others who hadn't heard the grapevine message may now begin thinking about it. On the other hand, to do nothing and assume the rumor will die in a few days may not be effective. It may grow as people begin to wonder why there are no statements being issued by the company. In many cases this issue results in "damned if you do, damned if you don't." Each instance must be taken on its own. Sometimes formal statements might be necessary (i.e. untrue rumors of a plant closing can cause problems within a plant, with the union, with community officials). Other times, action taken will include informal conversations with supervisors who spread the word, counter attack using the grapevine, and in some cases, patience and no response.

A further point—sometimes we lose sight of the fact that each individual wants to have the feeling that his boss has noticed what he has done. A kind word, and the tone of a conversation or note is very important. It doesn't take much time to indicate in a few words congratulations, praise, notice of unusual effort or the successful tackling of a complex task. All too often that is overlooked, particularly at the higher levels. Of course, one expects a well paid high executive to do well and to put forth extra effort, but while some top executives do well in praising lower officials, they sometimes forget that high officials also desire praise when they have earned it. Man needs the psychic income provided by notice and praise as much as monetary and status income. Executives, furthermore, are more conscious of other forms of communication. Are they invited to meet important customers, suppliers or legislators? Are they members of major committees? Do they have an opportunity to participate in Board of Directors discussions or make presentations to the Board? Are they invited to social affairs, or to lunch, dinner or coffee with the chief executive officer?

CLARITY

We end this chapter with a discussion of and plea for clarity in expression. The use of too many words, obfuscation and gobblegookism does grave damage to good communications. It also wastes time, effort and paper, causes eyestrain and headaches, necessitates more copying machines, increases costs of filing and record keeping and destroys one's love of the language. Each executive should strive to go on a word reduction program as assiduously as people go on weight reduction programs (hopefully with more success!). Increase your clarity time and score just as you seek to improve your jogging time or golf score. Take anything you write or tape some of your conversations, seek to reduce the words and time by 20-25-33 1/3 percent. Most people can, in fact, improve their writing and speaking by reducing words used by 25 percent. Some of you may only have to reduce verbiage by 15 or 20 percent; others may need to reduce by around 50 percent. It can be done and the rewards are great in terms of cost, time, clarity and the other factors cited.

The insurance and banking industries have long been known for their mastery of the ability to dazzle and daze the reader with their prose. In recent years, sometimes prodded by state legislation, they have begun to clean up and simplify their documents. Here are some examples:

Before: The company will indemnify the insured for all sums which the insured shall be legally obligated to pay as damages and expenses, all as more fully defined by the term "Ultimate Net Loss" . . .

After: We've designed this policy to give you and your family extra
          liability protection, above and beyond the coverage of your
          present auto, homeowners and other policies . . .
              Say you have a standard auto policy that covers you up to
          a $300,000 liability limit for bodily injury for each accident.
          With this policy you're covered even if a jury says you have
          to pay $1,300,000.

How to Tell a customer "You're in default":

Old Way: In the event of default in the payment of this or any other
          obligation or the performance or observance of any term
          or covenant contained herein or in any note or other con-
          tract or agreement evidencing or relating to any Obligation
          or any collateral on the borrower's part to be performed
          or observed; or the undersigned borrower shall die; or any
          of the undersigned become insolvent or make an assign-
          ment for the undersigned under any provision of the
          Bankruptcy Act; or any money, securities or property of
          the undersigned now or hereafter on deposit with or in
          the possession or under the control of the bank shall be
          attached or become subject to distraint proceedings or
          any order of process of any court; or the bank shall deem
          itself to be insecure, then and in any such event, the bank
          shall have the right (at its option), without demand or no-
          tice of any kind, to declare all or any part of the obliga-
          tions to be immediately due and payable, whereupon
          such obligations shall become and be immediately due
          and payable, and the bank shall have the right to exercise
          all the rights and remedies available to a secured party
          upon default under the Uniform Commercial Code (the
          "Code") in effect in New York at the time, and such other
          rights and remedies as may otherwise be provided by law.
          Each of the undersigned agrees (for purposes of the
          "Code") that written notice of any proposed sale of, or
          of the Bank's election to retain, collateral mailed to the
          undersigned borrower (who is hereby appointed agent of
          each of the undersigned for such purpose) by first class
          mail, postage prepaid, at the address of the undersigned
          borrower indicated below three business days prior to
          such sale or election shall be deemed reasonable notifica-

tion thereof. The remedies of the bank hereunder are cumulative and may be exercised concurrently or separately. If any provision of this paragraph shall conflict with any remedial provision contained in any security agreement or collateral receipt covering any collateral, the provisions of such security agreement or collateral receipt shall control.

In Plain English: I'll be in default:

1. If I don't pay an installment on time; or
2. If any other creditor tries by legal process to take any money of benefit of creditors; or a petition shall be filed by or against any mine in your possession.
   You can then demand immediate payment of the balance of this note, minus the part of the finance charge which hasn't been earned figured by the rule of 78. You will also have other legal rights, for instance, the right to reposses, sell and apply security to the payments under this note and any other debts I may then owe you.

In many cases a commitment to simple understandable English will involve beginning from ground zero rather than trying to rework an existing letter, document or brochure. A general I heard about in the Army had a reasonable technique for improving his clarity. He would have an enlisted man with less than an eighth grade education read all his non-classified speeches and memos. He would then ask the enlisted man to write a simple statement about what the general was trying to say. If the response captured what the general meant, he used the document, if not he had it changed, sometimes incorporating the enlisted man's comments. The general's rationale was that if the enlisted man understood, there was a reasonable chance (though no guarantee) that his officers would understand it.

The point is that you should be concerned about eliminating what is no longer necessary in contracts or other documents. In memos, plans, speeches, consciously attempt to simplify, get to the heart of the matter, reduce verbiage. It's amazing what one can do when forced to write an executive or a one page summary of a problem. Word processing equipment now available provides us with the technical ability to become more responsive in dealing with customers and general correspondence. It is also an aid in drafting various documents.

But just because we can produce the old material and approach faster or more easily, we should not give up on reducing the complexity of thoughts and number of words and, if necessary, starting from scratch.

In the Essay section we discuss, briefly, how to become a better speechmaker and presenter. Here, we shall just note some brief guidelines for improved business writing. Although it can be categorized in different ways, the basic guidelines are:

1. Concepts or thoughts
2. Appropriateness
3. Clarity
4. Coherence

Concepts would include thinking about what the report, letter or other type of written communication will be used for, by who and what factual material is necessary. Under this category is the analysis used and whether assumptions, data, observations and conclusions flow logically. Finally, the question of the persuasiveness of the communication is involved, whether the content, facts, concepts, clarity, coherence, tone, style, action orientation, management viewpoint, all make the document persuasive.

Appropriateness (this category will vary depending upon whether it is an upward or downward communication). Is the tone correct for the particular situation and for the differences in position between writer and the receiver(s) of the communication, is the communication tactful? Is the supporting material on target and suitable in detail? Are opinions supported by facts, and are opinions offered that are unwarranted or not even requested? Is there a sense of honesty or sincerity in the communication, so that the communication is not overly defensive, obsequious, paternalistic?

Coherent—Is there a logical progression of ideas and the application of the correct mechanics—sentence structure, paragraphs, grammar, punctuation? Is the format an accepted and helpful one in terms of normal company communications, the purpose of the particular communication, and in the appearance of the document?

Clarity—Is the communication readable? Is there sufficient concern for the purpose and focus of the report or letter, the background and knowledge the reader brings to the subject matter, paragraph and sentence construction, the language or words used, the amount of jargon, abstraction, wordiness?

By focusing on the basic concerns or principles of effective writing, you can improve your communication ability significantly. Increasingly, companies and individuals are stressing improved communications and writing ability. Some may feel they and their firm do not have a problem or have conquered the problem. If you think you don't have a written communications problem, look closely at the next twenty memos or reports you receive and the next twenty you send. If you or your subordinates pass that test, take a look at your company's fringe benefit booklets and their approach in communicating benefit information that the reader wants to know and use!

eight

Representing

Today's top executive spends a good deal of time representing his/her company to external audiences. All indications are that he will spend even more time doing this in the future. The representation function involves public relations, showing the company flag, explaining, advocating, defending and demonstrating concern and involvement. Increasingly it involves the chief executive. It also involves top officials in general and specific individuals such as the Vice President(s) for Governmental Relations, Community Relations, Public Affairs; Affirmative Action Officer and support staff, such as attorneys, accountants, auditors, occupational safety experts and a host of other specialists.

The demands and needs for actual personal representation by the Chief Executive Officer and his concern about the activities of others carrying on the representational function comes from a variety of audiences: the particular industry; general business community; unions; the regulatory, administrative, executive and legislative agents and agencies of government at all levels, local, county, state and nation. In addition, there are special interest groups, consumer advocate organizations, customers, stockholders, employees. Still other claimants on the executive's time and talent (and ofter personal and company money) are a variety of organizations—civic, cultural, athletic, youth, educational, charitable, recreational, religious, community development, special needs (minorities, women, elderly, handicapped, the poor), and even government organizations.

It is no wonder that many top executives complain that they don't have sufficient time to manage their business and that a fair amount of the time they find for business is while traveling to a meeting, conference, committee or speaking engagement for a non-directly, business related function or in representing the company. It seems that because of these non-strictly business demands where more and more groups want the top man or number two or three, but no lower, the most talented individuals in the company are spending less and less time on managing the company. Or else, they are working too many hours a week to be at maximum effectiveness over a long period of time. After finally getting to the top or very close to it, the executive is almost forced to give increasing amounts of time to pursuits that are difficult to equate to the bottom line. (Of course, representing strict business concerns to governmental agencies can have a real impact.) Some argue that they are now paid more for doing less executive work than when they were working their way up the organization.

In response to this line of reasoning one can fairly argue that in many circumstances only the most prestigeous members of the company can fully meet the needs of the organizations listed above. It is not only because of the individual's skills or knowledge that this is true, but also because of his prestige, power, ability to commit his organization, influence and attract others. Given the economic, management and competitive strains many organizations face, the top executive may have to carefully evaluate how his time and the time of his staff is spent. They may end up having to say "no" far more often to requests from a variety of sources and give their name to certain committees, drives and letterheads, but not their time or presence. Alternatively, of course, the Vice President for Community or Public Affairs might take on a more powerful and visible role and in an increasing number of instances be empowered to commit the organization to certain actions. But the demands on his time will grow too and ultimately there may be a need for more staff time and more staff.

Some yearn for the good old days when an executive made a speech to Rotary or the Chamber of Commerce once a year and that was it. But the present demands seem very much here to stay.

INVESTOR RELATIONS

A new area of concern in regard to representation is investor relations. Until 1975 publicly held corporations had very little to do with "marketing" themselves to the investing public. The corporation issued an annual report, met occasionally with groups of brokerage and research firms analysts and held an annual meeting. Essentially everything else was done by the brokers and the corporation aided them if necessary. But as of May 1, 1975, fixed commission for the sale of stock to the public was outlawed by SEC regulations. One result was that brokers couldn't afford as large a number of analysts as in the past. The number of analysts dropped appreciably as did the number of stock salespeople working in brokerage houses and the time these remaining people spent selling stock as opposed to other areas of investment offered by the brokerage firms.

In effect, investor relations has to be done by corporations themselves and significant efforts are underway. In fact, even though the very large companies are doing more, it is of even greater importance to smaller companies since the limited resources of brokerage firms will be devoted to the giant companies.

Some steps that have proven successful are:

1. Face-to-face contact with shareholders, not necessarily with the Chief Executive Officer or Chief Financial Officer.
2. Visits to company facilities.
3. Use of attractive, informative printed materials geared to the specific interests of investors, brokers and analysts, and use of the annual report as a communications channel with the investment community.
4. Changing the time of the annual meeting from the morning to the evening to encourage a larger audience.
5. The less than giant size companies may seek to be more agressive than just following the above points. This may involve going to the different cities where the investors, financial editors, analysts and brokers are and making presentations rather than waiting to be asked. Attempts can be made to interest the financial press in writing stories about the company as well as the local press in areas where company offices and plants are located. The company may choose to communicate: to shareholders with a "dividend-stuffer"; to analysts with fact books;

to those who attended meetings or expressed interest in the company with special materials; to analysts, brokers, registered reps and portfolio managers by advertising in various publications; to upper income communities by advertising and listing local brokerage firms that follow the company; to overseas investors by advertising.

There have been success stories of greatly increased attendance at annual meetings, much more active trading and rise in the price of stock, increase in the number of shares owned by individuals located in cities in which presentations were made or stories written. While the investment community continues its traditional role in regard to evaluating the investment value of companies, more and more companies of all sizes are spending increased effort at reaching out to individual investors and to the investment community to inform, to interest, and in effect, to sell.

SOCIAL RESPONSIBILITIES

The social responsibilities of business remain a continuing concern. What obligation does a particular firm or industry owe to its various publics, ranging from workers and stockholders, to the community, state, underprivileged, etc. Some years ago it was clear that many younger executives wanted to reform or improve society on company time. Under the pressure of tough financial and competitive conditions in the past few years this zeal has been generally abated somewhat, but the issue continues to be a strong one. Is the obligation of the firm to: make a profit, make a product or deliver a service that is safe; treat staff and customers fairly and civilly, obey the laws; be honest. Or is it something more? (Some might say the overriding task is it to be profitable.) Does a particular business firm owe particular concern and action in regard to: the environment; training and employing the previously unemployable; recruitment and promotion of women, minorities, the handicapped, former prisoners; giving at least a specified share of its business to minority contractors and suppliers; going against the mores of a particular country and the actions of foreign (and perhaps domestic) competitors by not offering "commissions," "finders fees" or other fees that may be bribes; refusing to do business or withdrawing its business from companies or nations that allegedly violate human rights, take certain political or economic positions, take strong, perhaps illegal actions, against union organizing attempts or are accused of being unfair to certain groups in the population? Should the executive be concerned about the utility and value of the product or service, the advertising messages he uses and the potential impact on children and others, the TV programs he sponsors and their impact? These and other questions involve issues of social responsibility, ethics, integrity. But "doing the right thing" may, at least in the short run, reduce one's income, productivity and profit, and increase expense and perhaps lead to layoffs, plant closings, etc. The needs of individuals working for the company, those who desire employment, those who live in the community and larger society and the broad range of social responsibility issues must be balanced against the need to be economically viable, to meet competitive challenges, to create profits for present and future uses. It is not necessarily an either/or situation, but there are costs, risks and benefits on both sides of the dichotomy. The tough decision for many executives may end up being how much in short term monetary rewards (and possibly long term rewards because one may end up at a competitive disadvantage, or "good guys" don't necessarily eventually triumph or get rewarded) am I willing to sacrifice in order to meet various goals of individuals, groups, society as a whole? It's easy to agree that one's employees should receive as good a wage, health benefits, pension, vacation and other fringes as possible and perhaps even that the firm should forego some additional profits in order to provide larger compensation packages for all employees and more pleasant and safer physical surroundings. In one way or another these can be justified or attempt to be justified in terms of productivity, morale, lower absenteeism and turnover, fewer accidents, the bottom line. But in an economic sense, it gets to be more difficult to justify the costs for hiring and training and "carrying" for awhile those who don't have the skills you need and would ordinarily not hire. (Of course, government may require you do do so and you, therefore, have no choice.) One can say, the government requires this; this is the cost of good citizenship; this is a down payment to keep order and tranquility in society, or whatever. It may appear easy to give company time and a sizable donation to the Community Chest or other charitable drives and to educational institutions located near company headquarters and plants. But, what should a company do if the economics department or political science department or student government and press in the nearby college is violently anti-business in general and the company in particular because of various company actions? As a university official, I can talk about academic freedom, but a business executive may want to give his dollars elsewhere.

We have just barely touched upon issues that will have enduring importance to business management and society. There are no easy answers. Each firm will have to develop its own philosophy, goals and policies in regard to the very broad spectrum of issues that can be categorized as social responsibility issues. In some cases it appears that all one has to do is follow the law because increasingly there are state and federal laws that apply to and regulate the areas mentioned. But the issue is whether both the letter and spirit of the law will be followed. What indeed is a "good faith effort"? How hard will we really try to hire, train, promote, reward those who were previously left out of the company and the executive suite? And, if laws don't apply, what shall we decide to do on our own, with how much zeal, with how much time and money? In my view, it is not enough to say the government through its taxing abilities and regulatory abilities will provide for and insure the various needs of individuals, groups, communities. Each business and industry will have to determine how far it wants to go, in what areas, with what amount of resources, beyond what is required by law. Profit yes, effectiveness and efficiency yes, concern for running the best business possible yes, but also a yes for those things that mark a person as not just a manager and executive but also a caring, concerned human being.

IMPROVING THE REPRESENTATION ACTIVITY

Many businesses are concerned about proposed legislation, taxes and regulation, interpretations of existing legislation, taxes and regulations, governmental decisions about product standards, safety requirements, increased costs of utilities, the post office, airlines, trucking and shipping regulations, environmental and occupational health issues, packaging, anti-trust, pensions, labor legislation, regulations governing banking, mortgages, interest payments, competition, information to customers, accountability for the use of governmental funds, patents and copyrights, depreciation, safe materials, food and drugs, standards and licensing for construction and various business practices, campaign practices, bribery, award of government contracts, location of governmental installations, public works and other construction activities, and so on. On top of this, there are always individuals and groups who in the old days would say, "I got a lemon." Today they say, "Sue." (For those who need a bit of levity after reading about the various pressures of government and others, remember that employment for congressional staff, accountants, lawyers, governmental relations people and technical specialists have risen very significantly because of all this activity, thus keeping the unemployment rates for professionals down considerably and salaries increasing.)

We discuss in the Essay Section the impact of government regulations. In this section we turn to how to improve executive performance as representatives of the enterprise and sometimes as representatives of the industry.

Basically, there are three ways to get better at representing. *First,* get the most competent staff you can. This can be a permanent staff on the company payroll or outside consultants or experts on an annual retainer or project basis. The complex business organization needs a wide array of specialists who in turn rely on professional organizations and information reporting services to keep abreast of changing regulations, interpretations, decisions, what others are doing, etc. You need to have access to specialists in the various areas outlined above and to create avenues of communication so that the knowledge and judgment of the expert is brought to bear on decisions reached and methods of implementation. Among the specialists needed is a person or group of persons skilled in dealing with legislative bodies and regulatory agencies.

Second, is development by those who represent the company (aside from the Vice President for Governmental Relations) of informed knowledge and judgment in regard to a variety of issues and processes. It may seem to a President of a company that he is being asked to take a Political Science 101 course, but to be successful he had better develop knowledge of the political process. His experts can provide this to him, but he has to be interested and be a good student. The political process is more than what a civics text describes in terms of how a bill is passed. He must develop a concern for: what motivates particular legislators, administrators and agencies; where is the momentum and power for certain changes; what arguments score well or badly; what is the impact on others in regard to plant locations; what are the public relations and political implications of actions and the administrative cost, job creation or layoff implications, tax revenue and environmental implications; where and when and what kind of pressure can be applied to whom; how should one deal with friends and enemies; what was the intent of the legislation or regulation, what facts indicate that there is misinterpretation or mis-application in practice or that the rule, law or application just doesn't make sense; what trade-offs or modifications are possible; how can face be saved? A city councilman, a state legislator, a U. S. senator or congressman, a high ranking and sometimes a low ranking bureaucrat are all quite important to the company and the Chief Executive Officer must be accessible to them and reasonably responsive to their requests. Some legislators are individuals the top executive would never hire or want to associate with, but he had better not show that when he represents the company. Aside from understanding the government process whether local, county, state or national, there are other systems, processes and issues with which one must become familiar and adept. These involve civic, community and consumer organizations and groups. And, not to be forgotten, are the actions one should take and activities one should engage in regarding the employees of the organization at all levels.

Third, learn and practice public relations and presentation skills (see the Essay Section). Top executives may regard themselves as production, marketing or financial wizzards, but what may be even more important in their present positions at the present time is their public relations skills. In addition to particular managerial and technical skills, their personality and ability to articulate, influence and impress, to be perceived as likeable, credible, concerned, a "good guy" will become critical to their personal and company success. They will be called upon to form coalitions (sometimes with unlikely partners), to gain support, to anticipate negative reactions.

A further ability to be learned is how to deal with the media. Most executives have had very little contact with newspaper, magazine, radio and TV reporters. As the firm becomes more newsworthy, as a result of action it takes (recalls, expansion, contraction, price increases, layoffs, plant closings, mergers) or actions taken against it (various types of lawsuits, hearings, regulatory actions, strikes) the top executives will be in much greater contact with reporters and sometimes editors. Depending upon the situation, it won't be the thoughtful and knowledgeable reporter of a business oriented publication or business section of a newspaper, but it may be the investigative reporter or electronic media journalist looking for a twenty second headline for the 6:00 news. Business executives will have to become more accustomed to the goldfish bowl of publicity that those in public life have long complained about. Explaining complicated business transactions and terms to reporters who, except in rare instances, are not familiar with economics or business practices and problems is a troublesome matter. Those interviewed often complain about the accuracy of what appears in the media. It becomes even more of a problem when very little in a reporter's training and experience have prepared him for dealing with business issued. However, one can expect reporters to spend more time exploring business issues because it is seen as having considerable potential for newsworthy items of interest to readers and also a reasonably ripe field for investigative reporting. How much and what to say, to whom, when, whom to trust, when to intentionally leak things, how to react to leaks or false stories, when to say "no comment," the use and misuse of the media, how to get the media on your side, how to get media attention, understanding media concerns and needs—all of these questions and others in regard to the media will become of more importance to many executives in the future years.

The business executive may at times disparage the skills a politician acquires in being elected and remaining in office. In today's world the successful executive must acquire some of the skills of a politician as well as the skills of a salesman, orator, actor and expert in various areas, armed with facts and figures. At the same time he must be credible, honest, true to himself, a broad person interested in people, the community and society, successful at running a profitable business and still be humble and modest!

nine# nine

Controlling

Controlling is a necessary management activity to insure that what is actually going on in an organization conforms to plans and policies and if not, that timely action can be taken before the situation gets entirely out of hand. Control is related directly to several of the other management functions such as planning and budgeting. The budget is a control tool, as well as a planning tool, but we shall discuss budgeting in a separate section. In a perfect world everything would go as planned and delineated in policies and procedures. But, often, unanticipated external events, as well as internal events, may make it very difficult, if not impossible, to carry out well-designed plans, and even our contingency plans. Despite the chain of command and clarity of communications, individual managers and subordinates may not implement plans in the manner prescribed.

In seeking to insure that results conform to established objectives, controlling involves three basic components:

1. Establishing standards of performance in sufficient detail so that actual results can be measured against them.
2. Measuring performance and comparing actual results to established standards.
3. Taking corrective action in regard to deviations from standards and planned objectives.

ESTABLISHING STANDARDS

It is helpful to first focus on what we hope to achieve. Although we usually focus on profits or share of the market, a more general way of looking at what constitutes good performance is in terms of productivity or output, expenses, utilization of resources. Good performance is itself difficult to define. Discussions among the leaders of a company as to what is a challenging but fair baseline for results is often equivalent to golfers arguing about what should be par for a particular hole. Clearly, since future promotions, salaries and bonuses depend upon results as compared to a standard, the individual manager is vitally interested in the definition of par performance. The company does not want to make par extremely difficult or extremely easy. Thus, in setting a standard, there should be a good deal of thought, analysis and discussion, with a concern about flexibility, individual performance and circumstances. In establishing standards we also seek to establish strategic checkpoints so that we can assess performance reasonably early while work is ongoing rather than wait for the work to be completed, or face the frequently impractical task of evaluating all the work by everyone.

MEASURING PERFORMANCE

In evaluating results, we seek to look at performance both in terms of quantitative measures as well as those aspects that are difficult, if not impossible, to quantify. Some things cannot be measured directly or, if measured directly, would involve considerable costs. Predictions, estimates, projections and sampling methods can be usefully employed as a way of highlighting problems ripe for corrective action. Some areas, such as technical staff areas, present very tough problems with regard to setting useful standards. Control, here, normally, must focus on work techniques rather than the usual results orientation, although one should still attempt to develop meaningful results standards.

The usual method of linking evaluation to corrective action is through various types of control reports (discussed later in this section). Control information should go to the individual whose work is being evaluated so that he can take timely, corrective action in the event of deviations from standard. In addition, the report provides valuable feedback to him even if there are no significant deviations. The individual's superior and those further up the executive ladder receive summaries of control reports as their way of monitoring and providing fine tuning, changes in direction or assistance. In devising a system of control reports, there is always a balance or trade-off between rapidity of information flow and the degree of detail and accuracy required. It is difficult to achieve a very high degree of timeliness or speed with a very high degree of detail and accuracy. Depending on the situation and area, one must be willing to accept minor variations in later data in order to achieve very quick information and response.

Although organizations have developed sophisticated, computerized control systems and reports, an effective manager concerned with controls cannot hide behind a computer printout. He needs to do a reasonable amount of on-site personal observation and personal contact to supplement the formal measurement systems and add a personal dimension to the evaluation process.

TAKING CORRECTIVE ACTION

Based on the reports and observations, corrective action may be necessary. Minor corrections or fine tuning may be necessary to improve results or some more major efforts (temporary redesign, overtime, more staff or equipment, another shift) to meet a particular emergency, rush order or project, unexpected bottleneck. At times, the poor performance results may be caused by standards that reflect a lack of realism or that were improperly or hastily determined or designed. Corrective action would then necessitate going back to the drawing board to re-design standards. Corrective action always involves isolating and evaluating the causes for results deviating from the established standards. Care must be taken not to over correct. There may be a temporary problem, rather than something basic requiring aggressive action. On the other hand, one cannot wait too long in taking corrective action. Judgment is necessary as to what and how to correct as well as what and how to control.

In correcting deviations, two routes can be taken. The usual one is to pinpoint a particular manager's responsibility for results falling behind plans in order to get him to take corrective action. This assumes that there is a reasonable degree of certainty in what was planned, that managers have an adequate degree of good judgment, solid knowledge and experience, that performance can be adequately measured in a timely fashion, that a feeling of personal involvement and responsibility for performance is present and that the individual involved is sufficiently motivated and able to make corrections in a timely way.

The other route is more difficult in the short run, but has greater potential for success in the long run for the units and for the organization as a whole. The idea is to select and train managers who have the necessary skills and motivation to manage well so that those undesirable results caused by poor management do not occur in the first place. Sometimes poor results have nothing to do with the particular manager, but may come about because of external or internal problems or forces over which he has no control or responsibility.

We shall identify various areas of controls and different ways of controlling. First, however, it would be helpful to establish some guidelines for effective control systems:

GUIDELINES FOR EFFECTIVE CONTROLS

Effective Controls:

1. Require effective leadership.
2. Require a reporting system that is objective, timely, accurate and reaches the right people at the right time so that corrective action can be taken.
3. Should serve the organization structure, style and needs of the company and of individuals.
4. Should be linked to the various levels of plans and should be modified as plans are modified.
5. Should stress exceptions and critical points at which to appraise performance.
6. Should be flexible and responsive to changing times and needs.
7. Should be cost effective and result in a minimum of adverse consequences.
8. Should be as simple, logical and understandable as possible.

9. Should result in timely, clear and decisive action when necessary.

AREAS OF CONTROL

Controls can be established in practically every area of an organization's activities. We shall highlight some of the most important areas for control measures and indicate some techniques that can be utilized. In effect, the controls help management determine what is happening, why, how plans are being met, what should be done about deviations.

Financial Controls

This area of control is the one with which most firms are familiar. There is a long history of various accounting, auditing and other financial control techniques and accepted practices. Budgets are the usual financial tools and they will be discussed in chapter 00. Other financial controls include:

1. Standard Cost Controls. Standard costs are the cost of materials and labor (direct costs) that go into each unit of the product or service plus a standard overhead or indirect cost. Actual and standard costs will almost always vary. The area for concern is what is causing the variance and can the causes be ameliorated (in some cases, in a practical sense, they cannot).
2. Profit and Loss Control. Each major unit calculates periodically a profit and loss statement (including overhead allocations) and compares it with previous periods.
3. Ratio Analysis. This analysis provides a quick fix on operations and a method of spotting problems. After preparing a ratio analysis at a particular time, normally regularly scheduled, the ratio should be compared with reasonable present and future objectives, ratios for previous periods, ratios for comparable companies, past and present.
    (a) Return on investment (ROI)—Relationship of profits, after taxes, to investment; the rate of return that a company or unit earns on the capital resources available or allocated to it. This is probably the most important ratio.

(b) Net sales to inventory—Normally one would expect that the greater the turnover of inventory the greater the profit on investment.

(c) Net sales to working capital—The optimum use of working capital is critical in determining the return on investment. The preferred ratio for each firm depends upon the nature of the product, such as whether the unit costs are high or low and the perishability of the product. For example, the annual sales for a perishable agricultural product, tomatoes, will be quite a bit higher in regard to working capital as compared with another product such as mattresses. For perishable products, there must be a rapid turnover in inventory leading to a continuous use of the same working capital.

(d) Net sales to accounts receivable—This ratio depends on the dollar amount of sales, the amount or percentage of credit sales to cash sales, the credit and discount policies of the organization and the collection policies and aggressiveness of the company. If one assumes a basically constant rate of sales, and that all sales are on a credit base, then the net sales in a given fiscal period should relate to accounts receivable in approximately the same way that the fiscal period length relates to the credit period length. For example, if the credit period is thirty days, the ratio of net sales to accounts receivable should be at least twelve to one.

(e) Current ratio—The ratio of current assets (cash, receivable, working capital) to current liabilities.

(f) Quick ratio—The ratio of assets that are immediately available, or quick assets, to accounts payable. In general, the goal is that the ratio is at least one to one so that the company is able to meet all its probable needs for payment.

(g) Percentage of accounts payable on which discounts are taken—The goal is for prompt payment of bills so as to take maximum advantage of discounts available for payment within the specified time, e.g., thirty days. The company controller should be very careful to install the necessary systems to meet the deadline, without paying early. Also, depending upon cash flow needs and rates of return available, it may pay *not* to take the discount and to have more cash available for short term investment or to be able to meet priority needs without having to pay higher interest for loans.

(h) Relationship between administrative expense and sales—A predetermined ratio might be set and carefully monitored.

(i) Long term debt to total capital—This must be carefully balanced in order to provide enough of a hedge for safety.

(j) Other useful ratios are: sales to net worth, sales to assets; sales to total sales in the industry (trend is important); input (e.g., hours worked) to output (sales made). For investors, brokerage firms and for a company management desiring to compare itself with other companies in the same industry, compilations made by various organizations in regard to the following may be helpful: profits in relation to sales, rate of sales growth, rate of growth in earnings per share, return on capital, net income per share as related to investor's equity per share.

4. Break-even Analysis. Helps determine what profits will be at a given sales level or alternatively the sales needed to meet fixed and overhead costs and then produce various levels of profit. This is a valuable tool for both planning and control. It is important to note that the break-even point may fluctuate. For example, a rise in fixed costs leads to the necessity of a rise in sales to reach the same level of profit. Because of possible rises in costs per unit due to increases in labor or material costs, a regular monitoring of actual break-even points versus projected is necessary during the course of a year in order to make informed judgments as to courses of action.

5. Analysis of Administrative Expense. It appears that whatever we try, it is very difficult to keep administrative expense from rising and the ratio of administrative staff to production personnel generally seems to be rising even though there may be fluctuations due to economic conditions. Parkinson appears to be right; *Parkinson's Law* indicates that staff begets staff and that work is accomplished according to the time available. The shrinking British Navy and British Empire as noted by Parkinson, needed more people in administration than when they were much larger. We can attribute the growth of staff: to good people identifying new, present or potential needs or better ways of providing service or we can perhaps cynically suggest that we often engage in empire building in order to justify our existence, status and salary.

In fairness, one must note that due to growing complexity and size in various organizations and industries, there is a greater increase in the need for specialized and technical skills than in the increased need for those directly involved in the production or delivery of the product or service. Further, various reporting requirements to governmental agencies and keeping abreast of new regulations and applications of law and regulations require far more specialists and support staff, space, equipment and materials than in the past. Labor relations also require considerable staff and resources not only in terms of negotiations, grievances, day-to-day labor relations, but also in terms of the work involved in managing fringe benefits. Another factor is that both company personnel and customers expect more administrative services than in the past and in order to be competitive in terms of customers or attracting or keeping staff, additional services, reports, information are required necessitating more staff, space, equipment, materials, etc. For example, in many universities even though enrollment (sales) is decreasing, staff and administrative expense is constant or even increasing. This is not necessarily poor management (though it could be), but may be due to the fact that there are many fixed costs. To be competitive one needs increased admissions staff and expenditures (marketing). It is very difficult because of tenure to adjust staffing to student enrollment; students expect expanded services despite declining enrollment, etc.

The goal always is that the increase in staff will ultimately lead to increased sales or decreased expenses per unit of output. The results vary from company to company. In the face of needs of government, unions, customers and staff, a company must often be satisfied with the thought that increased administrative expense minimized potential losses, law suits, damages and problems rather than resulted in a net gain in profit. Of course, one can suggest a decreased loss was in effect a contribution to net profit.

Quality Control

The two general methods, in industry, for controlling the quality of a finished product involve inspection of each part of each product and statistical quality control by inspecting a sample of the products in each batch. In general, statistical quality control is about as good as individual inspection and is certainly more cost effective. Continuous sampling may be used so that corrections can be made before many low quality units are made. Various types of quality control charts may be used to indicate tolerance levels with indications of when changes have to be made. Although general statistical measures can be applied to many industries, it should be noted that a number of industries require special tolerances and quality control standards, e.g., food industry.

Time Control

Wasted time or effort results in higher costs, delays in production, lower profits and probably lower customer satisfaction and sales as a result of delays in meeting delivery dates.

The focus in regard to control of time is not so much forcing workers to produce more or providing incentives for extra performance, but it requires the need to focus on the causes of delays or bottlenecks. The analysis of work methods described previously, work sampling, layout analysis and other techniques can help improve our understanding of the problems and point to solutions.

Other control methods range from the old Gantt charts that are still useful to more sophisticated techniques. PERT (Program Evaluation Review Technique), for example, integrates planning and control. But unlike another integrator—budgets—it focuses on time rather than expense control. Originated in connection with the production of the Polaris Missile, it is particularly useful for large, complex projects. The PERT Network is based on a careful description of the activities and events involved in the project, the sequence involved, various time estimates for each activity. The basic strength of the technique is its focus on interrelationships, sequences, and detailed delineation of the steps required. PERT allows for better control of complex programs through planning, replanning and progress evaluation, it serves as a scheduling tool. Through its sophisticated and timely reporting, it allows management to identify potential problem areas early enough for corrective action to be taken, and it identifies the probabilities that certain deadlines will be met.

The PERT Network is composed of events and activities (see Figure 1). Activities are defined in a time oriented network, activities and events are sequenced in the network and each activity has three time estimates, optimal, most likely and pessimistic.

As a result of the technique, an off-shoot was developed called Critical Path Method (CPM) which identifies the sequence of activities that require the maximum time and that a change in the timing of any activity on this path will result in a change of completion of the entire project. This allows us to focus attention and control on the critical path and take corrective action quickly (overtime, second shift, more staff or equipment). (One can imagine two friends, both engineers, who want to go on vacation together. Each asks the same supervisor for time off. The answer to one is "no," the answer to the other "yes." The reason is one is working on something on the critical path and the other is not.) PERT-Cost is another varient of PERT which adds estimated costs for each activity in the network.

Another useful tool is the line-of-balance technique which involves three components. The first is the objective chart which indicates units to be delivered at specific dates with actual deliveries depicted on the chart. The second indicates the steps necessary to complete the work in terms of number of working days. The third is the progress chart which depicts through heights of bars that represent specific parts, the number of parts that should be available or on order based on the supplier's lead time. The line of balance is then drawn to show the actual number of each part on hand or on order enough in advance to ensure delivery at the scheduled time. If things work right, the line of balance should run across the tops of the bars. One can regard LOB as a sophisticated version of Henry Gantt's contribution over 60 years ago in depicting a production schedule.

In addition to techniques, very important aspects of time control are to see to it that the necessary machinery is in good operating condition, that the work flow and work place layout is correct, that the raw materials and preceeding steps flow smoothly.

Personnel Control

This would involve techniques and reports in regard to effective recruitment,selection, training and utilization of personnel, turnover and absenteeism, promotability and development of individuals, performance evaluation, compensation review.

Logistical Control

Based upon contributions made by operations research techniques, techniques utilized would include various OR techniques as well as distribution matrixes, work scheduling, simulations, inventory models, systems flows and integrated operations control and logistics systems.

Facility Control

This area involves a concern for effective equipment and physical facilities utilization, productivity, costs, safety.

Policies and Procedures Control

This would involve review and controls (if necessary and cost effective) in regard to policy planning and implementation, improved procedures, standard operating manuals, work simplification techniques, records, reports, forms and correspondence management.

In addition, management controls are effective in areas of organization planning, product development, and information technology design and utilization.

DESIGNING AND IMPLEMENTING CONTROLS

An internal or external audit team can help design and implement the control systems necessary, focusing not only on the usual financial controls, but also on management controls. By management controls, we mean areas of control that management needs to monitor in order to get the job done, without overcontrolling and with a concern for cost/benefits. In designing controls one must be fully aware of the relationship between decentralization and control. One should not hamper decentralization by overcontrolling. Decentralization need not lessen control, it puts the focus of managerial attention on appraisal of results, rather than on control over operations.

In designing controls we must be fully aware of the cost benefits involved. You don't want to spend $100,000 to design, implement and operate a control system that monitors actions that can result in trivial dollar costs. Over-control or terribly burdensome control systems is a very real problem. Exception reporting or control by exception has been developed as a way of reducing cost and attention paid to control reports. In essence, if everything is on target or extremely close to target, no report or analysis is necessary. Management and the control system only focus on significant exceptions, either one time or a trend, from that which has been planned.

THE ROLE OF AUDIT

Some feel that the two biggest lies about auditors is captured in the following dialogue: Manager of a Department to the Head of the Audit Team,"We're glad to see you." The Head of the Audit Team replies, "We're here to help you." Despite the normal concern about auditors and their "detective" image, they can be very helpful. Chief Executive Officer and/or the Board of Directors, or to the Chief Fiscal Officer or Chief Operating Officer (organizational reporting relationship can be very important in terms of how auditors are perceived, how they see themselves, what their role is), reports of auditors are important aspects of control.

To maximize the effectiveness of the audit function there must be clear understanding of: what the auditors are charged with doing; how they are to do it; the need for frank discussions and full exchange of information between auditors and those being audited (unless the auditors suspect fraud); the need for letting the head of the unit know the findings and recommendations prior to their being put on paper so that he can correct any factual errors and provide information that may modify the auditors' report; the need for confidentiality where appropriate. For effective management one needs a management letter from the internal or external auditors that accurately states problems and suggests solutions or a range of solutions that are realistic. Mangement has the responsibility to see that a timetable is established for analysis of the auditor's recommendations, for reaching a decision as to how and on what schedule to correct deficiencies, for implementation and for monitoring the results.

In addition to the usual function of financial audits with importance placed on internal controls, increasingly it is of value for the firm to establish an operations audit capability. This could be a separate unit from the financial audit function. It would provide the means for evaluating whether and how various policies and procedures are being carried out, the control mechanisms at work, and in a sense, evaluate the effectiveness and efficiency of various operations. This is indeed a powerful role and one has to be concerned as to whether those performing operations audits are, in fact, auditors or consultants. It may be necessary to set up a unit that performs internal management consulting and services that is indeed separate from the evaluation, "audit" function since there may be a confusion in roles. How can you be very frank with someone who may include all the warts exposed in a report? On the other hand, to get full value out of consultants or auditors you need to provide them with all the facts as well as the nuances. Therefore, in structuring an internal audit function and in the use of external auditors, management must clearly decide what it wants from the auditors, how best to structure the unit and its relationship to others, what types of staff does it need for the unit. (For an operations audit staff, you need persons with technical knowledge, thoroughness, creativity and an ability to deal with others and be understanding of the constriants and concerns faced by operating managers. These traits and abilities are particularly necessary in operations auditors and internal consultants, but are also necessary for the traditional financial auditors.)

THE HUMAN ASPECT OF CONTROLS

We have discussed principles, areas and techniques of control, but end our discussion with a concern for the effect of controls on people and vice versa. The design and implementation of controls must be sensitive to how people react to them. Individuals may react negatively to control systems because of:

1. Their lack of knowledge about or disagreement over the stated performance objectives to be attained or the goals of the control system.
2. A belief that the standards and measurements established are in some way unfair or inappropriate in terms of quantity or quality and do not recognize the reality of the situation.
3. A view that the controls are being exercised by inappropriate people or an inappropriate level within the organization. This raises the issue of the role of staff units in setting and evaluating standards for performance by operating units (the role of staff should be approached carefully and particular attention should be paid to testing out staff ideas with operating personnel very early in the formation process).
4. A conflict between the pressures asserted by peer groups and those asserted by the company and its control systems.

Each of these problems can be met through recognition of their possible and real existence, sensitivity to the problems and planned action to meet the issues. Encouraging participation, explaining the needs and system; full discussion, responsiveness to concerns, suggestions and problems raised, flexibility in design and implementation attuned to particular needs and conditions; making adjustments as necessary; working with individual group members as well as the group; carefully planning the role of staff and insuring that operating personnel *not* staff are involved in corrective action—all of these will be helpful in reaching the goals of the control systems and attaining the understanding, cooperation and support of all involved.

Control techniques are vital to success but they cannot be heavy handed, overly burdensome or insensitive to the human element and to cost benefits. The power of sophisticated information technology and the latest advances in control techniques must not overshadow a need for flexibility, creativity, the motivation and satisfaction of individuals and the need for cooperation and commitment in achieving an organization's objectives.

ten

Directing

After all is said and done, the final test for all executives is how well did they carry out their objectives. Clearly, all the elements of management discussed previously are vital factors in determining success. At different times in an organization's history and an executive's career, major emphasis will be placed on one or more of the various managerial activities—planning, organization, controlling, etc. Increasingly, however, directing is assuming a greater role in evaluating an executive. By direction we mean the ability to work with subordinates in such a manner that they strive consistently to do their best to accomplish the unit's objectives. This implies that they know what's expected of them and that the person in charge aids them in developing and improving their skills and accomplishing their tasks. Thus, leadership, motivation, a concern for productivity, a concern for people, as well as results, are all involved in successful direction. But just working well with people or being a charismatic figure is not enough. To be successful at directing, one must also be successful at the other management functions. Your subordinates may love you as a "boss" because of your empathy, but they (and/or your superior) may fail to respect you because you did not plan for contingencies, emphasize meeting objectives, or seek to innovate, or organize the unit or company well. Being tuned in to people, motivation and morale is vital for success in practically all organizations, but one must not lose sight of the other aspects of management. The line between people concern and production concern or technical expertise can indeed be fine. The goal is to strive as much as possible for strength in both areas. It is not rare to find a top executive discharged because he could not work well with subordinates, he could not lead even though he may have technically been most knowledgeable and creative. The reverse can also apply.

The person who is successful in directing is able to build upon strengths in all the management areas within the context of a broad ability to lead, work with and motivate others. This chapter will focus on leadership, motivation, productivity, and some special aspects of directing.

LEADERSHIP

There are volumes of published materials that deal with the nature of leadership. Early attempts at answering the question of what makes a successful leader focused on listing leadership traits. Frequently listed are: intelligence; self-confidence; creativity; initiative; courage; forcefulness; drive; persistence; commitment; concern for others; integrity; communications ability, stamina; superior knowledge and experience. Other studies have dealt with the physical aspects of leaders.

Discussion about leadership progressed from trait theory to what is known as *situational theory*. That is, that leadership is specific to a particular situation at a particular time. A leader arises or is chosen because he is perceived to be best able to meet the organization's or group's needs at a particular time. At one point in an organization's history, the president may come from the marketing ranks or from production, finance, legal or some other area. His style may be production-oriented, human relations-oriented or some other general approach. When he retires, leaves or is replaced, times may have changed so that a different background and style are more suitable for the needs of the moment and for the foreseeable future.

Another area of investigation has been examining the behavior of leaders. This has led to looking at organizations and at leaders within them to determine whether they are "employee-centered" or "production centered." Of course, in this approach and in situational leadership approaches, one must also look at the group or organization in which the leadership tasks are to be carried out. Different tasks and times demand different leaders. Various studies have indicated that democratic leadership and participative leadership produce better results than authoritarian leadership regardless of the background of the leader.

In discussing leadership and motivation, it is valuable to take a brief glimpse at some contributions by human relations and behavioral science theorists and researchers. We will summarize some of the leading concepts next.

Human Relations—Behavioral Science Concepts

As background we should note that the prevailing prior philosophy of management was based on the scientific management movement led by Frederick W. Taylor and Frank Gilbreth in the early 1900s. Taylor was concerned about the concept of a fair day's work. His work in time and motion studies launched their use in industry. He was concerned with differential piecework and a sharp reorganization of supervision with emphasis on separation of planning and doing and use of a functional foreman. He also can be considered the originator of the *management by exception* approach. Gilbreth was concerned with the best way to perform a given task and thus, emphasized the improvement of efficiency through the reduction of effort achieved by eliminating unnecessary motions. This work is the basis of modern motion study techniques. His "therbligs" were the seventeen basic elements in motions performed on the job—search, find, select, grasp, position, assemble, use, disassemble, inspect, transport loaded, pre-position, release load, transport empty, wait-unavoidable, wait-avoidable, rest to overcome fatigue and plan. He also created the flow process chart as a way of analyzing an entire operation.

Elton Mayo—The Hawthorne Studies

In the 1920s and early 1930s a series of experiments were conducted at the Hawthorne plant of the Western Electric Company in Chicago. Elton Mayo of the Harvard Business School publicized these studies and developed interpretations of the findings which led to new understanding of how to increase productivity. This began the development of a human relations approach to management. The original experiments dealt with the issue of fatigue and the value of providing rest periods, but as the research developed it was clear that there were factors, other than fatigue, at work. The startling result of the experiments conducted over several years was that there was an increase in productivity regardless of the changes in rest periods and even when rest periods were eliminated. Even with changes in work schedules and with no financial incentives, productivity increased and sick days were markedly down as contrasted with workers in the regular assembly room. It was clear that those involved in the experiment felt differently about their work. Very little supervision was necessary. Mayo theorized that the work group was of great importance, that people wanted to develop a sense of belonging and cohesion, and that non-directive interviewing of employees and non-authoritarian supervision would yield important productivity results. While some of Mayo's conclusions have been questioned, there is no doubt that his efforts gave impetus to an indepth analysis of nonfinancial approaches toward understanding motivation and improving employee satisfaction and productivity.

Douglas McGregor—the X-Y Theory

McGregor, a professor of management and a college president, suggested in an important book, *The Human Side of Enterprise,* that managers' attitudes are critical to making human relations work. He divided managers into two categories, those who subscribed to Theory X and those who subscribed to Theory Y in regard to describing the nature of employees. Theory X holds that people naturally dislike work and will avoid it if they can. Most people regard security as their primary aspiration and seek to avoid responsibility. It then follows that employees must be coerced in one fashion or another to put forth an adequate level of effort. As opposed to this rather bleak view of human nature, McGregor proposed Theory Y. It holds that:

1. Mental and physical work effort is as natural as play or rest.
2. Individuals will exercise self-control and self-direction if they are committed to the objectives of the unit or enterprise.
3. Commitment to objectives is related to the rewards associated with achievement (the most significant rewards are satisfaction of ego and self-actualization needs).

4. The average person learns under proper conditions not only to accept responsibility, but also to seek it.
5. "The capacity to exercise a relatively high degree of imagination, ingenuity and creativity in the solution of organizational problems is widely, not narrowly, distributed in the population."[1]
6. "Under the conditions of modern industrial life, the intellectual potentialities of the average human being are only partially utilized."[2]

Abraham Maslow—Hierachy of Needs

Psychologist Maslow indicated in his book, *Motivation and Personality,* that in motivating individuals we should recognize that there is a hierarchy of needs and that once a lower need is satisfied, only a desire to satisfy a higher need will result in motivation. In ascending order the needs he indicates are:

1. Psychological needs—food, shelter and other needs critical for survival.
2. Safety from danger, threat, deprivation.
3. Social needs for association with others, for love and friendship.
4. Self-respect, self-esteem, status, the respect of one's colleagues.
5. Self-fulfillment or self-actualization—the ability to develop powers, skills and opportunities to use one's own creativity.

It is clear from Maslow's formulation that the highest two needs are the hardest to satisfy to any great degree, particularly self-fulfillment. But many jobs in society, particularly those on the assembly line, hold little hope for challenging the worker to improve once he has learned the basic skills or motions, unless there are great changes in job structure and environment. On the assembly line, the work pace is mechanically controlled; there is repetition—skills required or opportunities for new skills are minimal; there is a set use of techniques and tools, and very little attention or focus is necessary. Some of these are characteristics of many nonassembly line jobs.

---

[1] McGregor, Douglas, The Human Side of Enterprise. McGraw-Hill Book Company, Inc. (New York, 1960) p 48.
[2] *Ibid.*

Robert Blake—Jane Mouton—The Managerial Grid

Blake and Mouton developed the concept of the managerial grid. In their view, a manager's basic approach toward management is exemplified in his attitudes toward production and people, and can be rated on a 1-9 scale. A high concern for production or people would be 9, medium 5, low 1. There are various combinations that would indicate a particular manager's style. The five distinct types of supervision identified by Blake and Mouton were 9-1 — Task Management: "Produce or Perish," 1-9 — Country Club Management: "Try To Win Friends and Influence People," 5-5 — Middle of the Road: "Be Firm But Fair," 1-1 — Impoverished Management: "Don't Rock the Boat," 9-9 — Team Management: "People Support What They Help Create."

Frederick Herzberg—Job Enrichment

Frederick Herzberg formulated the motivation-hygiene theory, job "satisfiers" as motivators and "dissatisfiers" as "hygiene" or maintenance factors in the job. In his studies, he found that job satisfaction factors are quite distinct from factors that lead to dissatisfaction with the job. The factors are not opposite from each other. The satisfiers are those aspects of the job associated with job content, that draw upon the individual's need for achievement and to thereby experience psychological growth. The dissatisfaction (hygiene) factors are associated with the job environment. The motivator factors indicated by Herzberg that are intrinsic to the job are: achievement, recognition for achievement, the work itself, responsibility and growth or advancement. The hygiene factors that are extrinsic to the job include: company policy and administration, supervision, interpersonal relationships, working conditions, salary, status and security. His theory led Herzberg to stress job enrichment (vertical job loading) rather than job enlargement (horizontal job loading). In traditional job enlargement, the worker is given the challenge of increasing production, or adding tasks at the same level of challenge or skill, rotating assignments, removing difficult aspects of a job so that he can accomplish more of the routine. By job enrichment, Herzberg stressed the motivating aspects in a job that provide the opportunity for growth. This would include removing some controls (accountability would be retained), increasing the individual's accountability, providing the individual with a complete unit of work, providing additional authority and freedom in his job, providing information directly to the individual as to results of his efforts rather than to the supervisor, providing new and more challenging tasks, assigning specialized tasks which enable the individual to develop expertise and the recognition flowing from that.

Rensis Likert—System 1-4

Likert indicated the critical role of the supervisor in productivity and satisfaction. An important concept is the idea of work groups being linked to the rest of the organization by persons who are members of two or more groups (called "link pins"). Another important concept is his view of the principle of supportive relationships, that the supervisor and the organization is perceived as supportive of the individual and the individual's sense of personal worth and importance. Likert indicated the greater the influence the unit's leader is seen as exercising with his own supervisor and with his peers, the greater the likelihood that his directives will be carried out by his subordinates as a group. Likert developed four styles or systems of management which incorporate actions involving leadership, communication, motivation, decisions, goals and controls, and result in System 1: an exploitive—authoritative style; System 2: benevolent—authoritative; System 3: consultative; System 4: participative group. System 4, participative group is the system advocated by Likert. It involves the use by managers of the principle of supportive relationships, the use of group decision making and group methods of supervision, setting high performance goals for the organization.

Fred Fiedler—The Leadership Contingency Model

Fiedler suggested that depending upon important and variable elements of the situation, a particular leadership style may be effective or ineffective. By requiring a person to give a self-description and descriptions of his most and least preferred co-workers he derived "Assumed Similarity Between Opposites" scores (ASo) which indicated the differences or "distances" between the various descriptions. The "high" ASo individual tends to be concerned about interpersonal relations, has a need for approval from associates and is less "distant" in describing himself and others. The "low" ASo individual is relatively independent of others, less concerned about feelings about him and puts great emphasis on other individuals' ability to get the job done. In the leadership situation itself, Fiedler described the major factors as:

1. Leader-member relations — the degree to which the group trusted or liked the leader and were willing to follow him.
2. Task structure — how well the task was defined.
3. Position power — the formal power of the leader as distinct from his personal power.

Fiedler concluded that the favorableness of the group task situation determines the appropriateness of the particular leadership style in maximizing group performance. The leader will do best if he is well liked by the group members, has a powerful position and is directing a well-defined task. The least favorable situation is when the opposites hold — the leader is disliked, has little power and directs an unstructured task. This leads to Fiedler's view that the task-oriented leader will excell in those group situations which are at the extremes in terms of being highly favorable or unfavorable to the leader, while the relationship-oriented leader will excell in group situations which are neither highly favorable or unfavorable to the leader.

Herbert Mintzberg—Basic Managerial Roles

Mintzberg discussed the various methodologies used to study managerial work—secondary sources, questionnaire and interview, critical incident, diary, activity sampling, unstructured observation and structured observation. He presented research evidence indicating that the emphasis on a manager's job focusing on planning, information processing, basic, regular duties and scientific management concerns, are myths. His empirical observational study of five managers and subsequent research work led him to describe managerial work as consisting of ten basic roles: figurehead, leader, liaison, nerve center, disseminator, spokesman, entrepreneur, disturbance handler, resource allocator and negotiator. Mintzberg regarded managerial skills as including: developing peer relationships, carrying out negotiations, motivating subordinates, resolving conflicts, establishing information networks and subsequently disseminating information, making decisions in conditions of extreme ambiguity and allocating resources.

Some of the many others who can be cited as having made important contributions to concepts about leadership and motivation include: Chris Argyris and his views about integrating individual and organizational objectives; Warren Bennis, in his various books and articles has dealt with issues of leadership and has suggested that leadership is "an active method for producing conditions where people and ideas and resources can be seeded, cultivated and integrated to optimum effectiveness and growth"; Chester Barnard discussed three basic executive functions—providing a system of communication, promoting the securing of essential personal efforts, formulating and defining purpose. The executive functions, in his view, served to maintain a "system of cooperative effort"; James March and Herbert Simon discussed the relationship among satisfaction, level of aspiration and expected value of reward; Peter Drucker has talked about the internal self-motivation for performance.

A PERSONAL VIEW

There are no easy answers to leadership or motivation. Attempting to maximize results and attainment of performance objectives while at the same time maximizing individual and group satisfaction are goals long sought after but rarely attained. The pendulum swings from people orientation to production orientation. Styles and environments change as do the internal and external forces acting on individuals, groups and organizations. In our society's search for the right answer or approach to motivation and better performance, there have been attempts at:

1. Reducing the time spent at work or giving people more control over the work time through "flex" hours and four-day weeks.
2. Various types of incentive pay and profit-sharing plans.
3. Improved and creative fringe benefits.
4. Human relations, sensitivity, group dynamics, leadership training, quality circles, quality of worklife approaches.
5. Improved and increased communications from junior board of directors, suggestion boxes, newsletters and brochures to attitude surveys and group participation programs.
6. Job involvement and participation.

In seeking to work out one's own style of leadership, one should recognize factors within himself, within subordinates, within the organization as a whole and factors affecting the particular situation and group.

The individual in a leadership role or who aspires to such a role seeks to gain a better understanding of himself. What are his goals and ambitions, his values, his degree of loyalty to the organization, supervisors, peers and subordinates, his own self-confidence? What does he really know and like and where is he weak? What does he dislike? Does he really want the risks, rewards, stresses of leadership? How secure is he about himself, his life, the organization? How much confidence does he have in others? With what type of leadership style does he feel most comfortable? How much of a risk taker is he in terms of management style?

The factors one must consider in regard to subordinates depend upon needs and desires for independence, responsibility and job enrichment; willingness to assume some control over their work lives and the results of their actions; commitment to the group, the leader, the organization; their knowledge, abilities, ambition, tolerance for ambiguity; past experiences in the organization.

Within the organization, various factors involve the type of organization it is; its history, tradition, size, complexity, values; its corporate style and culture; its ability to deal with stress, competition, adversity and success; the managerial, competitive and economic problems and opportunities it has faced, faces now, and will face; its image of itself; the time frame of decision making, etc.

The particular time or situation in the organization also shapes the style of leadership that will be effective and the leaders who will emerge. Important also are the nature of the problems to be solved, time and competitive constraints, the personal and professional characteristics of those involved.

One's style may have to change or be modified, but each leader must seek to define for himself where he fits on the people-productivity issues, Systems 1-4, or other approaches that have been espoused. Success in an organization may come to those with very different styles depending upon the various factors. One may indeed have the right style at precisely the right time in an organization's life, but then time may pass you by, unless you can adapt.

This is not to suggest that a successful leader is a chameleon. Values are very important, and this includes a concern for the growth and satisfaction of others. Surveys of employees at all levels seem to indicate that basic concerns involve:

1. The nature of the work—is it interesting, challenging, satisfying in one way or another?

2. Does the organization provide the necessary assistance, equipment, resources, environment so that the tasks can be accomplished?
3. Is there sufficient information to accomplish the objectives?
4. Is there sufficient authority and responsibility to reach one's goals?
5. Is the compensation fair?
6. Does one have the opportunity to develop special abilities, to grow, to be recognized and rewarded?
7. Is there emotional and psychological security as well as security of maintenance of a job?
8. Can one get a sense of accomplishment, of seeing the result of one's labor?
9. Is there a sense of involvement, participation, consultation, control to some degree over one's fate?

The successful leader, while seeking to be fair and just to all, may have to use different approaches to different individuals and different situations. Some subordinates will need to be encouraged, praised lavishly, brought along slowly; others will have to be held back a bit, prodded, kicked in the rear. Some will need more attention and supervision, others more independence and freedom. Each individual is different; what motivates one might not motivate another. Though treating everyone alike may seem reasonable and democratic, without bias or favoritism one still needs "different strokes for different folks."

In the various situations, internal and external, that a leader faces, his pace, decisiveness, strategies and tactics will have to be adapted to the needs of the moment. The leader who is always a hard charger, tough guy, may enjoy great success, but there are times that such a style will be counterproductive. One can either moderate the style for the situation or have someone else with a more compatible approach deal with the matter. Within a particular organization's culture it may be good to be identified with a particular management style, but to have an ability to adapt, roll with the punches, read the situation and respond accordingly.

Some leaders pride themselves as working harder, longer hours, and better than anyone, as setting very tough objectives for themselves and others, as being very tough on themselves and others, as being one of the "ten toughest bosses in America." Others are just the reverse. Both types have a time and place in which they can be successful.

Whatever the style or the person in the leadership role, it is important to remember that these are people we are working with, not robots, machines, systems or numbers. It may not be quantifiable, but it pays off to operate with:

1. A basic decency toward others.
2. A concern about what is happening to others on the job, their challenges, frustrations, recognition and reward.
3. The effect that poor working conditions, atmosphere and supervision can have on the individual's physical, psychological, and emotional life, on their sense of self-worth and on their families.

These and other concerns about people can go side-by-side with seeking to excell in a highly competitive atmosphere. The leader need not be a slave master nor a saint. But in the long run, those who can inspire and motivate through precept and practice, through mind as well as heart, will be most likely to attain and retain high leadership positions.

If you seek to become more of a humanist, while still seeking to maximize objectives (a more humane organization can indeed become a primary objective), start by asking yourself some questions. What do you admire most/least in a supervisor, colleague, subordinate? Which of these attributes do you exhibit in dealing with subordinates, peers, superiors? What, to you, is the "ideal" supervisor, colleague, subordinate? How far do you have to go to reach or be reasonably close to the ideal? What do you have to do, how can you do it, by when? How can you encourage others to reach closer to the ideal? What do you have to do? What do they have to do? What does the organization have to do?

To answer these questions, many things have to be done that involve more than people relating to people. The organization's objectives, structure, communications, planning, controls, history, standards, tradition, processes and many other aspects may all be called into question. There may be a need to have fewer staff, but at higher pay, or fewer top staff. There may be the need to question how much participation and by which groups or individuals. There may be the need to put yourself in your subordinate's shoes. You may have to have an objective attitude survey, some one-on-one discussions, some willingness to be open, to admit you don't know.

In regard to focusing on human relations, some simple things can pay big dividends:

- Keeping an open mind and ear
- Encouraging departures from routine thinking
- Soliciting ideas, reactions, suggestions, advice
- Recognizing both effort and success in formal (as well as informal) ways
- Complimenting someone in writing or in a call
- Remembering a person's birthday or anniversary in the company or recognizing important events in their personal lives
- Inviting people to meetings or to various types of occasions or celebrations
- Encouraging good, timely communications upward and downward
- Encouraging teamwork
- Setting high standards
- Being concerned about the quality of life in the work environment
- Encouraging initiative
- Providing support
- Establishing realistic and measurable targets and deadlines
- Evaluating performance in an objective, timely manner and conducting periodic performance reviews with the goal of improving performance
- Tuning in to an individual's goals, aspirations, self-image, frustrations
- Helping the individual plan job and career objectives
- Providing a range of assignments and opportunities as well as times to recharge one's enthusiasm and energy.

The problem many of us will face is that there are only a few "good" or "potentially good" jobs in the organization. And there may be several potentially good people for each of those positions. At a time of a steady state or a declining economy, really challenging jobs may be available for only a few in the organization. We may have to deal with redesign of jobs in order to offset the blue collar blues, white collar woes and executive burn-out and blahs many organizations face. The economy and the future will have important roles to play. We must recognize that a job and title are important in determining satisfaction. Satisfaction with one's job may depend upon occupation, status, job content, supervision, compensation, personal and peer relationships, working conditions, mobility, growth or security. But the question is, can many individuals, particularly in some of our more traditional businesses and industries, have jobs that lead to real satisfaction or that really lend themselves to redesign?

Out of this turmoil and self-questioning, can come a stronger, more self-confident leader. Some people are "natural" leaders, most learn leadership through experience of dealing with the hard realities of a company or industry, and through insight, education and training. The best leaders tune in to problems and people. They have a vision of the future for the organization, for themselves and those who work with them. They seek to work with others to attain that vision. They are not satisfied with the status quo. They set high standards for themselves and others and provide the resources and environment for others to accomplish objectives. They strive to do today's efforts better, more creatively or inexpensively or with more quality. But they look to tomorrow and how to be ready for the challenges and, as far as possible, to shape the future. They take real pride in picking and nourishing good people, in letting them fly as high and as fast as they can. They share the glory, but not the blame. They are mentors as well as bosses. They are proud of their unit, their people and themselves, but never completely satisfied or complacent. Their subordinates know that they not only work hard, but they work smart, and after all is said and done, they care about the job, the company, the people.

PROBLEMS IN DIRECTING

Productivity *(See Essay Section)*

The issue of increasing productivity has been so frequently mentioned as a cure for inflation, balance of trade problems, foreign competition, creation of new jobs and a variety of other economic problems that many of us begin to tune out when it is mentioned. But the executive must be concerned about the rate of growth of productivity in his organization (just as a nation we must be concerned about it).

Some frequently cited approaches to increasing our productivity growth rate revolve around management's actions in regard to building new, more efficient plants and installing new, more efficient equipment, substituting capital and technology for routine labor, focusing on laborsaving and timesaving devices and methods, better marketing, etc. Government, it is suggested, should be involved in terms of cutting down on over regulating and in providing tax, research and development and other incentives to business. Increasing employee motivation is also cited as a possible cure.

It is helpful to indicate that there are a number of possible causes of the slowdown in productivity growth in recent years. The slowdown is indeed real. A generally accepted figure is that productivity grew by only 0.9% a year from 1973-79 and that it actually declined by 0.8% in 1979. This is in contrast, for example, with an annual growth of 3.2% during the period of 1948-65.

Some possible causes for our recent decline include:

- Inadequate investment in capital presumably because of scarcity of capital, tax disincentives, the benefits derived from adding cheaper, more plentiful labor to overcome capital risks. But management can be seen as at fault in using available dollars to buy other firms or to fund incentive plans that reward quick returns.
- Expansion of the work force—about 50 percent more new jobs were created in the 1970s than the 1960s, but this included a large number of untrained teenagers and housewives returning to or joining the labor market. The availability of labor served as a disincentive to management to attempt to substitute capital for labor.
- Soaring costs and shortages of energy created economic problems as well as the need to hire more people to search for or conserve energy. Consumption declines in gas and electricity cut back on the productivity of utility workers.
- Slowdown in expenditures for research and technology.
- Growth in the retail and service industries. The jobs in these industries are generally low productivity jobs as contrasted with steel, auto, etc.
- Growth in white collar jobs which traditionally have a low capital investment in each worker, and difficulty in measuring and evaluating productivity. We are just beginning to focus on the productivity of white collar professionals, for example, lawyers, bank lending officers.
- Life style changes and affluence encouraged some workers to be less concerned about earning more money and more concerned about getting satisfaction out of work or just enjoying life.
- Changes in family structure—more working wives, more divorced

people and single parents in the labor force had some effect on productivity because of the influence of family and personal problems and responsibilities on work time and concentration.

- Alcohol and drugs—there appears to be significantly more alcohol and drug abuse problems with effects upon absenteeism, lateness and quality of work produced.
- Crime and lawsuits—more companies and employees are concerned about security and safety, thus leading to dollars spent for security guards and devices. Shoplifting, employee theft, auditing all impact on productivity. Concern for safety of staff leading to sending salespeople and meter readers in pairs in certain areas leads to reduced productivity. Further, more money and employee time (not only attorneys, but staff throughout the organization) is spent anticipating, guarding against and defending a wide variety of lawsuits—personal injury, product liability, violations of various federal and state laws on age discrimination, affirmative action, etc.
- Governmental actions (See Essay)—Productivity has been reduced by the need to use company resources for nonproductive activities involved in complying with governmental regulations and reports. The extra cost for businesses has been projected as above $100 billion. The need to monitor, evaluate, comply, oppose, appeal, and report in regard to the regulations of the last decade has led to the need for employing many experts, consultants and support staff and for various new equipment purchases and plant and production modifications. OSHA and EPA have been the major agencies which have caused significant additional costs. Capital has been used to comply with regulations rather than for productivity improvements. The toll on managers and top executive time has been considerable. In addition, some would say that governmental action in regard to the economy, particularly its role in bringing about or controlling inflation, hurts productivity. The threat of wage and price controls and federal tax policies also have an impact on productivity.
- Employee motivation—Some believe there has been a decline in employee motivation whether as a result of turning away from the old work ethic, adaptation to new roles for women and minorities, a reaction to the Vietnam War, a reaction to different approaches to supervision, etc.

In this section we focus briefly on employee motivation. We have tried to indicate in a previous section problems of motivation and leadership. The point here is that management must begin to focus on the nature of the jobs people perform, the need for redesign in some cases, change in work environment and atmosphere, the problems of boredom and challenge on the job.

Beyond job enrichment, important as that may be, management should focus on attempting to involve workers as fully as possible in making decisions that influence their lives at work. Workers can be an untapped gold mine of knowledge about how to do things better or what things are unnecessary. There have been a few attempts at plants to develop full communication with workers. A concept that may have great potential is the Quality Control Circles (QC Circles) idea developed in Japan. Some would suggest that QC Circle concept is similar to QWL, Quality of Work Life. QWL is basically a concerted and sustained effort to give workers greater control over their jobs and working environment. QWL actions involve new pay systems, nonsupervised work groups, group developed work methods and systems, increased participation in decisions having an impact on work groups, etc.

Although the Japanese culture may prove to be more fertile ground for the concept than in the United States, QC Circles, with appropriate adaptation are worth detailed exploration.

The essence of a QC Circle is that it is a relatively autonomous unit of a small group of workers, generally led by a first-line supervisor or senior worker. QC members are taught basic techniques of problem formulation and problem solving including quantitative and statistical methods. Group membership is voluntary. The group focuses on solving quality problems on the job in order to improve production methods, thereby leading to cost reductions and increased productivity. Equally important in the QC approach is a concern for self-development of workers and improvement of the work environment. Basic assumptions in the QC approach are:

1. That the concern is for a continuous study and review process rather than a reaction to specific problems.
2. Analysis is needed to determine the causes and cures of poor quality and that those involved in the circle should receive appropriate training.
3. Those involved will be more committed to insuring successful implementation of those solutions which they have developed.

Of course, in Japan and elsewhere, there are departures in practice from the ideal stated above. QC can be imposed from the top and, thus, may not really be voluntary. The emphasis may be more on increasing productivity than worker potential and, thus, have little personal meaning for the worker. It may end up like any fad, losing its momentum and creativity and becoming bogged down in process and form.

The QC approach can be adapted to particular American companies. In our view, it should involve union cooperation and be applied to white collar and professional staff as well as hourly, blue collar workers.

LABOR—MANAGEMENT RELATIONS

We approach the discussion of this important aspect of directing by looking at two situations—labor relations without a union, and labor relations with a union. As a base for discussion we can look at the past decade and note that the pace of unionization has slowed in recent years, that white collar workers now constitute about 28 percent of all unionized workers, that in the past decade unions have been losing more National Labor Relations Board elections than previously and now lose more elections than they win. The proportion of the labor force in unions has been declining irregularly since the peak in the mid 1950s and as a proportion of the total labor force in the United States union membership is about 20 percent. If workers in employee associations are added, then the figure is about 23 percent. The growth in unionization in the last decade has been in the white collar area (28 percent of union employees are white collar workers), particularly in public service employment. Management, particularly in the private sector, but also in hospitals and universities, tend to vigorously fight unionization more often than ten years ago, often using attorneys and consultants specializing in preventing unionization.

Labor Relations Without A Union

For most non-unionized companies a major concern is creating a climate that would make unionization unlikely or very difficult. This approach tends to be defensive or preventative. If seen in another light, as a means of providing a better working environment, greater job satisfaction, less turnover and absenteeism, and possibly (though not necessarily) higher productivity, the steps taken can definitely enhance management and the work environment.

We would argue that some of the steps described lead to better management for both the company and the staff. An important fall-out effect is that it will probably make an organizing drive unlikely or unsuccessful. For whatever reason, either to improve management or defend against possible unionization these steps outlined below should be taken. We would also argue that even in an organized environment the steps would still be helpful.

If one assumes that most companies are reasonably competitive with their counterparts in the industry or area in terms of salaries and fringe benefits, it becomes apparent that there are nonmonetary aspects of work life that lead to discontent, absenteeism, turnover, quality control problems and possibly unionization.

A good management will demonstrate concern for:

- the individual
- the stress and strains on the job
- the work environment
- the type of supervision
- the role and personalities of first line supervisors (This is a critical element in labor-management relations)
- two way communication
- fair and prompt handling of grievances
- the cleanliness and safety of the work environment
- recognition of long service employees beyond pins and letters
- the fairness of wage differentials in relation to skills required
- the views employees have
- employee gripes
- the fairness of merit increases
- whether incentive rates are too "tight"
- how much overtime is required and how overtime is administered
- the role of seniority, how promotions, shift and job transfers are handled, whether salaries and fringe benefits are fair, updated and responsive to the needs of the work force
- how discipline is handled
- promotional and growth opportunities
- job enrichment opportunities

Management must be aware that the changing nature of the work force, the surge of younger workers who are better educated than in the past, the growth of the number of women and minorities, different life styles and attitudes or a desire for the good life—all of these have to influence the old ways of dealing with staff. Workers are concerned with the rapid pace of change. They do not necessarily fight change (though change makes most people at all levels uncomfortable), but they resist changes when they have had nothing to say, prior to implementation, about things that will effect them. Time spent in discussing changes, soliciting views, preparing people about why the change is being made and the impact upon them, is time very well spent.

This leads to another area of deep concern for workers, particularly younger workers, white collar workers and those relatively new to the work force—the need for good, continuous two-way communication. The worker needs an outlet, beyond the informal group, to indicate views, ideas, suggestions, gripes about what is happening to him at the work place and in his job. Newsletters and memos from the top down are not enough. This is where first-line supervisors tuned in to people as well as the tasks to be performed are of great importance. Beyond listening, the supervisor should be one who within his own authority makes necessary changes and, if beyond his authority, is willing to take matters to higher levels.

We have just noted another major concern, and that is the quality and style of supervision. Supervisors at all levels have to be carefully selected and trained to deal with people problems as well as task responsibilities. All too often, the first line supervisor is left out on a limb without concern by higher management for providing him with access to information, higher authority, training, specific objectives, ways to promote his subordinates, job satisfaction, etc.

Fighting a Unionizing Attempt

If all has gone well, as outlined previously, one need not worry too much about a serious unionizing attempt. But if such an attempt is made, often because of serious discontent by workers, management can be successful in fighting back. If management has treated workers unfairly, sooner or later there will be a unionizing drive.

The labor relations department, often with help from labor lawyers or consultants, can be successful in winning the National Labor Relations Board election (if the company falls within the National Labor Relations Act) legally without resorting to questionable or illegal activities. Often it can keep the election from ever being held because the union sees that its efforts will not succeed. A good deal of work is involved on the part of management at all levels, particularly supervisory levels. In a sense, it is a political campaign. One has to understand one's weaknesses and strengths and the weaknesses and strengths of your opponent (the union and its organizers and organizing committee). Normally management will try to delay a vote as long as legally possible to give it time to marshall its forces. But in planning the campaign and executing the plan, the idea is to influence people by knowing what the problems are and using all legal means to show them that things have been getting better, that changes are possible (it is illegal for management to make promises), that management is now tuned in to their problems.

In fighting a unionizing attempt, management must take account of the issues uppermost in the worker's minds, the mood of the workers, the mood and commitment of supervisors, past history in the company and the style and tone that is most suitable to the company. A too aggressive response by management may turn off those who will cast ballots and, in fact, end up in votes for the union. A too mild reaction may lose the election.

Management can fight fair, yet tough. It is important to let employees know what is in the union's constitution, bylaws, and signed contracts. Normally, a union does not fully inform individuals of its initiation fee, dues and fine structure, history of increases, its mandatory membership clauses, its requirement to give support to strikes at the company and elsewhere, its contribution to various political and union organizations, its salaries, fringe benefits and travel allowances for staff, as well as its staffing levels and administrative and organizational expenses, its actions before and during strikes and the number of strikes it has been involved in, its requirements for membership, how decisions are made in the union, number of disciplinary actions taken and fines imposed, the administration of its welfare and pension funds, its win and lose record in elections, the number of decertifications, salaries and fringe benefits in unionized organizations as compared with the company (after taking into account union dues and work stoppages).

At times, newspaper stories and legal actions involving the union and its leadership and the personalities and style of union leaders and organizers may also be of help to management. The tone and tactics used by union organizers, if pointed out to employees, and counterattacked when necessary, can aid management. Often union organizers overlook the changing composition and mood of the work force and, thus, hammer away at old issues which may have lost some or much of their potency—increased wages, benefits, job security and union solidarity.

Management must be alert to various illegal or close to illegal union practices which are rare, but not unknown. Examples of these include:

1. Forged employee signatures on union cards petitioning for an election;
2. Misrepresentation by the union that the signed card just asks for an election, rather than the fact that the card designates the union as the employee's bargaining agent;
3. Pressure on employees to sign because "you are the last one in your unit to sign";
4. Promises to eliminate or reduce initiation fees for those joining the union or signing cards prior to the NLRB election;
5. Various monetary and power inducements to individuals, such as offering "steward" positions if the union wins;
6. False union claims of wage and benefit gains at other companies;
7. Misrepresentation of management actions, earnings reports, salary scales; or
8. Harassment or threatened violence against company supporters.

One can easily list a number of actions by management that also violate the letter and spirit of the law and fairness considerations in fighting a union.

The point is that by understanding the situation, being reasonably aggressive in presenting one's case, playing up the positive and admitting blemishes in a way that is helpful to one's case, taking the offensive where appropriate against the union, by planning, organizing and following through, management has a reasonably good chance of defeating an organizing attempt.

Establishing a Good Labor-Management Climate

Despite management's normal reaction to fight the union, a unionization may still come about. In fact, at times unionization can indeed be helpful to management. The negotiations can lead to changes in policies, procedures and work rules that ultimately prove beneficial to both management and labor. Further, the sound administration of a labor agreement, while at times hampering management flexibility, can also do away with precedents that hurt management.

It is important that a good labor-management climate be created, otherwise a company can have a war waging within it—not only during bargaining, but after. From a management perspective, there are a number of basic steps that should be taken in regard to developing good labor relations. These apply to companies without unions, as well as with unions.

1. All levels of management, from the president to the first-line supervisor, should be concerned about creating a favorable labor relations climate, and top and middle level management's attitude and actions set the tone for all.
2. Those involved in negotiating and administering contracts and in carrying out day-to-day labor relations responsibilities should be highly competent, motivated, experienced, and sensitive to the concerns of management at all levels, the union, and the workers.
3. Good supervisors, particularly first-line supervisors, are a critical element in good labor-management relations. They should be carefully selected and trained. Their motivation, recognition and rewards, interpersonal and communications skills as well as technical skills are important factors in successful labor relations.
4. Good communication, upward and downward, with supervisors, union officials and workers are very important.
5. The company should learn about the union leaders' strengths, weaknesses and style. Management leaders should meet regularly with union leaders to discuss problems, inform them of planned actions, solicit reactions. The goal should also be to build both formal and informal relationships.
6. Training is important for employees so that they know their job, company policy and what is expected of them—for supervisors, so that they know their job, the company, interpersonal and communication skills, company policies, good industrial relations practices, understand the causes and ways of handling grievances, understand the union contract.
7. Those involved in dealing with grievances should know the procedures thoroughly and administer them impartially.
8. Employees and their representatives should have the opportunity to present complaints, ideas and grievances.
9. If management is wrong, if something should be done, if the agreement has been violated, admit the error and take remedial action promptly. Handle issues, if possible, before they become complaints or grievances.

10. Employees and their representatives should be treated fairly and consistently, with a sincere, continued interest shown in each employee.
11. Provide specific reasons for your decisions and answers when questions are raised as to your actions or company policies. If you don't know the answer, find out as soon as possible. Answer all complaints promptly and thoroughly.
12. When grievances or issues arise, carefully investigate, document and handle each matter in the expectation that it will result in a decision at the final stage of grievance or arbitration.
13. Where and when appropriate, higher levels of management should be informed as to actions taken.
14. Do not modify or amend the contract or existing procedures through informal understandings or agreements. Be mindful of setting precedents or acting in a preferential or biased manner on an individual case. Document your actions.

With these precepts in mind, every attempt should be made to forge a good working relationship with the union and its leaders. Give and take; reciprocity and accomodation; understanding the other's views, constraints, needs and pressure; the importance of making concessions, saving face, appearing to "win"—all of these are important elements of a healthy union-management relationship. Neither side can or will sell its constituency down the river, but both can understand each other and which things are possible now. The desire for accommodation, truthfulness, sensitivity to the other's concerns, reasonable compromise and small victories by both, rather than all out victory or defeat or humiliating or destroying the other side, should be the goal of both parties.

When companies and the nation, unions and their members, and non-unionized workers are undergoing difficult economic times, labor-management relations become even more important. It is tempting for either or both sides to cut corners, take advantage of a situation, to seek to make gains or correct past concessions. Increasingly, however, union-management cooperation will be necessary to deal with quality of work life, productivity and job satisfaction issues in a relatively reasonable and responsible manner. Particular situations—prestige, power, politics, rhetoric, emotion and irrationality; personalities; history and tradition; comparisons; grievances; economic conditions; working conditions and managerial prerogatives—will all influence the present and future labor relations climate in a particular company. However, even those who are somewhat battered as a result of battling in the labor relations arena for some years, continue to believe that relationships can mature so that legitimate needs and concerns of both labor and management can be at least partially met.

DEALING WITH THE TOPPED OUT
OR BURNED OUT EXECUTIVE

Often the senior executive must deal with subordinates or colleagues who indicate signs of being burned out or topped out. Although some of the problems are similar, there are differences and we shall, therefore, deal with each problem separately. It is also possible that being topped out may lead to burnout and vice versa.

The Burned Out Executive

At times, the climb to the top or near top of the organization and maintaining one's success is so tough, unrelenting, tension filled and debilitating that a base is firmly laid for a serious attack of being burned out. Burnout can also occur because of lack of challenge and stimulation on the job.

Signs or Effects of Being Burned Out

- challenge of the job loses its glow
- interest in the job decreases
- personal satisfaction declines
- family tensions increase
- heavy involvement in company, industry and community activities not directly related to one's job
- escape mechanisms abound such as drinking, gambling, lateness, sickness, absenteeism, long lunch hours, job hopping, divorce, separation or affairs
- decisions are reached too quickly or slowly or avoided
- erratic performance
- over delegation or great nit-picking
- decreased productivity and performance

- staff turnover, firings and demoralization
- ill health, headaches, stomach distress
- lack of eagerness to go to work or to plan ahead, great joy about approaching vacation or a Thank God It's Friday feeling or regarding lunch hour as the best time of the work day

The executive may spot these signs and symptoms in himself or in others. The organization must be concerned because often the burned out executive is one of the best performers the organization has had. Although the approaches to meeting this problem depend upon the individual involved, his supervisors and the organization, some general guidelines can be helpful.

From the burned out person's or potential burned out person's point of view:

1.   Look out for the telltale signs of emotional and physical drain, depression, boredom, the symptoms indicated above, remarks from family and associates about your appearance and attitude.
2.   Discuss frustrations or problems with your family and with your colleagues and supervisor. Just airing one's concerns can help relieve the burden, however, your colleagues or supervisor might be helpful in solving some annoyances or at least indicating support and concern.
3.   Change some patterns or habits at work, analyze how your time is being spent and whether it can be spent in a more productive or pleasant fashion. Leave time to evaluate the problems at hand, to plan ahead, to fight the tyranny of the in-box.
4.   Check out your health. Consider regular exercise not only for physical health reasons, but for a means of relieving stress. Analyze stress provoking situations and how to deal with them (professional help can be of assistance).
5.   Try to separate your work life from after work life. Rest, relax, seek hobbies and other forms of recreation, enjoy more frequent and different types of vacations and non-business related activities, conversation and relationships.
6.   Try to make your nonwork life stimulating and at least somewhat different from the skills or tensions involved in your work life. Community involvement, writing, consulting, teaching, hobbies, athletic participation or observation, jogging, can be helpful in kindling interest and letting off steam.
7.   Vary your work pace and assignments, seek out new opportunities and challenges within the organization and industry (al-

though one may need to change locale, company or industry.)

8. Make time to be involved with your family and friends. Try to involve them to an appropriate degree in understanding the challenges and frustrations of your job.

9. Look for ways to enrich your job and expand your knowledge and skills in the same or different areas through job or committee assignments, courses or workshops, reading and training.

10. Set realistic, yet demanding goals and challenges for yourself at work and in non-work situations. By focusing on the problem, by honesty with yourself and others, you can mount an attack on burned-outitis that will result in your finding out that you're still as good as you once were or thought you were and perhaps even better.

The Topped Out Executive

Many of the signs and symptoms and actions to be taken are the same for the topped out executive as it was for his colleague, the burned out executive. The topped out executive, while still filled with enthusiasm and vigor finds himself in a situation where it appears that he has gone as far as he can go in the organization and perhaps in the industry or in his career. It may be a matter of having come too far, too fast, having reached one's Peter Principle level of incompetence, having naturally progressed to the highest rung possible given the size of the organization or competition within it. It is also possible that one's salary, based on his contributions to the particular organization, is considerably higher than other companies or industries might pay. The issue then is what happens to the individual who sees that the next five to twenty-five years of his work life may carry with it relatively little increase in power, prestige, compensation or significant difference in scope of job responsibilities or job challenges. This can indeed be an increasing problem in companies or industries that are growing slowly, are static or declining. It can also be a problem in expanding companies when those on the fast track finally find no place to go. The topped out phenomenon may explain to some degree the problems of motivation, performance and satisfaction in those who have served in government, education and other nonprofit organizations for a long period of time.

Those who are topped out may seek to employ the actions suggested for burned out executives. But, they may also have to place more emphasis on creating new challenges and opportunities for themselves in the organization, seeking outlets for their energies in nonwork related activities, considering job, career or life style changes with all the risks, tensions and opportunities such changes imply.

LETTING PEOPLE GO

We have a general theme in this book in regard to the importance of setting high standards and not being satisfied with merely satisfactory performance. As the needs of an organization to perform better increase under competitive and economic pressure, some people will have to be passed over for promotion, reassigned, transferred, demoted, not given increases, or fired. A November 1980 report in the Wall Street Journal of a Wall Street Journal/Gallup Survey indicated that firing employees who don't meet performance objectives is significantly more acceptable to management than a few years ago (and it is even more of a change from the past that poor performers will receive no raises or small raises). In large firms, 59% of the chief executives said it was more likely now than a few years ago that their managers would discharge incompetent performers—25% said it was less likely—for medium size firms the figures were 48% more likely, 38% less likely—for small firms figures were 39% more likely, 50% less likely.

Through the evaluation process we should be able to determine those who need help in reaching their potential and the business' objectives and those who just won't make it. Frequently, the handwriting is on the wall for an individual when his performance indicates one or more of the following:

- narrow outlook and point of view
- significant weakness in understanding and/or working with others
- lack of decisiveness
- lack of initiative and self-motivation
- shying away from or failing to take responsibility or exercise authority
- weaknesses in regard to integrity and industriousness
- inability to meet objectives

Personal and family problems, as well as inability to deal with mid-life crisis, burn out or top out may also be underlying causes for termination of employment.

Sometimes it is difficult to spot those who should be fired since they may be successful in burying themselves in the organization or building strong defensive strongholds. The inept executive may avoid discovery or firing by:

1. Explaining away shortcomings by attributing them to his management style or unique requirements of the organization.
2. Performing very well in areas not critical to his primary job responsibility, thus, building some general support or a halo effect.
3. Relying on the old boy network, contacts in the organization or past contributions to the organization.
4. Being the recipient of too much praise being handed out for mediocre performance.
5. Controlling the flow of information and communications.
6. Covering one's rear well by either hiring strong employees who will make the manager look good or hiring weak employees so that the manager stands out.
7. Blaming poor performance on having too much responsibility, being involved in too many outside activities supposedly to bolster the public and community relations of the company, having too little responsibility, it's the fault of someone else, poor systems and policies.

Once a decision has been reached that someone should be fired either because of his own performance or because of economic, managerial or organizational changes in the company, a growing number of companies use "outplacement" firms, particularly when a large number of employees must be let go. The company pays the fee of the outplacement firm. The outplacement industry is about a dozen years old and has been growing rapidly. In the first few years of outplacement, counselors dealt with upper and top middle management on an individual basis, now the service extends to lower level management and white and blue collar layoffs. The goal of the outplacement counselor is to ease the shock of firing and assist the employee in regaining his confidence and planning for the future. The counselor does not find jobs for the individual, but does provide advice on how to identify personal goals and strengths, job opportunities, how to market oneself, how to search for a job.

Firing anyone, particularly a fellow executive, is one of the most difficult experiences a manager faces. One should carefully think through and rehearse what he will do and say. It may be helpful to get advice on conducting such interviews from the company's Personnel Office or from outplacement agencies. Inadequate attention to the delicacy involved in a firing could result in a negative public reaction or image, poor morale among other executives and lawsuits charging age, race or sex discrimination. Firing is a devastating blow to any individual and must be handled sensitively. Although it is tempting for the boss to have someone else do the firing in order to spare him the trauma involved, it is better for the person being fired that he get the word directly from the boss.

Once a decision is made about letting someone go, it should be implemented quickly before rumors get out or the atmosphere becomes poisoned. The actual termination meeting should be brief, no longer than ten or fifteen minutes. The reasons should be clearly and unemotionally stated. Although one should not be unduly harsh, it is important that the employee understand exactly what was wrong. This can help him in seeking other positions or in performing on a new job. In determining when it is best to inform the employee, the manager should check and be sure that the meeting does not occur near an important event in the employee's life—birthdays, anniversary, college graduation, wedding, etc. It is generally best to hold the termination interview in the fired employee's office or a conference room so that you don't face the awkwardness in trying to get someone to leave your office once you have delivered the bad news. It is also good to have a private, quiet setting in case there is a good deal of emotion involved.

If the company uses an outplacement firm (and even if not), it is probably better to overcome the usual temptation to fire on a Friday because the employee then has to face a very tough weekend. By firing early in the week, the outplacement firm can get to work immediately, perhaps right after the interview. If an outplacement firm is not used, if at all possible, it is reasonable to provide: (in addition to severance pay and continuation of benefits in accordance with company policy), an office, secretary, phone and duplicating services to provide assistance in job hunting; a number of contacts or the names of executive recruiting firms. And, despite the emotions involved in a firing, it is helpful to the employee if the supervisor demonstrates continuing concern and support by calling from time to time to see how things are going.

Most managers have very little experience in firing executives. Unfortunately, if we keep to high standards we will probably acquire more experience in this disturbing aspect of an executive' job. It is a difficult task that should be done with sincere concern about the impact on the individual and with honesty. Each of us, because of circumstances within or beyond our control, faces the risk of being on the other side in the termination interview process. In effect, the question for those who have to fire an executive or anyone is, if I got fired, how would I like to be treated?

USE OF EXTERNAL AND INTERNAL CONSULTANTS

Often, there is considerable value in utilizing the specialized skills of consultants to assist the organization in accomplishing one or more of its objectives. There are advantages and disadvantages in regard to use of either external or internal consultants. We shall discuss both types of consultants and how they can be utilized in an effective manner.

External Consultants

There are three basic reasons for using outside consultants:

1. To obtain professional, independent, objective advice and recommendations on issues and problems of major present or potential impact on the organization.
2. To enable execution in planning and/or implementing special projects when:
   a) internal staff cannot be made available to accomplish the project in the time frame necessary.
   b) The specialized skills are not available or readily available in the organization.
3. To secure highly specialized skills and services in sufficient quality and quantity to meet the needs of the organization or project when such services and skills are not available within the organization.

Since employing outside consultants can be expensive (billing rates of $40-$100 an hour for junior to middle level consultants and $125-$250 an hour for senior and partner level consultants) are common, there are a number of considerations that should be kept in mind in using such consultants.

1. The work to be performed and the results to be achieved must be clearly and specifically defined. If bidding is used, care

must be exercised that the specifications are carefully drawn so that one ends up with the task of evaluating reasonably comparable bids. In evaluating proposals or bids, selection criteria, weighted as necessary, should be developed to reflect the characteristics and skills necessary for maximum performance effectiveness.

2. The responsibilities and role of the consultants and the various units and individuals on the staff of the client should be specifically spelled out. It is important to designate one person as the chief liaison person to deal with the consultants or as the general coordinator of the project. As appropriate, depending on the type of assignment, it is valuable to involve some of the client staff in the study so that they learn from the consultants, are trained, and can help implement, follow up and evaluate results or apply their skills to similar projects.

3. In choosing a consultant, consider the consultant's demonstration of:
    a) Understanding of the project, situation or problems.
    b) Thorough, specific, solid and responsive approach and time-table to performing the tasks assigned and to reporting to management on progress and results.
    c) Experience in regard to the project and the environment in which the project will be conducted.
    d) Quality and experience of those who will actually perform, supervise and be responsible for the work (in addition to professional qualifications and experience, consultant style, personality and "chemistry" is also very important).
    e) Clear delineation of how much time will be devoted to the project by the senior people in the firm and the agreement by the consultant that the client must approve any substitutions for key personnel (at times a firm's most impressive people are used in a marketing role and don't have the time or are over booked so that they don't actually work on a project or else spend very little time on it).
    f) The firm's track record on similar or comparable assignments in comparable companies or environments—careful reference checking is necessary in regard to quality of work product; timeliness of product and reports; cost overruns; meeting client expectations; ability to work with people in the company; involvement of key consultant personnel; sensitivity to the company's particular problems, situation and

environment; work style; practicality of recommendations and plans; concern for implementation and evaluation; cost effectiveness of recommendations; thoroughness; analytic and communications abilities; accuracy, creativity and persuasiveness.

g) The firm's objectivity, professionalism and independence; its courage in standing up for what it believes correct, yet its ability to be flexible and explore alternatives; its willingness not to tell management only what it wants to hear.

h) Reasonable costs for the level of effort and skills required.

4. Management cannot abdicate its responsibility to be concerned about the project, involved in it, eager to get timely, periodic reports on progress and problems so that corrective action can be taken, if necessary. Consultant progress and efforts should be monitored and evaluated, yet the consultants must be given sufficient latitude and flexibility to carry out their responsibilities.

5. Management has the responsibility to carefully review interim and final reports, question the consultants, ask for additional or back-up material if necessary. If there has been involvement throughout between top management and the consultants, the final report should not be terribly surprising. Depending upon the specific assignment, management must be concerned that various alternatives, risks, and positive and negative consequences have been assessed, a sound implementation plan and plan for dealing with adverse consequences and contingencies have been developed and that a system has been developed for monitoring, evaluation and feedback. A consultant's report must be questioned and understood carefully. The action finally taken, in fact, may be a modification of the consultant's recommendation based upon the experience and judgment of top management or something quite different from what was recommended. Finally, management must be concerned about the cost/benefits and positive and negative consequences of the work performed by the consultant.

The advantage an outside consultant brings is broad and deep experience, expertise and the ability to tackle your problem with objectivity. However, the best people may not be available when you need them; the costs may be considerable; it may take too long for the consultant to understand the real corporate environment, the nuances and traditions; there may be insensitivity to the problems of implementing or living with the consultant's recommendations, etc. It is true that the consulting firm wants to do a fine job in order to live up to and enhance its reputation and because it wishes to be called back for other assignments or gets a good recommendation. However, there are alternatives to outside consulting such as assignment to a particular unit in the company, a task force approach, or setting up and assigning projects to an internal consulting unit.

Internal Consulting Unit

Internal consulting units may not have the expertise, breadth and depth of the outside firms and rarely are they paid the salaries outside consultants earn. There are also possible questions about their independence of judgment and objectivity since their jobs may be at stake. On the other hand, the internal consultants may know the problem and its nuances and the company environment far better than outside consultants, may be more realistic as to what is possible, and will almost always be substantially less expensive on a man-hour basis.

There is sometimes something of an adversary relationship between internal and external consultants. Some companies require an internal consultant to serve on each external engagement. It may be that the internal consultant emerges as a generalist, general practitioner with external consultants used as specialists. While there has been a growth in outside consultant use, there has also been a growth in the development of inside consulting groups (similar to the growth of corporate law departments).

In developing and maintaining an internal consulting unit, the following considerations are important:

1. To maximize its potential the unit must have top management support.
2. It should be carefully introduced into the organization with a clear indication of its scope, authority and responsibility.
3. The mission should be a broad based one. Each organization should determine whether the unit will have the authority to implement its recommendations or to coordinate implementation. Alternatively, other units can implement recommendations, assisted by the consultants, with the internal consultants performing followup evaluation studies.
4. Change and improvement should be the basic orientation of the unit and of the organization in which the unit is formed,

while at the same time, there should be a concern for the impact of change on people and organizations and how change should be introduced.

5. The organizational arrangements are important in achieving success. The head of the internal consulting unit might report to the President or executive vice president, but small units of consultants could report both to division or group heads and to the internal consulting unit head. How the group is organized and to whom it reports will depend on the particular organization. On one hand, there is the necessity for access to the top executives and the clout one has through formal authority as well as access. On the other hand, there is a need for operating management to have a sense of involvement and control over the internal consulting function. Since much, if not most, of the assignments will come from the users, there is the need for a feeling of involvement or authorship of the projects.

6. The staff should consist of highly qualified professionals who keep up-to-date through training and education. Depending upon the scope and size of the unit, various technical skills will be needed by the consultants. In addition to their technical knowledge gained through education, training, operational and consulting experience, they need to have: analytical and creative skills; thoroughness, flexibility and imagination; an open ear, eye and mind; an ability to communicate, listen and reason; an ability to work with and relate to people; a sense of realism and professionalism; a "passion for anonymity"; an understanding of limitations in consulting, an understanding of top management objectives; a high frustration level; an understanding of the impact of consulting studies on people and units.

7. The unit should incorporate good management techniques in its own management in order to enhance its credibility with other units—this would include the various points outlined in regard to use of external consultants. Clients of internal consultants should expect a comparable level of professionalism as they obtain from external consultants. A user should also exercise the same responsibilities as if external consultants were employed.

8. The unit should be evaluated in regard to what it has achieved, at what cost, and how well it has met the objectives of particular studies, top management, users, and its own goals.

COMPUTERS

By this time most organizations have gone beyond the use of computer technology for payroll accounting, clerical and recordkeeping transactions to an extended use of the computer for management information, budgetary planning and decision making processes. In a subsequent chapter we will discuss computer applications in the future. Our concern here is the role of direction in regard to computer facilities and use of computer hardware and software.

It is undeniable that massive computer power, small specialized computers, terminals, small computers at home, software packages, on-line, real-time applications, have been a tremendous resource for firms, large and small. The issue is, are we carefully evaluating the benefits received from the hardware, software, personnel, ancillary equipment, space and maintenance costs involved in installing, operating and maintaining new systems and maintaining and operating existing systems.

Although hardware costs have declined over the years and companies are able to buy, lease or rent significantly better equipment for less dollars than they did five or ten years ago, the combined expenditures for computer centers and systems are normally quite large. Faced with continuing major expenditures and requests for upgraded equipment, more terminals, more and better staff, and improved and new applications, top executives should be concerned about:

1. The need for increased emphasis on requirements reviews as an essential step in determining whether a software system (and hardware system) should be bought, leased, rented, developed internally, or whether a modification of a commercial or existing package should be made. User requirements of a system, the reasons for such requirements and alternative ways of meeting the needs must be developed, analyzed and evaluated. The costs and benefits of the systems proposed must be carefully evaluated.

    It is most important in developing new applications and maintaining present ones that the users and the providers of data processing services communicate openly and frequently with each other. All too often elaborate systems are developed or bought which ignore special needs of users because of lack of communication. The user has to learn to speak to the computer expert and vice versa.

2. Hardware and software measurement systems should be used to insure that the organization's needs are being met in an effective and efficient manner. By installing hardware monitors and software monitoring programs the computer system manager and top executives can determine how well the computer systems are being utilized and managed. Hardware monitors are small, special purpose electronic counting devices attached electrically to the computer. Software monitor programs are loaded into the core memory of the computer. They periodically check the contents of the various registers, thereby providing information on the status of each computer resource. By use of these monitoring devices, productive and idle time of various pieces of equipment can be determined, thereby leading to optimization of the equipment configuration and its usage. This should lead not only to possibilities for cost reduction, but also to cost avoidance. When it appears that capacity is lacking there is a demand for more computer power and programs. However, since capacity is based on the interaction among all pieces of equipment (which vary, sometimes radically, in operating speed and demand), increased capacity can sometimes be achieved by replacing or adding peripheral units rather than investing in a larger computer.

    In determining effectiveness and efficiency of computer use, demand must be carefully analyzed. Thus, through appropriate review, top management should know what applications are being run, at what cost and what priority, and what are the proposed new applications. Management can then determine whether the right priorities have been established and whether the computer use is cost effective. Often computerized reports (as well as traditional reports) get started and keep on going even when the need or use has long since disappeared. A review process of existing and proposed applications can help reduce demand.

3. Chargeback systems to users for their use of computer services can be an effective tool in managing computer resources and ensuring that the date processing operation is self-supporting. Some organizations integrate such systems with the budgetary process in which each user receives an allocation of funds for his budget based on a projection of needs. (If this approach is used, care should be taken to control any transfers of data processing funds by the unit to other categories of expenditure. Such transfers will result in "hard" money being spent

while the costs of the data processing operation may not be re-
covered.) The chargeback system discourages the user from
making unreasonable or excessively costly demands. It encourages the user to demand their money's worth from the data
processing unit in terms of responsiveness, service, effectiveness and efficiency. In fact, it may be wise to allow units to
have the internal computer operation compete with external
providers to assure users that they are getting the most for
their money.
4. Like any other resource, data processing must be evaluated
and managed. Even though computer experts have a jargon
that probably surpasses all other fields of management expertise and have whiz bang equipment, displays, bells and whistles,
as in the case of all other experts, management cannot abdicate
its judgment and evaluation. "GIGO" is a cliche in the data
processing field—Garbage into the computer results in Garbage
out of the computer. Unfortunately, we often overlook this,
and end up regarding the Garbage that went in, as the God
that comes out. System analysts, designers and programmers
sometimes make mistakes or don't understand fully or clearly
the needs and objectives of users and management.

Users and managers must become more knowledgeable about what
date processing systems can and cannot produce and how the expertise of computer people and equipment can be effectively and efficiently utilized. Computer personnel must tune in better to serving
the needs of users and exploring ways in which they can help users
define and articulate their needs and then proceed, working with users, to meet their needs and evaluate results.

DELEGATING

An important aspect of direction is delegating. Proper delegation
allows for work to be done more effectively and efficiently by the
appropriate person, saves time for higher ranking executives so that
they can focus on more critical problems; challenges, develops and
satisfies staff. What gets delegated to whom depends upon the personality, style, self-confidence and confidence in subordinates that the
delegator has and the talent, ambition, personality and style of the
person to whom he delegates.

Some supervisors are afraid to trust subordinates because the supervisors are ultimately held responsible. Some wish to hold on to the things they like or have performed well in the past even though they have advanced and should no longer be personally doing certain tasks. Others don't want to share the glory or have subordinates steal the limelight or look as if they can ease the manager out of his job. If subordinates are carefully selected, trained and motivated, delegation of responsibilities, with commensurate authority, can improve organizational performance, the manager's performance and the subordinate's performance and growth.

It should be noted that if one wishes to have subordinates who can take responsibility and grow, they must have the appropriate opportunities. Delegation provides the opportunity.

MANAGEMENT BY OBJECTIVES

There have been various techniques used as an aid in directing; performance reviews and evaluations, assessments centers, manpower development programs, carefully selected assignments for individuals, etc. One particular technique used widely is MBO (Management by Objectives). MBO is defined by Dale D. McConkey[3] as:

> MBO is a systems approach to managing an organization—any organization. It is not a technique, or just another program, or a narrow area of the process of managing. Above all, it goes far beyond mere budgeting even though it does encompass budgets in one form or another.
>
> First, those accountable for directing the organization determine where they want to take the organization or what they want it to achieve during a particular period (establishing the overall objectives and priorities).
>
> Second, all key managerial, professional and administrative personnel are required, permitted, and encouraged to contribute their maximum efforts to achieving the overall objectives.
>
> Third, the planned achievement (results) of all key personnel is blended and balanced to promote and realize the greater total results for the organization as a whole.
>
> Fourth, a control mechanism is established to monitor progress compared to objectives and feed the results back to those accountable at all levels.

[3] McConkey, Dale D., MBO for Nonprofit Organizations (AMACOM, Division of American Management Associations, New York, 1975) pp 10-11.

In essence, MBO views management as consisting of developing and establishing objectives, directing the accomplishment of those objectives, and measuring results.

The potential advantages of MBO to the manager are well known:

- greater role in determining what is expected of him and the content of his job responsibilities;
- greater latitude in how he manages his unit and more self-control and self-supervision;
- evaluation and reward based on the accomplishments of the agreed upon objectives;
- ability to determine whether additional tasks can be added to the unit as a result of higher management desires, or at least pinpoint the priorities that have to be placed;
- supports a concern for future planning and priority setting, promotes better coordination, communication, appreciation for others' responsibilities;
- assists in management development; and
- results in increased job satisfaction.

MBO can and does work. Often, however, mistakes are made in implementing an MBO system or after a while it may become routine and, thus, lose some of its effectiveness. Successful implementation and continued operation requires:

1. Thorough knowledge of what MBO is and how it works, and thorough briefings for all those involved.
2. Commitment and involvement by top management—MBO should not be delegated to a Personnel Department or Planning Department—it is a pervasive approach and requires support and involvement from the top down.
3. Planned implementation of the MBO system on a reasonable system.
4. Careful determination of priorities and needs.
5. Clarity and fairness in setting and programming objectives—objectives must fit within the needs and style of the organization, be realistic, specific, capable of being evaluated, be carefully planned as to how they will be achieved, be attainable, challenging, important.
6. Avoidance of overemphasis on techniques, procedures and paperwork.

7. A balance between short term and long term objectives.
8. Emphasis on a clear method of periodic review, communication and feedback.
9. A reward structure (salaries, recognition, promotion, job assignments) tied in an appropriate way to performance achieved.
10. Refresher training in the MBO system.

There are both economic and humanistic aspects of MBO. MBO has sometimes been oversold or overemphasized as a goal setting, performance appraisal, compensation program. An undue overemphasis on the economic aspects of MBO can lead to playing games with performance goals, numbers or results in order for the individual to survive economically or in terms of status, or do better in regard to bonuses, promotions, salary increases or competitive status. While performance evaluations and appropriate rewards should be based on performance in regard to objectives, the other aspects of MBO should not be overlooked or downgraded—open communication; concern for employees as people; confidence and trust in people; mutual support and reinforcement; teamwork and team building; periodic reviews and feedback; coaching and counseling.

IN SUMMARY

We have touched on a wide range of topics in directing. Clearly, it is a critical management activity requiring a full knowledge of both the art and science of management.

II

ESSAYS ON MANAGEMENT TOPICS

eleven

The High Achiever's Job Satisfaction— The Learning/Growth Curve*

The high achiever in business frequently finds himself/herself experiencing feelings of restlessness and lack of fulfillment. At a relatively young age, the high achiever has reached the division manager/vice presidential level or above, often in a series of rather quick promotions. Now that he/she is close to the top, and the executive vice presidency or presidency of the firm, if not yet reached, is perhaps a relatively long period of time away, is uncertain or unattainable (or has already been attained), there often are yearnings for something more out of the job or in life. The higher achiever may fall prey to being burned out or turned off and some, in effect, drop out literally from their jobs to seek other pursuits, positions or careers, or figuratively, in escape to alcoholism, broken marriages, affairs, gambling and other distractions and diversions.

The problem, then, for both the individual and the organization is how to keep the high achiever reasonably satisfied and stimulated, and productive at a level at least comparable to his/her past performance.

Motivation and job satisfaction have been of considerable concern to managers at all levels as well as to leading thinkers in the

*This essay was published in *Personnel Administrator*, January, 1981.

field of management.   Practitioners of management have been exposed in one way or another to the concepts of Herzberg, Argyris, Likert who stress man's emphasis on achievement and self-fulfillment, and to the thoughts of Skinner, Whyte, Homan, who stress that human behavior is a pursuit throughout one's life of pleasure and the avoidance of pain, the Benthamite view of motivation reinforced by various experiments. The individuals cited above tend to hold the view that all human beings are essentially alike in their sharing of common satisfactions and needs. There is another group of thinkers such as Bennis, Drucker, Bell and McClelland who see individuals as quite different in their needs and satisfactions. For example, David McClelland divides people into three types—those who stress achievement, those who desire power, those whose purpose is to like and be liked (affiliation). A manager's training and experience has exposed him/her to such concepts as McGregor's Theory X and Theory Y, Herzberg's satisfiers and dissatisfiers, Likert's Systems 1-4 and linking pins, Maslow's hierarchy of needs, management by exception, management by objectives and other concepts. Whether he has followed in whole or in part one or more of the theories or approaches has depended upon the individual manager's philosophy, experience and the environment in which he operates.

Based upon my own experience and anecdotal evidence from numerous discussions with individuals about what gets them interested in a position and keeps them interested, the usual factors that are common knowledge, and frequently discussed in the literature, often crop up. These are: interesting responsibilities, range of responsibilities, challenge, stimulation, impact on the organization, recognition, compensation, status, relationship with superiors and others, ability to innovate, being one's own boss or having one's own time, freedom to act, pace of the organization, quality of the organization and its people.

In addition to the above, I have been able to identify one other, not often discussed, concept. This factor, one of major significance to the ambitious, high achieving, high potential individual, is the importance of the Learning/Growth Curve.

I, therefore, suggest that one of the major factors in job satisfaction for middle and upper level managers is directly related to where they see themselves on the Learning/Growth Curve.

By Learning/Growth, I refer to new or incremental knowledge, skills, perceptions, abilities, attributes, experience. With learning/-

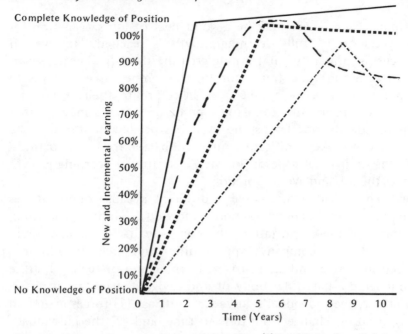

Figure 1   New and Incremental Learning Over Time (% Cumulative Growth in Learning). The line curve indicates how long it takes to reach the approximate 100% mark and the leveling off thereafter.

growth, the individual now knows, is successful at, feels comfortable with (at a more than satisfactory and often outstanding level) that which at some point before he had little or no knowledge of, or was able to do at a lower level of competence or not at all. The new and incremental learning provides a source of growth. The curve indicates the percentage of new learning added to one's abilities in a cumulative fashion up to thoroughly knowing all aspects of the job. The curve indicates that depending upon the person, position, company and environment, the executive may reach the 100% mark or close to it in one to five years. At that point, in most cases, there is no significant new learning, the curve has flattened and the zest may be gone. In fact, the curve may indicate a down turn because boredom, frustration, etc. may cause a decline in the application of one's knowledge and skills. Further, as the high achiever is able to look ahead a year or two or three, he can anticipate a slowing of progress up the curve or reaching the peak. Thus, the ambitious individual begins to think of new challenges within the organization or elsewhere.

Sample curves are drawn on the accompanying chart to indicate that in some situations there is very rapid learning and in others, less rapid. Often, there may be a good deal of job satisfaction for many years after "full" learning/growth is reached. However, if the focus is primarily on learning/growth, three-five years seems to be a common time frame for highly competent executives to feel that they are close to the peak in regard to their current responsibilities. From the company's point of view, it may be that the more quickly one learns and even has peaked in learning, the sooner he can make significant contributions and for longer periods. From the individual's point of view, continued learning/growth enhances the job and avoids boredom.

For each individual the curve is different because opportunities for learning vary depending upon individual abilities, position, the climate in the organization, the company itself, outside forces impacting on the company, opportunities and luck. In addition, each person's pace and standards of learning and of feeling that he has conquered a particular body of knowledge or new task is different. Further, the individual's curve can shift as: (1) forces in and on the organization change from time to time, and (2) the individual's needs, goals and opportunities undergo change.

The sense of newly acquired (or significant advancement of existing) knowledge, skills, accomplishments carries with it a feeling of excitement and exhilaration, of climbing a high often jagged peak and reaching the top. Many executives strive for that feeling, and the sense of accomplishment is indeed great. The feeling of exhilaration need not be felt every day, week or month, but for many, it is of considerable importance to perceive that they are on the climb up that mountain.

In an effort to gain physical and/or mental fitness and achieve accomplishments in areas different from normal activities, executives engage in a variety of sports and activities. The wilderness survival experience, jogging, squash, racquetball, tennis, golf, camping and a variety of hobbies and community activities fill very important needs. Accomplishment in these pursuits results in a glow of achievement, a sense of pride and exhilaration. The same can be true of learning, knowing and demonstrating new understanding, skills and abilities on the job. Once the mountain top of new knowledge has been reached, or having reached a plateau on the mountain, the high achiever will be exhilarated by reaching new plateaus or climbing new mountains. The plateaus or mountains may be more difficult, or even the same or lesser difficulty. Although there is a natural desire for the highly talented to desire to do something more difficult in the next climb, for most talented individuals, another climb (and certainly climbing higher) is sufficient to keep one happy and feeling that he is still ascending the curve.

It should be noted that usually the individual hopes that his own sense of ascending the learning/growth curve is recognized by others and that he receives appropriate attention and rewards in regard to his achievements. It is similar to the graduate student who believes he has mastered a difficult course and is capable of doing "A" work, but he needs the opportunity to demonstrate his ability—the test, research paper, case study, class presentation. After demonstrating his ability he wants someone in authority to evaluate what he has done and reward it appropriately. The Learning-/Growth Curve, therefore, is important to both the organization and the individual. The organization will have to focus on how it structures positions, responsibilities and communications; job enrichment and enlargement; reward and recognition systems and other actions indicated in this article. Recognition or applause, monetary as well as psychic income, is important to the high achiever. Many high achievers have a good sytem of self or internal applause (reality rather than ego based) and so they don't need an enormous amount of recognition. But most individuals cannot live with internal applause alone. They seek and need recognition from subordinates, peers and supervisors in their unit and company and sometimes even beyond to the industry, community, state, region or nation.

The issue then for individuals and for top management is how to keep the highly capable individuals on that learning curve at a slope and speed of ascent that meets both the needs of the talented individuals and of the organization.

Sometimes there may be an incompatible match. Someone may strive (assuming valid talent) to climb too fast—others in the organization may not tolerate it and the organization itself may not be able to accommodate it. And, at times, the executive might have an unfounded belief in what he/she is able to do and, thus, in reality, be unqualified for greater opportunities at this point in his/her career.

Whether we call it planning, human resource management, organizational development, or the need to fulfill the individual's various needs, management should focus on the learning/growth curve issue. This will involve careful matching of the individual's skills, goals, interests and concern for growth with the needs and opportunities in the organization (and in a static or declining organization this will be very difficult to do).

Possible approaches to putting one on the learning curve with a sense of accomplishment and still a long way to go include:

1. breadth and depth of assignments,
2. types of assignments,
3. scope of responsibilities,
4. special project assignments,
5. mobility assignments between and among staff and line functions and units,
6. ability to undertake supervisory responsibilities, staff, line, planning responsibilities; variety in assignments
7. new knowledge acquired through education, training, seminars, conferences
8. exposure to public and community activities, speaking and writing opportunities
9. opportunities to serve on and lead inter and intra-departmental committees or task forces, inter-organization, and industrywide activities, committees and task forces
10. opportunities for short or long term travel or relocation
11. part-time or full-time public or community service assignments
12. exposure in some depth with some hands-on experience to newest techniques and technology in fields of one's primary responsibilities and interests as well as in allied or related fields, or in potential areas of responsibility—this can range from product development to human relations to operations research, computer technology, etc.

Before hiring an outsider the organization might look to enrich the individual's present position by adding significant new responsibilities and scope to his current assignments. Opportunities for such action come about in the event of retirements, position vacancies, acquisitions, mergers, formation of new units, need to supervise new functions or activities. Totally unrelated functions should not be grouped under the same individual. However, by stretching things a bit, by regrouping and/or renaming a position, the individual can be given a real growth/learning, additional compensation opportunity. This will maintain his zest and interest and possibly save the organization some money that would have been paid to an outsider. The individual will then be able to break out of the box of present responsibilities and thereby enlarge his field of interest and continue to advance up the curve or start on a new curve. I suggest that the importance of the learning curve negates the old proverb "You can't teach an old dog new tricks." The point is that for the highly talented, creative and ambitious, at whatever age, one wants to enlarge his or her bag of tricks and learn new ones, in other words—to climb new mountains.

In my view then, both the organization and the individual should be asking: (1) What have I (has he/she) accomplished this year that is significantly better, different, or newer than last year? (2) Do these accomplishments demonstrate significant learning and growth in my (his/her) ability to deal with this and related areas, problems or issues and indicate a solid base for further learning and skills?

From time to time, the individual should take stock of where he has been, where he is and where he is going and growing. Years of experience of performing essentially the same tasks at the same level of difficulty, and applying knowledge or learning acquired in the first year or two is often found to be frustrating and stultifying for some or many of those of most value to the organization. The individual is likely to give up and coast (though he/she may still be of great value), get frustrated and not do anything beyond the routine. This in turn may have a negative impact on his staff and on their performance. But "trapped" by a high salary, good environment and status, and good general quality of life, he may elect or be forced to stay put. Or he may leave to seek opportunities and the zest and excitement of once again climbing the learning curve and the organization may thereby lose the dollars and time invested in a good executive and the potential high payoffs he/she had to offer. Even if he/she stays but with enthusiasm diluted or killed, the organization has lost a good deal. The three to five year itch that many capable executives demonstrate in changing from one organization to another is due in part to the flattening or even dipping of the curve. The goals for the talented individual often is "at least 95% of my brain cells going at least 95% of the time, my abilities being taxed to the utmost as often as possible, and my knowledge and abilities growing from year to year." However, once the curve has flattened, the individual is forced to settle or seek new opportunities, and most often, these are found outside his current organization.

Organizations are becoming increasingly aware of the high cost of recruitment of executives (including relocation costs, executive search services, bonuses and "upfront monies", etc.) and the high investment in new executives in their early years. Return on investment ratios for many executives become more attractive only after several years of good performance. Further, the demographics of the American population suggest relatively few senior executives positions. The retention of the best people in the company, therefore, is an economic, operational and demographic imperative. The philosophy, system, practice and track record in regard to learning/growth opportunities in an organization cannot be achieved quickly or under the gun of a particularly valued individual indicating that he/she is about to leave. It is important and prudent for companies to begin to develop ways and means to meet the learning/growth problems discussed above, to implement them, to evaluate their effectiveness and to modify their practices as necessary.

The organization that fails to deal with the learning/growth curve problem is failing to maximize the effectiveness and contribution of its most precious resource—the very talented individual. That individual, in turn, who does not look objectively at his/her needs in regard to the learning/growth curve, where he is on it and where it extends to, may well end up finding himself/herself feeling trapped and unfulfilled.

twelve

Executive Job Satisfaction

POSITION CONTENT, CONTEXT, CHALLENGE AND COMPENSATION

Outstanding talent is a scarce and expensive resource in all organizations. The competition for new and experienced executive talent is fierce. Newly minted outstanding MBA recipients from the top Business Schools can expect to start at $25,000-$40,000 and if they join major consulting firms, they can expect $30,000-$45,000. For those executives with an excellent track record, search firms are likely to indicate possibilities having 33-100% increases in compensation.

After the firm's and the individual's ego have been massaged and gratified by the pursuit and mating dance of a first or new position, the important question for the organization and the individual is what keeps an executive interested and productive on the job and content to stay with the organization. The same question can be asked in terms of what makes an executive choose to accept one position rather than another.

The major components of job satisfaction are: position content, the context or environment in which the executive will operate, the challenge offered by the position, and finally, the compensation received currently and the compensation expected in the short and long term.

Depending upon an individual's own values and needs, minor or major concern or dissatisfaction in one or more of the four criteria can lead him to look for another position, be receptive to feelers about changing jobs, or when job hunting, have him accept one job over another. For some, dissatisfaction only comes about if their grade for a criterion is a B– or worse, and they may need four B– grades in order to turn down a job or leave their current one. For some, even one B+ with the others all A or A– would lead to job dissatisfaction. For others, it would involve averaging the grades and assigning weights to the various categories with anything below (depending upon the individual) a C, C+, B or B+ average leading to serious discontent.

Some tell-tale signs of dissatisfaction, though often not recognized by individuals, and sometimes not recognized by their supervisors are:

- Boredom
- Frequent headaches or heartburn or rashes or ailments of various kinds that linger
- Increased use of sick leave
- Best part of the day is lunch
- Looking at your watch frequently to see how close it is to quitting time
- It's harder to get up in the morning than it used to be
- The Thank God It's Friday feeling comes more and more often—in fact, it becomes a Thank God It's Thursday, then Thank God It's Wednesday
- Hard to go to work on Mondays; start getting headaches or depressed or irritable Sunday evening
- More fights with people on the job or off
- Lethargic during off-times or hyperactive
- Manic depressive feelings in terms of work or life
- Don't have anything to say about your work
- Focus on good feelings, people liking each other, but overlook concrete achievements
- Spending more time, but accomplishing the same or less as you used to
- Spending less time at work
- Hate to come back from a vacation, or keep looking forward to vacations and keep counting the days
- Don't have a sense of wanting to accomplish anything important next week, next month, next 6 months or year—or as you look back, it doesn't seem important
- Feeling that a great percentage of what you do is trivial, can be done by someone else one, two or three levels below you

- As you look closely at what you do, it seems like busy work, too much attention to detail, being too finicky, sending things back to get them perfect, scheduling too many unnecessary meetings, prolonging conversations or meetings unnecessarily
- Measure the success of a day, week or month by nothing went wrong, rather than what went right

The individual can apply the following content, context, challenge and compensation factors to gauge current satisfaction (and check the tell-tale signs) or in deciding among alternative choices and offers. The company working to improve its executive recruiting, retention, and performance should also take these factors into account in structuring, organizing, enlarging and enriching positions, and in its training, advancement, evaluation, communication and compensation policies and practices.

CONTENT OF THE POSITION

The day-to-day activities of the position, what is to be done and how it is to be done are included here. What are the short and long range objectives, goals, tasks, plans and opportunities? How do the activities and objectives relate to, utilize and optimize the individual's skills, abilities, interests, experience, education and training?

Is this the type of position that one would like to hold for a number of years, that trains, gives you the credentials and positions you for further advancement? What is the status of the position, the power in the position, the ego gratification and self-actualization realizable immediately, short and long term?

How much trivial work or activity is involved in the position? How much time and effort will be taken up by tasks that involve skills and activities the executive regards as unappealing because he believes: (1) they are beneath his knowledge, experience and position level; (2) they are not interesting? (3) he is not particularly good at them or he just does not have the necessary skills and is unable or unwilling to learn them?

CONTEXT OF THE POSITION

How do your personality, management style, technical and managerial skills mesh with supervisors, peers, subordinates and others in

the organization and the organization's history, traditions and probable future? What is the leadership style of the organization? What
are the physical and psychological working conditions in the unit and
the organization? What is the climate, tone and mood of the unit, the
organization and the industry? What challenges does the organization
face? What is its reputation? How is the organization doing financially
and competitively? What does the short and long term future seem to
hold for the organization? What is the prestige, reputation and past
history of the position and the particular unit in the organization and
in the field—what does the future seem to hold? What resources are
available to you, directly and indirectly? What is your freedom to
change things? What is the "chemistry" between you and your superior and his superior—between you and those you will work with as
colleagues, peers and subordinates? What is the level of competency,
performance, motivation, drive and creativity of supervisors, peers
and subordinates? How high are the standards of performance and
how are they being met? Why is there a vacancy? Why are they interested in you? What job security is offered, e.g., a tight employment
contract? How and under what criteria will you be evaluated?

CHALLENGE OF THE POSITION

The evaluation of the challenge depends upon the position. Individuals at different levels will evaluate challenges differently. Some of
the evaluation differences will be based on individual differences—age,
personality, ambition, experience, etc. Does the position provide the
opportunity to make a significant difference to the success of the
unit or the organization as a whole, immediately, short term or long
term? Is there enough in the content and context of the position to
keep one's brain cells and energy cells going at full power both short
and long term? Is there enough to keep one's ambition, drive, fire in
the belly going at full blast? Are the problems real, tough, exciting,
and do they provide a sense of accomplishment, self-fulfillment and
self-actualization? Is there a sense of full utilization of particular
skills, interests and abilities? Does the position provide the opportunity to grow, to learn, to expand, to be visible, to be respected and rewarded? Does the position meet one's personal and family life style
and aspirations? Do the demands of the position conflict with how and
where one wants to live? What is the psychic income of the position?

COMPENSATION

What are the compensation arrangements for the position and how does it compare with similar levels in the organization, in the field, and with those who, for whatever reasons, the individual compares himself? How well does the package offered meet your particular concerns for disposable income, base salary, bonus, deferred compensation, fringe benefits package, stock options, time off, entertainment allowance and travel, various types of "perks," pension, insurance, early retirement.

How will relocation be handled (taking into account mortgate rates, costs of moving and buying and setting up a new home, tax differences, income tax, real estate, school tax, guaranteeing the sale of present home, need for private schools for children, differences in cost of living, availability in the company or in the new location of a position for one's spouse)? What are reasonable compensation expectations for the short and long term, assuming good or outstanding performance?

SUMMARY

Not every question in each category need apply nor will every answer be completely satisfactory. However, when making the critical and tough decision involved in choosing a new position or deciding to remain at his present one, the executive must take the factors outlined into account. He must carefully consider the facts as he knows them, as well as the perceptions and gut feeling he has about the position and the organization. Careful probing, thorough analysis, and objective introspection in regard to the organization and his own abilities, attributes, desires, needs and goals, immediately, short and long term will result in a solid and sound basis for reaching a most important decision.

thirteen

Evaluating Executive Perfomance :
Some Criteria for Judging Others
and Yourself

A boy about 16 telephoned a supermarket manager and asked whether there was a part-time stock clerk position available. The manager replied that it had been filled about three months ago. The boy asked "Is your present stock clerk hardworking, dependable, honest, does he show initiative, potential, follow instructions, accomplish results, get along well with people." The manager responded affirmatively to all the questions but was so impressed by them that he told the caller that another stock clerk position would be open soon and asked whether he wanted the job. The caller responded, "No thanks, I already have the job as your part-time stock clerk, I was calling just to find out how I was doing."

Moral: Evaluation and communication are important.

In an era of increasing concern for productivity and performance, many organizations are spending (or should be spending) a considerable amount of effort and money on developing and administering methods to evaluate the performance of their executives at all levels, junior executive, middle management and top management.

A thorough serious effort at performance evaluation and potential

*This essay was published by Braniff Airlines in-flight magazine *Flying Colors* in August 1979 and is reprinted through the courtesy of Halsey Publishing Co., publishers of Braniff's *Flying Colors* magazine.

assessment is difficult and it says as much about the evaluation and the organization as it does about the individual being evaluated.

Various techniques, quantitative and qualitative methods can be utilized. Some of these include: weighting factors; specific criteria for evaluation; ranking individuals in comparison with others; scoring by numbers, grades, choice of words, descriptive sentences written about performance, percentile ranking compared with similar positions, scoring on a curve, deviations from the normal; management by objectives; bottom line approaches; managerial grid; transactional analysis techniques, written justifications necessary for evaluation above or below average; self evaluations, evaluations by peers, superiors, subordinates or a combination of two or more of these; oral evaluations, written evaluations; annual, semi-annual, quarterly evaluations or at the end of specific projects. In addition, many systems include indications of particular contributions, accomplishments, strengths, weaknesses, specific ways in which an individual can improve or how a supervisor can help the individual improve.

In developing a new system or revising an existing one (and every system should be reviewed after several years), some general guidelines may be helpful.

I.   The evaluation technique, instrument, process and style should be responsive and suited to the needs and style of the particular organization. Much can be learned from "off the shelf" techniques or what is used in similar organizations. But, just as it is unwise to blindly copy a successful company's or textbook's organization chart, its evaluation system should not be transferred without thorough review and modification as necessary.

2.   The company should be clear as to what it hopes to achieve with an evaluation—it may want executives to understand better the strengths and weaknesses of their performance and to make improvements in their performance, to aid supervisors in identifying persons who should be considered for development and promotional opportunities; to provide supervisors with information in order to determine compensation increases; to measure commitment to equal opportunity/affirmative action. All, some or one of these goals may be the sole or paramount concern in developing a system and depending upon the objectives chosen, the form and process may be different.

3. To be successful, the system finally adopted (and a careful, thorough process should be used before adoption) must have the enthusiastic support of top management and levels below it.

4. To achieve credibility, it is wise that those affected—evaluators and evaluated—be involved in developing and assessing the evaluation system.

5. The individual who was evaluated should receive a written copy of the evaluation, should have an opportunity to discuss it fully with the evaluator, and should have the opportunity to respond in writing. The evaluation and the response should become part of the individual's personnel file.

6. At least at some levels, the evaluator's supervisor should go over the evaluations with the evaluator prior to submission to those evaluated. The supervisor may also wish to see any written responses and then discuss those with the evaluator. At times, the supervisor may want to add his written comments to the evaluation form and sign the form indicating that he/she has read the form and the response.

7. To indicate the importance of a careful application of the evaluation system, one of the criteria used by higher executives in judging subordinates should be their efforts at evaluating their subordinates (including working on improving performance as a result of the evaluation).

8. Those who do well (and those who do poorly) on the evaluation(s) should see some results in terms of compensation, promotional or assignment opportunities, job enrichment, training opportunities, or their future in the company.

9. As far as possible, there should be consistency in applying the process and criteria; high standards of evaluation should be set. It is recognized that some criteria may not be applicable or may need to be different for different units in the organization, e.g., the research and development department versus the sales department. The techniques may vary a bit depending upon level or unit. However, in fairness to all, the system should encourage uniformity and consistency in evaluation criteria particularly when salary increases depend upon one's score versus the scores of others. It must be recognized that there will certainly be differences among evaluators. "Grade inflation" extends not only to the "Gentlemen C" in

college that is now a "B," but also extends to how we evaluate in business. Thorough evaluation is difficult, time consumung and often stressful. It's so much easier to just run down a column marked excellent or outstanding and check every box rather than trying to exercise judgment and differentiate among abilities the individual has and among individuals. Aside from ease and speed, one is saved from hurting someone's feelings or having to explain it to the individual being rated, your superior, the personnel director and perhaps an outside investigator in regard to an equal opportunity—affirmative action complaint. The system should demand high standards and monitor evaluation practices. At the same time, it should provide a way of taking into account unnecessarily 'hard graders" or "easy graders" so that the individual evaluated is not particularly helped or hurt.

10. To insure all of the above, a successful system needs constant monitoring, concern and support. And like all other systems and processes in an organization, at regular intervals the evaluation system itself should be evaluated and modified to meet changing times and needs.

The broad goal in developing an evaluation system is to assess and then communicate the evaluator's judgment about the individual's performance. If the process works right, this can be built upon so that the supervisor gets information about how he can help or improve in helping the subordinate to perform better in the future. An important part of the evaluation is for both parties to work out why, how, when and where improvements can be made during the next and subsequent rating periods and how they can be measured and evaluated. This may involve specific actions such as setting objectives and goals, describing training programs or educational courses, different assignments, etc. The evaluation process should, of course, focus on what has happened during the past rating period (and evaluations should be timely), but it should also focus on the present and short and long term. By indicating on the form and after discussions various ways of improving performance, the evaluator and the evaluated are making a mutual commitment.

Suggested below are some criteria that can be used to evaluate executives at all levels. In fact, the reader may choose to do a self-assessment to see (hopefully objectively and with high standards) how he or she measures up and to identify areas needing further emphasis, concentration, development, training, or experience. Not all the criteria can be applied to every position or unit, some may seem to be similar to others, a few could be divided into separate criteria, but in one way or another, many of these criteria have been found to be very useful benchmarks for evaluation.

I. SKILLS, ABILITIES AND ACCOMPLISHMENTS

1. Puts forth hard, sustained full effort—accuracy—thoroughness
2. Professional/technical skills
3. Results achieved
4. Performance compared to goals
5. Planning abilities—immediate, short and long term
6. Organizational abilities
7. Coordination abilities
8. Allocation of resources
9. Budget planning and control—overruns, underruns
10. Communications abilities—upward, downward, lateral, internal, external, oral, written
11. Decision-making skills—makes timely well thought out decisions
12. Implementation abilities
13. Management skills
14. Supervisory skills
15. Analytical skills
16. Quantitative skills
17. Research skills
18. Effectiveness
19. Efficiency
20. Skills in recruiting staff
21. Ability to delegate
22. Innovative/creative abilities
23. Productivity improvements
24. Cost/savings improvements
25. Income generating improvements
26. Quality of personal work
27. Quantity of personal work
28. Quality of unit's work
29. Quantity of unit's work
30. Meets priorities and deadlines (sets them for self and unit)
31. Sets high performance standards for self and meets them
32. Sets high performance standards for subordinates and motivates them to achieve goals
33. Evaluates issues from a broad as well as specific perspective

34. Management of personal time

35. Reporting/briefing supervisor and others on problems, actions taken or to be taken

36. Other activities—successful involvement in committees, assignments, issues not necessarily limited to one's primary responsibilities

37. Abilities in regard to public/community/governmental/industry relations

38. Keeps on top of developments in field, organization, industry

39. Progress over last rating period

40. Potential for advancement, new challenges

II. ATTRIBUTES AND TRAITS

1. Self-confidence

2. Handles stress/pressures/frustrations well

3. Ability to influence/inspire/motivate

4. Aggressiveness

5. Ambition

6. Contentment/satisfaction with oneself, position, unit, organization, life, without being complacent

7. Maturity in judgment, action, style

8. Congeniality/convivality

9. Integrity/honesty/ethics

10. Persuasiveness

11. Courage in making decisions, taking action, sticking one's neck out

12. Decisiveness

13. General attitude—cooperative, team spirit

14. Enthusiasm/zest

15. Appearance/mannerisms/habits

16. Vigor/vitality/stamina

17. Articulate

18. Desire for responsibility

19. Concern for results

20. Concern for people

21. Intelligence

22. Action-oriented

23. Dedication/commitment/loyalty to position, organization, superiors, peers, subordinates

24. Flexibility in thinking and action

25. Social skills—adapts to social situations, people—good

representative of organization

26. Able to work harmoniously with others

27. Dependable—diligence, consistency takes on added work and tough tasks

28. Able to relate to peers and high officials—internally and externally

29. Seeks to expand knowledge, responsibilities, skills

30. Commitment to equal opportunities/affirmative action.

CONCLUSION

Evaluation is a major management responsibility. A good evaluation system takes considerable time and effort to develop, implement and operate, but it has very significant benefits for the individuals involved and for the organization.

fourteen

Time and Stress Management

Two of the most popular current topics among executives is how to deal with stress and how to manage your time. Many seminars, workshops, books, pamphlets and columns are offered to help the executive overcome problems in these areas. In this brief essay I shall attempt to summarize the current thinking in each area.

STRESS

Concern about stress on the job in a personal sense, and also as part of one's responsibilities as a manager, is of increasing importance. Stress can also have some major cost implications since about 15 states, following court decisions, now make disability payments where work stress has caused depression, severe anxiety or other mental problems. Courts in six states have ruled that stress accumulated gradually on the job which leads to emotional illness also qualifies for awards.

Some types of personalities and job situations are more prone to stress. Generally, the most stress producing factors in the work situation are: work and time pressures, the gap between an individual's personal and professional objectives and the requirements and objectives of the organization, the managerial and "political" climate of the organization, uncertainty about how one's performance is being evaluated. Stress off the job may involve unusual events such as death of a spouse, parent, child or others close to the individual, divorce or separation but most often it involves everyday happenings, financial worries, problems with spouse and children, illness, vacations, change in residence, changing jobs.

It is important to note that despite the large number of articles and discussions about stress, most people handle it rather well and that the amount of stress on the job on a continuous basis is not that great. Stress, within reason, can be helpful in bringing forth personal growth, creativity, performance and teamwork. But a steady and increasing diet of stress can indeed be harmful. Some symptoms of stress are: headaches, backaches, muscle tension, diarrhea, nausea, difficulty falling asleep, drug or alcohol abuse and nervous habits.

DEALING WITH PERSONAL STRESS

Here is a list of ways to deal with stress:

1. Analyze the stressful situations you face and decide what is important to worry about and what is not. Delegating work to subordinates and setting priorities to meet important objectives are ways to alleviate stress.
2. Decide whether the company culture and environment is one you wish to work in. A highly charged, emotional and performance atmosphere may be one that is unsuited for you.
3. Develop, if possible, a work pace that minimizes physical, mental and emotional fatigue. Try to have variety in topics, pace, tempo, challenges on the job.
4. Achieve a balance between work, relaxation and play, a balance between the office and home and outside interests, involvements, activities and hobbies.
5. Develop a program of regular exercise and relaxation and recreation activities.
6. Use lunch breaks, when possible, as a time to refresh yourself by non-problem or non-business conversations and contacts.
7. Use some type of relaxation exercise two or three times during the work day. This might involve a quiet setting, a

comfortable position, a breathing routine (e.g. breathe easily through the nose, filling the stomach with each breathe and exhale somewhat longer than the time spent inhaling), keep your eyes closed and think of yourself as jello or as a puddle on the floor. You might do this for about five minutes, gradually open your eyes, and then remain relaxed for a minute or two before beginning activities. Yoga, transcendental meditation, and biofeedback are other useful techniques.

8.   Perhaps once an hour use deep breathing as a natural tranquilizer, take 3 or 4 deep breaths.

THE MANAGER AND STRESS

The manager should be concerned about stress produced in the organization and in his subordinates, whether his style of leadership is increasing stress for others (unrealistic deadlines, overlooking individuals, lack of feedback or praise), whether there is a feeling of security in employment, clear definition of job responsibilities, opportunities for advancement, authority commensurate with responsibility, a sense of joy in the job. Company policies and practices concerning relocation can also be examined since relocation often carries with it high monetary costs for the company and the individual as well as high stress costs for the individual and his family. These costs are often related to monetary costs, but are equally related to the stress involved in changing one's home.

Top leadership provides a role model for coping with stress and for indicating recognition of its existence. Programs and information about stress can be provided to the staff, exercise programs and gymnasium facilities at the work location can be encouraged, regular medical check-ups, job counseling and "relaxation-response breaks" can be instituted.

TIME MANAGEMENT

Before discussing what time is wasted on and how to attack the time wasters, it is interesting to note the findings of an American

Management Association Survey Report, *Executive Time Management*, written by Dr. Philip Marvin of the University of Cincinnati and published in 1980. Dr. Marvin surveyed 1,369 managers, about 40% of whom were chief executive officers or vice presidents. He found that only 47% of their time was spent on managerial activities, 31% in a specialist/technologist role, 16% in mentor activities, and 6% in other activities. In terms of time spent in managerial activities, the following list indicates the division of time as an average of all respondents: (It should be noted as indicated elsewhere in the book that Mintzberg and others would question the validity of using the traditional categories listed below.)

Decision-making	19%
Planning	19%
Organizing	13%
Implementing	13%
Delegating	12%
Evaluating	12%
Controlling	12%
Innovating	10%
Staffing	7%

Basically, if you are going to improve your use of time you will have to see what you're spending your time on (by keeping a time log) and then deciding what's important, what's not, is the distribution of time correct in categories such as the ones above, how does your managerial and personal style and objectives influence your use of time and what are the things that waste your time.

Various studies have indicated that the most frequent time wasters are:

Telephone—too many calls, calls are long-winded, difficulty placing calls

Meetings—too many, some are unnecessary and ineffective, lasting too long

Visitors—too many unannounced or drop-in visitors

Reading—too many memos, reports, journals to read and handle

Poor Delegation—work not delegated to subordinates appropriately, sometimes spend too much time checking subordinates

Paperwork—deluge of reports, memos, letters

Crises—unexpected problems arise that disrupt schedules (won't be able to eliminate those, except for problems that should have been solved prior to becoming a crisis)

Special Requests—usually come from higher echelons and must be met

Delays—you meet your schedule or are ready to perform but have to wait for others

Procrastination—hesitation in taking action or performing work— you will have to resolve this by taking charge of yourself. You can talk with others about this and use power or persuasion to make improvements.

The time problem can be attacked on an individual and corporate basis. Basic to understanding how to make an improvement in time management is to remember that the goal is not time "saving" per se but rather reallocating hours for more important tasks. This involves understanding what is important and what is not. Further, it is helpful if a company-wide concern and training in time management is instituted. In this way, bosses, peers, subordinates can reinforce each other in utilizing time. Finally, it should be remembered that time management training takes time. Involved are: briefings as to what is to be done, time log preparation and problem analysis, an in-depth workshop, follow-up and evaluation after two-three months. It will also take time to see results, because habits are not changed easily or quickly, feedback and review are necessary.

GENERAL TIPS ON TIME SAVING

1. Try to eliminate as much work as possible, both for you and your subordinates. Delegation is helpful, but you may just be passing on unnecessary work to someone else.

2. Be clear about your job objectives and results expected. This will help shape your decision about what's important, what you should be doing and how you should allocate your time.

3. Try to take control of your time by scheduling about 50-60% of your time (including thinking and planning time) and leaving the rest for interruptions, crises, responses to the needs and demands of others.

4. Analyze, through time logs or time work sheets, activities: that you are spending too much or too little time on; that do not need to be done at all or that can be done more effectively or efficiently by others; that lend themselves to significant

savings; in which you can help others save time. Establish
goals for yourself, adjust and allocate your time, evaluate
the results.

SPECIFIC WAYS TO SAVE TIME

We shall focus on some major time wasters which you have some
direct power to correct quickly.

Telephone

Have your secretary screen calls and refer them, where appropriate,
to other persons or answer some questions herself, try to avoid interruptions by setting aside a set time to return all incoming calls (some
calls you will have to answer immediately) and perhaps even a time
when you will place calls. Try to work with your subordinates and
colleagues to have notes on what information they want to convey
in a telephone call or problem or action they wish resolved so that
calls are not unnecessarily long and meandering. One can be polite
and friendly and still be short winded in telephone conversations.
The important thing in handling calls (and unscheduled visitors)
is to improve the quality of your time by eliminating interruptions
which break your train of thought and momentum. There can be
agreement among managers who interact frequently with each other
not to place calls during a set period each day.

Meetings

A great deal of time can be saved by eliminating unnecessary meetings, cutting down on the frequency and length of meetings and
number of key people and staff people attending meetings. Each
regular and special meeting and committee should be carefully evaluated as to purpose, results to be gained, risks or loss if the meeting
wasn't held initially or held again, who must be present, who should
be present, who might it be good to have present (the "should"
and "nice" to be present persons might be eliminated or be present
only a portion of the time), how frequently must meetings be held.
Depending upon the meeting, a set agenda should be circulated

well in advance. Work papers and other materials to be discussed should be provided well in advance of the meeting with responses to any questions that may arise about the material prior to the meeting so that time is not taken up answering minor questions (if there seems to be a broad question, the chairman can mention the question and the answer at the meeting). The chairman or convenor should be alert to ways to keep on schedule and reduce unnecessary digressions. It is generally valuable to have a set time by which the meeting will start and end. Sometimes the importance of the discussion will cause an extension of the meeting, but this should happen rarely if there has been good estimating of the time needed, necessary preparation has gone on prior to meeting, and the meeting is well run. There is very little excuse for meetings failing to start exactly on time with everyone present. (A delay of a meeting of ten top executives for ten minutes because eight are waiting for two, ends up in a potential of hundreds of dollars lost in 100 man-minute delay to start the meeting.)

Delegation

This can be improved through concentrating on what's important and who has to do what. Your fundamental style may have to be changed. Of course, the subordinate must be qualified, understand his responsibilities and have the necessary resources to carry them out and the manager must be secure enough about himself and the subordinate to delegate appropriately.

Visitors

There will always be some interruptions that will occur, a higher executive may drop in, a crisis involving a colleague or subordinate may arise, etc. However, a good secretary can screen most of the un-scheduled visitors and handle their problems, refer them, or schedule an appointment.

You can also indicate to colleagues and subordinates that unless an emergency arises you would prefer a scheduled appointment or a telephone call. The point here is that you won't necessarily save much time in dealing with the visitor and telephone problem but you can save fragmenting your time and interrupting your work flow.

Scheduling

Before scheduling anyone or a meeting, your secretary should
have received general guidelines from you as to who or what issues
to schedule, what non-job related meetings or events you will attend
or which non-essential job functions or social functions to accept.
If in doubt, she should delay accepting an invitation or scheduling
something without checking with you.

Paperwork

Ideally, there should be a company-wide war on paper with the
goal of eliminating unnecessary writing, typing, copying, reading and
filing (a handy wastebasket can be very helpful, instead of the normal tendency to file everything). One can argue that the invention of
copying machines and now faster, cheaper, two sided and color
copying ones, for all their great value, has created the problem of
too many people being copied on too many items of little or marginal importance. The goal should be identifying those reports, memos,
studies, forms, procedures, minutes, etc. that are necessary (they
may have been necessary in the past and just kept flowing in), in
what detail, with what frequency, to be read or used by which individuals. Significant savings can be achieved in this area not only in
time savings by executives but in material costs and in time spent
by secretaries in typing and copying.

On an individual basis, it is worthwhile analyzing what comes in
regularly. You can then determine what: (a) you must see, (b)
would like to see, (c) find some value in seeing but might wish to
receive in a different or more concise form or with less frequency,
(d) do not need to see. My guess is that most individuals can eliminate 10-25% of the paperwork flowing to or from them.

SUMMARY

By following the steps and approach I have suggested, assuming
serious concern, attention and action by individuals and organizations, I believe that most individuals can save between 60-90 minutes

a day. In using this time for more important aspects of one's job and for thinking and planning, we can improve productivity, performance and job satisfaction of a very important corporate resource, the managerial group.

fifteen

Preparing for Executive Position Interviews: Questions You Might Ask or Be Asked*

Through hard effort, a proven track record, initiative and/or luck you have been able to arrange to be interviewed for a middle or upper level executive position. This article seeks to help you prepare for a very important 60-120 minutes in your career by looking at both sides of the desk, table or couch. It suggests interviewers' questions, some typical, some tough, that you should be prepared to answer as well as some questions the candidate should consider asking.[1] One cannot anticipate all questions, but having at least prepared yourself, you're less likely to be caught off guard by initial or follow-up questions by the interviewer. Further, frequently an interviewer allows time for the candidate to ask questions by saying, "Can I answer any questions for you?" The goal of the candidate, assuming he/she is not desperate for this or any job, is to ask questions that will help him/her decide whether this is the right job and, at the same time, impress the interviewer with one's perceptiveness, clarity of thinking, analytical ability, high standards of performance and aspirations.[2]

---

*This essay was published by *Personnel* in September 1980 in slightly different form.
[1] Interviewers should find the questions listed helpful to them in preparing for interviews.
[2] No questions regarding compensation are listed based on the assumption that such questions would be asked and resolved at a subsequent meeting if the interview went well.

I. **Questions the Applicant Should Be Prepared to Answer[3]**

1. What are you proudest of in terms of your accomplishments at your present position or former positions?

2. What are you proudest of in terms of personal accomplishments and attributes?

3. What was your schedule or goals for accomplishment at your present position for the next year, for the next two or three years?

4. What would you have liked to accomplish in your present position that you did not accomplish, in whole or in part? What prevented you from accomplishing these things?

5. Why do you want to leave your present position?

6. From what you know about the company and the position, what characteristics and accomplishments should we expect from the individual we hire in the first six months, the first year, the first two years, the first five years?

7. What do you think will be the toughest aspects of the job if you were to accept the position? What will be the most enjoyable aspects—the least enjoyable?

8. What do you think your greatest contribution will be or what aspects of the job or the company do you think you would be able to make your greatest contribution to?

9. What are your personal goals in regard to this job in the next year, five or ten years, and in regard to the rest of your working career?

10. From what you have been able to learn of the company and the position, what do you think are the problems you will face short-term and long-term and how would you deal with them?

11. What problems do you think this organization faces in the next year, in the next two years, in the next five years, and what do you think you can contribute to the identification and/or solution of those problems?

12. How long do you think the challenges of this job will excite and interest you? How do you deal with the problem many executives face that after two to four years on the job, when they have conquered most of the interesting problems or have set in motion a way to conquer them, their enthusiasm wanes? When will you be ready for your next job?

---

[3] It should be noted that some of the questions are more appropriate for upper level executive positions than for middle level positions.

13. Assume we had to have a significant cut in expenditures on the order of ten to twenty percent within a year or two. How would you go about planning and implementing such a cut in the areas of your responsibility?

14. Assume that we expected significant growth in your area of responsibility and ask you to give us a plan in regard to growth opportunities. How would you do that?

15. Assume that the company was going to be merged or bought by another company. In terms of your own area of responsibility and in terms of a company as a whole, as you know it, what kinds of things would you like in the merger agreement and in the administrative operations plan?

16. I assume that at some point you were in head-to-head competition with an individual in your present company for promotion or for status or project managership or something of that type. What would your competitor say about you in terms of your strengths and weaknesses?

17. If you are selected for this position, how would you deal with the situation of individuals in the company who have been competitors for the job for which you are being interviewed and who may feel that they are better qualified? (Some of them may now be your subordinates.)

18. If you were conducting the selection process for this position, what would you have done differently and why?

19. If you were promoted to the next higher position in the company, how would you select your successor and what would you be looking for?

20. What criteria would you use in evaluating your subordinates' performance? How would you conduct an evaluation process? What philosophy and techniques do you use in motivating subordinates and energizing them and, when necessary, in disciplining them? Do you vary your approach for subordinates who are outstanding, good, satisfactory, mediocre? If so, how?

22. What factors are: (a) most important to you personally in job satisfaction? (b) most important to your subordinates in job satisfaction?

23. How would you deal with a subordinate who does not appear to: (a) measure up to increasing demands of the job; (b) whose enthusiasm, motivation and performance seem to be going down; (c) who seems under personal stress or tension?

24. What skills or attributes do you think the following should have: an outstanding subordinate; an outstanding peer; an outstanding supervisor of someone at your level? What skills or attributes do you possess that you think others would regard as being outstanding as compared with other individuals of your rank, experience and accomplishment?

25. How do your spouse and children feel about the change of position and the relocation of your home?

26. What gives you the most satisfaction in using free or vacation time?

27. How do you motivate yourself? How do you deal with stress, tension, boredom?

28. How do you set priorities for your own time? For your subordinates' time?

29. What is your expectation of the social and public relations demands of this job? How do you react to them both in terms of yourself and your family's involvement?

30. What business, community and social organizations do you belong to and why? What business, community and public policy issues interest you and why?

31. If a number of executive training sessions or continuing education sessions or conferences were to be scheduled, what types of sessions would you: (a) care to attend and why? (b) feel competent and interested in serving as a panelist, discussion leader, speaker, or teacher?

32. If you were able to do things differently, from age 18 on, what would you do that is different from what has gone on in your life since age 18?

33. From whom have you learned the most in your management career and why?

34. If you were able to meet with an outstanding management expert for (a) a one-on-one three-hour uninterrupted session and (b) an uninterrupted week or two, what kinds of things would you ask him/her and hope to learn from that experience?

35. Why do you want this job? Why should we hire you?

II.   Questions the Applicant Might Consider Asking

According to Julian Kien, President of the New York human resources management consulting firm of Kien & Associates, Inc.,

"Too many companies, consciously or unconsiously, tend to over-sell the picture and promise of opportunity and challenge. Test the reality aggressively. It reflects your judgment, analytical ability and seriousness about this most important decision."

1. What specific responsibilities of the position do you regard as most important? What are the other responsibilities?
2. What criteria will you use for my performance evaluation and what is the time schedule for performance evaluations?
3. How frequently and in what manner will we meet on a regular basis and how shall we deal with particular problems?
4. How do you like to operate in terms of assignments, delegation of responsibility and authority, general operating style, characteristics that you like in a subordinate, characteristics you don't like?
5. What are the company's goals, your area's goals, your goals for the area I might be in charge of, your personal goals, your superior's goals—short-term and long-term?
6. What short and long-term problems and opportunities do you think exist for: (a) the company, (b) your area, (c) your superior's area?
7. What problems and opportunities do you think my area faces—short-term and long-term? What will I face in the first week, month, 3 months, 6 months, 1 year, 2 years?
8. What do you hope I would accomplish within 3 months, 6 months, 12 months, 3 years, 5 years, 10 years?
9. What are the major frustrations, as you see it, of my job, of your job, of your superior's job, my subordinate's job?
10. What are the major challenges/rewards/stimulations of my job, your job, your superior's job, my subordinate's job?
11. What are the strengths and weaknesses of my subordinates as you see it?
12. What are the responsibilities of my peers (other subordinates to you) and what are their strengths and weaknesses?
13. Whom will I be interacting with most frequently and what are their responsibilities and the nature of our interaction? What are their strengths and weaknesses?
14. What are the limits of my authority and responsibility? What do I have to get your and other people's permission for, inform you or them about after the fact, discuss with you or them prior to action?

15. What freedom do I have to act and what budget is available to me in regard to: (a) changes in staffing, promotion, salary increases; (b) use of consultants, requesting or purchasing software and hardware systems, venture capital for new ideas and approaches, implementing planned growth, implementing planned cutback, (c) changes within my area in regard to policies, procedures, practices, performance expectations?

16. How frequently and on what matters do you interact with your superiors on a regular basis and how are particular problems or crises handled? How would you describe your personal and professional relationship with them?

17. What contact will I have with your superior, his/her superior and others above him/her? And what issues will de discussed?

18. What particular things about my background, experience and style interest you—make you think I'll be sucessful—give you some amount of concern? What experience, training, attributes, operating style, accomplishments, personality factors would the "ideal" candidate for this job have?

19. What opportunities are there for growth in my area of responsibility and advancement in the company, on what kind of timetable?

20. What social requirements are there in regard to the job for me personally and for my spouse and family?

21. What professional, industrial, community or public policy involvement do you feel it necessary for me to have and in what depth?

22. How do you think the company and its top leadership is perceived in the industry and in the local business community and why? What are its perceived strengths and weaknesses?

23. Why did my predecessor leave the position, what were his strengths, weaknesses, accomplishments, failures (or if this is a newly created position, what factors led to the decision that this position should be created)?

24. Why did you come here? Why do you stay?

25. After 6 months, 1 year, 2 years, 5 years—how will you know you made the right decision in hiring the person for this position? If the position were offered, why should I accept it?

Preparing to ask or answer these questions will take a substantial amount of time. But, for both the interviewer and candidate, the questions and the answers are important factors in making the decision to offer or to accept a position of challenge and responsibility.

sixteen

Lifelong Education for Executives and Potential Executives*

The dynamics, complexities, and rapidity of changes in today's business environment require managers to be up to date in their knowledge of managerial concepts and techniques. If we focus on the education that present top managers received as contrasted with business education being offered since their graduation we find very significant differences. A recent survey of 1,708 senior managers in Fortune 500 companies (35% of the respondents were in the Fortune 50's) reported in *Management Review*, July, 1979, indicated an average age of 53, with approximately 18% of the individuals having earned MBA's. If we assume that the average college graduate in that survey earned a baccalaureate degree at age 21-22, and obtained the MBA at 23-24, or perhaps at age 26-28, after having worked awhile, we are talking about individuals who "ended" their "formal" education twenty-five or thirty years ago.

Since the mid-fifties when most of the top managers in business had already graduated, there have been several waves of changes in management education.

1st Wave - Mid-1950s — began stress on rigor, mathematical and analytical approaches. Schools began to add to the business

*This essay was published by Braniff Airlines in-flight magazine *Flying Colors* in October 1979 and is reprinted through the courtesy of Halsey Publishing Co., publishers of Braniff's *Flying Colors* magazine.

faculty mathematicians, operations researchers, statisticians and engineers.

2nd Wave - Mid-1960s — Increased concern for the behavioral/ people-side of management. Business Schools hired as faculty members, psychologists, sociologists, organizational development specialists and even anthropologists.

3rd Wave - Early 1970s — Stress on international business, international marketing and finance with some attempts at exchange programs with foreign universities.

4th Wave - Currently — Stress on ethics (social responsibility issue had been around a long time) with some schools hiring philosophers for their faculty. In addition, stress on the context of business including nonbusiness organizations and professions. Now many schools offer courses, programs and sometimes joint degrees involving business and engineering, business and law, public sector and nonprofit organization management, health care management, fine arts management.

Some other differences:

- Ten to twenty years ago, a typical undergraduate business major would take 80%-90% of his courses in the business college and the business college would frequently have its own English, history and math professors. Today, approximately 50% of the undergraduate curriculum in the better business colleges are outside the business college with a concern for developing a broad perspective in business majors.

- Current textbooks even in traditional areas such as marketing, finance, production assume a knowledge of statistics, calculus, computers, all of which would not have been assumed a decade or two ago.

- As compared with 20-25 years ago, there is much more of a broad, decision-oriented approach as contrasted with the former stress on techniques, technical aspects, tradesman approach. Most MBA programs today assume a broadening experience in earning one's BA or BS and now seek to apply principles, once the student's background knowledge is verified.

- As contrasted with even 10 or 15 years ago and certainly with 25 or more years ago, courses are structured more on a decision-making orientation rather than a technique orientation. They are integration oriented among disciplines and departments rather than oriented to a particular field. They are also oriented toward policy making and the environment in which decisions are made rather than toward a stress on technical analysis.

To sum up, Dean Albert J. Simone, Dean of the University of Cincinnati's College of Business Administration described management education today by stating:

> Managers at all levels have to be increasingly aware of the complex environment in which decisions are made. In the past, concern about the decision-making environment was the exclusive purview of the Chairman, President, Executive Vice President and a few Senior Vice Presidents. At the present time, that concern affects decisions at much lower levels so that there are many levels of managers who must take account of such factors as international aspects of business, ethics, governmental requirements, consumerism, etc. if they are to be effective decision-makers. Today's management education seeks to develop in the student the perception and skills necessary to function in a decision-making, multi-faceted, multi-disciplinary, dynamic and environmentally complex atmosphere.

But all is not quiet in regard to management education. An unusually large number of business school deans in the last three years have retired, resigned or been forced to resign, perhaps an indication of responsiveness to the dynamic nature of management education. Business Schools are undergoing dramatic changes from within. For example, Harvard will begin to provide greater stress on theory and concepts in addition to their long heralded case study emphasis, and the University of Chicago, highly regarded for its theoretical research, now offers "laboratory courses" that send students to local companies to work on actual problems. In addition, and perhaps causing the internal changes, there is mounting criticism from those who employ Business School graduates. The issue is the fine line between theoretical approaches traditionally stressed by academics and the practical and new needs of business. The trend appears to be more "practical" offerings in the curriculum without turning the clock back thirty years in terms of narrow vocationalism.

What is clear is that unless the top executive has kept current through continuing education, his formal education of twenty-five or more years ago has not adequately prepared him for the challenges of today. We, therefore, turn to describing some approaches that an organization might take to develop new managers, and to retrain and refresh middle and upper level managers. Many firms do all or more than what is indicated below. Unfortunately, however, there are still a large number of organizations that do very little, in fact, even though there may be a "management training and development program" in the company.

The first step in creating a sound program is the formulation of a coordinated and communicated training and educational development plan for various levels in the company, with necessary involvement of those concerned. A good plan will be cost effective and will anticipate needs rather than being a reaction to a crisis situation. It will have a very important advantage of playing a major role in developing capable individuals for greater responsibilities (in coordination with progressive position assignments.) The plan is a means of motivating individuals and of indicating company concern about their abilities and growth.

In developing a plan, the company must determine what it needs to have its executives learn or have updated (based on each individual's prior education, training and experience) and what amount of time, effort and cost is required and available. This will depend, obviously, on the nature of the organization and its products or services, the environment in which it operates including a concern for competition and regulation, its current and future needs and challenges, its current and future staffing. Periodically, the plan must be updated to meet changing conditions, times, staffing and needs. This will call for different training approaches and topics of courses.

There should be a plan for the organization as a whole, each unit, each executive and each potential executive. In most executive groups, at the present time, there might be the need for in-depth or refresher training ranging from such relatively simple things as speed reading and time management to computer and operations research, analytical applications and techniques for managers; international marketing; behavioral science knowledge, techniques and skills; motivation and supervision; communications; handling stress; dealing with governmental regulation and consumerism; foreign language and culture training, etc. For those who are identified as potential executives, more basic training in conjunction with college degree programs can be developed.

There are various vehicles for training and development: (1) a training unit and program in the organization or specialized knowledge available from individuals in the organization; (2) outside training organizations or individual consultants or trainers; and (3) a university or college or consortium of colleges and universities. There are costs and benefits to each approach and one exclusive pattern need not be chosen. One or more of the alternative vehicles can be utilized depending upon the skills and knowledge to be gained, the immediacy of need, the level and number of individuals to be trained, the facilities, equipment and time available and required, the costs involved, the results achieved by the particular training vehicle and student reaction.

It should be noted that in addition to formal training and education in a variety of settings—lecture, seminar, case analysis, programmed instruction, etc—there are other means of training and development which improve the individual's capabilities. These include: attendance at conferences, meetings and workshops; involvement in different types of committee and project work—departmental, intra and inter organizational, industry, community, regional, state, national, international; job enrichment; job enlargement; rotational assignments between and among various line and staff assignments including operational, research and development, and planning activities; speaking, writing, training and research assignments.

The vehicles described above are all valuable means of advancing and broadening skill, knowledge, perspective, and providing an understanding of interrelationships within the organization and between the organization and its environment. Of particular importance is the assistance that a university or college, particularly its business school, can give to the company.

Universities and colleges in their desire to be responsive to business and community needs and the income and reputation such service can generate, are more open to suggestions and more flexible in approach than was true years ago. They can offer short- or long-term courses and training sessions, some for academic or continuing education credits, others not for credit. Their courses can be at the company's locations, at a central campus or satellite campus, basically at home through use of programmed instruction, television programs, cassettes or video tapes and even by teaching on commuter buses or trains, or using tapes or cassettes in one's own car. Courses, geared to the level of the participants and tailor-made for the company's needs, can be given early morning, during the day, evenings, weekends, during the Summer or in Summer Alumni Colleges or as vacation and learn programs.

There is more flexibility when certification can be given as to the nature of the course rather than the need to grant academic credits, although special B.A. and M.B.A. programs with academic rigor and integrity exist or can be modified or created.

A sound "Executive Program" can be described as one structured to meet the needs of executives who require a total systems approach to the accounting, finance, human resources, operations and marketing functions as these functions interface with the economic, political, legal, human factors, social and ethical environment. It might consist of the following highlights:

1. Selection of executives either from one company or several companies, industries or sectors of the economy who possess a diversity of experience (the advantage of individuals from more than one company in the classroom is the various differences in perspective and the knowledge "students" get from each other).
2. An emphasis on outstanding lecturers and discussion leaders who are skilled and dynamic teachers and are excellent in their understanding of both theory and practice in terms of the real world of executive decision-making.
3. Emphasis on involvement of students and faculty through discussion.
4. A variety of teaching and discussion methods and settings.
5. A faculty advisor assigned to each participant throughout the program to assist in a variety of ways including helping the executive establish goals and evaluate progress.
6. High standards and a high degree of commitment and involvement, expected of the instructors, the program administrators and the executives.
7. Frequent evaluation and communication, and if necessary, well thought out modification or fine tuning of the program, to meet university, company and individual objectives.

Based on the concept that organizations are systems and that various functions should be treated in the way they affect the systems, an Executive Program of twenty weeks duration, four or six hours per week given in one or two sessions (with or without dinner and appropriate breaks) might consist of:

First Ten Weeks   *Second Ten Weeks*

- Management
    Top management
    perspective
    Time management

- Personal Business Planning for Executives
- Oral and written communications by/for Executives

Management effectiveness
Managing teams
Complex environments
Organizational behavior
Organizational diagnosis
and design
- Marketing
- Operations Management
- Accounting a Manager
Can Use
- Financing
- Labor and Industrial
Relations
- Information Systems
for Executives
Design and effectiveness
Models and techniques
Business forecast for U. S.
and the particular region

- Strategic Planning for all Parts of the System—Short- and Long-term
- The System in International Business Management
- Special Topics for Managers
Political, social, and economic awareness of issues and responsibilities of organizations and their top management, such as: The impact of government attitudes about business and the reaction of top management
Environment and pollution issues
Dealing with inflation
Energy management
Productivity
Limitations and opportunities for top management in the 1980s.
- Analysis and Discussions of some of the Reports prepared by Executives
- Future of the Free Enterprise System in a Capitalistic Society.

Of course, shorter or longer programs could be devised. It should be noted again that in terms of the Executive Program or any program the company is engaged in with a University, the company as well as the University should be concerned about communication and evaluation.

Some special fee arrangements might be negotiated that reduce the company's outlay for usual tuition payment benefits depending upon: 1) the program; 2) the number of participants from the company; 3) whether the courses are given on the company site; or 4) the company's involvement in various logistical and administrative tasks involved in recruiting students, lump sum payment, communication, etc. (all subject to the usual University standards). For potential executives/or those who have not received a baccalaureate degree, a company might explore with a local University or college whether a program geared, in part, to company and student needs, and a special reduced fee, could be obtained. This might be based upon a guarantee of the number of qualified students either in separate classes or intermingled with other students (on site or on campus) and take into account the other factors cited above. Any courses, programs, or students enrolled would naturally have to meet all usual University standards and requirements.

A number of universities and colleges provide life learning credits as they evaluate the knowledge and experience the individual has gained in relation to the equivalent knowledge gained in regular academic courses. Life learning credits are somewhat controversial in the halls of academe because of a concern for academic standards and quality and attempting to insure that credits are given for relevant and related knowledge to that covered in the academic setting. However, if one's life learning is reviewed by faculty, with clear guidelines and appropriate standards, some of the learning obtained through equivalent company courses, self-teaching, practice and experience, college courses taken some years before, etc. can be equivalent to college courses. The credits legitimately granted can be motivational in getting an individual to complete a degree.

The company concerned about keeping its good people current, challenged and contributing to the company's challenges and success can thus offer, in addition to varied position assignments and duties:

- Specific skills, knowledge and perspective courses using various vehicles described and various methods of instruction

- Total or part tuition and book payments that may or may not depend upon: a) grade achieved, b) needs of the company, c) level of the individual, (with or without a commitment as to the time the individual will stay with the company).

- Special arrangements with particular colleges or universities in regard to time and place of teaching, nature and type of courses (with due regard for academic freedom and integrity), fees charges— either for regular academic credit, certificates, continuing education credits or non-credit.

- Time off from work at full pay to attend particular courses or programs full-time.

Lifelong education for executives and advancement toward a learning executive group and a learning society is not a fringe or luxury to be cut back or out when profits decline. It is, rather, a necessity for: achieving the present and future objectives of the organization; maximizing the challenge for, potential and contributions of, the individuals in the organization; and advancing the quality of life in America.

seventeen

Business Internships: Tapping the Skills of Outstanding Students*

In today's highly competitive climate, all organizations are concerned about recruiting the most talented college and university graduates. Although there has been a great increase in the number of students receiving undergraduate and graduate degrees in business and management, there is strong competition for hiring the best among them. There is also strong competition for outstanding graduates trained in the sciences, engineering, computer sciences and other current high-demand disciplines. As a result, business, public sector and not-for-profit organizations mount various types of recruitment and selection strategies and campaigns. The goal is first to identify the best possible applicants in terms of their abilities, interests and potential based upon the organization's present and future needs. Then, those involved must "sell" the position and the company so that the organization's first choices join, and hopefully, remain. The cost of recruitment and selection can be considerable, but it is a vital investment for any organization.

There is a way that a company can get a running start on employing outstanding baccalaureate and advanced degree recipients and do much to insure that its selections have a higher probability

*This essay was published by *Management Review* in January 1981 under a slightly different title.

of success than at present. A Business Internship Program can accomplish the results desired by giving the student, prior to graduation, "hands on" experience in the company, a sense of what the company is really like, how he fits in and what his future might hold. Similarly, the company will have a record of job performance to review prior to making an offer, in addition to interviews, recommendations and college performance. It might also be noted that with a large number of women returning to the labor market after their children are in school or graduated, or women now in business striving for advancement, a similar program can be developed for them. This would tap the talent, motivation and maturity of these women who, while often not trained or experienced in business, might indeed have much to offer.

There are a number of different approaches to utilizing university students prior to their graduation. Generally, student employees are seen as another pair of hands and not given particularly taxing assignments. The usual summer job is an example of this. A better approach to the employment of students is the Cooperative Education Program. This approach, first begun at the University of Cincinnati in 1906 and now in over 1,000 two-year and four-year colleges, has students alternating between going to school full-time and working full-time. Approximately 200,000 U. S. college students and 30,000 companies are involved in such programs. For example, at the University of Cincinnati today, there are approximately 4,000 co-op stucdents, employed in 1,235 organizations in 35 states, and in 1978 these students earned over 12 million dollars in their co-op jobs. Government has been particularly successful in the use of Internship or Fellowship Programs. The White House Fellows Program, Congressional Intern Program, The Urban Corps are some of the successful programs. Of particular interest to those starting a business internship program would be the New York City Urban Fellowship Program. This program conducts a nationwide competition to select twenty outstanding seniors or graduate students who serve a full academic year working in very responsible positions in government and earn academic credit. Aside from their contributions during the year a number of Fellows remain in City government, return to it after completing their education, or go on to other governmental positions.

The goals for the Business Internship Program should be to provide challange, stimulation, responsibility, learning, growth, experience and prestige to the student. At the same time, it should provide the company with the means to attract superior students, to decide which students should be offered permanent employment, and to benefit from the students' efforts during the internship period. Major law firms and Big Eight accounting firms have long used summer or academic year internships for this purpose.

As a guide for establishing such a program and for giving it a high probability of success, several principles based on the author's experience have been developed:

1. The goal should be to recruit from among the best available students. The selection process should be rigorous, thoroughly planned and carefully implemented.

2. There must be top management concern, interest and involvement in the program. It cannot be treated as merely another program of the Personnel Department or that top management's involvement begins with the welcoming speech and ends with the farewell speech.

3. A general co-ordinator should be appointed, a high level official who will spend some of his or her time directing the program and serving as a counselor to the interns. Interns should receive a detailed orientation to the company, the intern program, their responsibilities and assignments, performance expectations, etc.

4. A mentor relationship should be established for each intern. The mentor should be a high level official who is concerned about the intern as an individual and who serves as a teacher and supervisor of the intern. Mentors should be carefully chosen for their interest in the Program and young people, for their ability as role models and for their high standards of performance and expectations of performance.

5. Intern assignments should be developed based on challenge and interest for students and value to the company. High standards of performance should be stressed with reasonable frequency of evaluation by the mentor and the intern. Interns should have a choice among various assignments.

6. Assignments can be varied to expose the interns to various aspects of the company, to several officials and to different staff and line activities. The use of rotational assignments among interns is very valuable if the length of the program allows for more than one assignment. Such assignments ex-

pose the interns to more activities and also allow the company to evaluate a variety of capabilities and the flexibility of the student.

7. Assignments should involve matters of considerable importance that can be measured and evaluated in a specific manner. This is not only valuable for making judgments as to intern performance, but will also provide satisfactionfor the intern.

8. In addition to specific assignments, the interns should be exposed to other aspects of a professional's job—attending meetings his mentor goes to, etc.

9. There should be ways in which interns meet with each other and as a group to discuss their experience, jobs, and exchange information. Further, there might be specific group projects for all interns in addition to their regular assignments or the same problem given to teams of interns in order to see what alternative solutions can be developed.

10. The interns should meet from time to time with the Chief Executive Officer and other top officials to discuss the company, problems, plans and programs. Weekly or every two weeks there might be informal discussions focusing on a particular problem or issue or just for questions and answers. An intern might be the presenter, panel chairman or discussion leader. Alternatively, leading officials in the company might play these roles.

11. There should be a thorough evaluation of the program, the assignments, the interns and the mentors at the end of each year, or during the intern year. Modifications and fine tuning should be made when required.

12. After the initial year, former interns should be used in the recruitment program and selection process of new interns and as informal advisors to the Program and to interns. As they progress in the company, former interns might serve as mentors and as director of the program.

The time arrangements for such a program might vary considerably. It could be (a) full-time during one summer and 10-20 hours a week during the academic year, (b) two summers or (c) two summers and 10-20 hours a week during the academic year. A more ambitious program would involve cooperation with various universities. The student would spend full-time in the company for one summer and the quarter/semester preceeding and/or following the summer.

In order not to delay the student's graduation, he might be expected to amass extra credits during his regular academic work.

An innovative approach would be to allow the intern to receive some to full academic credit for the time spent at the company. This might involve independent study credits for the student based upon his work and readings. There could be weekly or twice a week regular academic classes or seminars or special seminars for interns. Depending on the academic credit arrangements, the student could graduate at the same time as if he had not been in the program or, he might have to attend summer school or one extra quarter or semester. If the program is challenging enough and recognized as providing very solid training and experience, the ambitious student will be eager to make the investment of time.

Salaries should be adequate and competitive, paid at a rate equal to a junior professional. However, the major factor for the student is the opportunity to gain real "hands-on" experience and exposure to high executives and tough problems. Outstanding performance should result in a challenging and well paid job offer surpassing opportunities available to those who did not participate in the program.

It should be noted that a Business Internship Program need not be limited to specific companies alone. There could be an industry-wide internship program or a general program sponsored by a local, regional or national organization such as the Chamber of Commerce.

If planned and implemented carefully and with enthusiasm, a business internship program as described above can result in significant benefits to the companies and interns involved. The benefits that are likely include: actual accomplishments and results during the internship period; attracting for permanent employment highly talented individuals who have proven themselves; providing prestige throughout their careers in the company for those who were interns and thus fast-tracking them; enhancing the reputation of the company and its ability to attract outstanding individuals. A quality internship program requires an investment of time, effort and money. The results can very well be one of the best returns on investment the company achieves on any of its activities.

eighteen

Attacking the Productivity Puzzle

"Declining American Productivity" is so often mentioned in magazines, conferences, newspaper stories and editorials that we are almost becoming immune to its importance. Although the parade of statistics and discussion of possible "solutions" seem endless, the remedy appears nowhere in sight.

The low level of American productivity is, in fact, a major cause of the current inflation and of serious concern for our economic well-being in the future. A few stark statistics will suffice: from 1965 to 1973 American productivity rose at an annual average growth rate of 2.1%, from 1973 to 1978, the annual growth rate was 1.6%, a decrease of about 24% in the rate of growth. In 1979, although the third quarter productivity rose one tenth of 1%, the Department of Labor reported a 3% *drop* in the 1st quarter of 1979, and a 2.2% drop in output in the 2nd quarter of 1979. The American worker is 11th in the world in productivity increases. Japan leads the world. In 1950, it took 7 Japanese workers to equal the productivity of 1 American, today it takes just 1. It took 3 West Germans to do the work of one American, now it takes 1.3. (It is true Japan and other countries had a long way to go and thus could make dramatic increases as compared with us, but still the difference in growth rates is startling.)

Before we deal with the causes of low productivity and some possible solutions, given our high inflation it is at least worth mentioning the relationship among productivity, wage increases and inflation.

Generally, wage increases sought by employees attempt to deal with two factors. First, the erosion in one's standard of living caused by inflation since the last wage increase or as a cumulative effect of prior years. Second, the employee or union seeks to take into account the employee's share of previous productivity gains. (A third factor can be the meritorious performance of responsibilities but this can be linked to productivity.) Sometimes it is said "strong unions never settle for anything less than 3% (as a productivity offset if 3% is the usual figure for productivity increases) plus the rate of inflation." Union settlements tend to set patterns for the entire labor market whether organized or not.

If a 7% increase in wages is matched by only a 1% increase in productivity, unit labor costs will rise by 6%. This rise in unit labor costs is for the most part passed on in higher prices. Higher prices fuel the inflationary spiral which fuels the demand for greater wage increases and we keep going around in circles. To take one industry, the paper industry, from 1974-78 the annual productivity increase was 1.7% per year, while the average hourly earnings per production employee were increasing at 9.8% per year. Clearly, unit labor costs increase and so must prices. One other factor, as a protection against inflation, it is very common for unions to negotiate cost of living adjustments (COLA). These adjustments, which attempt to play catch-up with inflation, in effect help fuel inflation in the industry and the economy as a whole and the cycle continues on its destructive path.

The causes of our low productivity are complex. As compared with other societies, we have moved to a manufacturing economy from an agricultural economy many years before they did. It is, therefore, more difficult to keep up with the gains in productivity that are made soon after a society moves toward a manufacturing economy. We are much more of a service oriented economy than other societies, and productivity is considerably more difficult to improve (or even measure) in service industries than in manufacturing. The United States has seen a phenomenal growth in employment and regulation at all levels of government during the last quarter of a century. A large labor force in government, and the difficulties of substituting capital for labor and increasing productivity in a governmental service setting, constitutes a considerable drain on productivity growth. Regulatory actions of government, necessary as most may be, also constitute a drain on productivity by increasing costs and time involved in doing business. Another impediment to productivity growth is our vast expenditures for military hardware, research and development, installations and personnel necessitated by our defense requirements and our status and objectives as a super-power.

Two major issues involved in our productivity gap deal with U.S. investments in new plants, equipment and technology and the question of worker satisfaction and the work environment.

As a nation, Americans tend to save less than some other developed societies and there is, therefore, less capital available for investment. Our major companies tend to utilize less of their profits for investment in the long range future than do companies in other countries (either as a result of their own decisions or in coordination with the government). In effect, the relative shortage of capital stemming from individual savings and corporate "savings" bring about less of an investment in future plant, equipment and technology than we need. Some would argue that the corporate "underinvestment" may be a result of the short term perspective of the company president or chairman. They have a relatively short average term of office, five or seven years, to make their mark on company history and, therefore, may tend to maximize profits, acquisitions and dividends. Others would argue that the basic factor is government tax policy or lack of incentives. Whatever the reason, the U.S. has been slowing down its investments in the future. To cite one area of investment, technological improvement and innovation, the following indicates the relative deemphasis on technological supremacy. In 1964, we spent 3% of our gross national product for research and development. In 1978, we spent 2.2% (granted that the actual amount for R&D is greater). Another important indicator is capital expansion. From 1966-76, capital investment in the U.S. was 13.5% of Gross National Product, in Japan it was 26.4%, in West Germany 17.4%, Canada invested 17.2%, France 16.6% and Great Britain 14.9%.

We must recognize, however, that limited and more expensive energy resources, greater competition from more countries for both domestic and foreign markets, domestic pressures for resource conservation, the political climate in the world which may require greater investment in a "non-productive" sector of the economy, armaments and larger armed forces, the demand for increased governmental services, and changing American definitions of the "good life," will all affect the rate of and climate for economic expansion.

The other significant concern is individual worker productivity while fully recognizing that the presence of modern competitive plant and technology will have a profound impact upon individual productivity.

In understanding the people side of productivity, we should be aware of demographic changes in our population and their effects. From 1979 on we will have relatively fewer young people expanding our labor force as compared with the last quarter of a century. Women and minorities have been and will continue to enter the work force in higher numbers and percentages than in the past and they, as well as white males, will be better educated than in the past. Our mature population, senior citizens and senior, senior citizens will grow to an all-time high of about 12% of our population. Our lower fertility rates will mean relatively fewer infants and adolescents. We face an excess of college educated individuals in relation to job positions traditionally requiring such education. Within 20 years, the median age of the work force will rise by 25% from 28 to 35. This in turn will impact upon income, consumption, employee benefit costs, and attitudes toward work. Perhaps, we shall face a generation of individuals, college educated, women and minorities who find that society does not offer the promised opportunity. We might even face the split in society between the old and young in regard to social security costs and benefits, pensions and health cost, the retirement age and equal opportunity programs.

We must further understand that all levels of employment, blue collar, white collar, executives, are a better educated work force who strive to make life more meaningful personally. They want greater control over their work hours, what they do and what happens to them at work and in their work years. They find increasingly attractive their leisure time. Couple this with two career families, the role of government regulation, the state of the economy, the questioning of authority and the decline of the Puritan ethic and one then begins to understand the complex and fundamental dimensions of the problem.

When looking at possible approaches toward solving the productivity puzzle we begin with a very simple definition of productivity as getting more out for less as compared with a standard or previous period.

First, let's look at the people/organization side of productivity. Some have suggested that we now face the reality that American leadership in business has been based on technology rather than management and as other countries' technology and investment philosophies have caught up or surpassed ours, our managerial weakness in regard to concern for people is exposed. Japan is pointed to both for technology and investment but also for their emphasis on worker involvement. In the U.S., the Quality of Work Life (QWL) approach has become a major movement rivaling the MBO emphasis of the 60s and

70s. By QWL, we mean a continuous, sustained approach to give employees greater control over their jobs and working environment. This includes: new pay systems; nonsupervised work groups; increased participation in decision making; job enlargement and enrichment; group developed tools, systems, procedures and work methods; design of jobs, work and work groups.

The Quality of Work Life approach can be helpful in increasing productivity but, while it can reduce turnover and absenteeism, it is no guarantee of increased productivity or job satisfaction. It should not be oversold. Other approaches might include cooperative ventures between management and labor in regard to job design and workplace design, rewarding merit and plant wide gain sharing plans. Individual reward systems might be utilized such as cafeteria style fringe benefit plans allowing the individual to choose and package fringe benefits of most meaning to him or lump sum salary increases. Individuals might be given more realistic descriptions and exposure to jobs before they are assigned to them or employed. New technology should be analyzed well before introduction in order to evaluate the impact on individuals and groups and to make necessary changes and/or undertake information and discussion sessions. More emphasis could be placed on individual, group and sub-group design of jobs and functions.

Another approach, too often overlooked, is the need for sustained emphasis on high quality and high standards of performance at all levels within the organization with a reward structure corresponding to the quality of performance. Merely satisfactory performance is not quite enough for an individual, unit or company in a highly competitive climate. We tend to demand too little of ourselves and of others. In today's society with an emphasis on litigation, malpractice claims, consumerism it is clear that increasingly and at times vehemently the customer expects to get his money's worth. Business should set considerably higher standards of performance and criteria for promotion and increases so that it too receives its money's worth from the person on the assembly line to the person in the executive suite.

We must also consider developing and tapping new resources for executive leadership. Although there are significant differences among industries and between the profit sector and the public/not-for-profit sector, there are also great similarities in the management skills necessary for success. Thus, in looking for outstanding executive talent, a relatively scarce resource, a business firm might look outside its particular industry to other industries and other sectors.

There must be a growing recognition of the need for a change of work attitudes in order to achieve a productivity breakthrough. Stress can be put by both management and labor on reducing "down-time" of machines, strikes and excessive repairs and maintenance. There can be increased analysis of work and the use of various monetary and non-monetary incentives and compensation plans to reward productivity. An analysis of manning levels, work scheduling, work flow, flexible assignments of specialized skills can lead to improvements. Shared work assignments, flex-time, looking at improved methods and productivity of professionals such as Detroit Edison is doing for its lawyers, engineers and accountants, emphasis on increasing productivity in office operations through utilization of the later generations of word and information processing techniques and technology, may well result in significant improvements.

On the financial front in regard to productivity increases, we might consider a rather controversial approach of concentrating our energies and investments on industries that rank high in regard to productivity, wages, technology and exportability. Less emphasis or energy might be given to strengthening or even saving inefficient industries. In other words, this approach would call for primarily leaving the manufacture of certain products to other countries.

Less controversial actions involve the reduction of corporate taxes, if money is applied to R&D or capital investments, applying more widely the 10% credit on capital investments and perhaps increasing the credit, faster depreciation write-offs could be approved, double taxation of corporate dividends could be eliminated.

We need both a financial and a people approach to productivity involving industry, unions and government. Immediate, short and long term actions are needed to match our rhetoric and concern. We must implement what we already know and devise new ways to motivate employees at all levels to want to do a better job. We must insure that they are able to do so through providing the necessary: plant, equipment, technology; knowledge; processes; sound management; organizational and work design and environment. The clock is ticking ever more rapidly. As a nation and as a society we can do better, we must do better.

nineteen

Impact of Governmental Regulation*

The nature, scope, interpretation and implementation of the avalanche of governmental regulations affecting every aspect of American life is of increasing concern to the business community and other groups in society. Traditional regulations and those involving the relatively recent areas of emphasis such as occupational safety and health, the environment, affirmative action, handicapped persons have a major effect on American life. We will sketch the impact of governmental regulations and what business might do to appropriately and effectively register concern about current practices and trends in order to assist in accomplishing the worthwhile goals of regulation without unnecessarily overregulating business and society.

Governmental leaders are well aware of widespread discussions about the burdens of regulation as indicated in the following statements:

> By now, regulation almost parallels the taxing and spending powers of Government in terms of its importance in the life of the nation. Finding ways to improve how it goes about regulating is the most important managerial task now facing the government.

Charles L. Schultze,
Chairman of the Council of Economic Advisers,
Carter Administration

*This essay was published by Braniff Airlines in-flight magazine *Flying Colors* in December 1979 and is reprinted through the courtesy of Halsey Publishing Co., publishers of Braniff's *Flying Colors* magazine.

President Carter in a speech in March 1979 declared "it is time we take control of Federal regulations in America" and outlined regulatory revision proposals "to reduce, to rationalize and to streamline the regulatory burden throughout American life."

We begin with the premise that there is general agreement that regulation has been very important and necessary in assuring the health, safety and protection of Americans in terms of food, drink, medicines, the workplace, the home, items purchased, travel, physical structures, the environment, and other areas.

The defenders of regulation argue strongly that the various governmental regulations have produced major public benefits and protection and that costs of regulations are often exceeded by the savings. For example, the White House Council on Environmental Quality asserts that about $22 billion dollars were saved in damages prevented as a result of $13.1 billion spent to meet Federal air pollution standards, a rather significant return on investment. Further, proregulation advocates will assert that it is impossible to put a value on certain things such as saving human life or reducing debilitating diseases through control of cancer producing agents. They say that in effect the current wave of anti-regulation advocates wish to repeal, diminish and destroy several decades of vital and progressive changes for the good of American society and its citizens.

Those who believe that there is too much regulation argue that excessive regulation: creates a drain on productivity and the economy; adds to inflation, unemployment, number of bankruptcies and negative balance of trade; hurts incentives for expansion, capital formation, new product development, innovation and improved production processes; effects the company's rate of return, profitability and the stock market; costs a great deal both for the regulators and the regulated.

Our emphasis will be on regulatory impact on business, but every aspect of American life is affected by regulation. A general example of the pervasiveness of regulation can be seen in a typical day for many Americans: getting washed and dressed, eating breakfast, driving to work, working, relaxing at home. The mouthwash, toothpaste, electric toaster, vitamins, toast, eggs, cereal, artificial sweetener for coffee, seat belts, unleaded gas, 55 mile speed limit, the workplace and work environment, mortgage, home improvement loan, television programs, cigarettes smoked—all and much more are regulated in varying degrees by one federal agency or another. The federal agencies involved in the above scenario are (in addition, state, county and municipal laws, codes and regulations apply in some instances): FDA, FERC, NLRB, NHTSA, EPA, FHLBB, FHA, FRC, FCC, ATFB, DHEW. At work, one or more of the following agencies will have regulated some aspect of the job environment or content: OSHA, EEOC, ERISA, NLRB, IRS, ICC, CAB, SEC, etc.

A specific non-business example is higher education. In the field of postsecondary education alone, the growth of government involvement has been dramatic. There are now 34 Congressional committees and over 70 subcommittees with jurisdiction over more than 430 laws affecting higher education. In 12 years, the number of pages in the Federal Register dealing with their regulation has grown more than 1,000%. A fairly recent Harvard study shows that, during one school year, its faculty spent over 60,000 hours complying with just five federal regulations at a cost of over $8,000,000. A university may experience having several investigating teams from the government, sometimes more than one at a time and from different sections of the same agency. For example, the Department of Labor can send in three separate teams dealing with the University's workforce and the Department of Health, Education and Welfare may send in three separate teams concerning a University's actions in regard to students.

When we look at business, we readily note that the number of laws, rules, regulations and administrative decisions and interpretations affecting business have expanded at geometric rates over the last two decades. Traditionally government sought to regulate economic matters with a concern for markets, rates and obligations to serve. But in the last 10 to 15 years we see the full force of what might be called social regulation which deals with conditions under which production of goods and services takes place and the characteristics of manufactured products. Every business leader today is armed with an arsenal of facts to show the costs of compliance with the deluge of governmental regulations. Such costs include: executive manhours spent; staffing–professional, support, outside experts; record keeping, files; computer processing and time; efforts to head off further legislation or regulation. The increased governmental regulatory thrust has necessitated the employment of large numbers of attorneys, accountants, various specialists, and consultants as well as thousands of support staff, both within and outside of government. They are all employed in order to be on the offense, defense, or in compliance in regard to various laws, rules and regulations. And beyond the costs, one has to consider the impact of regulation on innovation, risk-taking, decision-making, flexibility, prices to consumer and world trade competitiveness.

Some Facts and Interpretations in Regard to the Growth of Gevernment Regulations

1. Dow Chemical Company is a pioneer in the field of measuring the impact of government regulations. It analyzed its spending for the period 1975-77 in regard to regulated costs and came up with the following figures categorized into what it regarded as appropriate, questionable and excessive spending.

REGULATED COSTS (In Millions of Dollars)

Year	Total Spending	Amount (%) Appropriate	Questionable	Excessive
1975	$147	$ 87(59.2%)	$10(6.8%)	$ 50(34.0%)
1976	186	103(55.4%)	14(7.5%)	69(37.1%)
1977	268	139(51.8%)	14(5.2%)	115(43.0%)

It is interesting to note that, according to Dow, there was an 82%, or $121 million, increase in the cost of regulations during the period 1975-1977, and the "appropriate" spending rose by 130%, or $65 million.

2. A study for the period 1970-75 indicates that the number of major "economic" regulatory agencies grew by 25%, the number of major "social" regulatory agencies grew by 42%, the expenditures growth for major economic regulatory agencies was 157% and for major social regulatory agencies was 193%. The number of pages in the Federal Register grew 210% and the number of pages in the Code of Federal Regulations grew by 33%.

3. Currently it is estimated that over $6 billion a year is spent, in total, by 56 regulatory agencies not including the recently proposed energy regulatory agencies. It is estimated that there are more than 4,000 different types of government forms (excluding tax and banking forms) that require more than 140 million man-hours a year to fill out.

4. The Business Roundtable (composed of the chief executives of almost 200 of the country's largest corporations) in March,

1979 issued its report on the costs of regulation. The study, conducted by Arthur Andersen, measured the actual financial impact of six federal regulatory agencies and programs in 1977 on 48 Rountable firms, including AT&T, General Motors, Eastman Kodak, Exxon, Procter & Gamble. The total cost was $2.6 billion which was equal to 40% of their R&D budgets, 16% of the companies' net profits and about 10% of their capital expenditures. IBM chairman, Frank Cory, who supervised the study, thought the $2.6 billion figure extrapolated to cover the entire economy would be in the range of $79 billion. The Environmental Protection Agency accounted for 77% of the cost, EEOC—8%, OSHA—7%, ERISA—2%. Some would say that with the snowballing effect of regulation and inflation since 1977 and with the potential of rigid and literal enforcement of EPA, OSHA and other laws, the cost in 1981 would be from 35%-75% more than the 1977 study. The study did not deal with secondary costs such as losses or increased costs due to construction delays caused by environmental or OSHA regulation. It is important to note that the study did not deal with the considerable benefits of regulation. Mr. Cory agreed that many regulations are necessary, but noted that the expenditures demanded by the regulations can "often be wasteful and non-productive." In his view, companies should be given more discretion in how to achieve stated goals and that economic impact statements should accompany proposals for new regulations so that the costs could be weighed against the benefits.

Some Examples of Questionable Aspects of Governmental Regulations

- An Iowa Public Library barely escaped from being required to install facilities for the handicapped even though no handicapped person lived in the town and the cost involved was greater than the library's total annual budget.

- In Maryland, a state law requires hospitals to keep hot water in patient's rooms at no less than 110 degrees while a Federal regulation requires that it be kept at no more than 110 degrees.

- Children's pajamas are a concern. To maintain the flameproof quality of sleepwear, it is best to use detergents containing phosphates except a number of states have banned phosphates for environmental reasons.

- Dow Chemical cancelled in January, 1977, plans to build a $300 million petrochemical complex in California because of red tape. After more than two years, it had obtained less than 10% of various permits needed from all levels of regulatory agencies.

- It took Standard Oil Company of Ohio more than four years to obtain the 700 permits required to construct a terminal and pipeline from Long Beach, California to Midland, Texas.

Some Examples of Improvements In and Concern About the Regulatory Process

- In 1975, under pressure from a very unhappy public, Congress changed the law it passed in 1973 that all new cars contain an interlock device that forced the driver to buckle his seat belt before the car could be started.

- Alfred E. Kahn, former chairman of the C. A. B., was successful at cutting back on the regulatory power of his agency, and thus allowed airlines to serve the cities they choose at competitive prices. He was also successful in getting legislation providing for the abolition of the C. A. B. in 1985.

- When Dr. Eula Bingham, then head of OSHA, was able to press for revision, rewriting, and repeal of some minor regulations, e.g., 25 pages of national fire protection rules were replaced by a single paragraph. Paperwork requirements have been cut in half and in the same week that the heaviest civil fines in the agency's history was imposed on a company for exposing workers to lead, over 900 trivial regulations were repealed.

- In President Carter's speech referred to previously, he indicated that his proposal would require cost benefit analysis of proposed regulations, reductions of paperwork, review of existing regulations every 10 years.

An Interesting Side Effect

Federal regulations can't be all bad. A survey of 28 vice presidents of big Fortune 500 companies who deal directly with government regulations showed that 86% had their positions upgraded because of their importance to top management. About 82% had increased their staffs, 75% had been upgraded to vice president in the last five years, about 50% had their positions created in the last five years.

Although interest in regulatory reform seems to be sweeping the nation, progress is rather slow. And there are some very tough policy questions that have not been answered. Some of them are: How much regulation can the economy, jor opportunities and inflation stand? How can costs be evaluated as to different approaches by different agencies to controlling, for example, particular pollutants, from different sources? How can government regulation control control dollars best be spent? Should we marshall our resources for attacks on particular things or spread available funds as widely as possible; in other words, the very difficult political decision of choices among many goods or evils and the allocation of scarce resources? How do we determine, for example, that it's worth several hundred million dollars to reduce the level of sulfur in fuel burned in regions of the country?

We conclude with suggestions of possible ways of meeting the goals of regulation while attempting to improve effectiveness, efficiency and economy in regulatory activities and lessen the unnecessary burden on business and society.

The business community should consider taking action through individual firms, trade associations, lobbying, political activities within the limits of the law; acting in coordination and cooperation with other groups when appropriate such as labor unions and non-profit sector organizations, to accomplish:

1. Encouraging industries to formulate their own regulations and enforcement procedures subject to governmental review and audit.

    If these prove ineffective, the government should issue its own regulations.

2. Applications of the Sunset Law concept to existing and proposed regulations.

3. Bringing about cost/benefit analysis and economic impact statements by the Congressional Budget Office in the federal

government and its counterparts in the States in regard to existing and proposed regulations, with public discussion of the
results of the studies.

4. Setting priorities for the formulation of new and the application of existing regulations and providing maximum flexibility and incentives (positive and negative) for business and
   other institutions to meet the serious problems indicated in
   the priorities.

5. Mounting a campaign for public, legislative and executive
   branch discussion in setting priorities of the short-term and
   longterm needs of the country and the choices that may have
   to be made, i.e., increased production of energy sources vs.
   increased environmental regulation.

6. Urging consideration of possible alternatives to regulations
   such as special taxes or fees that would be beneficial to those
   who comply with the standards and priorities.

Regulation is necessary, important and here to stay. But, as in
any worthwhile effort, there can be excesses and unnecessary burdens and costs. Business should strive to be responsive to governmental and public needs and supportive of those regulations, sensitively and sensibly administered, that meed reasonable objectives.
At the same time, business should strive to improve its communications and be more effective in marketing itself and its concerns
about the impact of governmental regulations.

twenty

The Business Executive in Government *

The punishment which the wise suffer who refuse to take part in government, is to live under the government of worse men.

Emerson

My experience in government is that when things are non-controversial and beautifully coordinated, there is not much going on.

John F. Kennedy

Government is too big and important to be left to the politicians.

Chester Bowles

I like to start articles about government and politics with a joke but the worst thing about political jokes is that some of them get elected.

The only way to make a government official see the light is to make him feel the heat.

*A slightly different version of my essay was published by *Management Review* in February 1980 entitled "The Business Executive in Government: Look Before You Leap".

Tom Connally running for re-election was asked by a belligerent listener, "How do you stand on the cotton issue?" He
quickly replied, "I'm okay on that one, are there any other
questions."

One of the things we have to be thankful for is that we don't
get as much government as we pay for.

Charles F. Kettering

With increasing frequency, government at all levels, city, state,
county, federal, is attempting to attract successful businesspersons
for voluntary or paid part-time, temporary, short or long term service
as governmental executives. The hope is that the skills acquired by
experience and training in business are transferable and will aid
governmental units in becoming more effective, efficient and economical.

For the businessperson, there is a challenge of something new and
different and also the considerable ego gratification of being asked
by his/her city, state or country to serve. Thus he/she enters government service with high hopes of accomplishment.

It doesn't take long for those flushed and flattered with the prerogatives and responsibilities of power to recognize that there are at
work within the governmental system forces and constraints which
impede, dilute, delay, modify, mangle and sometimes destroy the
introduction, implementation and lasting effect of changes in governmental policies and practices. The businessperson who seeks to be
effective and a change agent must be prepared to expend his/her
energies, thought, time and reputation in grappling with these
forces. Depending upon the level of government, some of these
forces may be less prevalent or powerful, but practically all of these
are factors that have had very little, if any, impact on the individual's
business success or in his/her training and experience. This article
attempts to describe some of the factors that the businessperson
turned government administrator should be prepared to face.

1. *Politics.*   Any elected chief executive is fundamentally concerned about his political success and his chances for re-election.
Even if he chooses or is forced not to run, he wishes to leave a good
record behind and be able to influence the selection of his successor.
Thus, despite cost/benefit analysis and modern management techniques, the paramount question often is, "Will this enhance or
diminish my political power and base and add to or subtract from

my chances for re-election?" This is not to deny political courage or that good management can coincide with good politics or even override good politics. However, it is to affirm the realities of power, partisan politics and political pressures and priorities. An example— one budget director in a major city almost cost the Mayor re-election by not approving overtime for police and sanitation workers prior to an election because of the city's budget crisis. Finally, "wise" political heads prevailed and there were police all over and the streets were never cleaner than for the few weeks before the election. After the election, things returned to normal. (The Mayor was re-elected.)

2. *Publicity.* The goldfish bowl of publicity in political life is very distressing to the neophyte political appointee. Rumors, leaks, charges, counter-charges, professional and personal questions at all hours of the day and night, the sometimes potentially politically fatal desire to see one's name or thoughts in print or on television— all combine to divulge too early, frequently distort and often serve as a means of expressing dissatisfaction with one's opponents, subordinates, colleagues and leaders. The government manager needs the news media (and vice versa) and thus often uses and misuses the media (and vice versa).

The inherent conflict between the roles of the reporter and the official should be recognized. The reporter fights for the public's right to know; the official wants the public to know what's right about governmental programs. The news media look for the expose, scandal, stupid act that will rate page one and its electronic equivalent, good things rate hardly any coverage. Knowing the deadlines and practices of the media, governments tend to operate and innovate by press release and not all the time by actual practice since it is rare that the media will follow up a year later to see what happened. Finally, it should be noted that in this post Watergate era, a reporter may have a personal self-interest in the expose that might result in a Pulitzer Prize, fame, money, a book, movie, etc. Thus, a natural inquisitiveness and role can be heightened to unreasonable proportions because of personal self-interest.

3. *Interest Groups* are a powerful factor in governmental decision-making. They come in many forms—pressure, citizen, community, good government, geographic, particular issue, professional, religious, racial, sexual, ethnic, etc. Their pressure and power, from pickets to press headlines, their cooperation, competition and conflict, have

a profound influence on change and action. An administrator must consult, listen, be accessible or else lose an opportunity to be effective.

4. *Bureaucracy.*   Depending on the governmental jurisdiction (the federal service after its recent civil service changes is probably the best but still has problems), the bureaucracy with their families and friends constitute a significant portion of the electorate. Generally, in most civil service systems, the new adminstrator will find: inadequate performance standards and appraisals, very little relationship between performance and reward and great difficulty in firing anyone. Performance and productivity have often not kept pace with increasing pay, pensions, benefits and job security. Most civil service systems need to be changed for changing times and needs but this will be a long and very difficult process. The newcomer will find it difficult to work in the rules, laws, red-tape infested government departments. In addition to the various constraints cited in this article, and the difficulty of making and seeing progress, low compensation for top talent is a problem. A cabinet secretary or undersecretary position may make up in prestige what is lost in dollars, but for the equivalent of division managers or vice presidents, the compensation packages are generally very significantly below private industry and the legal profession. Thus, many of the best people leave and the businessperson doesn't stay long.

5. *Societal Problems.*   Many of the nations's problems are well beyond the resources of the particular city, county, region or state and are even beyond a quick solution by the federal government. These problems include poverty employment, education, crime, energy, pollution, health, race relations, transportation, housing. For other than the federal government, they place unmeetable demands upon out resources and pose the awesome problem of choice among vital needs. Many of the societal problems are closely related and, at times, attenpting to solve one is like grabbing a balloon—you attempt, let's say, to solve the employment problem, and the education and/or housing and/or transportation problem, etc. pops up or bursts out. The administrator will have to live with the frustration that he can "solve" very little, but he can, of course, make significant progress.

6. *Budget.* Large as governmental budgets are, the administrator often finds that his particular area's budget is inadequate. Other

pressures and priorities may prevent getting what is necessary. The current allocation may contain money locked in and mandatory expenditures protected by tradition and vested interest, thus leaving little or nothing for change or innovation.

7. *Unions.* Unions of public employees are the most rapidly growing sector of the union movement. In some areas of the country, their fringe benefits, work rules and salaries exceed private sector comparisons, although in prior years they may have been behind their counterparts. The issue for the governmental administrator is that unlike what he could do in business in terms of closing down a plant or moving to another area or taking a long strike, he cannot do this for some services in government. Some powerful unions can just about bring a city or county to its knees. Another factor is that many unions are very powerful politically in terms of influence, funds and manpower that can be supplied for a campaign. Their efforts and the voting power of their members, family and friends can spell electoral victory or defeat for a mayor, county executive or governor.

8. *Concern and Caring.* At times it will appear that no one really cares what happens to his/her city or state or nation. People may care about a block or neighborhood but it is difficult to get concern and commitment in regard to broader problems. The responsiveness and concern of government, citizens, and the various organizations and institutions in society are of vital importance but often it appears that the narrow self-interest is all that is operating.

9. *Measurement of Results.* Trained as he/she is in the "bottom line" approach, or "every tub on its own bottom," the business-person finds it very hard to measure results in government. There is no profit motive, bonus incentive or at times even an efficiency or effectiveness incentive. It is almost impossible to answer, "how well am I doing?" in the same way as is done in business. Some new programs may have been started, efficiency and service may have been improved, some cost savings made, good newspaper stories have appeared (or at least few bad ones) good relations established with the legislature, executive departments, interest groups, etc. If all that happened, the governmental manager should regard himself as a great success.

10. *Planning and Investment.*   Given the short time perspective
of political leaders because of their need to focus on re-election,
four years away, it is very difficult to get sustained interest and commitment to planning. Why use your best people and scarce resources
on things that will bear fruit (if successful) when someone else is
Mayor, Governor or President? Thus long range planning and the
heavy investment in research and development that business is
accustomed to, just does not occur with any real frequency in
government, except for crises (space program) or defense needs. The
time and need is ripe for the application of technology for new or
improved methods and equipment in the areas of solid waste disposal,
housing, transportation, air pollution, energy, etc. but short of
crisis, for private industry it may seem unprofitable and for government, too far down the road.

11. *Organizational Structure.*   Too often the structure of government has grown in a haphazard fashion as a response to political
needs, interest groups, the fad, scandal or crisis of the period, or the
particular style of the chief executive. The result often is lack of
effectiveness and efficiency, partisan and parochial departmental
interests and constituencies, separate fiefdoms, independent agencies,
and a wild goose chase for information or action for citizens, governmental officials and chief executives. Two examples from New York
City history: 1) at one time paving of streets fell under the jurisdiction of three departments: Highways for regular roads, Public Works
for bridges, and Parks for parkways; 2) well-baby clinics were under
one department and sick-baby clinics under another, with the sick-
baby clinics very crowded and the well-baby clinics underutilized.
Since they were under separate departments, medical staffs could
not be transferred to the sick-baby clinics and sick babies could not
be sent to the well-baby clinics.

12. *Jurisdictional Relations.*   Regionalism, creative federalism,
public authorities, by-passing the states in direct negotiation with the
federal government, revenue sharing, are all attempts to make things
happen despite the turf problems, politics and personalities involved
in our federal system of government. From the non-federal level,
there is a view that the "feds" (executive and legislative branches)
are too remote, non-responsive, tied up in red-tape, unconcerned,
distrustful, only interested in making rules that are impossible to
follow or prevent progress being made. From the "feds" point of

view, "lower" levels in our federal system are weak or not concerned enough about thorough planning, various controls, professionalism, effective and efficient performance, too prone to political and pressure group interests and, at times, even open to questions of honesty. The newcomer may thus get involved in long standing distrust and antagonism on both sides.

13. *Leadership*. The businessperson may wonder how in the face of all the above, anyone can truly lead and be effective. The short answer is, it's very difficult.

CONCLUSION

Although this article has attempted to describe the thicket and thorns, I end by saying that for the businessperson, the governmental unit and society, it is important and valuable that as many competent individuals as possible get involved. It is hoped that what has been written will be helpful and increase one's chances of success.

twenty-one

The Executive at the Podium*

My friend was recently appointed to a top executive position which requires a considerable amount of time devoted to making important speeches. As a gift, I gave him three envelopes labeled 1, 2, 3 containing advice as to how he should explain any particularly poor performance in his speechmaking to his superior. Though he does not know it, I will tell you what is in the envelopes. The first envelope, to be used after the first bad speech, contains this advice— tell your superior that the audience was dull, hostile, not receptive because of too much partying or expectation of later partying, the acoustics, seating or lighting were bad, you followed a very boring speaker who put people to sleep, you followed the star of the meeting and you just could not match him. The second envelope suggests—tell him the speechwriter left out important material or missed the point, the audio visuals were of poor quality, you did not have adequate time for preparation and rehearsal. The third envelope states—begin to prepare three envelopes.

Today's top business executive is increasingly called upon to deliver speeches to a variety of audiences. In addition to ritualistic speeches before the typical audience on a typical non-controversial topic, he must speak on controversial topics before antagonistic

*A portion of this essay will be published by *Personnel Administrator* in 1981.

or neutral groups. Although one can attempt to avoid the tough assignment, the demands grow. Crises arise—bribery issues, kickbacks, sharp increases in prices, sharp decreases in supply, layoffs, plant closings, strikes, recalls of products, variances in zoning for a new plant, location of a new plant, etc. Potentially hostile audiences want to listen and probably want more to shoot questions, barbs, make comments. These audiences might be composed of consumer advocates, environmentalists, equal opportunity advocates, community groups, governmental hearing or legislative groups, etc. The top executive's ability to communicate to a variety of audiences is of considerable importance to his company and to his own success in the company.

This article seeks to help the executive be more at ease and successful at the podium.

In accepting an invitation to speak or in seeking such an invitation, you must be clear as to your objective. What do you want to accomplish in your 15-20 minute talk (going much beyond 20 minutes is an invitation to lose your audience)? You should be able to state the specific objective or goal of the speech in one simple sentence. If the topic suggested to you just does not seem right, try to reshape it with the consent of the inviter. If you are not able to do so, consider turning down the invitation. If you are really uncomfortable with a topic, you are likely not to do it, yourself or your company justice. And for all speaking invitations and opportunities the cost/benefits should be evaluated. In deciding to tackle a topic you should also gain an understanding of the nature of the audience, their size, mood, knowledge of the topic, expectations, general views. You should also be concerned about the time the speech will be given, what place it occupies in the program (what it precedes and follows), the physical facilities, whether there will be a question and answer period (if there is, prepare yourself to answer a number of questions), whether there will be media coverage, etc.

The secret formula for successful speechmaking is simple. It is preparation and rehearsal. The idea is to avoid the canned speech and to try to make news or provide insights with what you're saying. It need not be news carried by the media, but should at least be news or food for thought for the audience. Your speech is part of an overall public relations approach of the company and, as such, what you say and how you say it can result in either positive or negative public relations on a small or large scale.

In planning the speech, develop in your own mind the theme and the major points you want to make. You then should turn to the company's speechwriter (whether the in-house individual or a free lance writer) for assistance. The professional speechwriter is a very valuable asset, but should be used properly. He or she should be involved in the entire process and if you make frequent speeches, a personal relationship should be established. In this way, the writer gets a good sense of how you approach things and what you would be comfortable with. The result will be fewer misunderstandings and drafts and better speeches. The writer (and in cases where there is no professional speechwriter available, either a subordinate of the executive or even the executive himself may turn out to be the "writer") can do research and provide the framework, words and rhetoric, but the basic concepts or theme must come from the executive and those he consults. Plenty of time should be set aside for researching, drafting, consulting and re-drafting, but with deadlines set for first draft, second draft, etc. Good and appropriate audio visual aids can be helpful. Leave ample time to develop them and to integrate them into the speech.

The writer and the speechmaker should tap the knowledge and comments of other key company officials, both for the initial draft of the speech as well as for subsequent drafts. After final re-writing (often taking several drafts) in language and tone that is the executive's, the speech is ready. But then the second part of the formula comes to the fore-rehearsal. The speech should be rehearsed often enough so that the executive feels comfortable with it, that it is indeed his speech, but it should not be memorized. A videotape or tape should be made so the executive can see and/or hear himself and make necessary corrections in style, tone, mannerisms, volume, gestures, speed of talking, etc. The use and integration into the speech of audio visuals should also be included in the rehearsal.

Now you are ready for the delivery of the speech. The minutes before the actual delivery and the first two or three minutes of the speech itself are very important. Therefore, the executive should arrive at least a few minutes before the speech to get a sense of the place and the audience. When approaching the podium, he should do so briskly and confidently, dressed appropriately. In the first few seconds after the introduction (or before the introduction), be sure that you are comfortable with the lectern and microphone positions. Look at the audience for a few seconds to establish eye contact before you begin speaking. Work carefully on your opening remarks in order to capture immediate interest. During the speech instead of scanning the room, try to make eye contact with individuals in different parts of the room.

Some DO's and DONT's:

DO
- vary the length of sentences—keep them, as far as possible, short and simple
- speak clearly, distinctly, and at moderate speed
- use appropriate gestures and pauses

DON'T
- lean on the lectern
- drink water unless absolutely necessary because of dryness in your throat
- accentuate the written text by loudly or very noticeably turning pages or cards

Remember that you can kill a speech by talking too much, giving a commercial for yourself or your company, talking yourself up or the audience down, throwing in unrelated items, speaking too fast, too slow, or in a monotone.

The issue of humor in speeches is an important one. Somehow we have all learned that we have to respond to the introduction with some humor and then begin the speech with one, two or three jokes. Humor can be helpful and effective if used properly and appropriately. If you do not have anything funny to say in response to the introduction, don't try it. At the beginning and elsewhere in your speech, humor can be utilized if it ties in to the speech. The joke or story that is used should be brief, flow out of the personal experience of the speaker (if possible), be appropriate to the topic, audience, or occasion. Most of all, you should be able to deliver it effectively. There are some people who cannot tell a funny story if their lives depended on it. Do not force humor if you are not comfortable with it or if the joke isn't suitable for the topic or audience.

Quotations from living or dead well-known persons, literature, historical documents, newspapers and magazines, etc. can be helpful in making a point, but they must be used carefully. They should not be overdone or overrelied on. Most important in deciding whether to use quotations is whether they help make the point or set the tone or mood. The same caveats can be applied to the use of statistics. A string of statistics, even in five color graph form, do not guarantee a successful speech.

You should conclude strongly, look at the audience for a second after your last word and then express your thanks for the opportunity to express your views or whatever other specific reason seems pertinent. In question and answer periods, you can politely bring the question period to a close by noting that there is time for just two or three more questions.

Successful speechmaking takes time, thought, effort, coordination, preparation, rehearsal, experience and good techniques. As the demands on executives mount, the ability to speak effectively will be an increasingly important aspect of an executive's performance.

As a bonus for reading this essay, I offer several jokes that may be helpful in getting your speech off to a good start or for use in the speech. Remember, tell them well and make sure they are appropriate to the topic and/or the audience. Change them as you wish.

If you are a substitute for a big name person who was supposed to deliver a talk, but could not make it . . .

> I know that many of you are disappointed that I am not the President of XYZ Company, Secretary of Commerce, the Governor, . . . well, frankly, I'm disappointed that I'm not the President of XYZ Company . . . the Governor.

> I was pleased to learn that you don't issue a newsletter outlining what the speaker said (or, I'm a little concerned about your newsletter that outlines what the speaker said). The last time I spoke before a large group I tried to explain how the use of psychology in management helps the executive achieve better performance by subordinates. The newsletter had as its lead story, in a big headline, "Ginsburg shows need for psychological help."

> The last time I spoke before a professional group it was in the evening to police officers, some of whom had worked a shift prior to coming to the meeting. It was a long lecture in a warm room. I got carried away at one point and banged the lectern. Three men in the back, awoke and reached for their revolvers. Please check your revolvers at the door, listening to me may be hazardous to my health.

> I'm glad to be home and speaking before people I think I understand. I just returned from New York and saw a very strange thing. I was in a prestigeous watch and clock store having my watch repaired. A man came in and purchased a huge grandfather clock. It seems that he had been searching for that exact clock for many years. The salesman asked where it should be sent, but the man said,

no he was in a hurry, he would carry it. The salesman protested it was too heavy, the man insisted that it be strapped to his back. He left and I was so amazed I followed him for about half a block. Just as he reached the corner, someone came running around the other side, banged into him and the two individuals fell to the ground. The grandfather clock owner surveyed his broken clock and angry beyond words, sputtered, "Why don't you watch where you're going?" The other man, upon whom the clock had fallen said, "Why don't you wear a watch."

A staff member came in demanding a large increase. He was well known for thinking too much of himself and for straddling on any tough issue, never taking a definite stand. I asked him, "How often do you make major contributions to this organization?" He said, "Now and then." I asked, "What specifically do you do in making innovations?" He said, "This and that." "Where can I see the results of your contributions?" "Here and there," he said. He then asked me, "When do I get my raise?" I said, "Sooner or later."

On my trip here today, the pilot announced, "I've got good news and bad news. The good news is we're making excellent time, the bad news is, we're coming in for a crash landing."

San Francisco is getting wilder. A visitor to San Francisco ordered eggs and the counterman asked how she would like them. "However's easier for you," said the pleasant visitor. The counterman handed her two eggs in the shell.

The computer is of great importance in business and can be used for a variety of functions. Computer dating is one use of the new technology. A guy told the computer that he was 28, attended prestigeous schools, was tall, good-looking, made $25,000 a year and carried $1,000 bills around with him. The computer mugged him.

When I was promoted to Vice President, my daughter, who is not terribly impressed by such things said, "Good, daddy, now you're like the man in the supermarket; he's Vice President for Prunes." I was furious and said there was no Vice President for Prunes in the supermarket. She insisted. Furiously, I called the supermarket and said I wanted to talk to the Vice President for Prunes. The response was, "Which Vice President, sir, for packaged prunes or bulk prunes?"

A boy about 16 telephoned a supermarket manager and asked whether there was a part-time stock clerk position available. The manager replied it had been filled three months ago. The boy asked,

"Is your present stock clerk hardworking, dependable, honest, does he show initiative, potential, follow instructions, accomplish results, get along with people?" The manager responded affirmatively to all the questions, but was so impressed by them that he told the caller that another stock clerk position would be open soon, and asked whether he wanted the job. The caller responded, "No thanks, I already have the job as your part-time stock clerk, I was calling just to find out how I was doing."

We are all concerned about the impact of the economy on business today and listen to various economists with their prophecies about what's going to happen. We should listen carefully to knowledgable economists, but before we take everything being said as the gospel, I would like to tell you a story about economists.

An Engineer, a physicist and an economist were shipwrecked. All they found on the sand was a large can of beans, a book of dry matches and some sticks.

The Physicist said, "Let's build a fire and heat the can of beans. The can will explode, we'll lose some beans, but still have most of the beans to eat."

The Engineer said, "Let's improve your good plan. We'll build a wall around the fire and recover some of the lost beans."

"No, said the Economist, I have a much better plan. First, assume a can opener. . ."

Role Ambiguity—A $20,000 prize Texas bull was sent over to Saigon under the U. S. AID program to improve the breed of Vietnamese cattle. Put into a field with local cows, he displayed no interest at all. The bull's Texas breeder was flown out, walked out to the bull and held what appeared to be a whispered conversation with him. The beast promptly began making vigorous approaches to the cows. Afterwards, U. S. and Vietnamese officials asked what had happened. "Well, drawled the Texan, I was able to clear up a misunderstanding. He thought he was over here purely as an adviser."

Like the Egyptian mummy—I'm pressed for time.

Poor air traveler—Stewardess: Turbulence is no problem—it is like a boat in rough sea—Traveler: But I'm a better swimmer than flyer.

Knowledge—The man who knows *how* will always have a job; the man who knows *why* will always be his boss.

Degree—The college that gets richer by degrees, knows to whom to give the honorary ones.

College—a student I knew boasted that he had graduated from college without taking a course above the first floor.

Most college courses are alike; the notes of the professor become the notes of the students without passing through the minds of either.

Another disadvantage of going to college is that it slows up your education for four years.

College is a fountain of knowledge where some students come to drink, some to sip, but most come to gargle.

Another virtue of postgraduate courses is that they keep the boss' son out of the business for another few years.

Office—In some businesses, the office force is like one big family, nobody is congenial.

The man who gets to the office after nine o'clock is either an executive or will never be one.

Office hours are the hours during which an office is normally open for gossip.

Profit— Business prophets tell what is going to happen, business profits tell what has happened.

Boss— Don't envy your boss: remember he has to get up early to see who comes in late.

The boss is the man whose son is the most likely to succeed.

Nothing improves a man's jokes like being a boss.

Machine— One machine can do the work of 50 ordinary men, but no machine can do the work of one extraordinary man.

Computer— The real danger is not that machines will begin to think like men, but that men will begin to think like machines.

Executive— There are two kinds of executives; one tries to get around him better men than himself; the other tries to get around better men than himself.

A successful executive is one who delegates all responsibility, shifts all the blame, and appropriates all the credit.

An executive is a man employed to talk to visitors so that the other employees can get their work done.

My niece and her husband were talking. My niece said, "If we were rich, I don't think we would live any better than we do now." "You're right" her husband said, "we can't afford to live the way we do now."

A politician running for re-election was asked by a belligerent listener, "How do you stand on the cotton issue?" He quickly replied "I'm okay on that one. Are there any other questions?"

Official— "Young lady, you have all the qualifications for the job— background, training, personality—but frankly I prefer men."
Young lady—"I don't hold one's sexual preferences against him; frankly, I prefer men also."

A young fellow took a job in a small general store. A guy came in and asked about stove pipes and the young fellow said, "We sell it in 6 foot length." The tough customer asked for ½ a stovepipe. The young man said, "We don't sell it that way." "Well you sell half a baloney, sell me half." "Can't sir." "Are you the boss?" "No sir, I'm not, it won't help, but I'll check." So he told the boss, "I've got a tough, arrogant, unreasonable S.O.B. who wants to buy half a stovepipe." He then noticed the S.O.B. standing right beside him and said, "this fine gentleman wants to buy the other half."

Maine farmer asked by the Texan the size of his farm, "starts by the brook, goes to the clump of trees and back to the brook." Texan: "Why my ranch, if I got in my car in the morning and drove all day, I might come to the end of my ranch by sunset. What do you think of that?" Maine farmer: "I once had a car like that."

Someone died—looked up at his headstone with its glowing words and said, "Either someone is an awful liar, or I'm in the wrong hole."

Hen and pig are walking. They see a truck with a panel "Ham/Eggs." Hen says, "Look—that proves we're strong colleagues—what we do, we do together." The pig said, "You're right but please remember— for you, it's a day's work, for me it's a life committment."

Don't worry when a speaker looks at his watch. Start worrying when he starts shaking it.

Mark Twain told those requesting him to make a speech—$25 if you pick the topic. $10 if I pick the topic—in either case, you'll get exactly the same speech.

I want to start my speech by mentioning the name of an outstanding person and superb speaker, Tom Keating. I note this does not have any effect on you. I should say why I mention the name. Last night, I met someone in a cocktail lounge who was making a speech elsewhere in town. After a few drinks, we agreed that I would mention his name, if he mentioned mine.

I approach talking about this topic to those who have more knowledge than I with some humility—my approach is like the Johnstown flood person who saved many people and talked about it for years and then died. St. Peter in Heaven gave him his request. He asked for a large audience to describe how bad the flood was and what he had done. He saw thousands of people gathered in the Heavenly Amphitheatre. St. Peter called him over just before he began to speak and said he wanted to just mention that NOAH is in the audience.

I shall do the best I can but ultimately the blame for my shortcomings must be shared by the Program Chairman who invited me. That reminds me of the story of the Easterner who was invited to address a large group of ranchers in the West. The talk was a dismal failure. At the end, he saw three very large Westerners, with guns and lassos marching to the podium. He began to tremble and the man sitting next to him said, "don't worry, son, they don't want you. They want the program chairman."

At this point, the speaker usually summarizes his talk. I shall not do that because such a summary assumes that:

1. No one listened to the body of the speech
2. Or, the speaker could have everything much more concisely.

If You are Unhappy

Once upon a time there was a nonconforming sparrow who decided not to fly south for the winter. However, soon the weather turned so cold that he reluctantly started to fly south. In a short time ice began to form on his wings and he fell to earth in a barnyard, almost frozen. A cow passed by and crapped on the little sparrow. The sparrow thought it was the end. But, the manure warmed him and defrosted his wings. Warm and happy, able to breathe, he started to sing. Just then a large cat came by and hearing the chirping, investigated the sounds. The cat cleared away the manure, found the chirping bird and promptly ate him.

The moral of the story:

1. Everyone who craps on you is not necessarily your enemy.
2. Everyone who gets you out of the crap is not necessarily your friend.
3. And, if you're warm and happy in a pile of crap, keep your mouth shut.

Dealing with employee dissatisfaction:

There's a story of a woman who joined a religious order that demanded poverty, chastity, good works and silence, except that every 10 years an individual was permitted two words.

After 10 years, and an outstanding record, the woman appeared before the head of the religious order. "Well, my daughter, you have been outstanding," said the head. "What two words do you have to say." The woman pointed to her collar and said, "too tight." The head said, "we'll correct that immediately," and got her a proper fitting collar.

Ten years later, again after an outstanding record, she appeared before the head. "Well my daughter, you have kept up your excellent service and performance. What two words do you wish to say." The woman pointed to her shoes and said, "too loose." The head said, "we'll correct that immediately" and got her a proper fitting pair of shoes.

At the 30th anniversary, after another fine 10 years, the woman appeared and in response to the head's question of what two words do you have, she said, "I quit."

The head of the order responded, "I'm not surprised, you've been complaining ever since you got here."

Decision-making

A poor island community, isolated from the mainland, sought to increase tourism by building a bridge. But they had little money to spend so they hired rather inexperienced architects and engineers. When the bridge was about completed, they wanted to test the 10 ton limit. So they sent an 11 ton truck across the bridge. The bridge collapsed and the truck and a major portion fell into the river. They then had to spend a great deal of money to rent a special derrick to retrieve the truck and the major portion of the bridge. They re-inforced the part of the bridge and this time sent a truck with 10½ tons across the bridge. It collapsed again with the truck and portion of the bridge falling into the river. Again, they had to rent the very expensive equipment. They reinforced the portion of the bridge and sent a ten ton truck across. Again, a collapse. This time the City Council, Mayor and special consultant met about the problem. They reached a new decision. Rather than renting a derrick, they decided to buy it.

Writing

A friend of mine publishes a lot of articles, actually he publishes a few ideas many times in many different forms and places. Being a plagarist is bad enough, but he goes one step further—he's a self-plagarist.

There was a Controller of a major corporation who every morning for forty years opened the left hand drawer of his desk, took out a slip of paper, read it and returned it to the drawer and then proceeded to run the corporation. After he retired, they were cleaning out his desk of the few things he had left behind and found the slip of paper which said, "Always remember, debits on the left, credits on the right."

I was congratulating a young friend who has just been elected to the State Assembly. I asked him what the normal career pattern was for a young State Assemblyman. He said, "Congress, the Bench, Prison—not necessarily in that order."

"I have been asked by the Program Coordinator to keep my remarks short. There's a story about the President of Yale, who was asked to give a short graduation speech. So he took as his theme Y A L E and spoke for 20 minutes on Youth, 20 minutes on Attitude, 20 minutes on Learning and 20 minutes on Education. At the end, he said—are there any questions about my theme on Yale? One student rose and said—thank God we're not graduating from the Massachusetts Institute of Technology."

Advice

I left my successor (or gave a good friend) advice on how to handle serious crises on the job. I put a card in each of three envelopes, numbered Envelope 1, 2, 3. The first envelope for the first serious crisis he'll face contains the advice—"Blame it on your predecessor." The second envelop for the second crisis contains a card—"Tell them you'll re-organize." The third envelope to be used only when his job is at stake contains a card—"Begin to make out three envelopes."

twenty-two

The Executive and His Spouse

Buffeted by the winds of change in terms of women's liberation or the male mid-career crisis (which can also apply to women), the relationship between the executive and his spouse and family is of increasing importance to the executive in terms of his personal life, but also in terms of his effectiveness at work.

This discussion will deal with the issue of relationships from the perspective of the male executive, although some of the points would apply equally to female executives.

The typical upper middle level or upper level executive in the mid-forties to mid to late fifties faces the normal issues of children growing up, going or not going to college, college and career choices and performance, relationships with their own and the opposite sex, questions regarding drugs, alcohol, social and political standards and causes, earning a living, general maturity, etc. Difficult as the relationships with children may be, of more impact is the relationship to one's wife.

Our typical high achieving executive will probably have a wife between 40 and 55 (even though with the divorce rate growing among executives, the individual may have a second or third wife, our discussions center on the person who has remained married to the individual he married in his twenties or thirties). Just as changes in the executive's life may be quite profound, (turning 40, 45, 50 or 55, loss of a parent, children leaving home, topping out or burning out on the job, etc.), changes in his spouse's life may be very major and thus have a profound effect on her and her spouse and family. A new force in many women's lives is the effect of the women's liberation movement. More than ten years after Betty Friedan's path breaking book, The Feminine Mystique, the effects of women's liberation may finally be sinking in, perhaps brought home or exemplified by a daughter or friend. Having reached a milestone birthday, 40-45-50-55, she may now begin to question in great depth, what am I going to do with *my* life. Though not a typical women's "libber," the executive's spouse is likely to have developed a job or career for herself in the last few years, or may have continued a career throughout her marriage, or may now be looking to start something on her own, beyond voluntary organization activities, as rewarding as these may be.

She (as does the male executive for some of these points) faces major upheavals in her life at this stage:

1. Children no longer needing her as much as previously.
2. A growing feeling of getting old—that milestone birthday can really hurt.
3. Death of one or both parents.
4. A sense that she was born ten, fifteen, or twenty years too early and, therefore, did not have the advantages that younger women have today in regard to a wider range of initial job opportunities, educational options, and opportunities for promotion. Changes in life style and culturally accepted norms also effect her—marriage is not as important as it was twenty years ago, single and divorced women are much more common and acceptable, two career families are much more accepted.
5. There is a growing sense that "just" raising a family, being a housewife and being active in community and voluntary organizations does not offer enough personal satisfaction and recognition from spouse, friends, family or society in general.
6. There may be the cumulative or initial effects of relocation, frequent travel and periods of absence by her husband, the strain of business social obligations, the strain of living with an individual who may be overworked, overtired, overstressed, burned out, frustrated or dissatisfied with his job.
7. There may be cumulative tensions in the marriage, one or both parties may feel they have outgrown each other, reached their tolerance levels for annoyance, dissatisfaction, unhappiness or

boredom with each other, going through a mid-life or mid-career crisis where change is desired.

8. If active in a career or contemplating a career, she may feel that marital life and family responsibilities may be significantly less stimulating, rewarding and enjoyable than a career. She may then wish greater freedom to reach professional and personal goals which may require her to be less hampered or totally un-hampered by family responsibilities.

Although these problems may occur in any marriage, the executive and the organization must be concerned about a degenerating marriage, not only for personal reasons, but also because of the impact on work effort. It should be noted that many of the above tensions on the executive, cumulative work tensions or stresses of the moment, the mid-career crisis, the temptations and opportunities that a powerful position, travel funds and high salary can offer in terms of relationships with other women, all of these can make the male the major cause of a disintegrating marriage.

For the executive and spouse in this emotionally scarring situation, one hesitates to advise action. Clearly understanding where one has been, is at, and is going, as individuals and as a marriage is important. Letting the hair down and frank discussions are necessary and perhaps some time and space together or apart to think about the marriage is necessary. Professional assistance in the form of clergy-men, marriage counselors, psychiatrists or psychologists can be help-ful. Medical checkups might be in order as well as an assessment whether there are some troublesome issues at home or at work that are causing significant distress or depression, but are not fundamental enough to shake the foundation of the marriage.

The divorce and separation rates grow and it is now fairly common to see people go apart after 10, 15, 20, 25 years and more of marriage. People tend to wait less often than in the past for the children to grow up, and companies are more understanding of having divorced top executives and those who lead a somewhat swinging type of existence.

One can approach the troubled marriage as a problem solving situation. Attempt to identify the problem through introspection and communication. Assess causes and remedies and the negative and positive consequences of action. Develop a solution and a detailed implementation plan and schedule. Gain acceptance and hopefully enthusiasm for the plan and then put the plan into action. Monitor results, fine tune or make major changes as necessary. One can also employ outside consultants (marriage counselors, psychiatrists, etc.).

But after all is said and done, logic, reason, management approaches can go just so far. Emotion, the heart, the gut, past history, will tend to prevail. It may well be that for whatever reasons one must regard tomorrow as the first day of the rest of your life and plan accordingly how you want to spend the rest of your life. One can, of course, seek to improve the home situation so that it changes from a negative effect on one's self and one's career to a positive stimulus. Accomodation, compromise, reasonable levels of tolerance and new understandings can be reached.

This might call for more discussions or less discussion about work problems or more involvement or less involvement in company related activities. But it may also require a greater interest and involvement by the executive in his wife's problems, concerns and aspirations. More sharing of family responsibilities may be necessary, more help for one's wife in advancing her goals and aspirations may be required—funds for education or travel, taking over some home duties while she is pursuing her interests, understanding of her need to work and to be working at night and on weekends, and to travel, understanding of the pressures and social requirement for *her* and for *you* caused by *her* job.

The high achieving executive may seek to achieve in his family life the same levels of success and satisfaction he is accustomed to at work. But it may require far greater effort, understanding and commitment than he is accustomed to providing or consider worth providing given the results he expects. And, thus, more in sorrow than in anger, either or both the executive and his spouse may finally decide to cut their losses, declare bankruptcy or close down the business.

The strain of executive life and the relationship with the executive's spouse who may indeed have significantly different needs and aspirations than twenty or even a few years ago, is a topic that deserves greater consideration than heretofore.

twenty-three

Successful Convention Planning

Considerable time, effort and money are spent by many organizations for convention planning and implementation. Conventions are a multi-billion dollar industry. There are well over 10,000 associations and groups in the United States. They hold scores of thousands of conventions and mini-conventions annually for their local, regional, state and national needs. Company meetings and workshops for introducing new techniques, products, continuing education needs and governmental requirements also add significantly to the number of conventions.[1] Attendees at conventions include association members, professionals, partners, salesmen, dealers, volunteers, workers, buyers, top executives, staff, distributors, etc.

A well-planned, organized and well-run convention can have a significant impact on the present and future operations and success of a company, organization or association. It can have a positive or negative effect on the image of the organization, its ability to accomplish its objectives, motivate staff and attendees, improve morale and espirit de corps, create a sense of excitement and progress. This article suggests ways in which the convention planner or planning group can achieve a successful convention. At the same time, it outlines aspects of their work that should concern top executives.

The first and primary step in having a successful convention is being clear as to the exact goals top management and those attending

---

[1] A reasonable estimate of the number of annual meetings held by companies and associations totals close to 1,000,000 meetings annually.

wish to achieve through and at the convention. The goals or objectives should be a major factor in determining: where the convention will be held, when, whether spouses will be invited; the length of the convention; the topics, format, style, speakers and methods of presentation; the mix between work and vacation, formality, informality and fun.

Most conventions seek to achieve one or more of the following objectives: provide, establish or review new information, directions, policies, plans and practices; discuss ideas and experiences; provide the means for attendees to make contacts; provide the ability to meet socially and informally with colleagues and to have an enjoyable break from the usual routine; conduct the organization's business; introduce new leaders; motivate and energize all involved.

There are many reasons why a good number of conventions are not worth the time and money involved. They may, in fact, harm the organization. The root causes of failures basically flow from a lack of thorough planning including serious concern for the audience's goals and expectations. Often, the goals of the planners are simply unrealistic or beyond attainment. The physical facilities and meeting setups are poor or inappropriate for achieving goals or audience needs. The material and presentation formats are inadequate. The speakers are poorly prepared, boring and talk down to the audience. From the audience's point of view, all too frequently they were not consulted about the meeting objectives and don't understand or agree with them. They are sometimes uninterested in the material and manner of presentation. Often, they don't feel involved, concerned or responsible about the outcome of the meeting, its success is not important to them.

In order to avoid these frequent pitfalls, planners must formulate clear, specific objectives for the entire convention as well as for each session. Top management must be consulted as well as those who will attend the meeting. The audience's interests and expectations must be ascertained and related to the objectives of the meeting. Specific actions must be taken to assure that prior to, during, and after the convention, those attending believe the convention is concerned with their interests and is, therefore, important for and to them. Whenever possible, a broad spectrum of audience members should be involved in planning the convention. Physical facilities and arrangements must be carefully checked and evaluated and presentation methods focused on the materials to be presented, the situation and the audience. Effective communication, before, during and after the convention, must be developed, designed and tested.

Site selection for any convention is a very important decision. There are two basic categories of questions that must be answered prior to site selection. One, is an analysis of the membership or audience and its needs. The second is the style of the meeting.

In looking at the audience involved, the following must be answered:

- How important is geographic location and time of year—is it important "politically" to rotate sites among various areas of the country during different seasons of the year?
- Would your audience prefer a resort atmosphere or city, are they recreation and/or sports minded, sightseeing oriented, interested in nightlife entertainment or cultural activities, interested in outdoor activities such as golf, tennis, swimming, picnics?
- Should the convention be considered as a convenient place for pre-or post convention vacation or tour tie-ins, and if so, which areas and sites are best suited for this idea?
- Is there interest and concern about areas off the beaten tract that are ordinarily not visited or are not the usual convention site?
- Is there a particular concern about going to a very well known location, or about safety, or about beautiful surroundings?
- Does a potential site meet the economic interests of the arrangers and the audience?

Often the answers to these questions must be obtained through a questionnaire of many or a sample of members.

Meeting style is also a critical factor in site selection. A heavy emphasis on exhibits will involve concern about shipping and transportation as well as the labor situation and costs. A concern for on-site visits or inspection of various facilities will demand concern for the number of available facilities, transportation, logistics. If it is indeed to be a "hard work," education, and results oriented convention, you might want a self-contained or relatively isolated site where there is little other competition or temptation for the attendees' attention. If the convention is seen as a combination of work and play, a large city or well developed resort area might then be the appropriate choice at an appropriate time of year. If at all possible, the site should harmonize with the goals, mood and style of the convention.

Once determining the answers to the primary questions, a particular location's convention and visitors bureau, hotels and arenas can be contacted for detailed information. Wise planners will personally check out sites and be concerned about general conditions of meeting places and hotels, the accommodations offered, facilities, equipment, meeting rooms and meeting setups, parking, food, exhibit space and audiovisual facilities, services, transportation, accessability, dates available, costs, efficiency in administrative procedures at the hotels and meeting sites, recreational and entertainment facilities, quality of staff, and security.

In reviewing various administrative details of the convention, attention should be paid to: notices, signs; material recording, duplication and distribution; registration, tickets and information procedures; recordkeeping; supplies; communications; charges; badges; messages, emergencies, outside activities such as sightseeing, car rentals; special gratuities; convention accounting; preconvention briefing and post convention evaluation.

Of necessary concern is the spouse program. The old fashion show and luncheons approach may be a disadvantage in attracting spouses and, in fact, the convention goer him or herself. By gathering information about the spouses, by asking them what they would like through a questionnaire, an exciting program can be arranged. Such a program may include sightseeing; various types of entertainment including theatre, concerts, museums, spectator sports; social functions at the convention including a hospitality room; sports for participation; baby sitting service. Interesting speakers on current events or the area's history and culture can be arranged. Self-improvement courses can be given in such things as speedreading, time management, bridge, gourmet cooking, photography. Mini-academic or continuing education courses can also be given over a three or more days convention in conjunction with a local university.

Promotion and publicity are of considerable importance to those sponsoring and attending, and possibly to the trade, exhibitors and the public in general. The goal should be motivating individuals to be interested in the convention. A schedule of attractive and interesting mailings should be set up to reach a crescendo at convention time. The timing, extent and the excitement of promotional effort can have a major effect not only on attendance but on the spirit of the convention. The local convention bureau and the hotels can provide very useful material about the community and the area, unique attractions, special events, headliner entertainment if available, etc.

What has been outlined are some of the benchmarks for planning a convention. But the most critical factor is where we first began, the objectives and the program to carry out the objectives. A well-administered convention with all administrative details carefully planned is, of course, a plus. But if the convention does not accomplish its goals both for the arrangers and the attendees it is, in the final analysis, an expensive failure.

A good program committee that designs a detailed program plan is crucial to the success of the convention. The committee should include as many views as possible. Their focus should be on what do they want the typical attendee to carry away with him overall, and from each particular session or event. Well in advance, attendees at the convention might be asked what they want discussed, with how much emphasis and detail, in what types of formats, and what they hope to get out of the convention both in content and atmosphere. This brings about a feeling of importance on the part of the delegates, causes them to focus on the forthcoming convention and increases interest in attending. The planners will receive valuable information to set priorities, subject matter, time allocation, methods of presentation and speakers to be contacted. Committee members and others should be assigned specific duties in regard to coordinating sections of the program, getting speakers, etc. A successful convention is not a one man show.

Each potential item on the program should be subjected to various tests. What is the nature of the material (controversial, quantitative, technical, informational, philosophical)? What is the setting for the material (what comes before and after it, what is the level of audience interest and knowledge about the subject, what do we want the individual to carry away with him, is it "important" to a large number of listeners)? Depending upon the material and the audience, a variety of platform presentation methods can be employed to convey information, elicit responses and maintain interest. Presentations can include speeches, speeches with audiovisual aids, demonstrations, situation presentations, dramatic action presentations, films and case studies, panel-symposium-forums. Opportunities should be provided for maximum participation of attendees. This can involve ample questions and discussion time at each session, breaking down into "buzz-groups," providing question and note pads and sufficient time for informal and casual conversations over drinks, coffee or around a swimming pool. Sending material out well in advance so that attendees have the opportunity to think and then respond at the convention is another valuable way of encouraging interest and participation.

The objectives, size of group and time available have major impact on the schedule. In scheduling, the right mix among types of formal and informal meetings, relaxation and entertainment, is of great importance in attaining both the objectives and mood sought.

Evaluation of effort is very necessary and often overlooked. Such evaluation need not wait for the end of meeting questionnaire or be limited solely to that. Preconvention consultation was suggested above, but during the convention a sample of delegates can be queried as to their reactions. If necessary, and possible, some changes can be made. If there are several sessions on a particular topic, knowing the reactions to the first or second session can be very helpful in shaping the rest of the sessions.

At the end of the meeting, a questionnaire might be used. Or, a small group of individuals could be interviewed before and after the convention in regard to their expectations and their reactions as to what actually occurred. A few weeks after the convention a questionnaire might be sent to all attendees asking what particular items in the program (and other aspects of the convention) stand out in their memories, what has been most useful to them on the job, what would they change for next year? By taking seriously what is said, before, during and after the convention, the planner has an opportunity to improve both the present and future conventions. Those involved in planning and execution should keep a file on what occurred and write a review of actions taken with suggestions for those involved in planning the next convention.

If conventions are to be more than just a break from the routine and a chance to relax and talk with colleagues (and these are worthwhile goals in themselves), careful program and administrative planning, implementation, communication, evaluation and follow-up must be done. The effort and costs will be considerable, but for all those involved in a truly successful convention, the benefits will far outweigh the costs.

twenty-four

Evaluating Educational Institutions

Corporations have a notable record of contributions to higher education institutions. In addition to capital, operating and scholarship fund monetary contributions by the corporation and its leaders, many corporate leaders and staff serve on various university and college boards, committees, projects and state coordinating bodies. Corporations serve as sources of revenue by providing tuition remission programs for their employees and by working out arrangements for university courses on company sites and for university research studies. Corporations also serve as a source of internships and jobs for a university's students.

Since significant corporate money and time may be spent in regard to a particular institution, it may be beneficial for a corporation to evaluate whether the particular educational institution is using the money and time wisely and well (of course, academic freedom and institutional missions should be respected). In essence, aside from direct evaluation of particular research studies performed for the company and reactions of their employees to courses given by the institution, the corporation may wish to evaluate whether the particular educational institution is worth a general investment or whether another institution is a better investment opportunity. Some criteria and factors for consideration are suggested in this article.

CRITERIA—FACTORS FOR CONSIDERATION

Academic Quality

1. How high are the academic standards, for students as well as in hiring, promoting and tenuring faculty—how are they enforced and are the standards and enforcement reasonable.
2. How good are the professors as teachers, researchers and individuals who contribute to the generation of new knowledge and to the dissemination and transmittal of new and existing knowledge.
3. How available are the professors to students.
4. How flexible are the programs and the professors in regard to student needs and academic challenge and innovation.
5. How good, modern, and accessible are the various library and support services, facilities and instructional equipment.
6. Is there a real concern for quality of effort rather than just saying so, are the various programs really first rate.
7. Does the student feel he truly earned his degree.
8. What research and training contributions has the institution made to the community, area, region and nation.
9. What are the publications, research, training and community service records of particular departments and the institution as a whole.

Students

1. Are the administration, faculty, trustees tuned in to student concerns.
2. What avenues are there for students to express their views and grievances.
3. Are students involved in governance—how so.
4. What's the track record in regard to responsiveness to student concerns.
5. What's the attitude toward students by various categories of staff—administrators, faculty, secretaries, security officers, etc.
6. How good are the various student support services—counseling, placement, etc.
7. How well the students do on the job and in their careers.
8. How tuned in is the college to non-traditional students.

Responsiveness to Change

In response to changing times and needs, what have been the changes in regard to university goals, programs, courses, majors, interdisciplinary approaches, instructional methods, community needs, student services, recruiting and advertising, out-reach to nontraditional students.

Governance Structure of the University

1. Who has authority to do what in what time frame—Trustees, President, Vice Presidents, Deans, Chairpersons, Faculty, Students, Alumni.
2. Who has the power to delay or veto. Are decisions made thoughtfully yet in a timely fashion.
3. How is the institution organized and how recently have changes been made; how realistic is the organization.

Budget

1. How does the institution plan, monitor and control the budget—who is involved—how are decisions made.
2. What's the track record of actual vs. planned in regard to the bottom line.
3. What reserves are there.
4. What's the percentage of scholarships to income and has the ratio changed.
5. What percentage of expenses are spent in instructional costs, plant upkeep, support services and how have these varied.
6. What's the backlog in regard to deferred maintenance and how will it be funded.
7. What's happened over time to research, grant and gift support.
8. What strategies have been adopted for increasing income and decreasing expense—and what's happened.
9. What do the trends show in regard to actual expenditures and income over the last few years and what are the projections for the future.
10. What's the staffing ratios and how have staff numbers changed in relationship to enrollment and income.

Staff Relations

1. Morale—as measured by what staff members say about the institution and its officials, turnover, accessibility of top officials.
2. Unionization—which groups, if any, are organized—why or why not; what is in the contract that hampers good management or seems excessive, what did management "get," what did it "give."
3. How does the institution measure and reward performance—how high are the standards of performance.

Plant and Facilities

1. How does the place look and how does it really look beyond the usual spots that one focuses attention on.
2. Is there a planned maintenance schedule and replacement and refurbishment schedule and is it adhered to.
3. How adequate are the facilities in terms of adequate space for libraries, study, recreation, athletics, offices, student activities, laboratories, classrooms, seminar rooms, etc.
4. How good is residential space in terms of size of dorm rooms, various kinds of dorm facilities, maintenance and upkeep.

Systems and Procedures

1. Are the systems and procedures in all areas of the university— whether it be registration, admissions, payments, housing, grades, transcripts, diplomas, etc.—modern, accurate, timely, and concerned with a service approach toward meeting student and other needs rather than just living by the rules, which may be rather inflexible and not tuned in to concerns of consumers.
2. Is there a concern for effectiveness, efficiency, and economy.

Neighborliness

Is the institution truly part of the community, providing services and access to the immediate community and to the wide area surrounding the university or college.

Identity of the Institution

1. Is there a sense of what the institution is all about, its strengths and weaknesses, its unique aspects, its areas of particular value to its students, or to the community, including students.
2. Is there a sense of identity with the institutions' goals and programs and activities and aspirations that is shared among all members of the community, including students.
3. Is there a sense of a loyal and dedicated and interested student and alumni body as well as faculty and administrators.

Governmental Relations

1. If it is a public university, how is it able to relate to the legislature and executive branch. Whether public or independent, how is the university able to relate to the various governmental regulations and laws that effect it.
2. How is it in obtaining research grants and financial aid for students, special appropriations from various governmental bodies.
3. How does it relate to governmental jurisdictions in terms of fire, police, safety and building inspections, etc.

Style of Management

Summing it all up, what is the style of the institution. Is it open or closed; is it straight forward; is there a sense of good and responsive management; does it encourage free expression and dissent; does it encourage innovation and questioning where we are and where we are going; how confident is the management about itself and the future of the institution; how participative or authoritarian is management; how does it communicate, consult and coordinate; does it know where it's going, where it's been and how it has performed; is it able to react well to crises and anticipate most of them. In effect, how does management put everything all together.

HOW TO RATE

You may want to give each category a value of 10 points and assign a grade of 1-10 for each category, thus the most an institution can earn is 100 points in a category or 1,200 in total. Remember, be at least as tough in evaluating the institution as it was (if you graduated from there) or would have been in evaluating you. Out of a total possible score of 1,200 you may decide (depending on how easy a marker you are) to assign 1,080 or above an A, 960-1,079 a B, 840-959 a C, 720-839 a D and below 720 a failing grade. If you like to be more exact, add pluses and minuses. If you graduated from the institution and are daring, you may want to submit your analysis for a grade to the Dean of the Business School or President of the College, but watch out, he or she may try to revoke your degree!

III

QUESTIONS AND RESPONSES ABOUT WORK-RELATED PROBLEMS

INTRODUCTION

During 1980, I answered listeners questions at 12:55 p.m. on "The World of Work" on WGUC, the University of Cincinnati and national public radio station in Cincinnati, Ohio. I have selected some of the questions asked and my answers in order to give a flavor of some concerns that people have about work related issues.

I am a secretary who frequently uses a duplicating machine. While my sense of humor does not include making a xerox copy of my "buns," I believe that firing a person for having an off-beat sense of humor is very harsh treatment. (This letter refers to the secretary who was fired for making a xerox copy of her rear). Shouldn't a company respect an employee's right to have an off-beat sense of humor? The whole idea of firing an otherwise efficient secretary for duplicating her "buns" on a xerox machine makes me very angry. Sign me. . . .

Hot Cross Buns

Dear Hot Cross Buns:

This is a rather unusual question. As one who usually deals with the bottom line on financial statements, I'm not sure that I am expert in regard to other kinds of bottoms. I used to be, but my children are growing up.

I assume this letter is based on the story widely carried in the newspapers of a secretary who photo copied a part of her anatomy and when other employees began talking about it, management fired her presumably because she lied when asked whether she had done so.

I think an appropriate sense of humor is very important to success in management. Employees usually feel better about working for a company that does not appear to be overly staid or stuffy.

In this particular case, one has to decide whether this was indeed appropriate humor. I think not. But, I also believe that on the facts of the case itself, firing was not called for. Lying in and of itself is grounds for dismissal. If the individual had "confessed" prior to an accusation and said after thinking about it she realized it was the wrong thing to do, I believe an oral or written reprimand or other discipline would have been sufficient. Similar or somewhat stronger action, short of termination would have been warranted, if when accused, she admitted the act. But lying was sufficient grounds for dismissal. The company might also want to indicate in a memo to all staff that copying machines were to be used only for company business and use of the machine for personal business would be considered as grounds for disciplinary action. One other thought, punishment in a corporate setting should not only fit the crime, but also take into account the employee's past record in regard to performance and disciplinary actions and the circumstances surrounding the infraction.

I'm under a lot of stress and tension at work—deadlines, a lot to do, not enough help, a tough boss. It's hurting my performance and home life.

What can I do?

Tense

Dear Tense:

People often get in the situation you describe. Sometimes there may be physical health problems involved or family or personal problems. Just as work problems effect home life, the opposite is also true.

If we focus on the work issue, it's important to realize that every job has frustrations and tensions and sometimes these may get to be too much to handle. It may also be that you are burning out or bored or unhappy with your work, promotion opportunities, salary, boss, or company.

If you don't take steps to attack this problem, you may get into real difficulty.

I suggest that you may want to discuss this with your spouse, a co-worker or colleague or friend just as a way of relieving anxiety and tension. It is possible that you may want to discuss the problem with you boss or someone in the Personnel Department. Some supervisors react well when a subordinate indicates that there has been a lot of pressure lately and perhaps he can talk about how to accomplish the goals with less tension and pressures. Other supervisors will mark you as a person who is a complainer or cannot take the heat—so be careful in deciding whether to talk to your supervisor.

There are things you can do for yourself. List the specific problems or tension building incidents. Think about what caused them and why they occurred. Then, think of ways you could have reduced the tension or handled the matter differently. Also, just by listing these upsetting things on paper, you can begin to say, that's not so bad, I can deal with that, this one's not that important, don't get emotional about small stuff.

One other area of attack—you may want to take a coffee break with a friend just to get away from it all and talk about something else, or relax more at lunch by non-business talk, or plan a long weekend vacation. Some people find it helpful to do various types of relaxing exercises during the day or jogging or athletic endeavor at lunch, before or after work to conquer tension.

Instead of letting these feeling roll over and knock you down and perhaps out, you should recognize that all of us have varying degrees of stress at various times. You then should be aggressive in looking at the problem and learning to deal with it.

A key supervisor in my company appears to be seriously ill. . . I think he will probably have to stop work in the next few weeks. I'm a supervisor in another area and I think the boss may ask me to step in to complete the very important project he was on. There are other well qualified people who can also be asked to step in. If I am offered the opportunity should I accept or should I try to find a way to get out of it? (Since there are other people available, I'm sure the boss won't hold it against me if I get out of it in a nice way).

Undecided

Dear Undecided:

We have all been conditioned by two opposing proverbs, "take advantage of every opportunity," and the military service warning of "don't volunteer." In our Walter Mitty dreams, we frequently have visions of stepping into the break and doing such a great job that we're promoted to Vice President and marry the boss' daughter. I propose another proverb to guide you, "look before you leap," although I recognize that "he who hesitates might be lost."

I would suggest that you neither accept hurriedly or try to find a way to get out of it. Buy time is my advice, take a look at the pluses and minuses. Don't be too much of a gambler, the rewards may be terrific but the odds may very well be against you.

If the boss comes to you, it's a great compliment and you will have considerable visibility. Clearly there are pluses. But consider the following possible negatives:

1. *Are you really competent enought to step in and do a better than satisfactory job?*
2. *Do you have enough time to learn the job and skills required— if you do a poor job, your reputation may be hurt for a long time.*
3. *How competent and interested are the people you'll have to work with, will they really cooperate?*
4. *What's going to happen to your own responsibilities while you're taking over the project?*

If you think the odds are stacked against you, try to find a way out by indicating that you won't be able to do the job expected on such short notice. Also state your willingness to be of help to the person chosen.

If there's no way out and you have to accept, try to get whatever help you can. Ask for people to be assigned to you temporarily, try to extend the schedule, see if you can get an outside expert to help you. In short, don't have your head turned by Grade B move versions of what great things can happen to you but face the decision making process realistically.

I am young, ambitious, and frankly, very talented. I've just landed a "pre-executive" position with a good company, just two years out of college. But I don't want to stay at this level for long.

Tell me, how can I "get off the mark" quickly? I want to make a strong impression right away without seeming pushy.

Young and Ambitious

Dear Young and Ambitious:

Ah, to be young and ambitious. My advice is to be careful that you don't appear either too young or too ambitious. Often, talented young people try to prove in everything they do, how outstanding they are and end up antagonizing others and falling on their face. And sometimes, even though bright eyed and bushy tailed, the young hot shot really isn't as good as he or she thinks he is, and ends up like a shooting star that appears quickly, moves fast and luminously and then just disappears.

To get off the mark quickly I suggest:

1. *Learn your job thoroughly and do it in a solid and, where possible, creative way. Don't just do the flashy things well, but also do your homework and meet the nitty gritty, routine aspects in the same manner as you do the more noticeable aspects of your job.*
2. *Before you ask for more assignments or more challenging assignments, make sure you've established yourself as very good in all aspects of your present assignments, including personal relations.*
3. *Seek to establish good working and personal relationships with superiors, subordinates, peers, support staff by tuning in to them as people and reacting sensitively rather than holding yourself aloof.*
4. *Put forth extra effort willingly, whether weekend or evening work, short lunch hours, etc.*
5. *Not only meet your deadlines on assignments, but try to beat them.*
6. *Review what you have done before you hand in completed work.*
7. *Set goals for yourself and strive to accomplish them—these should also include goals in regard to operating style and human relations.*

Once you've done the above well and on a continuous rather than one shot basis, seek out opportunities for further growth, learning and challenge—whether additional training or extra or different assignments.

In short, the odds are that if you keep a sense of wanting to be ambitious and deliver performance rather than banking on potential, you will indeed fulfill your ambitious goals.

M y husband seems about ready to become an executive drop out. I've tried talking with him about the problem, but I don't think I'm getting across. Please advise me on understanding the state he is in, and what I might do to help.

Concerned Wife

Dear Concerned Wife:

Temptation for the executive to drop out is an increasing problem for individuals, their families and their companies.

It might help you to know that there are some common causes for this problem.

1. *Fatigue—a feeling of mental, physical, even spiritual exhaustion. The executive feels that a change of pace, a long vacation, a new assignment won't provide a remedy and thus he wishes to drop out.*
2. *A sense of little time remaining in life or in a career. This is sometimes regarded as the mid-career crisis. It may come about because of some perceived failure on the job or in one's career. It may also result from one feeling that tomorrow is the first day of the rest of your life and that one's goals and lifestyle should be reassessed.*
3. *Some type of personal shock or grief or unhappiness.*

Frequently the executive gets conflicting advice. He's lambasted— "you're throwing away a good job or career," "you're a fool," "you're sacrificing your family." Others will say, "you're right," "I wish I had your guts."

You might urge him to talk with people he respects in business, his friends, a physical to check whether there are physical problems, a clergyman, and perhaps seek counseling and psychiatric help.

The executive contemplating dropping out should focus on such questions as:

1. What happens if he's unhappy with his new life.
2. What are the chances of coming back to the company or his career field—he may indeed find it very difficult.
3. Is there another approach rather than the all or nothing dropping out—vacation, professional help, different assignments.

For some, starting a new path is the best thing to do and the sooner done the better in terms of one's enjoyment of life and of one's family. However, this major step should be carefully and calmly thought through, preferably after a good deal of conversation, rest, and if necessary, professional counseling. For you as the concerned spouse, it is indeed a very difficult and perplexing time, but your understanding, involvement and support are crucial.

I am a generalist and receive quite a few reports and recommendations that contain a great many "facts." How do I make sure that a fact is a fact?

Truth Seeker

Dear Truth Seeker:

The higher one goes in management, the more remote you are, generally, from the basic data that produces the facts. Normally, you have to rely on the competence, judgment and integrity of your subordinates and their subordinates as well as your own knowledge and hunches.

To strengthen the chances that the facts are indeed facts, I suggest:

1. Be careful of absolute statements unless you're 100% sure. Even if facts are facts, there may indeed be different interpretations. Thus, without overdoing hedging you may want to say, "it appears that" rather than "it is certain that," or you may want to state assumptions and margins of error.

2. *Watch out for vested interests that may blind those coming out with the facts to other alternatives or approaches or inter- pretations—ask for assumptions, alternatives, pros and cons.*
3. *Check with others—ask for evaluations by knowledgeable peo- ple in and outside the company.*
4. *Take you time, something may seem certain today and not so certain three days from now. But remember, you normally can't delay too long and often decisions are made without 100% of all the information you may want to have.*
5. *Encourage and reward independent and creative thinking so that your subordinates and you don't always take the obvious path or follow the same line.*

By doing what I've sketched, you are likely to build a climate that produces better facts, interpretations, analysis and ultimately better decisions.

I have a number of employees who are very sensitive to getting directions from me and accepting criticism. What can I do?

Trying to Tame Touchy People

Dear Trying to Tame Touchy People:

First, make sure you're not getting touchy or super sensitive to touchy people. You should try to be objective to determine whether you have offended the individuals by word, action, tone, body lan- guage or whatever. However, if you can honestly say that you've done nothing to offend a person with a reasonably thick skin, then don't get yourself in a stew just because someone else is very thin skinned. There are some things you can do to try to soothe the prob- lem for the thin-skinned person:

1. *Try to find out if there's a particular thing, circumstance or time of day that he or she is more sensitive to—and work with that knowledge.*
2. *If you think something you've said or done is bothering him/ her, discuss it. Try to get him or her to open up—maybe it's*

*an expression you use that he/she just doesn't like, or maybe
you like to kid and he/she doesn't have a sense of humor or
thinks you don't. .*

3. *Try to get your point across without getting the other person's
    defenses up. If you disagree with what his reaction or idea is,
    don't just shoot it down, spend some time talking about it,
    suggest alternatives.*
4. *When they deserve it, praise them. But don't just throw away
    praise, you'll cheapen the value.*

*With some planning on your part and assuming mutual good will,
you can solve much of the sensitive people syndrome.*

I am in middle management and I'm taking too much work
home from the office. It's hurting my family life and relaxing time.
Can you advise me what and what not to bring home? Thank you.

Homeworker

Dear Homeworker:

*In days gone by, and even today, there are the workaholics who
for a variety of reasons come in early, work late and spend much of
their evening and weekends working. The two bulging attache cases
to be taken home each evening or weekend is a way of life for many.
But increasingly, the sense of wanting to enjoy something more in
life than work, is taking hold in the United States. You may have to
take work home during peak load periods or due to various emergencies, but it is better for you, your family, and your company, if you
tried to cut down the amount. You therefore should analyze what
you have been taking home to see if it was indeed important or
whether it could wait for the next day or be delegated to someone
else. It is true that many executives find that they need the quiet
time at home for reading complicated material or for thinking through
tough problems.*

As to your specific concern as to what to take home and what not:

Consider for homework:

1. *Things you want to think about in a quiet setting away from the usual pressures of work.*
2. *Something that you don't really like to do and just keep putting off.*

Bar from homework:

1. *Work you have to do by questioning or working with colleagues or subordinates or by checking reference material.*
2. *Non-essential work that eats into your family time or relaxation time.*

Assuming that some work has to be brought home, you have to consider the needs of your family:

1. *Over time your spouses concerns and needs may have changed and he or she either needs your involvement in certain problems of his/her own career or in managing the household.*
2. *Recognize that there are some very important matters, events, or emergencies at home that rightfully take precedence over work—and don't feel guilty about it.*
3. *Plan your home time—work, relaxation, family time as well as you can to minimize conflicts and make the most of your time.*
4. *If you have to miss something important at home, try to explain it well in advance of the particular event.*

There's more to life than going through a bulging briefcase. By looking at the work you take home, the needs of your family, and your own needs for non work related time, you can meet the formidable challenge of balancing work and non work.

I have just been promoted to my first managerial position. I have always thought that when I got to be a manager I would try to be a supportive and people oriented boss rather than a tough boss. Can you give me some tips on what I can do to be regarded by subordinates as a people oriented boss?

New Manager

Dear New Manager:

It is a very good indication of future success that in your first managerial position you want to establish a commitment, philosophy and style of being a people oriented manager. However, don't forget that you also have an obligation to obtain good results and high productivity. High morale and job satisfaction doesn't necessarily go along with high productivity. Therefore, be careful that you don't lose sight of the fact that you have to produce in terms of the bottom line. With skill and knowledge you can obtain good results and still feel good about how you deal with your subordinates. Even more important, your subordinates can feel good about their relationships with you.

You can indeed be a results oriented boss and a nice person to work for if:

1. *You insist that people have the facts and do their homework.*
2. *Treat everyone fairly and don't single out favorites or persons you're always down on.*
3. *You fight for your subordinates—you back them up, try hard to get the resources they need, try hard to get them salary increases commensurate with their performance, advance their ideas with full credit to them and involvement by them.*
4. *Demonstrate personal concern about people and their personal interests—their health if they've come back from sick leave, or are in the hospital, their children, etc.*
5. *You are serious about the results expected of the unit and of the individuals in the unit.*
6. *Your subordinates should feel they have access to you and that you welcome their interaction with you.*
7. *You are candid with your subordinates, concerned about their problems and avoid placing blame on them.*
8. *You encourage your subordinates in regard to promotions, opportunities in the company or in regard to further training.*

I think with these general guidelines in mind and your successful implementation of them, you will be on a fast track to success.

I have a severe absenteeism record in my unit and my supervisor is on my back. What can I do about absenteeism among my subordinates?

Time Checker

Dear Time Checker:

Often high absenteeism is a symptom of dissatisfaction, poor morale, discomfort about the physical working conditions, unhappiness about what people are doing, how they are doing it or who they are doing it with. Therefore, you may have to probe deeper and deal with even tougher problems than absenteeism.

As far as absenteeism itself is concerned, I suggest:

1. *Keep good records, find out who is out, how often, and whether there are particular patterns—Mondays and Fridays for example.*
2. *Let people know that you are keeping records and are interested in good attendance as one factor in promotions, salary increases, choice assignments.*
3. *Talk with individuals who have poor records but do so in a manner that indicates you need them and that they're important to the work effort of the unit.*
4. *Try to motivate people about the deadlines ahead, productivity needed, goals to be achieved so that they feel that their presence is important.*

You have a tough task ahead but by talking with individuals and showing you're interested in their attendance and efforts, the odds are that there will be a significant improvement.

I 'm 28 and a single woman. My boss is 35 and recently legally separated. He asked me out and I said I was busy. I think he'll ask me again. If he wasn't my boss I'd like to go out with him, but somehow I think it wouldn't be good for my career in the company if I go out even once. What do you think?

Interested But Wary

Dear Interested But Wary:

Instead of Dear Sig, I feel like Dear Abby. I think you're right. Generally, dating one's boss has the risk of leading to some difficulties for both parties. If all works out well and you get seriously involved, that may seem fine. And it is for both of you, but if others find out about it, it is impossible to change perceptions that you are getting better assignments or increases because of your relationship. Or, he may be forced to bend over backwards and give you less than you deserve. If you get married, it is probably against company rules that you serve in a position where he determines your salary increases or promotions. If it turns out to be a casual relationship which either or both of you stop, there may be some bad feelings that effect your working relationship. Those bad feelings may be harmful to you if he turns out not to be so interesting and you break it off.

This may seem like a lot of long-range planning over a simple first date. Many people just go ahead and don't worry about the first date and just see what happens. If you're a risk taker, or don't plan to be in the company that long or if he's really great—go ahead and enjoy it. But, if you're a cautious individual, and he doesn't seem to meet an "A" rating, don't run the risks of a C+ kind of guy.

You can hear from what I've said why I'm a manager and not a counselor.

M y boss has offered me a choice of an 8% increase in salary or the equivalent amount of cost to him in an increase in fringe benefits of my choosing. What do you suggest I do? Thanks.

Choosy

Dear Choosy:

This is a fine choice to have and it is what is called in the trade, a cafeteria approach to benefits, namely you choose what you want and need. You may need some amount in cash but remember the tax aspects. In essence you would like to minimize your tax liabilities and choose non-taxable benefits. But, don't make your own assumptions as to what's taxable, have the company check it out.

I'll suggest some ideas, if the company is able to provide them. Some they may not because it may set a precedent, or not be available except on a group basis.

1. *A better health, dental, life insurance, disability insurance or optical plan*
2. *More vacation and personal days*
3. *A company car*
4. *Released time for education and full payment of educational costs*
5. *Attendance at conferences you would not ordinarily attend with all expenses paid, perhaps also for your wife (her portion would be taxable)*
6. *A supplementary retirement plan*
7. *Company payment of employee share of social security, retirement or health, disability and life insurance plans.*

You have some nice goodies before you, now go ahead, carefully analyze what you need and the take home benefits for you.

What advice would you give a college student who is looking for an internship opportunity for the Summer semester between his junior and senior years?

Planning Ahead

Dear Planning Ahead:

You are off to a good start by beginning your search early. Competition is very keen for anything more than the usual summer job and, in fact, keen for the usual job—counselor, busboy, waitress, fast food store worker, lawn maintenance, lifeguard, etc.

I suggest you carefully look at what you want to get out of the summer—a specific experience or skill—something that's interesting and/or can help you on your resume or in your application for graduate school, or provide one foot in the door in the organization in which you want full-time employment after you graduate.

Once defining a specific goal, figure out what contacts you have in the area, or access provided by parents, relatives, neighbors, acquaintances, friends, teachers. Then ask those who are assisting you to guide you as to how to meet the contacts. Prepare a good resume and cover letter and seek an interview. Better yet, seek an interview and bring your resume with you.

If the contacts don't pan out, you can try the straight cover letter and resume approach, but the odds aren't good. Good organizations receive hundreds of inquiries. But, if they are nearby you may want to stop in to see if you can get an interview, rather than relying on your letter.

The task is a tough one. But, if you plan your approach carefully, geared to your particular access and/or to the company itself, you have a fighting chance. Sometimes you may want to have something highly specific in mind and hope to capture the company's interest with the concept and the contribution you might make. At times they won't particularly like your idea, but they may be interested in your thinking ability as expressed in your idea, and hire you for something else. Other times, you may want to present yourself as a bright, eager, flexible person who is willing to do anything useful.

Planning, creativity, persistence, optimism and some luck may land you a very interesting summer job.

I own a small company and have lately begun to suspect that several of my employees are drug users. What should I do?

Drug Fighter

Dear Drug Fighter:

Drug abuse, by all levels within an organization—not just lower levels—is an increasing problem in companies. The problem is not just heroin. It includes marijuana, cocaine, amphetamines, barbiturates. Sometimes the drugs, such as barbiturates, are legally prescribed, but they are overused. And don't forget that alcoholism is the most serious problem of all the drugs in terms of effect on American industry.

I suggest:

*Announce a clear policy against drug use and abuse, including al-
cohol and stick to your policy.*

*Indicate that abuse is injurious not only to the health and safety
of the employee, but in the health of the organization. It can affect
performance, safety of others, quality of the product, productivity
due to sick days, reputation of the company.*

*You may want to offer help, except if you're a small company
you probably don't have a medical department. You may arrange
help through a physician or appropriate service agency indicating
that the employees relationship with the agency or physician will be
confidential.*

*Indicate clearly and specifically the actions that will be taken in
the event of possession of use of drugs on the job or on company
premises.*

*You will have to use your supervisors in leading this campaign.
They should be fair and not be more harsh on drug users than on
any other individual who is not performing. Warnings should be employed prior to dismissal as well as offers to help.*

*The drug problem, including alcoholism, is a sufficiently serious
risk to all businesses, that care and concern should be taken to combat it.*

M y son is entering college next year and is interested in management. What kinds of jobs are likely to be plentiful when he graduates and how can he prepare for them?

Concerned Father

Dear Concerned Father:

*It is very hard to predict what field will need graduates four years
from now. One should also be concerned about ten, twenty and thirty years from now. It is true that voluntairly or otherwise, increasingly, individuals change careers one or more times. Further, most
technical knowledge gained in college or graduate school is likely to
become somewhat or greatly outmoded within three to fifteen years
after graduation depending on the field and the rapidity of change.*

Education for most managers and indeed for all people should be a continuing, lifetime commitment.

As for your son, I would suggest that he take courses other than straight management, economics, accounting and math. He should take some of these, but also expose himself to the social sciences, physical sciences, arts and humanities. If he wishes, he can get the more technical management courses in graduate school. College should be more than job preparation, it is also helping to prepare for life. One should take courses and get involved in activities that will broaden one's life, in addition to positioning oneself for a career.

As to career fields in management, computer sciences and information technology, government and regulatory affairs, affirmative action, financial management, planning, non-profit sector management, hospital and health care facility management are all likely to be areas in the next five or ten years that will need well trained individuals.

I am a relatively new manager and now that I know the operations of my unit thoroughly I plan to make some significant changes. I know about the usual resistance to change people have. Please advise me as to how to make changes without upsetting people unduly.

Change Agent

Dear Change Agent:

No matter what the level in an organization, there is often a conscious as well as unconscious resistance to change.

It is good that you have studied the operations of your unit carefully and are thinking about the problems of making changes. Often new managers move too quickly without concern for the effect on people. This usually creates significant problems. Your approach so far gives you a reasonable chance for success.

Here are some things you might do to increase your chances for success in introducing changes:

Carefully plan each change—what do you want done, why, by what date, by whom? Think of what may go wrong in implementing the plan or what objections might be raised prior to implementation—have contingency plans ready.

Be prepared to discuss the changes with those effected directly as well as with the entire unit. Oral discussion would be helpful followed by a memo. This enables people to ask questions, make comments. Show how the changes help achieve reasonable goals. Be careful that the schedule for implementation is realistic and reasonable. Keep open about the changes so that as a result of discussion you may want to drop some and modify others. However, after discussion, if you think you're right, be prepared to go ahead after explaining why. Alternatively, you may want to delay controversial actions to build credibility based on success of less controversial ones.

Make sure everyone is clear as to the new procedures, work flow, etc.

After the implementation date, monitor the results. Talk with people about the changes to see if the goals are being reached. Be prepared to modify the changes as necessary.

People should feel that they are truly involved and committed (and not just for show). They should know that their views will have some influence as to what the changes will be, how they will be introduced and when, and how they will be evaluated. If they do, and you plan carefully, you have an excellent chance to overcome the normal resistance to change.

O ne of my unit heads is excellent, but he does too much himself. He isn't developing his staff properly and I worry that if he leaves or becomes ill, work in his unit will really suffer. What can I do to help solve this problem?

Supervisor of a Star

Dear Supervisor of a Star:

Your problem is not unusual. Often managers are blessed with unit heads who are able to personally produce quality and quantity results in quick fashion. It is natural that we like these high achievers who get things done. But the problem is, are they doing too much personally and not managing enough or developing their staff. If one of the stars gets promoted, leaves or becomes ill, his unit and you and possibly the company as a whole, may suffer serious consequences.

I suggest that you get the star to manage the job more and work it less by the following actions on your part:

Press him to appoint someone as second in command and to make sure that the person is capable and can handle all aspects of the unit's work—be careful that this request is made with sensitivity because you don't want your star to feel as if he is being pushed out. Explain the importance of having a good back-up supervisor.

You should encourage the unit head to spread some of his great energy on other pursuits of value to the company and to him—you can have him attend various training courses, attend more management meetings. This might encourage him to delegate and develop more than he has been doing.

Look for new responsibilities for the individual—delegate to him some appropriate tasks that you now do—this will enrich and enlarge his experience, but with your advice, he should then delegate some of his present tasks to his subordinates. Be careful, however, that in regard to the last two points that he doesn't continue his old habits and try to do everything himself. Watch out for signs of fatigue on his part.

Ask who in his unit is available for special assignments—this will indicate the importance of delegation.

You have a mixed blessing in your star. What you have to do is bolster his weak areas in regard to doing too much himself. If you are successful, you will have someone very close to a truly outstanding subordinate and manager.

I have normally been able to communicate well with my subordinates, but lately one of them is unresponsive to any of my questions. What can I do to encourage him to be responsive?

Unzipping a Tight Lip

Dear Unzipping:

Sometimes it is best not to overreact if a subordinate suddenly clams up. He or she may be having a tough time at work or in his personal life. It may be best to give it a chance to work itself out assuming that performance does not slack off.

At some point you may have to take action. Don't add to the subordinate's stress by pressing him too hard in trying to find out what's wrong. Try to be subtle. Here are some things you might do to get him to open up:

Drop in on him at his work—you shift from your turf to his and he may be busy so don't overstay your welcome.

Ask his advice about a problem you are facing—he may then feel more comfortable about discussing his problem.

Try to talk with him more often—out of the increased contact you may get some clues as to what's bothering him and then be able to discuss it, or he may just be more likely to discuss his concern.

Make a list for yourself of activities you think may be bothering him—it may be difficult personalities, a new organization, turnover, lateness of delivery of supplies, etc. When and where appropriate you might mention these to indicate your knowledge and concern about some problems. This would give him the opportunity to get things off his chest.

Channels of communication are very important. Every once in a while they need some lubrication.

I have noticed that I have some free time each day—perhaps 15 minutes to an hour in snatches, some as little as three or four minutes. Can you suggest some use of time when they come in small chunks?

Time Watcher

Dear Time Watcher:

Time is your most important resource. You can train yourself to use each available minute. Here are some ways to use rather than waste free time:

Have a small pocket pad or 3 × 5 cards handy and a pad by your telephone. While waiting for calls to be put through, at random times during the day, jot down things that occur to you about current efforts or future plans.

If you drive to work or to business meetings during the day, attach a dictating machine so that you are able to drive safely, but still dictate thoughts.

Train yourself to focus on major concerns during free intervals. Even one random thought that pops into your head that can be written up in greater detail later, is worth a great deal. You may want to focus on less major concerns also, ones that have been hanging around for a long time.

Keep in touch with people—just a short telephone "hello" or brief drop-in, can be helpful.

Keep a pile of short individual items that you have to read—you should try to have only those things that take under three minutes each, so that you can complete the individual item.

Do whatever file cleaning and housekeeping is necessary.
Prepare for future meetings or assignments.
Establish weekly, monthly or annual goals.

These eight areas provide for effective use of time. Of course, you may also wish to do some type of relaxing exercise, regular exercise, or another means of providing a break that helps you relax and prepare for the rest of the day.

By using time wisely, one can become a much more effective manager.

I've been told that sometimes I can be as effective in being silent as I can be in speaking out. Can you advise me what is meant and how to do it?

Wary of Silence

Dear Wary of Silence:

I am not sure what the person who spoke to you meant, but I can tell you that silence can convey a message. I can also tell you about how to use silence.

Silence is a communication tool and is often used with body language. It also gives you an escape hatch since you haven't said or written a word.

Here are some techniques you can use to "say" things without words:

I'm not taking sides—if you want to avoid siding with one or the other in an argument, slouch a bit, perhaps fold your arms, and just follow the action with your eyes or by turning your head from side to side as the argument flows.

I'm not going to tell you where I stand—keep a bland expression— a poker face—and alert posture so that the listener can't get any information about what you're thinking.

I'm bored or uninterested—keep changing positions, draw doodles or keep handling things, let your eyes wander.

I'm opposed to what you say—keep your jaw set, posture rigid, eyes and expressions hard, shake your head indicating disapproval.

I'm tuned in and turned on—establish frequent eye contact, lean forward, take notes, nod approval.

I'm waiting for a response—after you make a request or comment, you can look at the person, assume a relaxed position and wait for a response. Don't oversell your case—don't break the silence or eye contact.

Silence and body language can be helpful tools in gaining attention and respect for your views. Don't overdo it, but don't shirk from using a valuable communications tool. Also, recognize the signals that are being sent to you.

My boss is big on the importance of communications, but he stresses writing memos and questions. He thinks conversation ends up in a lot of wasted time and gossip. How can I convince him that conversation can be very helpful?

Talker

Dear Talker:

You're right! Conversation can be a helpful means of gaining information. I suggest that you write your boss (he'll be happy about a memo) about the values of conversation and include the following:

Writing is important, but at times conversation is a better way of finding out things, particularly when people don't want to commit things to paper. For example, some people don't like to write about the real power structure, the informal organization, who listens to whom, where to get help.

Although there may be written procedures, often you want to talk with someone who does the exact task as to: 1) how it is done, 2) what isn't written down, 3) more effective ways of doing it—this can apply also to using equipment and machines.

There are some things that are only in peoples' heads rather than in books or files—it may be historical—what was done in the past, why something failed, who did what to whom.

There are some topics that you want to gauge peoples' expressions, reactions, pose follow-up questions.

These are just a few uses of conversation. If you're really daring, you can encourage your boss to do a real turn around by encouraging more conversation. You can appeal to his instincts as a good manager to encourage people to use the knowledge of others. To do so, he might also encourage informal get togethers, brief talks by individuals about their units or projects, or even joint assignments, mobility assignments or referrals to others.

In many instances, one conversation is worth ten pictures or memos.

I have been told that there are some steps one should follow in reaching a decision. Can you outline them for me?

Trying to Improve

Dear Trying to Improve:

Although there are different stages one can follow in making a decision, the following is an approach that is often used:

Recognize that there is a problem that requires a decision or solution.
Identify what the problem is in a specific way.
Develop alternative decisions or solutions.
Choose the best among the alternatives focusing on meeting the specific elements of the problem and on the possible adverse consequences of each alternative.
Draw up a plan for implementation including contingency plans if things go wrong.
Implement your decision.
Monitor and evaluate results—fine tune or modify your decision if necessary.

If you get in the habit of following these steps it is very likely that your decision-making ability will improve as well as your confidence.

I have a number of problems at work I just haven't been able to resolve. They are not major problems, but they keep hanging on and popping up. How can I approach solving these problems and getting rid of them once and for all?

Tired of Trivia

Dear Tired of Trivia:

Often, the minor problems can cause the most distress. They're annoying, they seem trivial and they don't disappear.

You have to force yourself to reach closure on each problem. I suggest the following:

Commit yourself to reaching a solution—rely on your judgment and the information available; don't yearn for the perfect solution.

Commit yourself to taking time to solve the problem or parts of it—focus on what annoys you the most about it.

Use problem solving techniques—identify the problem, possible causes, possible alternative solutions, choose the best one, recognizing the advantages and disadvantages.

Work out the details of implementation of your choice—give yourself a deadline.

Implement your decision.

Evaluate the results.

You may have to force yourself to take the time to do all this, but it will be well worth it to get rid of some long-lasting headaches.

I am a clerk in a company and believe that I have the capability of doing a great deal more. I have assisted people higher than me and they rely on my knowledge and advice. However, since I don't have a college degree, it seems to me that my supervisor regards me as just a clerk. Can you suggest how I can demonstrate that I have the capability and knowledge to do a great deal more and, in fact, become a supervisor or manager.

Trying to Climb Higher

Dear Trying to Climb Higher:

The problem you describe is a common one whereby supervisors stereotype people and often don't look at the individual's own skills and motivation. We also tend to over credentialize when we expect a piece of paper like a college degree to substitute for individual judgment. I suggest that you do an objective analysis of specific contributions you have made, specific people who can attest to your going beyond your current job duties, specific skills that you have or think you can develop quickly. I would also consider enrolling in an appropriate college program in the evening or on weekends. You should find out if your company has a tuition remission program or time release program for a college education. It might be helpful if you enrolled before you talk with your supervisor, you should then talk with him and present your case.

You may prefer to have something in writing that you give him after you meet but it would be valuable to try to discuss the situation face to face. You should be specific as to what things you would like to emphasize and what things you think you can do to demonstrate your ability.

If you follow the plan that I have suggested, I think you have a good chance of getting his attention and interest. Most supervisors look for ambitious and motivated staff members. He might be able to give you what you want immediately but I think it is likely that you will find opportunities for development and making contributions coming your way in the future. You may even want to reach out and suggest a bit more than you do now and thereby demonstrate your knowledge and creditability and maybe rather quickly you will get more and more to do at a higher level of responsibility. Good luck.

I am supposed to make a major presentation and will want to use various exhibits and charts. Can you give me some suggestions as to how to be effective in using charts?

Chart Wary

Dear Chart Wary:

Successful presentations are important to one's career. Frequently a person is a good speaker and organizer of presentations but doesn't work on the charts and visual aids as well as he or she might. Here are some suggestions to make sure your charts help you make your points and reinforce the verbal report you are making:

Carefully check the materials before you use them and also have someone else check them—you may be too close to the material and miss an error.

Have a separate and, if possible, distinctive exhibit or page for each important point you want to make—don't have too much on one chart.

When you're not talking about a chart or page of your presentation, cover it up. Otherwise, people's attention will be distracted.

Pencil in clues to yourself on the exhibits—you can clue yourself in to the next page or to additional material so you don't have to leave the easel to check your notes.

Know your exhibits and your material so you don't keep going back and forth from the easel to your notes.

Use your exhibits to highlight—don't just simply read the exhibits thereby repeating exactly what's on the chart—this will annoy listeners—they can read as well as you.

Careful attention to exhibits and weaving them into your presentation will reinforce your efforts. It's well worth the effort.

I am to advise my boss on which of two candidates is the best for a major promotion. They are very, very close in ability. Can you advise me as to how I can break the tie and recommend one person.

Can't Decide

Dear Can't Decide:

You are facing an important decision for the individuals involved and the organization. Unfortunately, you can't resolve the tie by a sudden death overtime period common in some sports. I would suggest that you investigate the areas I shall suggest and score each person on a 1-5 basis, 3 is average ability, 1 and 2 below that, 4 and 5 above. Be careful in your evaluations and don't be afraid to give them both the same score in a category.

How well does the individual create confidence in his/her judgment or actions, does he act consistently and fairly and take responsibility for mistakes?
Makes decisions promptly and without hesitation and anguish.
Encourages candid discussions and dissenting views, doesn't place blame unduly when there are errors.
Keeps subordinates and supervisors informed about what's going on in the unit.
Develops subordinates skills, encourages growth and learning in individuals.
Sets realistic priorities.
Has a high energy level, stamina, ability to take pressure.
Has a concern for bottom line results as well as subordinates' personal satisfaction.

The score may indeed be close but by looking at these factors you have an opportunity to break the tie.

I think my boss is wrong on a tentative conclusion he's reached on a major project for the use of outside consultants. How can I convince him he's wrong, although I have already expressed my view in writing. Thank you.

Would-be Advisor

Dear Would-be Advisor:

This is a tough question. Some bosses don't like to have their judgment questioned even the first time and you are proposing a second shot at your boss.

However, if you feel strongly about it (assuming you have some time before the consultants are hired) you may want to wait for an informal occasion to bring the issue up. It may be at the end of a meeting on something else, particularly if the meeting has gone well and you have made a good contribution. Or, it may be at a chance meeting at coffee. You may also want to fire off a new memo but don't just repeat your old arguments. If you have some new information or ideas, express them in a non argumentative way. Or, you can just write a simple note saying, "I have some further thoughts on the consultant study that might be helpful to you. Please contact me if you want to discuss them."

One way or another present your case as well as you can. But once the decision is made, try to be as helpful as you can in making the decision work. If the boss, in the end, turns out to be right, tell him so. If he's wrong, keep quiet and hope that if he's big enought about it, he'll mention something to you.

I manage a small unit and keep hearing people saying nasty things about my unit's work and staff. What can I do to change what is being said?

Thin Skin

Dear Thin Skin:

At times jealousy and unfair perceptions of a department by others can hurt the morale and effectiveness of a unit. Your unit may have received praise or better space, or more bonus money or have different working conditions or style than others. This may lead to the comments you find objectionable. On the other hand, there may be a real problem. Your unit may not be holding up its fair share, it

*may be delaying others, your people may not be particularly coop-
erative or productive.*

*You should move quickly to clear up the attacks on your unit. If
you don't, the negative perceptions may get deeper and more widespread and you'll find it increasingly difficult to turn things around.
I suggest:*

- *Discuss the issue with people—indicate you've heard negative
  things and that you want to hear about them specifically. You
  then will have a chance to provide facts, figures and different
  interpretations. The odds are that you will increase understanding of the problems faced by your unit.*

- *Talk about past, present and future activities, progress, changes
  and plans. Invite comments, show how your plans relate to the
  other operations in the company. Offer to have joint task forces
  work on some mutual problems. Invite people to visit.*

- *Try to widen your contacts and the contacts of your top staff
  so that others get to know you and your staff.*

- *Where other units or top management can be helpful, ask for
  help and support.*

*It's natural to say, "I'm not going to spend time fighting rumors
and jealousy." In this case, I suggest that you reassure yourself that
it's not something more—either misunderstanding of what your unit
is supposed to do, poor communications, or poor efforts by your
unit. I believe that if you follow what I have suggested you have a
good chance of making your unit very much talked about—but in a
very positive sense.*

I'm very interested in getting into food management. I've
worked in several restaurants in the kitchen and enjoy it, but I'd
much rather be in the management department instead of the cooking department.

I've talked to my employers, but I can't get any advice on what to do in order to get the position I want.

Friends have told me I have to be good in math and get a business degree before I can get into management. I don't entirely agree. I feel the experience I've had in the kitchen is better than a business degree. Can you please tell me what to do?

I don't want to do the wrong thing and I'm extremely anxious to get my career started. Answer as soon as possible.

                                                                              Overmixed

Dear Overmixed:

I admire your desire to get into food management, but it may be that the world needs great chefs more than it needs great restaurant managers. Depending upon how good you are or become in the kitchen, you may in fact earn more, have more challenge and more mobility and marketability than most food managers.

However, I assume that you have decided that management rather than cooking best meet your goals and abilities. Clearly the knowledge you have gained in the kitchen will be of help.

I suggest that if your ultimate goal is ownership and/or management of one or more restaurants or an executive position in a restaurant corporation, you should take courses in the various areas I shall indicate. You may want to eventually get a Master in Business Administration which would be particularly helpful if you joined a large corporation. Some companies won't hire you without at least a B.A. or B.S. degree. Remember your advantage will be the kitchen experience but you do need additional knowledge and experience.

Areas in which you should acquire fundamental and advanced knowledge—sometimes by courses, sometimes by on-the-job training:

- *interpersonal relations, human relations and principles of supervision.*
- *some understanding of accounting, budgeting and costing principles and techniques*
- *marketing and advertising principles and techniques*
- *inventory control*
- *planning principles and techniques*

On the job experience outside the kitchen but in other aspects of the restaurant business will also be helpful. These include customer relations, bartending, buying, restaurant design and layout, etc.

The food business is a tough one with many people failing in their dream to have a beautiful, fine and profitable restaurant. The more you can do to prepare yourself the better your chances for success. I've given you the basic recipe for success, you'll have to stir and modify to taste.

I am a division manager and have had increasing problems with my first line supervisors. They have not been performing as well as I expected. Their moral seems low and I have not been getting the productivity needed from those they supervise. I know a first line supervisor's job is a tough one. What can I do to help make them more effective?

Manager

Dear Manager:

First line supervisors are critical to the success of any firm but the supervisor's problems are often not noticed or acted upon.

Higher management should tune in on the problems of the foremen and other first line supervisors and on the demands that are placed on them.

The first line supervisor of today must be more of a manager than in the past. He or she must excel in interpersonal skills in dealing with a better educated workforce, a multi-generational workforce and one that has a higher percentage of women and minorities. There is increasing pressure for administrative efficiency and on good human relations and solid technical skills.

The first line supervisor position combines a master craftsman outlook of the past as well as that of the lead man. He is caught between middle management and the workforce, and often bears the brunt of union attacks. Frequently, the first line supervisor has too little authority, does not know the policies or objectives of top management, is far removed from the decision making process and is often in a dead end position.

Managers can help the first line supervisors:

- *By becoming aware of their actual working conditions and problems.*

- *Keeping supervisors informed of decisions, policies, objectives, priorities, and plans.*
- *See that means are provided so that they are educated about new technological and management processes that may impact upon their jobs or help them perform better, such as training in interpersonal skills, motivation, discipline procedures, etc.*
- *Evaluate them in an objective manner and inform them as to how well they are meeting management's goals.*
- *Provide a way for them to express their views to higher management, and to get together with their peers to discuss mutual problems.*

I find myself getting bored on the job and I know that unless this stops, it can effect my work and future. What can I do?

Bored

Dear Bored:

Everyone, in every job, faces moments and often long periods of boredom and frustration. You're right, if boredom goes on for a long time with no end in sight, your enthusiasm, energy, and self-esteem are bound to suffer and so will your performance.

Sometimes boredom may be the result of being burned out; you may have tussled with the same problems, met the challenges and strains; and you may just be tired. Or, as you indicate, the challenge and stimulation may be gone, your learning and excitement may have hit a plateau. Fundamental to approaching the problem is analyzing why you are bored, what you, if you had power to do so, would do about it. It could be you are at a stage in your life where you want to radically change things; where you are questioning what you want out of a job and out of life. This is sometimes called the mid-career crisis. Be thorough in your analysis, don't act quickly or emotionally because if you're in the midst of the mid-life crisis you stand a great risk of making a bad decision if you react emotionally. Aside from looking for a job outside the company which I don't recommend at this point, I suggest the following:

- *Talk with your supervisor about possibilities for additional responsibilities or a new assignment or one or more special projects*
- *If some position is vacant or someone is going to retire, you may indicate that you would be interested in taking part of the position's responsibilities in addition to your own or transferring to that position.*
- *If your company is quite progressive, it may offer mobility assignments for staff so that you can spend a tour of duty in a different area.*
- *You may want to acquire new knowledge and skills, therefore, discuss with your supervisor and/or the Personnel Department in-company training programs, or special seminars, courses and university courses.*
- *You may, of course, be at a stage where you want significantly different responsibilities. If you believe you have the capabilities necessary, talk with Personnel about opportunities in the company, or ways in which you can acquire the necessary skills and experience.*

If all these actions do not produce results, you should then consider looking for positions outside the company.

In my view, you should make every effort to structure a job that stimulates you, that gives you satisfaction, that you feel your brain cells and energy cells are at close to full capacity a very high percentage of the time. If a company wants to get the most out of its most precious resource, its people, it will try to accommodate and encourage what I just described. It is difficult to do it for everyone, but a good company will seek to provide job satisfaction which requires tuning in to individuals with different needs. You can overcome your present feelings by the actions I have suggested, but it will require thought and effort.

I am a new department manager in a medium size company. We have a new hot shot Controller who is asking us to submit our preliminary budgets for next year. The instructions are, "Explain what you need and why and how does this compare with your spending over the last three years in the categories you are requesting?" Can you advise me on the best strategy and tactics for getting the most money for my department. We are in something of a financial crunch and I want to be able to get at least my fair share of the available dollars.

Gearing for Battle

Dear Gearing for Battle:

This is a difficult question for me to answer because it puts me on the spot. You're asking a budgeteer to tell you how to beat him at his own game. I may help you but end up losing my effectiveness on the job and then be writing in to someone asking for tips on a new job.

Seriously, I think the best thing you can do with a new hot shot Controller or other budget person is establish a record for honesty, accuracy, and thoroughness. If the new person is really a hot shot, I doubt whether you can con him, or con him more than once. I would give him the exact facts and figures with clear, non-defensive and non-propagandistic explanations for what your expenditures have been, why they have gone up or down, what your specific needs are for the next year and even suggest your plans for the next few years. You should present comparative data that is helpful to your case in regard to what you have done with your budget allocations versus other units (in a non derogatory way), or your productivity figures or sales, etc.

In short, be clear, concise, persuasive. Indicate that you are concerned with effectiveness, efficiency, economy, and do not play games with figures or interpretations. If you are able to indicate to the Controller in your first dealings with him, that you do your homework, are well prepared, don't ask for the moon or play games, can carefully defend your requests and have explored all alternatives, you will probably come out ahead.

Finance types are human, believe it or not, many are much broader than being the traditional green eye shade types—you may even want to establish a personal relationship with the Controller or at least a very good professional one. Deep down, Controllers want to be liked for something other than their money!

think I deserve a raise. I'm the most productive member of my work group and have an excellent attendance and overtime record. My annual ratings have been the highest given. However, due to the economic crunch in my company, we all get standard increases. The boss has said that he won't give any more. I understand the boss' problem, but I think I am underpaid in comparison with what I produce compared to others. How do I go about getting what I deserve?

Deserving

Dear Deserving:

The record of performance you cite certainly demands attention and recognition. However, many companies find themselves unable to grant merit increases because they have only a limited amount of money available during a period of economic recession. They reason that they should spread all that is available across-the-board so they can please as many as possible. If they make exceptions for you, they might have to make exceptions for others.

I think you should indicate to your supervisor your concern as well as your understanding of the problems involved. Ask what alternatives there are. Although the boss might be fearful of setting a precedent, based upon your outstanding performance and the company's inability to give you more than a standard increase you might make some suggestions to him. You might ask:

1. *To be given priority for overtime or special assignments that carry supplementary compensation.*
2. *Is there another job classification you can qualify for which would provide more money and prestige—perhaps you can serve in an acting capacity to demonstrate what you can do.*
3. *Can extra vaction or personal days be granted in lieu of extra compensation?*
4. *See if you can get a commitment to a special salary review at a time earlier than the usual salary review time.*
5. *At the very least, a notation should be made in your personnel file that you would have qualified for an additional X% or Y dollars if funds had been available.*

You may be unhappy with the response to the above suggestions or with any other alternatives proposed by your boss. In fact, your boss may just say, "you're a good person, but I can do absolutely nothing." You then have to face the issue of how long you can live with this situation psychologically, as well as financially. Be careful that you don't live with it too long because you may do damage to yourself and your performance as you become disgruntled. It may be that things will improve in a year, but if you see yourself locked into a bad situation, begin to look for a new job.

I caught your program while driving the other day. Please answer this problem I have. The Personnel Department in my company reclassified some jobs in another unit that are similar to mine. I'm very upset because I should be reclassified also, but my manager doesn't like to make waves. What should I do?

Yearning to be Reclassified

Dear Yearning to be Reclassified:

Feelings that other people in other units are doing better in terms of classification or salary occur quite often in organizations. Sometimes the rumor mill about this matter is inaccurate. Or, the reclassification may have been the result of a reorganization in the other unit and/or additional job responsibilities being added to the individuals. You should try, informally, to get as accurate information as possible. There is no sense stirring up a fuss and then being blown out of the water because your facts are wrong. If the information you get seems to support the view that they have a higher classification than you for doing essentially the same task, you should speak to your supervisor. You should ask whether your job also qualifies for reclassification given what has happened in the other unit. If he is wise, he will look into it and then press for your reclassification, citing the other unit as precedent. If for some reason he wants to bury the issue, and maybe you, take the next step. Go to the Personnel Department to raise questions as to whether your job should be reclassified. Asking a question, rather than making a demand, is an effective approach. You can demand later through appeal or a grievance procedure. By going to the Personnel Department you should know that many supervisors do not like staff to go around them. Therefore, if you seem to be at impasse with your supervisor, offer him an out—before he says absolutely no, suggest that maybe you can talk with Personnel to get clarification on this matter. This gives him a way out because Personnel will then be the ones saying it should be done. Just to complicate your life, he may say I don't want you to go to Personnel. You will then have to decide on the risks of going over his head.

There are times in large organizations that the squeaky wheel gets greased. It may be that someone else's supervisor was more concerned about his classification structure than your supervisor. Therefore, if the facts are correct, you should squeak also, but give your supervisor an opportunity to look as if he is doing a good thing.

I am *so* excited I can barely begin this letter. The other day I got my first job—computer programming trainee. I'm enthusiastic, hard working, and unfortunately nervous.

I was hoping that you might give me some advice on how to do well at my job. I know there are certain things that are a must on the job, but this being my first one, I don't know what to do; and I *don't* want to mess it up!

If you could give me some suggestions, I would really appreciate it. Thank you very much.

Shaky Trainee (In need of a new program)

Dear Shaky Trainee:

Your excitement and enthusiasm are delightful. If you can keep that up and your nervousness down, you are bound to be successful. By the way, it is very natural to be nervous about a new job and it is natural to be doubly nervous about your first job. So, don't get nervous about being nervous.

I suggest that you follow some simple guidelines for success on your first job:

1. *Learn as much as you can as fast as you can, listen more than you talk—and listen carefully.*

2. *Ask appropriate questions—not questions just for the sake of saying something.*

3. *Be sure you have mastered the basic fundamentals before reaching out for more complex assignments.*

4. *If you don't know something, if something is difficult or unclear, ask and if necessary, ask again. No one expects you to be perfect very early on. Take notes on the answer to your questions—list things you have to check or recheck and write down the responses.*

5. *Set some goals for yourself in terms of things you want to accomplish and evaluate your progress.*

6. *Develop good work habits—such as punctuality, adhering to time allotted for lunch or coffee break or quitting time.*

7. *Appropriate style of dress is important.*

8. *Even though as a programmer you work with models, equations and machines, don't forget your co-workers and superiors. Try to develop good professional and personal relationships by being yourself, by being eager to learn and to admit lack of knowledge and by thanking those who help you.*

If you follow these guidelines and are true to yourself, I think you will enjoy great success.

I am about to retire from a governmental job and with my pension and savings I would like to fulfill my dream of owning my own business. I'm thinking of a stationary store, small restaurant, tobacco store, cleaning store or something like that. What advice can you give as to what kind of store to open and how to succeed?

Eager

Dear Eager:

The best advice I can give is don't be too eager! Many people lose their savings, time and self-esteem by failing in a small business. In fact, the odds are against success in a small business if you have never worked in that particular endeavor before. Many dreams about being our own boss, doing things right, setting our own hours and making a lot of money—but few, very few achieve it.

Running a small business is very hard work. I think you should do a lot of careful planning. What do you like to do and what don't you like to do? What do you really know how to do? Location, good help, adequate cash flow, knowing what to buy, etc. are very important. You should assess what you are willing to risk in money and number of hours of work, do you have enough money to hire adequate help or to buy into a going business with the successful owner continuing to run the operation with you. Each of the examples you cite require some specialized knowledge, some more than others. Try to narrow your field of interest, talk to a lot of people in the various businesses. Perhaps you can work part-time or even at no pay in a particular line of work to learn the ropes.

In short, I'm urging you to learn a lot more, to talk with people in the business you think you may like, talk to your local banker, to suppliers, customers, etc. You've worked hard to save enough to try to achieve a dream. Be very careful, take some chances but not wild chances because all too often a dream without careful planning becomes a nightmare.

I have worked for my company for three years and have a better than average record and better than average increases. Six months ago a new supervisor, from outside the company became head of the unit. We haven't gotten along well and last week he indicated that if I don't improve within 30 days, he'd fire me. He refused to give me any details. All he said was I'd better improve my attitude and performance. I need my job. What shall I do?

Worried

Dear Worried:

I suggest that you try to evaluate your own performance—what's good, what's bad. Be tough on yourself, but fair. If there are weak-

nesses, try to think how to improve them. You may be getting in late, or there may have been reasons why you were taking a longer lunch hour or leaving early. You may have been late meeting deadlines due to some factors under your control and some not under your control.

Once you have this list and what you can do to improve things, as well as a list indicating what you have been doing well, contact your supervisor. Calmly suggest to him that you have done a self-inventory of both good and bad points and how you plan to improve. Also indicate what you have been doing well—he may not be aware of them.

Ask him to add to the list, to indicate objectives and goals and a timetable to be met. Also inform him of your previous record. Suggest that it is important for both of you to understand each other and that you want to know what he wants, how he wants things done and that you will do your best to meet his goals.

Be frank and be yourself. I think the self-assessment you do will demonstrate seriousness and concern and will probably receive a good reaction from your superior. It is clear to me that you and he have been unclear as to his expectations and style. If he is a good supervisor, he has an obligation to communicate better. I think he will, once he sees how you have approached the problem.

What you do and how you do it in regard to this problem will help you out of a sticky situation and will also prove valuable to you in the future.

I enjoy your program. Here's my question. There's been a cutback of staff in my organization and my boss has told me that I have to tell a good employee who has been with us for five years that we will have to let him go. There are no other vacancies in the organization for which he is qualified or can be trained. He is the most junior person in his category. We can offer a reasonable amount of severance pay and time to find a job. I have never fired or let anyone go before. Please tell me how to perform this distasteful task.

Ax Swinger

Dear Ax Swinger:

Firing someone, particularly because of no fault on the individual's part, is one of the toughest, if not the toughest, thing you will have to face as a manager in terms of impact upon your emotions and conscience. Some managers find this so distasteful that they avoid taking action, delegate it to someone, or try to get it over quickly by a letter or memo so that they don't have to face the individual. In trying to be brisk, they often end up being brusque.

Though it will be difficult for you to do the things I suggest, remember, how much more difficult it is for the person at the receiving end of the bad tidings, particularly if there has been no forewarning. At the very least, think how you would like to be treated if roles were reversed.

I suggest:

1. *Deliver the news personally and express your own feelings that you wish that this action didn't have to be taken or there were some way to avoid the action because of the individual's fine efforts for the company.*
2. *Listen to the person's reactions—let him ventilate his feelings if he's not shocked into silence—he may want to talk about it at a later time—he probably will become quite emotional and resentful so be prepared for it.*
3. *It is normal for people to inquire—why and why me—so you should be prepared to give an accurate, succinct response that indicates why this was necessary and the fact that all possible alternatives were explored in an attempt to avoid laying off the individual.*
4. *Offer to soften the impact—termination pay, vacation pay, perhaps sick leave, help in finding another job—contacts, resume writing, a telephone or office or secretarial assistance for a reasonable period.*

These actions may seem inadequate given the enormity of the effect on the individual, but at least they demonstrate a concern for the individual and places management in the proper light of being concerned about people.

I am a married woman with two children, ages 16 and 19. My husband has an excellent position in Cincinnati, for which we have waited a long time. I have just received an advanced degree in a highly specialized field and cannot find employment in Cincinnati, although I have tried very hard. Should I seek a job out of the state, even though this might disrupt our family life, or make my husband have to move from his job?

Worried Woman

Dear Worried Woman:

Twenty or even ten years ago, a male might have tried to be cute in answering this question by quoting the bible, "Wherever thou goest, I shall go." But today there is a question of who is the thou, and who is the I, the husband or the wife.

Cincinnati and other medium size cities are not easy areas for highly skilled women to find responsible positions. As an aside, I might mention that you could contact the Women's Opportunities Program at the Central YWCA. It attempts to identify specific positions available, help women decide on their job and career goals and prepare for finding a suitable position.

Basically, this complex issue deals with each of the spouses' goals and objectives, the strength of the marriage, the needs of the children. There are a growing number of two career families separated by wide geographic distances with reunions on weekends, monthly or even less frequently (commutation is expensive and time-consuming!). It takes a strong marriage and family life to survive the separation.

In some cases, depending upon the skills of each partner, the wife may be more likely to find a job easily in a new city than the husband because of the pressure on many organizations to hire qualified women.

I think you and your husband have to talk about the matter in great detail and then discuss it with your children, if you choose an alternative which involves relocation for you or for the entire family.

A first step may be that you explore what is really out there in other locations. Are there really excellent jobs for you and what positions might be available for your husband with your company or with other companies in the new location. And, of course, is the new place one that you and your family would like to live in. It may be that after looking around elsewhere and looking for jobs in Cincin-

nati that may not be exactly what you want but reasonably close to it, you may decide that its best all around to remain here.

I should also note that some companies are progressive enough to realize the problems in recruiting married women and thus make serious attempts to help the husband find an appropriate position. Given the growing number of two career families, companies are also being asked when recruiting the husband to also employ the wife or help in locating a suitable position for her.

I don't mean to paint a rosy picture. You will probably find a good position somewhere, but the company or city might not offer a good position for your husband. In that case, the two of you must decide on your priorities. In the worst case, one of the partners in the marriage may have to sacrifice more than the other.

I am a writer; at least, I am trying to become a writer. I have been through 4 years of college, and have done a *lot* of writing. Now I am on my own and trying to make some money for once. I have sent some of my short stories to several publishers and have been rejected by them all. I do not want to give up writing so I can get a job just to make money. I need the money but I love writing—WHAT SHOULD I DO!!!! Please help me.

Tired of Writing for Nothing

Dear Tired of Writing for Nothing:

Being a successful free lance writer is very tough. Thousands of people believe that the world is just waiting for their novel, short story, poetry or non-fiction. So, be realistic. You may want to get a regular job or one that leaves you with some free time and use your evenings and weekends for writing. Once you have some paid publications and know the ropes, you can then decide whether to spend full time on writing.

I assume you have writing talent. You may be getting rejections not only because of the great competition or your weaknesses in writing but also because you have not carefully looked at the market. You may want to single out particular publications that publish material somewhat in the same general area or similar in style to what you write. In other words, target your submissions rather than shot-gunning them. Also, you may want to contact several editors and describe in outline form or with a few paragraphs what you're planning on writing. Gauge their interest and solicit their ideas. If they get interested you have at least one foot in the door when you send your final draft.

As I've said, you have some tough, frustrating times ahead but I urge you to continue trying to follow the routes I've indicated. Try to get objective criticism on what you've done and try to find out why a specific manuscript was rejected. You may want to try to get a few articles published in journals that don't pay you just to build a publication track record. Writing can be exhilarating and fun and even, but unfortunately, rarely, profitable.

Good luck!

Your advice sounds good on the air . . . but level with me. We all know that good work habits, industriousness and competence won't get you ahead in the business world as quickly as having the luck to be in the right place at the right time, brown-nosing, or being related to the boss. It's been my experience that advancement follows those kinds of activities, rather than the kind of conscientious work habits you advise. Right?

Skeptic

Dear Skeptic:

You pose a tough question and you deserve a frank answer. It doesn't hurt to be related to the boss! And it certainly doesn't hurt to be in the right place at the right time. Luck does play a role in most people's lives. But to some degree you can try to make your luck.

If you develop the work habits I have suggested in my previous answers and an attitude of confidence, enthusiasm, a zest for tough challenges and an expectation of success, you can help shape your future. There is no guarantee that the best person will get the job or do well, history and personal experience is replete with stories of bad luck or favoritism or power plays that hurt the "good guys." And often you have to be reasonably aggressive and market yourself and plan ahead, perhaps attach yourself to a rising star or to an area in the company or an industry that seems to be on the rise.

You can't wait for fortune to shine upon you or for the chance meeting with someone who will do great things for you. In my view, you have to do all you can to make yourself as competent as possible and then look for and make your lucky breaks.

In my experience, "luck" seems to happen more often to those who seem well prepared and with a good track record behind them. I would suggest you do all you can to become good so that if luck does strike, you can capitalize on it. Just standing around hoping for that "one break" decreases your odds of success, and even if you get it, if you're unprepared you'll flub your big chance!

My husband's company does not have a formal early retirement program. He would like to retire next year, at 65. (His company will allow him to work until he's 70.)

We have a fair amount of savings and plan to sell our house at a large profit. The company has made some early retirement settlements, all on individual bases. I think they'll be fair, but not overly generous. What things might my husband ask for that won't upset them, but would still be fair to him?

Green Pastures

Dear Green Pastures:

In a time of inflation, before one heads for those pastures, you have to be very sure that the pastures are indeed green. Many people jump at early retirement and then find themselves bored, unhappy and worried about finances. Some people also retire expecting that they'll find some kind of part-time work to make ends meet. But, depending upon the economy, competition from those seeking employment, and where you live, it may be impossible to get extra income from part-time work.

You and your husband should plan carefully in regard to where you'll live and what you will be doing in terms of your use of time and your income needs—not only six months after retirement but for the next ten or more years. In regard to a fair early retirement settlement, I suggest that you:

1. *Calculate your monthly income if your husband retires at 65 based upon pension, social security, savings and investment income, interest earnings on proceeds of sale of your home.*
2. *Calculate what these same figures would be if your husband retired at 70.*
3. *Try to determine whether the company's replacement for your husband would earn significantly less than he does over the next five years—or if your husband won't be replaced. This is an effective argument for showing how much the company would save in salary and fringe benefits if your husband retired five years earlier.*
4. *Determine what your monthly expense is as you see it for the next five years (remember, if you rent an apartment to anticipate rent increases, and general increases of perhaps 10-12% per year or maybe more.)*
5. *Determine the gap between income and expense.*

I suggest that you consider proposing the following reasonable package to the company:

1. *Continuation of all existing health care benefits you now enjoy under the same terms as present until age 70—with the usual company procedures continuing after 70.*
2. *A provision that any improvements made to the retirement or health care system after you retire early should apply equally to you.*
3. *Either a lump sum, or probably more acceptable, an annual supplement to your pension for the next five years. This might be paid monthly along with your pension. Depending upon what's most beneficial to you it could be based on years of service, your final salary or final three year average or highest three year average, and the savings the company might have by not replacing you or replacing you at a lower cost. If you can show an appreciable savings to the company by your retiring early, you are in a good position to ask for a significant share of that savings.*

In all that you do plan very carefully. The more carefully you plan, the greener those pastures are likely to be.

My boss has criticized my oral and written presentation at staff meetings and in reports. What can I do to improve?

Poor Communicator

Dear Poor Communicator:

Many individuals, often with advanced degrees and at senior levels, are poor at communication. In fact, business writing and effective speaking are two of the most popular courses in business schools today.

In order to deal with your particular problem you should find out from your boss what specific aspects of your communications he finds weak. You might then want to take company run courses or courses at universities dealing with effective writing and speaking. You may also want to talk with your company librarian or public librarian as to what books are available that can help you.

In the meantime, prior to taking courses or reading books, I can make some general suggestions about effective business presentations whether oral or written. Of course, focus on the specific weaknesses cited by your boss.

Written Communication

1. *Before you put a word on paper think through a) who is your audience, b) what do you want to accomplish with your written communication.*
2. *Think through the approach or format you will use—choose the one that most clearly and succinctly presents the problem or issue, the alternative solutions, the advantages/disadvantages of each, and your recommendations and reasons for your recommendations.*
3. *You may want to use a one page executive summary in your major reports. Whatever the format, remember you want to capture and hold attention—too much detail may cause boredom, one chart may be worth ten pages of description.*

4. *Style is important. Use action words, short sentences, short paragraphs, try to avoid too many commas, colons, semi-colons and parenthesis. Your first sentence is important in each paragraph and the rest of the paragraph should logically follow the first sentence. Try to avoid over-use of pat phrases and cliches. Of course, grammer, punctuation, spelling, typos should be carefully checked. In short, read your material several times before you send it forward. As a good exercise for yourself, force yourself to cut 25% of the words you use in everything you write. You'll find that most people tend to write too much or use three words when one or two will do.*

For oral communication, I would follow the same principles as to what you want to accomplish and the words you wish to use. You'll want to try to be crisp but remember to have the detailed knowledge. Learning to summarize is important. Other important aspects involve manner of presentation, tone of voice, when to pause, eye contact, tie-in with charts and audio-visual aids. Also, rehearse carefully.

It'll take time and effort to improve what you say and write and how you do it. You may want to tape yourself and perhaps even film a practice presentation. More and more, success as an executive will come to those who are outstanding communicators.

I am a 24 year old woman who wants to get a good managerial job. I am married and have a 2 year old child. I expect that potential employers will ask about how I can hold a full-time job with a young child and/or whether I intend to have other children. How can I handle what I consider unfair questions?

Worried

Dear Worried:

There's a reasonable body of opinion that states that questions about child care provisions or intention to have children are improper and illegal questions. I have never heard of anyone asking a male applicant for a job how he intends to take care of his children or

*whether he intends to have more children. Therefore, one can reason-
ably claim that such questions directed to women are discriminatory,
unfair and illegal. However, some interviewers will either directly or
indirectly raise the issue. An indirect approach would be, "There
may be considerable overtime, evening or weekend work, does this
give you a problem?". Or, "We need someone we can count on for
full-time, continuing employment for the next three or five years
since it's an important function and we are investing a lot in training—
can you make a commitment to our needs?".*

*You may want to attack the problem directly by volunteering that
the employer may have some concerns about the issue, but you want
to assure him that adequate provisions have been made for child care
and that you don't intend to have other children in the near future
or if you do, that if it occurs, you will be able to arrange to be back
to work with minimum interruption and that you may even be able
to do some work at home. I would suggest that you see how the
interview goes and have your responses ready if it comes up. You
may want to say, "Do you ask that of male employees?", with a
smile. But you have to judge the interview mood to determine how
you will handle it. Most employers have learned that if the individual
is a good candidate, the organization and the individual can work
things out. Employers are more accustomed than in the past to dealing with young women with children in the work force and can deal
with the problem.*

*In short, don't be defensive or too concerned. Fly under your own
colors and let the employer see that he's missing a good opportunity
if he lets the children issue stand in the way of making a good
selection.*

I am looking to change jobs, but have not filled out a resume
for many years. Can you give me some advice?

40 and anxious

Dear 40 and anxious:

*In preparing a resume, evaluate your strengths and then decide
how to present your strengths and experience in the most favorable*

light. You may wish to have a general resume and use your cover let-ter to highlight specifics geared to the particular position and/or company. Or, you may wish to have two or more resumes geared to different positions or industries. Certainly if you have the time and resources you may want to tailor make each resume you send for the particular position.

You can find very helpful information in regard to resumes in a number of standard books. They will discuss the traditional resume as well as the functional resume which highlights particular skills. Clarity of expression, succinctness, neatness, excellent typing, format, presentation and paper selection will be appropriately stressed.

Let me suggest some points that interest me as one who has read literally hundreds of resumes.

1. *The resume should be responsive to the company's position announcement—I want to focus on what you can do for me in filling the particular position—what are your skills, accomplishments, experience, education and training.*
2. *I want to get some idea of you as a person—this can come from the resume and the cover letter, not only the content, but the style and manner of presentation.*

You should do several drafts of the resume, have someone else read it for clarity, crispness, accuracy. After you have sent it out or even in your cover letter, you should indicate you will follow up. A phone call a week or two later will indicate your interest as well as providing information as to where you stand.

Take your time, plan the resume, use good language. Regard it and the cover letter as a marketing piece for yourself. And after all is said and done be prepared for a number of rejections. But if you have a good story to tell, and tell it well, you have a good chance for success.

IV

MANAGEMENT IN THE 1980s AND 1990s

The executive of the 1980s no longer faces the winds of change of the 60s to the mid 70s, but rather for now and the future he is buffeted and occasionally thrown off balance by hurricanes and typhoons of change. Some of the problems facing the executive of the next decades revolve around the effect of legislative and regulatory action taken in the last 10-15 years; other problems will result from new forces, at work in the United States and the world as well as forces as yet unidentified.

It is no wonder that executive stress, burnout, changing jobs (voluntarily or otherwise), early retirements are all current discussion topics. Thus, for today and in the foreseeable future, high level executives will be faced by internal and external challenges and problems that are wider in scope, larger in number, and deeper in terms of potential impact than in previous years.

These challenges, problems, issues, frustrations may be grouped into two broad categories: (a) external to the organization involving industry, region, country and international settings; and (b) internal or within the organization. Many of the issues have both external and internal aspects and interrelationships.

External to the organization are such factors as international competition, the world economy, governmental legislation and regulation, anti-trust activities, productivity, the public perception of business, societal trends and the nature of American life, reindustrialization of America and concern for government.

Internal to the organization are areas such as human resources management, planning for the present and the future, dealing with change, technology, commercial intelligence.

We shall discuss briefly in this overview each of the factors mentioned, beginning with the external factors.

EXTERNAL FACTORS

Competition and Productivity

The ability of the United States to compete in the world economy is a major concern to American business and the American government. It is also of major concern (or should be) to America's unions and workers because in the absence of an expanding productive, efficient economy, dislocation of people results, the worker's investment in his job is lost or undermined, and economic opportunity and mobility is lessened.

There are profound implications of unfavorable balance of trade situations continuing over long periods of time. A large continuing trade imbalance indicates in fact and/or perception an inability to compete successfully and/or to moderate our dependence upon foreign goods, raw materials, and energy sources. This affects the value of the dollar, our cost of living, our economy as a whole, our rate of inflation or recession, our employment and profits. The United States' economic weaknesses have significant impact on the economy of the entire world. Ultimately, the trade balance affects our political and military standing, respect and influence in the world with the potential of considerable risk to our national security and the security of those allied with us. The risk need not culminate in war. There can be the threat of military actions or other ways of taking advantage of an economically weakened United States, such as attacking our vital interests; seeking to change the status quo; pressing situations which cause us to back down or back off; extracting unreasonable concessions in negotiations. One or more of these actions can combine to weaken the political and military strength and independence of our country.

There has been much discussion of why United States productivity is slowing down (see other sections of this book). These changes have been attributed by the Council of Economic Advisers to:

(a) the demographic makeup of the work force—much younger workers proportionately than in the past and early retirements removing experienced workers from the labor force;

(b) decline in the growth of capital per man hour of labor—in 1948-1966 capital per man hour grew each year by 3.1%, but it was 2.8% in 1966-1973 and only 1.7% after 1973 (Economic Report of the President—Washington, D.C. 1977, pgs. 45-48);

(c) shift in labor from agriculture to industry—industry is more productive but since much of the shift from agriculture to industry has already taken place, any additional shift is slowing down;

(d) declining progress in technology—R&D has declined in real terms since 1970 and has declined over the last decade as a percentage of the gross national product.

Others would attribute declining productivity to:

(a) no new national purposes which result in technological breakthroughs as exemplified by the post Sputnik era;

(b) social legislation and expanding restriction of legislation and regulations;

(c) the impact of an unproductive and large military sector in the economy;

(d) worker discontent over the content and conditions of their work;

(e) Club of Rome-type predictions as to the limits of growth, thus indicating that continued economic growth is impossible;

(f) the absolute and relative growth of the public sector which is a relatively low productivity area.

Some countries as a result of large pools of cheap labor, or better, newer, cheaper equipment and technology, and/or aggressiveness in innovation, sales or marketing, have outproduced or outpaced us per man hour, out bid us and out sold us. Of course, some of the advantages particular industries in particular countries may have is in their access to or control over natural resources and raw materials and active support of their government for their enterprise. Further, many foreign industries do not face the considerable expense of compliance with governmental regulation as is true of United States firms and there may be considerably less governmental and public concern over types of business practices which may not be considered acceptable for Americans, i.e., bribery. The issue is not a hopeless one and one can do more than have songs that sing about "look for the union label" (though this approach does not hurt). In fact, foreign markets can be broken into and the only good news about the fall of the value of the American dollar is that it makes our goods cheaper in relation to foreign products so that sales of commodities increase as well as sales where price is a major factor (such as textiles). High technology is what the United States has been good at, but we also need the aggressive, hard sell.

The businessman should be concerned about the possible need for mini-Marshall plans for various areas of the world and the need to employ the billions of dollars that are available in pension funds, money market securities, general investment means to meet the many current investment needs of the poor nations. (We also have a significant need for investment in many areas and industries in the United States.) And, to get even more basic, don't all of us need to be concerned about who will feed, clothe, house, provide services for and employ the approximately 200,000 people added to the world's population every single day and the possibility of a 7 billion world population by the year 2000 and possible doubling of that to 14 billion in 2050.[1]

Governmental Regulation

Governmental legislation and regulation is currently a major concern of business and industry, but also in the non-profit sector, notably hospitals and education. The number of laws, rules, regulations and administrative decisions and interpretations have expanded at a geometric rate and something of a counter-revolution is at hand. Traditionally, government sought to regulate economic matters with a concern for markets, rates and obligations to serve, but in the last 10 to 15 years we see the full force of what might be called *social regulation* which deals with conditions under which production of goods and services takes place and the characteristics of manufactured products. The power this has given govenrment is immense and thus leaves open the possiblilty of abuse. A President may employ not only "jawboning" to get a company into line as he may have in the fifties or early sixties (and perhaps threaten IRS or antitrust investigations), but he now can see to it that various regulations are enforced with a vengeance. OSHA and EPA regulations to cite just two areas, can effect immense strain on any company. Every business leader today is armed with an arsenal of facts to show the costs of compliance with the deluge of governmental regulations: number of manhours spent; costs involved for professional, support, outside experts, recordkeeping, files, computer processing and time; and efforts

[1] Benton, Lewis, ed., *Management for the Future*, McGraw-Hill, New York: 1978, p. 1.

to head off further legislation or regulation. It seems as if the government has another aim, perhaps unintentional, of keeping up employment levels of attorneys, accountants, various specialists, consultants, as well as thousands of support staff, both within and outside of government, in order to be in compliance with various laws, rules, regulations, etc. And beyond the costs, one has to consider the impact of regulation on innovation, risk taking, decision making, flexibility, prices to consumer, world trade competitiveness, etc. (See Part IV, the essay on the *Impact of Governmental Regulations*).

Today and in the future, the nature, scope, interpretation and implementation of occupational safety and health matters, environmental matters, affirmative action and contract compliance, and handicapped persons regulations, as well as the more traditional areas of governmental regulation, will be of major concern to organizations.

Demographics

In the past 50 years, we have faced three significant shifts in population growth:

1. "Birth-dearth" of the Depression years where the fertility rate dropped to 2.1, close to the zero population growth level, with about 2.5 million births a year as opposed to 3 million a year.
2. The "Baby-boom" era from about 1945 to 1963. In the mid-1950s, the fertility rate increased dramatically to about 3.8 and the number of births increased to above 4 million a year.
3. The "baby bust" of the 1960s and 1970s with the fertility rate progressively falling so that it reached 1.76 in 1976, far below the population replacement level, bringing the number of births down to about 3.1 million in 1976.

The size and age distribution of the population has a major impact on society, the economy, manufacturing, life style, migration from certain areas and jobs. In terms of management in the 1980s, a very large number of well educated younger men and (increasingly) women will be on the first rung of the executive ladder while the number of experienced executives to supervise and develop them will not grow at the same pace. In the 1990s, the situation will be dramatically different with more fully qualified individuals available for upper management positions than the number of positions available. The demographics of executive availability may cause some significant changes in the next twenty years in regard to trying to attract and retain senior management with bidding wars among firms, significant differentials in pay between levels of management, greater concern for job security, etc.

In the 1980s, we will have to fact the problem that with one out of four workers having a college degree, when they reach a mid-career period in 10 years they may be overcredentialed for the position they hold. This may be occurring just as they are in or begin to approach the mid-life "career crisis" stage. Further, projected patterns of occupational demand for middle managers indicate a decline in the opportunities for advancement in a narrowing organizational hierarchy. There is likely to be great competition from the large baby-boom group of the 1950s for the limited middle management opportunities. The age 70 mandatory retirement law (and possible extensions beyond that) will also create limitations on the opportunities for advancement. Another factor will be the sizable increase of women and minorities in the labor force and managerial ranks.

It is clear that in many companies there is a tension between the outlook of the managers with their stress on productivity and profits and of the changing concern of workers from the blue collar to recent college graduates in junior management positions.

But there is another source of job tensions and that is the oversupply of college graduates. According to the Bureau of Labor Statistics, between 1974 and 1985 there will be an oversupply of about 950,000 graduates, that is, graduates will exceed the number of positions available that require degrees. What will happen is that the college graduates will move into blue collar or white collar service jobs that traditionally did not call for a college degree. In 1976 about 650,000 graduates were in blue collar jobs compared with about 28 percent of that number in 1970.

In terms of all levels of workers, we will have to deal with stereotyped thinking as well as the reality of how older workers' needs on the job, (job satisfaction, concerns, productivity, absenteeism, compensation priorities) differ from younger workers. The new mandatory retirement age of 70 in the private sector will, of course, bring changes in terms of job definitions, standards and evaluation. In a sense the need for evaluation will be good for management because it will not be emphasized only when the worker is around 65, but throughout the individual's career (not only for reasons of good personnel practice, but also to avoid age discrimination charges).

The new retirement age will also have an impact on unions in terms of their current and future membership and the demands likely to be placed on the table in regard to early retirement provisions and cost of living and other supplementary benefits for all retirees.

In regard to the greying of our work force, there are two counter-vailing pressures at work. On one hand, unions and individuals will press for better retirement plans available at an earlier age than 70— 55, 60, 62, 65—so that retired individuals in good health can enjoy life. On the other hand, there is increased understanding that activity after 65 is important to one's psychological and physical health. Whether for economic reasons (and inflation is, of course, particularly burdensome on pensioners with fixed incomes) or for psychological and physical reasons, many "retired" people are often looking for some type of part-time work.

The Public Perception of Business

American business and industry, so capable, in general, of marketing their products and services, are not terribly successful at marketing themselves as worthwhile organizations, as vital forces in American economic life and as important factors in the totality of American life. Thus business executives must strive to increase understanding and acceptance among various strata of society of: the role of business and businessmen; the competence of business leaders in terms of knowledge, skill, contributions to society; the prestige of the business profession. Business must examine and reform itself with reasonable regulation by government in regard to business ethics and practices, product safety and acknowledgement of the rights and concerns of consumers. Business naturally has a concern for maximizing profits, but many firms have a laudatory record, not often publicized, of concern for their present and former employees, customers, the community, region, state and nation.

Government Investigations

The increasingly restrictive legal theories that have developed in anti-trust, price fixing and bribery investigations are another major pressure for executives. Anti-trust investigations normally capture the headlines, but increasingly price-fixing and bribery investigations will occupy the time and resources of the large corporation. (Although it seems highly unlikely that it will happen, from time to time suggestions are made to reduce the exemptions of labor unions from anti-trust laws. On the other hand, some emerging court decisions seem to imply that "employers" do not share this "anti-trust exemption" under the National Labor Relations Act. Advocates say, subject to fierce opposition, this would reduce the effects of union monopoly—higher prices and lower output, and help reduce inflation and increase employment.)

Societal Trends

   Societal trends and the nature of American life pose a great challenge for the executive. Ours is increasingly a service and knowledge economy. And though we often moan about low American productivity growth as compared with other countries or our past history, we must recognize that in a society where most of our labor is used to provide services rather than goods, there's bound to be a declining rate of productivity growth. This comes about because: service work involves a much greater degree of labor intensity, there is difficulty in mechanizing or automating service work; there is a greater number of managers and supervisors required in a service economy; there are more white collar workers and more decentralized operations and smaller firms than in manufacturing. It is also quite difficult to measure white collar productivity.

   With a technology and productive capacity based upon knowledge rather than manual labor, we need a better educated and continually educated work force. The nature of work and workers also leads to questions of employee motivation and the human-social values of society. The work ethic still abounds, but increasingly employees at all levels are concerned about things beyond the work place and regard work as satisfying in and of itself, but also in that it provides for a better life in off hours. Thus, the idea that there's much more to life than merely dollars earned on the job, will lead increasingly to concern about job security, hassles on the job or in the work environment, and the concern for the "good life" whether it involves factors at work or outside the work place.

   Societal trends are bound to influence the types of leaders that emerge in society as a whole and in business, industry and the non-profit sector. They may well emerge from among those who are best tuned in to and able to lead a society that is likely to emphasize:

   1. The quality of life rather than the quantity of goods owned or produced.

2. Interdependence rather than independence among organizations, institutions, and political bodies.
3. A trend toward cooperation rather than competition.
4. Increased stress on participatory management and development of individuals and individual and organizational unit job satisfaction.
5. A return to recognition of work as a major way of self-actualization.
6. Concern for leisure and relaxation as valid in their own right.
7. Concern for restoring a sense of optimism about the future.
8. Striking a balance between nature and civilization's needs.

This list underscores the need for nontraditional leaders for the future. Leaders will then have to have a concern for people, high personal and business integrity, ethics and individual responsibility, more effective and efficient institutions in society (including government), the importance of national and international problems.

REINDUSTRIALIZATION OF AMERICA

At the moment, "Reindustrialization of America" is a vague concept that means different things to different people. However, it is quite concrete in terms of generating considerable income to those writing books, stories, supplements, essays and giving speeches and seminars about it.

The mounting call for revitalization of the American economy or reindustrialization of America is based upon our significant relative economic decline in the past decade. Our overall economic growth was about 2.9% per year in the 1970s as contrasted with 4.1% in the 1960s and 3.9% in the 1950s. Our manufacturing market share at home and abroad has been declining in a number of key industries. At home, autos, steel, apparel, electronic components, consumer electronics, farm machinery, textile machinery and many others have declined significantly. Abroad, there has been marked decreases, for example, in autos, aircraft, agricultural machinery, nonelectric machinery and appliances. We have hurt ourselves by cutting back on expenditures for research and development. In constant dollars, in a decade, 1979 as compared to 1969, industrial R&D expenditures only went up by 8%. Another dismal indicator, in 1978 real industrial R&D expenditures as a percentage of real gross national product was at 1.6% as compared to 2.1% in 1964. There has been a decline in the growth of technical manpower. Our rate of savings is very low as compared to our major competitors. Although our productivity is still the highest in the world, other nations are rapidly closing in. The array of distressing statistics can be enlarged, but the point is, we are in serious trouble.

It is important to understand the causes of our problem. Some of the causes are:

Government

1. Policies in regard to overregulation, with resulting increased costs and inefficiencies in organizations, hurdles in foreign trade, contradictory policies that confuse and hurt industry (e.g., The National Highway Traffic Safety Administration requires safety equipment on cars that add weight. The Transportation Department requires lighter vehicles to save fuel).
2. Governmental actions or inactions in regard to lack of industrial promotion, questionable anti-trust suits, governmental restrictions on exploration and development on public lands, governmental deficit spending policies and taxing policies.

Corporation Weaknesses and Failures

1. Failure to plan ahead and an emphasis on maximizing short-term results. The automobile industry, rubber industry and some aspects of the fast food industry are examples of failures to plan ahead or of opportunities foregone.
2. Plants that are outdated and outmoded.
3. Declining investment in research and development.
4. Failure to concentrate on foreign markets.
5. Failure to fully recognize the impact of inflation on the real meaning of corporate financial measures.
6. The zest for entrepreneurship and risk taking has decreased as we have maximized short-term results and emphasized quantitative measures.

Labor Unions

Have pushed their power and muscle to the extent of having a considerable impact on costs (and, thus, prices and inflation), and on restrictions of managerial prerogatives which has led to slowdowns in productivity and flexibility.

Society as a Whole

Society's views affect reindustrialization. These include: views on the work ethic; the need for savings; the concern for correcting inequities in society; a psychology of affluence; a belief that opportunities and economic growth had no limits and would go forever upward and onward.

Though some would shy away from the term *economic planning*, if we are indeed going to reindustrialize or revitalize the American economy, we will need to consider much greater coordinated economic planning than the United States has had. Thus, reindustrialization should involve concern for:

1. Actions in each of the areas outlined above to soften or solve the problem. This would involve a greater interaction and involvement among government, business and labor, in order to build an economic and social contract. Regulatory reform is a primary goal, but the other areas cited constitute very important needs.
2. A tax climate favorable to capital formation and investment and long-term planning and investment including concern for depreciation and investment tax credit policies.
3. Policies, governmental and corporate, that encourage and reward research and development. It is true that managers and presidents focus on short-term results because their salaries, promotions and bonuses depend on it. But evaluation systems can be built, and Board of Directors encouraged, to focus on the individual's performance in regard to long-range planning and commitments. There can be improved linkages among government, industry and universities in regard to research and development.
4. A focus on investment for the future over consumption of today which includes heavy emphasis on production of capital or producer goods rather than consumer products.
5. Easing regulations regarding obtaining venture capital.
6. Developing United States energy sources.
7. Emphasis on technological innovations, high technology, microelectronics, computer aided design and computer aided

manufacturing, information processing.

8. Increased investment in people—to upgrade skills, provide greater job satisfaction, job enrichment, provide incentives for work rather than reliance on various welfare and entitlement programs.

9. Greater concern with productivity, with emphasis on labor saving devices, technology, productivity of managers as well as workers and better, smarter management.

10. An emphasis on good, creative management, concerned with the long as well as short-term, higher standards in recruiting and in on the job performance.

THE IMPORTANCE OF COMMERCIAL INTELLIGENCE

An important part of planning for the future involves understanding the environment, particularly the increasingly competitive environment. Paying sufficient attention to "commercial intelligence" can be most helpful in providing information of importance. By commercial intelligence we don't mean bribery, theft of secrets, various types of spying or other acts that are unethical and/or illegal. Commercial intelligence involves gathering publicly available information about present and potential competitor capabilities, intentions and goals that can be useful in your company's formulation of defensive and offensive goals, objectives, strategies and tactics for short and long range planning. Good intelligence can have an impact upon prices, advertising, priorities, packaging, product response strategy, sales and marketing techniques and strategies, legal and patent problems, etc. (At the same time that you focus on intelligence, you should also focus on counter-intelligence, defending as far as possible against competitors gathering a great deal of information about your company.)

The costs of performing at least some level of commercial intelligence functions can be affordable even for small size companies. The more money spent, the more detailed the activity can be, but some things cost very little.

The following list is a preliminary check list of what can be done at relatively small cost:

1. Get feedback from field personnel about activities and views of competitors, suppliers, customers.

2. Have key officials spend some time each week or month talking with customers—this will provide valuable information about competitors.
3. Know what information is available through the Freedom of Information Act by knowing what reports your firm submits to the federal government.
4. Get as much information as you can from press releases, news and trade magazine stories, annual reports, etc.
5. Make sure your internal security and concern for secrecy is as effective as possible.
6. Buy competitors' products, break them down, analyze and evaluate them. Determine their strengths, weaknesses, cost and marketing advantages and disadvantages.

Getting into commercial intelligence need not cost very much. Some actions that can be taken are: (1) purchasing a few shares of a competitor's common stock; (2) subscribing to the *Wall Street Transcript* and *Official Gazette of the United States Patent and Trade Mark Office*; (3) subscribing to a full scale clipping service, economic newsletters and forecasting services and trade publications; (4) use of computerized information data banks such as Dow Jones News Service or the New York Times Information Bank which are available from the companies themselves, information companies, or from large university or public libraries. One might carry the above out through use of a good part-time or full-time staff trained in research or data gathering or market research. In addition, or as an alternative, an annual contract with a market research firm to provide a great deal of information and analysis can be of considerable help. Further, contacts by top corporate staff with security analysts, bond analysts, stockbrokers and economic analysts, and journalists who specialize in the particular industry can be of significant assistance.

A solid commercial intelligence operation should yield valuable information in regard to: competitors' financial statements; labor relations activities; acquisition, merger, divestiture, R&D, patent, new plant expansion and closing activities; actions against or by the company—anti-trust, stockholder, lawsuits, governmental agencies; personnel matters—compensation, turnover, top executive biographical and compensation information, numbers of staff, assignments of staff; new product announcements and possible product production and sales data; new equipment and plant announcements; advertising expenditures, etc.

Technology

Technology is a vital factor in shaping a manager's environment. Although improvements and changes in the use of the telephone, television/telephone, word processing, copying and sending information, recording and storing information, are very important, computer technology advancements will have the most profound effect. We can expect that with increasing sophistication in our knowledge of not only the hardware and software of computers, but the management of computer technology, we will move from "computer management" to "data resource management." In data resource management, the end user and the data processing or data resource center are equally accountable for the quality of the data effort and for the design of new applications. Computer hardware technology will become much less expensive, continuing the trend ever since its introduction. But purchasing effective software, having enough of the right people in the right jobs, and getting trained data system administrators will be increasing problems.

In terms of technology we can expect:

1. Magnetic bubble memory which in the next few years will enable us to store on a single chip smaller than the size of a penny, as many as 500,000 characters or 4 million bits, or about 60 times what we are now able to store on our most powerful semi-conductor chip.
2. Increasingly, a paperless office with some reduction in clerical work force and a net cost savings (more machinery/design/programming/maintenance vs. people) or approximately 10-15%. It will be a word processing world with more investment in capital costs for white collar workers. The hardware will include electronic memory typewriters, stand alone design systems, shared logic systems. The office of tomorrow will have terminals, printers, magnetic storage systems, electronic mail computers. All this will lead to increasing productivity in the white collar force which presently has a very low productivity increase rate.
3. An attempt to computerize specific technical or general knowledge individuals have gained through experience, education and training.
4. A stress on having the management information system produce management information (understand trends, spot symp-

toms, allow for timely, corrective actions before a crisis), rather than data produced more accurately and/or quickly.

5. Greater use of interactive processing at various levels of the organization and at various locations (at home, while in transit).
6. Use of the computer for: transmission in billing/invoice information; machine readable, transmission of business correspondence; employee identification; transmission of manufacturing designs; also electronic fund transfer, tax information to IRS on magnetic tape, census data on tape, etc.
7. Use of market research techniques employing "answer-back" capability on television sets that the Warner Qube system and competitiors can provide.
8. Increased ability to have electronic display of printed pages and televised, interactive long distance conferences, thus saving significant costs in travel time and expense and speeding up decision making.
9. Increased use of computers and microprocessors to: direct conveyor belts with the human voice, to transport material to a specific destination; dial telephone numbers; print records and checks.
10. Considerable progress in producing "intelligent machines," ones that can talk and listen.

Of great importance to the technology and economic health of the nation in the 1980s and 1990s will be the increased use of robots. The Robot Institute of America offers a definition of a robot as "A reprogrammable, multifunctional manipulator designed to move material, parts, tools, or specialized devices, through variable programmed motions for the performance of a variety of tasks." The robotization of American industry, now in its infant stages, owes its existence to the technology of microprocessors and the inflationary thrust in wage rates. Although capital investment costs in robots is high, typically $7,500 to $175,000 (and coming down), it can be paid for and operated at about $4.80 to $5.00 an hour. The cost of a worker in industry, with fringe benefits, ranges from $10-$20 an hour. The economics of robotization are starkly clear.

Thus, the demand for robots will increase greatly driving down present costs of robots by 50% or more. The time on the job of a robot can be approximately 95% while the average blue collar worker with lunches, coffee breaks, vacations and sick leave is at work 75% or less. (This does not include using a robot for two or three shifts versus a one shift worker.) Robots are already in use in the automobile, electronics and other industries. We can expect this use to multiply significantly in the next two decades in regard to:

1. Assembling, handling, moving, inspecting parts or materials.
2. Working in areas or handling materials too dangerous for humans or very unpleasant or fatiguing for humans—nuclear power plants, coal mines.
3. Use in medical applications—to replace limbs or assist physicians.
4. Use in military defense activities.
5. Use in space exploration.
6. Use as "white collar" assistants in laboratories, medical and technical offices and even in "administrative assistant" type operations.

While Japan is outproducing the United States in robots by about 5 to 1 (we currently have about 3,000 in operation; they have 10,000), it is expected that we will grow at about 30-40% in this decade and by the end of the decade the industry will be at a $2-$4 billion level.

In this decade we are bound to advance in constructing "smart" robots that can "see" and "touch" and thus, make decisions. They can be made to hear, to perceive infrared light and ultrasonic sound. By the end of the 1980s, we can anticipate that 15-20% of all assembly systems will use robot technology, and perhaps 50% of the work involved in small compact assembly will be done through robots. The use of robots has important ramifications for management and unions, employment figures, productivity, profits, salaries, individual workers, the number of jobs available, job satisfaction. We are on the threshold of a revolution, one that must be approached with optimism, yet care and concern for individuals.

A CONCERN FOR GOVERNMENT

Business executives have normally been concerned about governmental regulation, tax and other legislation affecting the operations of companies and industries, economic policies and programs of the President, Congress, Federal Reserve Board and other agencies. But as government gets involved in developing "industrial policies" or "economic revitalization" or "reindustrialization" policies, business will have to have a broader outlook and understanding of government and vice versa.

Some executives and middle managers may serve in the federal, state or local government for a period of time or on various government advisory committees. Executives may choose through their associations and personal contacts to lobby for ideas that are helpful to their organizations, industry and the business community as well as to the nation. Whether as individuals, company representatives or members of associations, it is important for the intelligence and energy of executives to be focused on governmental problems. Beyond vested interests, it is important to have some of the brightest and most energetic people in American Society, the executive group, analyzing and speaking out on governmental issues that affect society as a whole.

The agenda for discussion is indeed important. Some of the results of a close scrutiny of governmental policies and practices may hurt profits of a particular company or industry as well as its employees in terms of jobs available. But the issue should be what is best for America. True enough, sound managerial analysis might be vetoed by political power, expediency and the need for re-election, but it is time for executives to speak out more forcefully than they have on broad public policy issues. I believe the 1980s will see more analysis and speaking out in regard to, for example:

1. Review and evaluation of the various income transfer programs and their vast impact on the budget (currently about 49% of all federal expenditures). The programs include Social Security, veterans benefits, food stamps, child nutrition, federal pensions. These and other programs that aid the aged, infirm or children, would not need major changes aside from insuring that they are properly funded (e.g., Social Security), and administered effectively and efficiently. But programs that transfer income to those who could be working (female family heads with school age children, single individuals and male heads of household) deserve very careful scrutiny as to whether they are providing the right incentives for people to find employment. One can reasonably argue that many income transfer programs discourage job seeking.
2. Evaluation of defense strategies and costs.

3. Review governmental procurement and research policies to determine whether they add unnecessary costs.
4. Question the staffing levels in government—if we indeed decrease the number of regulations as has long been discussed, and also combine and eliminate governmental agencies and committees, significant staffing reductions should result. This review of staffing would also apply to staff in Congress and State legislatures since there has been an astronomical growth in committee staff and legislative aides in recent years.
5. Suggest that government buy more services instead of supplying them directly. Government can monitor, control, evaluate, but need not supply all that it does. The presumption is that the taxpayer would get more value for the dollar.
6. Suggest that legislatures limit themselves in writing laws to policy questions rather than to specific administrative detail. The tendency of legislatures to specify considerable administrative detail creates inefficiency in implementation and administration. Congress and State legislatures may want to consider what would happen if no new bills were introduced for the first six months of the year so that current legislation could be evaluated. It may be that legislative bodies could set goals of 50% less new legislation in the next year. Regulatory agencies might set a similar goal for the next few years.
7. Insist on basic improvements in public management regarding: how we hire, reward, evaluate, motivate, discipline, fire; the application of business management and management science techniques; the need to reduce the layers of review and re-review that exist in government, thus, delaying action and increasing staff and instead relying on individuals taking responsibility; continuing constant vigilance in regard to incompetents or those of marginal competence on the payroll; questioning civil service rules, regulations, tenure, pension and fringe benefit costs; suggesting that while fewer employees and more management systems are necessary, there may be a need to pay the highly qualified and productive more than current rates and systems allow; advocating the need for sunshine and sunset laws on regulations, programs, activities and tough evaluation of cost/effectiveness of programs and activities; suggesting concern for higher salaries for those at departmental manager, deputy assistant secretary and above levels in order to attract very capable people without forcing them to make a signifi-

cant economic sacrifice, or limiting the field to those who can afford to come into government; suggest a careful review of present conflict of interest legislation, suggest a careful review of travel expenditures, expenditures for consultants, expenditures for furniture and office decoration; suggest emphasis on merit systems and evaluating productivity.

8. Continue concern for deregulation and against logrolling, pork barrels and politically expedient programs.

9. Show concern for the level of governmental spending and whether a lid should be placed on such spending.

10. Be concerned about prevailing wage policy in regard to blue collar workers.

11. Be concerned about federal and state regulations and laws and the effects on productivity, flexibility, profits, services and paperwork. Over 1¼ billion hours a year are spent on filling out governmental forms, with almost half that amount of time by employees working in businesses and other institutions.

12. Speak out on a broad range of public policy issues such as the economy, tax policy, foreign policy, defense policy and spending, energy, environmental concerns and controls, Social Security, aid to cities, welfare, public transportation, support for research and development, incentives and assistance in foreign trade.

The list can be expanded many times. The frustrations are great, but for the good of society it is time for us to be very seriously concerned about the planning, decision making and managerial effectiveness of government. We may have to put our time, energies and income levels where our mouths are.

ADAPTING AND RESPONDING TO CHANGE

Social change is a phenomena each organization must take into account. For example, costly mistakes have resulted from failure to take into account early warnings that have led to tougher safety, liability and environmental standards. Although it is difficult to get managers away from focusing on financial plans and economic forecasts, an increasing number of companies are turning to forecasts of the future in regard to economic, social, community, technological, political, life-style and work-style factors.

Many companies, in the face of competition, will have to focus on what business are they really in or what business should they really be in and how do they change to meet competition, changing technology, changing times. The momentum toward deregulation and generally tougher competition, foreign and domestic, will force a variety of changes in how traditional companies and industries compete and do business and, in fact, face competition from non-traditional rivals.

The banking industry is an important example of an industry facing very significant changes brought about by deregulation, competition and technology. There will be major changes in the banking industry during the next decade. The forces of change will be deregulation which will bring about increased competition and financial pressures on a number of institutions, and technology already available. The most sweeping piece of financial legislation in American history is the primary cause for a whole new ballgame in banking. The Depository Institutions Deregulation and Monetary Control Act passed in March, 1980 parallels the important strides in deregulation in the transportation and energy industries. But it has even more widespread effects because of its impact on every company and individual.

Competition will increase because of the likelihood of banks being able to offer full banking services statewide and across state lines. Savings and loans institutions already offer practically all banking services (they too are becoming full service banks). But in addition to the traditional competition among banks and now between and among savings and loans and banks, there are a variety of other competitors. Securities firms like Merrill, Lynch provide checking, savings and loans services. Sears Roebuck and American Express offer bank style deposit services and loans—and these firms operate nationwide. Foreign banks are increasing their number of branches and activities. Money market funds draw off significant sums from traditional savings accounts and they offer checking services. Organizations such as Comdata Network Inc. allows a neighborhood gas station to become a 24-hour teller.

Technology through powerful computers and their terminals, toll-free long distance lines, automatic teller equipment and sophisticated equipment for banking by phone are vital aspects in forging the banking revolution.

The point is that it is no longer a banking industry that we are talking about, but a financial services industry. Bank holding companies, savings and loans institutions, credit unions, foreign banks, securities firms, insurance companies, retailers and other organizations offer several or many financial services—checking, savings, credit cards, debit cards, real estate lending and brokerage, nationwide branching, underwriting securities, insurance, investing. Banking, or better said, financial services has become one of our most competitive industries.

The big questions for traditional bankers are "What is banking?", "What business are we in?", "How can we compete with others including those not so highly regulated?"

As a result of the competition, deregulation and technology, we are likely to see in the current and next decade substantial movement toward: significantly fewer banks, absorption of smaller banks and savings and loans into larger groupings leading to huge banking conglomerates, electronic funds transfers leading to less geographic segmentation, a checkless society or no return of checks, large scale paying by telephone or over telephone lines, and large scale use of automatic tellers in a variety of locations, less market segmentation in types of services offered (although some institutions may specialize in order to differentiate themselves from the competition and thus servive), decreasing differentiation between commercial banks and thrift institutions, "one-stop, full service" banking for individuals and corporations, a wide variety of mortgage instruments available, "true cost" will lead to higher borrowing costs, but efficiency in providing money to corporate and individual borrowers and more creative loan approaches, higher interest rates for savings and checking accounts and even more competition after 1986 when all interest rate ceilings are lifted.

Internally, individual banks and conglomerates will have to focus more on their management, their services and the abilities and training of their staff. They will need to become, for example, more concerned about team effort in a bank, improved communications, long range planning, preventing burnout, enriching and enlarging jobs, job satisfaction, career opportunities for women and minorities, a marketing, entrepreneurial and innovative spirit, and an increased service orientation.

INTERNAL   FACTORS

People

James G. Affleck, Chairman, American Cyanamid Company, has said, "The future of Management is 'nonmanagement.' It will be the development and utilization of people organized to employ all of their individual creative talents to the maximum, within an environment of continuous and dynamic change. The rigid and highly structured organizational framework of the past will be replaced by a cohesive interdependence of thought and action, perhaps without conscious direction or apparent leadership as we have understood it. Management's main job will be the exercised sensitivity and an educated intuition to draw the maximum from a highly skilled and intellectually sophisticated force of managers and workers."[2]

Thus, motivation and supervision will be of major concern to the executive. The demographics indicated earlier will necessitate a concern for keeping people challenged and interested with appropriate recognition and rewards.

We shall have to understand more about ourselves as human beings and our employees at all levels, their needs, wants, desires, satisfactions and dissatisfactions.

Individuals in a corporate setting need occasional shots of adrenalin, whether as a result of their own aspirations having been reached, the wear and tear of corporate life bringing about restlessness, fatigue or being burned out, or that one's learning/growth curve has flattened either because of one's own attributes or as a result of impediments in the organization itself—size, structure, growth potential, competitive standing, staffing, etc.

To deal with this problem, both individuals and organizations will have to focus on: breadth and depth of assignments; types of assignments; scope of responsibilities; special project assignments; mobility assignments between and among staff and line functions and units and among various divisions of a company or companies within a conglomerate; ability to undertake supervisory responsibilities, staff, line, planning responsibilities; new knowledge acquired through education, training, conferences and seminars; exposure and involvement in public and community activities; speaking, teaching and writing opportunities; opportunities to serve on and lead inter and intra-departmental committees or task forces; opportunities for short or long term travel or relocation; exposure in some depth with some hands-on experience to newest techniques and technology in fields of one's primary responsibilities and interests as well as in allied fields or fields related to one's primary interest, or fields of potential responsibility for the individual.

The policy makers in an organization will have to deal with the increasing frequency of the dual career/dual income family and the impact that a desire to have an individual move to another location will have on that family. Whereas ten or more years ago a job relocation was strain enough in terms of impact on children and one's wife, now with more and more women in the labor force with increasingly more prominent and well-paid jobs, relocating the male may cause major problems in the family and in the family's income. In the future we shall have to deal with many more instances of—"I can't take the job unless my wife or husband finds an equally good job in the new location." Even without disruption of a dual career, executives are more prone now and in the future than 10 years ago to say "no thanks" to job relocation because of disruption of life style and relationships established. And, whereas "no" in the past tended to freeze or destroy one's career advancement, most companies have to be more understanding of this and willing not to block the individual's advancement. Correspondingly, and perhaps conversely, where one lives, the "sun-belt syndrome," schools, recreation, cultural facilities, leisure time opportunities, crime, cost of living, beauty of a place, may well play increasing importance in ability to attract or retain executives and staff to the area in which the organization is located.

In our concern for people and for productivity, we shall have to tackle once again the longstanding problem of absenteeism. Absenteeism costs workers and the economy over $20 billion a year in lost pay alone. Furthermore, industry spends about $10 billion a year in sick leave pay and $5 billion annually on fringe benefits that continue even though the employee is absent. According to a U.S. Bureau of Labor Statistics report, work hours lost due to absenteeism generally ranges around 3.5%. The traditional methods of discipline or bonuses have not been particularly successful in controlling absenteeism and more emphasis is now being placed, correctly, on various types of job enrichment approaches involving discussions with employees, attitude surveys, employee involvement in developing absenteeism control policies and procedures. (Lateness, an attitude of not caring, alcoholism and drug abuse are also important concerns.)

The concern for human resources has necessitated an attempt at measuring the human return on investment, the allocation of more time and resources to developing and managing compensation and performance appraisal and training and development techniques, and career planning methods. Due to failings in personnel development efforts, an individual's own shortcomings, changes in needs of an organization or because of mergers or acquisitions, good "out-placement" programs have become a more common concern. The manager has to deal with greater involvement of employees in company activities, and increased concern for improved communications.

As I hope is evident throughout this book, the concern for managing people will be of even greater importance in the next twenty years.

The Personnel function has traditionally been under attack as a function that costs money (rather than adding to profit), is overly concerned with making employees happy, is not sufficiently concerned with the operational problems of the manager and is not staffed with the most competent, creative or hardworking individuals. In recent years, the deluge of governmental regulations, OSHA, ERISA, equal opportunity, affirmative action and contract compliance and the growth in technical aspects involved in labor relations, benefits administration, training, salary surveys, etc. have given personnel experts greater prominence. But the danger in this is that Personnel can now be viewed as a "necessary evil." The human resources function, like many staff functions, has a difficult line to balance between service and control. Personnel often approves raises, promotions, reclassification, grievances, affirmative action plans, salary increases and other aspects which can put it in an adversarial role.

If the human resources function is to play the role it should (while maintaining its concern for employees) it must become more management minded in the sense of: assisting in increasing output, helping operating managers achieve their goals, helping managers make better decisions through providing research analysis and evaluation assistance, joining with others in helping the organization prepare for the future and in the proper utilization of people to attain organizational goals, formulating strategies, objectives and plans for maximizing the effectiveness, efficiency and job satisfaction of those employed by the organization at all levels.

The human resources function of the 80s and 90s should be more concerned than it has in the past with:

- employee motivation, productivity, growth and learning
- the interrelationship between people and organizational structure and climate
- managing managers and professionals and evaluating and motivating them

- relating people to organizations, particularly those who are relatively new to the work force, women, minorities, the handicapped, etc.
- placing greater emphasis on conceptualization, planning and control and knowledge of and involvement in organizational development and design and management information systems
- concern for greater participation by employees in decisions and factors influencing their work life, including use of work teams, physical aspects of the workplace and the impact of workplace design, scheduling and layout
- advising management, before decisions are made, as to possible effects of what are sometimes not considered personnel functions—major changes in systems, procedures, organization, creating a department or position, building a plant, impact of cost or reductions or plant closings, dealing with public and community relations problems, etc.

The coming years can be very important ones for executives in the human resources field and for corporations concerned with more effective human resources management. The human resources manager must demonstrate the capacity and drive to be more involved in meeting the changes and challenges of the future.

ORGANIZATIONAL CONCEPTS

It seems probable that Boards of Directors will be restructured to include more "true" outside directors who cannot be charged with even remote conflicts of interest. The directors may spend considerably more of their time (compensated appropriately) in fulfilling their Directorship function. In addition, one might consider the possibility of more organizations having an independent audit and analytic group serving as staff to the Board. Another development may be different models and combinations in regard to centralization and decentralization and more frequent shifts among organizational concepts in terms of organizing by purpose/product, function/activity, area or clientele served. The group executive concept is likely to expand as a means of providing top management direction, although in practice the concept will have to deal with role definition, impact, and how the group executive achieves recognition and reward.

Planning

Planning for the future of the enterprise is a major concern now and will become even more of a vital concern. As John Galsworthy said, "If you do not think about the future, you cannot have one." Arthur Schopenhauer put it, "Every man takes the limit of his own field of vision for the limits of the world." Peter Drucker suggests, " . . . the first job of a business manager is to convert social needs into profitable opportunities." John Dewey put it well in stating, "The brain is the organ of last resort." Herbert Simon's concept of "satisficing" has great value. In Simon's view, economic man chooses the best alternative from those available to him, while administrative man (the real-life executive) satisfices—looks for a course of action that is satisfactory or good enough.

In a *Management Review* interview published in January, 1979, Simon said "Satisficing is intended to be used in contrast to the classical economist's idea that in making decisions in business or anywhere in real life, you somehow pick, or somebody gives you, a set of alternatives from which you select the best one—maximize. The satisficing idea is that first of all, you don't have the alternatives, you've got to go out and scratch for them—and that you have mighty shaky ways of evaluating them when you do find them. So you look for alternatives until you get one from which, in terms of your experience and in terms of what you have reason to expect, you will get a reasonable result." However, the issue in the 1980s will be what is "good enough."

Thus, the executive is faced with the question of planning, not only in regard to human resources, but to all resources of the enterprise and the larger environment in which the organization must function. The executive group should be continually wrestling with what we want to be, what business are we in, where are we going, as well as long range planning and day to day decision making.

The executive must grapple with the environment, costs, results within his own organization, planning, and how such planning relates to the industry, the region, the country and when necessary, other countries. In terms of his company's product or service, concern should involve: (a) the products or services being made or offered, (b) the present and potential needs and demands of the market for the company's current products, (c) potential products or changes in needs and demands, in society now and in the future for various products and services, (d) how does technology and the company's current productive, sales, marketing and distributive capabilities impact upon the present and potential products or services, and (e) the role of competition and external forces.

Planning involves a need to manage within a framework of constant change, with changing values, pressures and perceptions. Executives will have to be evaluated as to their ability to deal with change. Some criteria might be:

1. Do they have the time and does the organization permit them to concentrate on anything except the immediate and short run problems and issues?
2. Do they have conceptual knowledge and insight to perceive future broad and specific problems facing society, the industry and the organization, motivation necessary to tackle problems whose time frame extends beyond their tenure of office or position?
3. Do they have the self-confidence, motivation, long range outlook and organization support to deal with problems, the impact, analysis and/or solution of which extends beyond their term of office?
4. Do they have the information and information system necessary to provide relevant data for problem and issue formulation, analysis, solution, feedback, monitoring and evaluating results in an effective, efficient and timely manner?
5. Does the organization's structure, procedures, processes, recognition and reward system assist them in formulating, analyzing and solving problems?

The external and internal forces briefly discussed in this chapter constitute some of the factors that make up the environment in which management today and for the next twenty years must be planned, implemented, evaluated, fine tuned, and when necessary, changed. Beyond the powers of intellect and analysis there must also be the will to deal with a vastly more complex society and, in fact, more complex individuals because of rising educational levels, job and life expectations, and societal trends.

Despite the increasing pressures and problems described here and elsewhere in this book, the manager of today and tomorrow must "dare to dream things that never were, and say, why not?"

V

CONCLUSION

We have tried to convey the concepts, issues and opportunities in management, the challenges of today and tomorrow. Throughout this discussion there has been a concern for excellence, for ethical conduct, for striving to do more and better, for creativity and intelligence, and above all, for concern about our objectives and goals and the people in the organization who work to accomplish these objectives. Organization structures and cultures can be created, in most—not just a few—organizations, that encourage people to cooperate with each other to meet organizational objectives because it is in their best interest—personal and professional—to do so. Personal cooperation and team effort in achieving organizational and individual goals is not only enriching and nourishing in a monetary sense, but also in the sense of self-esteem and satisfaction.

American business has been concerned with short-term profits and too little concerned with the future and with their employees' motivation, job satisfaction and ideas they can contribute to the profitability of the company. In general management style, we too often forget that there is more to management than numbers, computers and quantitative analysis. Professional managers have become fixated on financial analysis, but a successful manager really needs to know more than theories and applications of discounted cash flow and return on investment. The managers of today and the MBA's produced in our schools seemed to have lost or never acquired the entrepreneurial spirit, the zest for risk taking and bold decision-making. Many managers are too remote from the heart of the enterprise they manage. They are wrapped up in numbers and management information system reports rather than tuned in to the technology, markets, processes and workers.

We beat our breasts about productivity but the largest part of the blame is poor management planning, commitment and decision making. We worry about foreign competition and at times seek various protectionist defenses, but the problem is due, in part, to our lack of emphasis on how to sell abroad.

Critical observers can reasonably complain of lack of American pride of craftsmanship and quality, of a society that produces large numbers of people who expect a gratuity, promotion, bonus, large pay increase for inadequate or barely adequate performance, of a nation that has come to accept a standard of performance or production that is barely or merely satisfactory or at the most, above average. That is not enough for the world we live in! We ought to ask much more of ourselves, our organizations, our staffs, our corporate and national leaders, our nation as a whole. We seem to be running at slow motion or jogging, saving ourselves for some future event. But the future is now, we ought to be sprinting and running full out!

From a person's first day in the organization to his last, at every level, we should set high standards, assist him, provide the opportunities, resources and training, but for him and ourselves the goal should be consistent, outstanding, superb performance.

Bringing about excellence is not that difficult. It involves thought, concern and caring. A recent study by McKinsey & Co. of ten well-managed companies identified eight points that characterize their management style and culture:

1. An action orientation—don't study things to death—"do it, fix it, try it."
2. Keep things simple and lean—simple form, lean staff.
3. Emphasize the customer—stay close to him.
4. Improve productivity through people—motivate people, reward them.
5. Encourage entrepreneurship through operational autonomy.
6. Place stress on a particular business value—it could be customer relations, cost reduction, productivity, new products or whatever. The value permeates the company.
7. Do what you know best—build on your strengths, don't leave

your base of knowledge in acquiring companies or getting into new product lines.

8. Maintain simultaneously, both loose and tight controls—control some variables tightly but allow maximum looseness and flexibility in others.

As managers and executives, we are rightfully concerned about maximizing our own monetary income and that of our subordinates and all who work in the enterprise. But man lives not by bread alone. Increasingly, an important aspect of motivation, satisfaction and productivity, is psychic income—recognition, job challenge and stimulation, learning, growth, utilization of one's abilities, meeting high standards, sense of mission and accomplishment, sense of team effort. It can come about for ourselves and others as a result of organizational climate, culture and concern and the efforts of managers throughout the organization focusing on human needs and aspirations.

Management can indeed be challenging. In striving for higher organizational and personal goals and standards, and in developing, leading, motivating and working with others to reach for the top, there can be great exhilaration and joy in meeting great expectations. A well managed organization that is concerned both with outstanding results and optimum job satisfaction and growth for its staff, from a candy store to General Motors, exemplifies both the art and science of management and the results of an entrepreneurial, creative spirit.

To reach the goals set forth is indeed difficult, requiring the best we have to offer as individuals and as organizations, but it can be done. We need a renewed passion to succeed, to take chances, to make our particular organization a better, more productive, more challenging and satisfying place. We need to emphasize a performance/ self-actualization ethic which consists not only of hard work and efficiency, but also of learning, growth, pride and a concern for quality, craftsmanship and high standards of production and service.

Our credo, for the tough mission sketched might well be based on Theodore Roosevelt's statement, "To the Man in the Arena":

It is not the critic that counts nor the man who points out how the strong man stumbled or where the doer of deeds could have done them better. The credit belongs to the man who is actually in the arena: whose face is marred by dust and sweat and blood; who strives valiantly . . . ; who knows the

great enthusiasms, the great devotions, and spends himself in a
worthy cause; who, at his best, knows the triumph of high
achievement; and who, at his worst, if he fails, at least fails
while daring greatly, so that his place shall never be
with those cold and timid souls who know neither victory nor
defeat.[1]

---

[1] *The Works of Theodore Roosevelt,* National ed., vol. 13, (New York: Charles Scribner's Sons, 1926), p. 510.

APPENDIX

Important Books in Management

Ackoff, Russell L., *The Art of Problem Solving: Accompanies by Ackhoff's Fables,* New York: John Wiley, 1975.

―― and Patrick Rivett, *A Manager's Guide to Operations Research,* New York: John Wiley, 1963.

Albert, Kennth J. (ed.), *Handbook of Business Problem Solving,* New York: McGraw-Hill, 1980.

Allen, Louis A., *The Management Profession,* New York: McGraw-Hill, 1964.

Appleby, Paul H., *Big Democracy,* New York: Knopf, 1945.

――. *Policy and Administration,* Univ. of Alabama Press, Univ. of Alabama, 1949.

Appley, Lawrence, *Management in Action: The Art of Getting Things Done Through People,* New York: American Management Association, 1956.

Argyris, Chris, *Personality and Organization,* New York: Harper, 1957.

――. *Organization and Innovation,* Homewood, Ill.: Richard D. Irwin, 1965.

――. *Integrating the Individual and the Organization,* New York: John Wiley, 1964.

――. *Executive Leadership,* Hamden, Conn.: Archon Books, 1967.

――. *Management and Organizational Development,* New York: McGraw-Hill, 1971.

―― and Donald A. Schon, *Theory in Practice,* San Francisco, Calif.: Jossey Bass, 1974.

Bakke, E. Wight, *Bonds of Organization,* 2nd Ed., Hamden, Conn.: Archon Books, 1966.

Barnard, Chester L., *The Functions of the Executive*, Cambridge, Mass.: Harvard
    Univ. Press, 1938.
——. *The Nature of Leadership*, Cambridge, Mass.: Harvard Univ. Press, 1940.
Bassett, Glen A., *Management Styles in Transition*, New York: American Man-
    agement Association, 1966.
Beer, Stafford, *Cybernetics and Management*, London: English Univ. Press, Ltd.,
    1968.
Bell, Daniel, *The Coming of Post-Industrial Society: A Venture in Social Fore-
    Casting*, New York: Basic Books, 1973.
Bennis, Warren G., *Changing Organizations*, New York: McGraw-Hill, 1966.
—— and others, *Interpersonal Dynamics*, 3rd Ed., Homewood, Ill.: Dorsey Press,
    1973.
——. *The Planning of Change*, 2nd Ed., New York: Holt, Rinehart, Winston,
    1964.
—— and Philip E. Slater, *The Temporary Society*, New York: Harper & Row,
    1968.
Benson, Herbert, *The Relaxation Response*, New York: Avon, 1976.
Benton, Lewis (ed.), *Management for the Future*, New York: McGraw-Hill, 1978.
——. *Private Management and Public Policy: Reciprocal Impacts*, Lexington,
    Mass.: D. C. Heath, 1979.
Berle, Adolf A. and Gardiner C. Means, *The Modern Corporation and Private
    Property*, New York: Harcourt, Brace and World, Rev. Ed., 1968.
Berman, Eleanor, *Re-entering*, New York: Crown, 1980.
Berne, Eric, *Games People Play: The Psychology of Human Relationships*, New
    York: Grove Press, 1964.
Blake, Robert R. and Jane S. Mouton, *The Managerial Grid*, Houston, Tex.: Gulf
    Publishing, 1964.
Blau, Peter M., *The Dynamics of Bureaucracy*, Rev. Ed., Chicago, Ill.: Univ. of
    Chicago Press, 1963.
Bolles, Richard N., *The Quick Job-Hunting Map*, Berkeley, Calif.: Ten Speed
    Press, 1979.
——. *The Three Boxes of Life*, Berkeley, Calif.: Ten Speed Press, 1978.
——. *What Color Is Your Parachute*, Berkeley, Calif.: Ten Speed Press, 1978.
Boorstin, Daniel J., *The Republic of Technology: Reflections on Our Future
    Community*, New York: Harper & Row, 1978.
Bork, Robert H., *The Antitrust Paradox*, New York: Basic Books, 1978.
Brammer, Lawrence M., *The Helping Relationship: Process & Skills*, Englewood
    Cliffs, N. J.: Prentice-Hall, 1973.
Broron, Deaver, *The Enterpreneur's Guide*, New York: Macmillan, 1980.
Burger, Chester, *The Chief Executive: Realities of Corporate Leadership*, Boston,
    Mass.: CBI Publishing, 1978.
Burnham, James, *The Managerial Revolution*, New York: John Day, 1941.
Burns, James McGregor, *Leadership*, New York: Harper & Row, 1978.
Buskirk, Richard H., *Modern Management and Machiavelli*, Boston, Mass.: Cah-
    ners Books, 1974.

Cantor, Rosabeth, *Men and Women of the Corporation*, New York: Basic Books, 1976.

Carnegie, Dale, *How to Win Friends and Influence People*, New York: Pocket Books, 1975.

Carroll, Stephen T.F. and Henry L. F. Tosi, *Management By Objectives: Applications and Research*, New York: Macmillan, 1973.

Catalyst, *Marketing Yourself*, New York: G. P. Putnam, 1980.

——. *What To Do With The Rest Of Your Life*, New York: Simon and Schuster, 1980.

Chamberlain, Neil W., *The Limits of Corporate Responsibility*, New York: Basic Books, 1973.

Chambers, John C.; Mullick, Satinder K.; Smith, Donald D., *An Executive's Guide to Forecasting*, New York: John Wiley, 1974.

Chandler, Alfred D., Jr., *The Visible Hand*, Cambridge, Mass.: Belknap Press, 1977.

Churchman, C. West, *Challenge to Reason*, McGraw-Hill, 1968.

Cleveland, Harlan, *The Future Executive: A Guide for Tomorrow's Managers*, New York: Harper & Row, 1972.

Cochran, Thomas C., *Business In American Life: A History*, New York: McGraw Hill, 1972.

Cordiner, Ralph J., *New Frontiers for Professional Managers*, New York: McGraw-Hill, 1956.

Cornish, Edward, *The Study of the Future: An Introduction to the Art and Science of Understanding and Shaping Tomorrow's World*, World Future Society, 1977.

Corson, John T., *Business in the Human Society*, New York: McGraw-Hill, 1971.

Cyert, Richard M., *The Management of Nonprofit Organizations*, Lexington, Mass.: Lexington Books, D. C. Heath, 1973.

—— and James G. March, *A Behaviorial Theory of the Firm*, Englewood Cliffs, N. J.: Prentice-Hall, 1963.

Dale, Ernest, *Management: Theory and Practice*, 3rd Ed., New York: McGraw-Hill, 1973.

Dalton, Melville, *Men Who Manage*, New York: John Wiley, 1959.

Davis, Keith, *Human Behavior at Work: Organizational Behavior*, New York: McGraw-Hill, 1977.

deMarc, George, *Corporate Lives*, New York: Van Nostrand Reinhold, 1976.

Dertouzes, Michael L. and Joel Moses (eds.), *The Computer Age: A Twenty Year View*, Cambridge, Mass.: MIT Press, 1979.

Diebold, John, *Man and the Computer*, New York: Praeger, 1967.

——. *The World of the Computer*, New York: Random House, 1973.

Dimoch, Marshall, *The Executive in Action*, New York: Harper & Row, 1945.

Downs, Anthony, *Inside Bureaucracy*, New York: Little, Brown, 1967.

Dreyfack, R., *How to Delegate Effectively*, Chicago, Ill.: Dartnell, 1964.

Drucker, Peter F., *Age of Discontinuity: Guidelines to our Changing Society*, New York: Harper & Row, 1969.

——. *The Concept of the Corporation,* New York: John Day, 1972.

——. *Effective Executive,* New York: Harper & Row, 1967.

——. *Management: Tasks, Responsibilities, Practices,* New York: Harper & Row, 1974.

——. *Managing For Results,* New York: Harper & Row, 1964.

——. *Managing In Turbulent Times,* New York: Harper & Row, 1980.

——. *The Unseen Revolution,* New York: Harper & Row, 1976.

Dunlop, John T. and Walter Galinson (eds.), *Labor in the Twentieth Century,* New York: Academic Press, 1978.

——. *Business and Public Policy,* Cambridge, Mass.: Harvard Univ. Press, 1980.

Dyer, Wayne W., *Pulling Your Own Strings,* New York, Avon Books, 1978.

Emerson, Harrington, *The Twelve Principles of Efficiency,* Ann Arbor, Mich.: Univ. Microfilm, 1971.

Etzioni, Amitai, *Modern Organizations,* Englewood Cliffs, N. J.: Prentice-Hall, 1964.

Fayol, Henri, *General and Industrial Management,* Translated by Constance Stons, London: Pitman, 1949.

Fear, Richard A., *The Evaluation Interview,* New York: McGraw-Hill, 1973.

Forrester, Jay W., *Industrial Dynamics,* Cambridge, Mass.: MIT Press, 1961.

Friedman, Meyer and Ray H. Rosenman, *Type A Behavior and Your Heart,* Fawcett Books, 1974.

Friedman, Rose and Milton, *Free to Choose,* New York: Harcourt, Brace Jovonavish, 1980.

Fritschler, A. Lee and Bernard H. Ross, *Executive's Guide to Government: How Washington Works,* Englewood Cliffs, N. J.: Prentice-Hall, 1980.

Galbraith, John Kenneth, *The Affluent Society,* Boston, Mass.: Houghton Miflin, 1971.

Gantt, Henry Laurence, *Gantt on Management: Guidelines for Today's Executive,* Alex W. Rathe (ed.), New York: American Management Association and American Society of Mechanical Engineers, 1961.

Gellerman, Saul W., *Management By Motivation,* New York: American Management Association, 1968.

——. *Motivation and Productivity,* New York: American Management Association, 1963.

George, Claude S., Jr., *The History of Management Thought,* 2nd Ed., Englewood Cliffs, N. G.: Prentice Hall, 1972.

Gilbreth, Frank B. and Lillian Gilbreth *The Writings of the Gilbreths,* William R. Spriegel and Clark E. Myers (eds.), Homewood, Ill.: Richard D. Irwin, 1953.

Goldberg, Philip, *Executive Health,* New York: McGraw-Hill, 1978.

Greenwood, James W., Jr., and James W. Greenwood, *Managing Executive Stress: A System Approach,* New York: John Wiley, 1979.

Greif, Barrie S. and Preston K. Munter, *Tradeoffs: Executive, Family and Organizational Life,* New York: New American Library, 1980.

Gulick, Luther and Lyndall Fownes Urwick (eds.), *Papers on the Science of Administration*, New York: Institute of Public Administration, 1937, repr. Clifton N. J., Kelley, 1969, in Reprints of Economic Classics Sciences.

Hackman, I. Richard and Greg R. Oldham, *Work Redesign*, Reading, Mass.: Addison Wesley, 1980.

Harragan, Betty Lehan, *Games Mother Never Taught You*, New York: Warner Books, 1978.

Harris, Thomas A., *I'm OK—You're OK: A Practical Guide to Transactional Analysis*, New York: Harper & Row, 1969.

Heaton, Herbert, *Productivity in Service Organizations: Organizing for People*, New York: McGraw-Hill, 1977.

Heilbroner, Robert L., *Beyond Boom and Crash*, New York: Norton, 1978.

Henderson, Richard, *Performance Appraisal: Theory to Practice*, Englewood Cliffs, N. J.: Prentice Hall, 1980.

Hertz, David B., *New Power for Management*, New York: McGraw-Hill, 1969.

Herzberg, Frederick, Mausner, Bernard and Synderman, Barbara Black, *The Motivation to Work*, 2nd Ed., New York: John Wiley, 1959.

Hessen, Robert, *In Defense of the Corporation*, Stanford, Calif.: Hoover Institution Press, 1979.

Hollander, E. P., *Leadership Dynamics*, New York: The Free Press, 1978.

Homans, George C., *The Homan Group*, New York: Harcourt, Brace, 1950.

Howe, Robert Franklin, *Scientific Management and Labor*, Reprints of Economic Classics, Clifton, N. J.: Kelley, 1966.

Huber, George P., *Managerial Decision Making*, Chicago, Ill.: Scott, Foresman, 1980.

Hunt, J. G. and L. L. Larson (eds.), *Leadership: The Cutting Edge*, London: Southern Illinois Univ. Press, 1977.

——. *Leadership Frontiers*, Kent, Ohio: Kent State Univ. Press, 1975.

Jacoby, Neil H., *Corporate Power and Social Responsibility: A Blueprint for the Future*, New York: Macmillan, 1973.

—— and Peter Nehemkis, Richard Eells, *Bribery and Extortion in World Business*, New York: Macmillan, 1977.

James, Muriel and Dorothy Jongeward, *Born to Win: Transactional Analysis with Gestalt Experiments*, Reading, Mass: Addison-Wesley, 1976.

Jay, Antony, *Management and Machiavelli*, New York: Holt, Rinehart and Winston, 1967.

——. *Corporation Man*, New York: Random House, 1971.

Jongeward, Dorothy and Muriel James, *Winning with People: Group Exercises in Transactional Analysis*, Reading, Mass.: Addison-Wesley, 1973.

Josefowitz, Natasha, *Paths to Power: A Woman's Guide From First Job to Top Executive*, Reading, Mass.: Addison-Wesley, 1980.

Joyles, Leonard and Margaret K. Chandler, *Merging Large Systems: Organizations for the Future*, New York: Harper & Row, 1971.

Karrass, Chester Louis, *The Negotiating Game*, New York: Crowell, 1970.

Kaufman, Herbert, *The Limits of Organizational Change,* Univ. of Alabama Press, 1971.

Kepner, Charles H., and Benjamin B. Tregoe, *The Rational Manager,* New York: McGraw-Hill, 1965.

Kiev, Ari, *A Strategy for Success,* New York: Macmillan, 1977.

King, B., S. Streufert and F. Fiedler (eds.), *Managerial Control and Organizational Democracy,* New York: John Wiley, 1978.

Korda, Michael, *Power: How to Get It, How to Use It,* New York: Random House, 1975.

———. *Success,* New York: Random House, 1977.

Leavitt, Harold J., *Managerial Psychology,* Chicago, Ill.: Univ. of Chicago Press, 1972.

Leighton, Alexander, *The Governing of Men,* Philadelphia, Pa.: Saunders, 1945.

Levinson, Harry and Others, *Men, Management and Mental Health,* Cambridge, Mass.: Harvard Univ. Press, 1962.

———. *Executive Stress,* New York: Harper & Row, 1970.

Likert, Rensis, *New Patterns of Management,* New York: McGraw-Hill, 1961.

———. *The Human Organization,* New York: McGraw-Hill, 1967.

———. *New Ways of Managing Conflict,* New York: McGraw-Hill, 1976.

———. *Systems and Organizations,* Ann Arbor, Mich.: Univ. of Michigan Press, 1976.

Lilienthal, David E., *TVA: Democracy on the March,* New York: Harper, 1944.

Lindblom, Charles E., *Politics and Markets: The World's Political-Economic Systems,* New York: Basic Books, Inc., 1977.

Lippitt, Gordon L. and Edith W. Seashore, *The Leader Looks at Group Effectiveness,* Falls Church, Va.: Leadership Resources, 1972.

Lombard, George F. F. (ed.), *The Elusive Phenomena* by F. J. Roethlisberger, Cambridge, Mass.: Harvard Univ. Press, 1977.

March, J. G. and H. A. Simon, *Organizations,* New York: John Wiley, 1958.

Marrow, Alfred J., David G. Bowers and Stanley E. Seashore, *Management by Participation: Creating a Climate for Personal and Organizational Development,* New York: Harper & Row, 1967.

Maslow, Abraham Harold, *Motivation and Personality,* 2nd Ed., New York: Harper & Row, 1970.

Mason, Edward S., *The Corporation in Modern Society,* New York: Atheneum Ps., 1966.

Mayo, George Elton, *The Human Problems of an Industrial Corporation,* Boston, Mass.: Harvard Business School, 1933.

McClelland, David Clarence, John W. Atkinson; Russell A. Clark; and Edgar L. Lowell, *The Achievement Motive,* New York: Irvington, 1976.

McConkey, Dale D., *No-Nonsense Delegation,* New York: AMACOM, 1974.

McCoy, J. T., *The Management of Time,* Englewood Cliffs, N. J.: Prentice Hall, 1970.

McGregor, Douglas, *The Human Side of Enterprise,* New York: McGraw-Hill, 1960.

McLure, Charles E., Jr., *Must Corporate Income Be Taxed Twice*, Washington, D.C.: The Brookings Institution, 1979.

McSweeney, Edward, *Managing the Managers*, New York: Harper & Row, 1974.

MacKenzie, R. Alec, *The Time Trap*, New York: AMACOM, 1972.

Maier, Norman R. F., *Problem Solving & Creativity in Individuals*, Belmont, Calif.: Brooks-Cole, 1970.

———. *Psychology in Industrial Organization*, Boston, Mass.: Houghton Mifflin, 1973.

Margolis, Diane Rothbard, *The Managers: Corporate Life in America*, New York: William Morrow, 1979.

Martin, Thomas L., Jr., *Malice in Blunderland*, New York: McGraw-Hill, 1980.

Marvin, Philip, *Executive Time Management: An AMA Survey Report*, New York: AMACOM, 1980.

Meadows, Dennis L. (ed.), *Alternatives to Growth-1: A Search for Sustainable Futures*, Cambridge, Mass.: Ballinger, 1977.

Meadows, Donela and Others, *The Limits of Growth: A Report for the Club of Rome's Project on the Predicament of Mankind*, Secaucus, N.J.: Univ. Books, 1972.

Metcalf, Henry C. and Urwick L., *Dynamic Administration—The Collected Papers of Mary Parker Follet*, New York: Harper & Bros., 1941.

Miller, Elwood, *Inflation Accounting*, New York: Van Nostrand Reinhold, 1980.

Miner, John B., *The Management of Ineffective Performance*, New York: McGraw-Hill, 1963.

Mintzberg, Henry, *The Nature of Managerial Work*, New York: Harper & Row, 1973.

———. *Structuring of Organizations*, Englewood Cliffs, N.J.: Prentice-Hall, 1979.

Mooney, James D., *The Principles of Organization*, New York: Harper, 1941.

——— and A. C. Reiley, *Onward Industry*, New York: Harper, 1931.

Myers, M. Scott, *Every Employee a Manager: More Meaningful Work Through Job Enrichment*, New York: McGraw-Hill, 1970.

Nader, Ralph, *Whistle Blowing*, New York: Grossman, 1972.

Niles, Mary Cushing, *The Essence of Management*, New York: Harper, 1958.

Odiorne, George S., *Management by Objectives: A System of Managerial Leadership*, New York: Pitman, 1965.

———. *How Managers Make Things Happen*, Englewood Cliffs, N.J.: Prentice-Hall, 1961.

Ogilvy, David, *Confessions of an Advertising Man*, New York: Atheneum, 1966.

Osborn, Alex F., *Management Decisions by Objectives*, Englewood Cliffs, N.J.: Prentice-Hall, 1969.

———. *Applied Imagination: Principles and Procedures of Creative Thinking*, Rev. Ed., New York: Scribner, 1957.

Ouchi, William, *Theory Z: How American Business Can Meet the Japanese Challenge*, Reading, Mass.: Addison-Wesley, 1981.

Paluszek, John L., *Will the Corporation Survive?*, Reston, Va.: Reston, 1977.

Parkinson, D. Northcote, *Parkinson's Law*, Boston, Mass.: Houghton Mifflin, 1957.

Peter, Laurence F. and Raymond Hull, *The Peter Principle*, New York: Morrow, 1969.

Phyrr, Peter A., *Zero Base Budgeting—A Practical Management Tool for Evaluating Expenses*, New York: John Wiley, 1973.

Ramo, Simon, *Management of Innovative Technological Corporations*, New York: John Wiley, 1980.

Randall, Clarence B., *The Folklore of Management*, Boston, Mass.: Little, Brown, 1961.

Redding, William J., *Managerial Effectiveness*, New York: McGraw-Hill, 1970.

Roethlisberger, F. J., *Man-in-Organization*, Cambridge, Mass.: Harvard Univ. Press, 1968.

—— and W. Dickson, *Management and The Worker*, Cambridge, Mass.: Harvard Univ. Press, 1956.

Scheele, Adele M., *Skills for Success*, New York: William Morris, 1979.

Schultze, Charles L., *The Public Use of Private Interest*, Washington, D. C.: Brookings Institute, 1977.

Scott, William G. and David K. Hart, *Organizational America*, Boston, Mass.: Houghton Mifflin, 1979.

Seir, R. G. H., *The Master Manager*, New York: John Wiley, 1980.

Selznick, Phillip, *Leadership in Administration*, Evanston, Ill.: Row, Peterson, 1957.

Shein, Edgar H., *Organizational Psychology*, 3rd Ed., Englewood Cliffs, N. J.: Prentice-Hall, 1980.

Sheldon, Oliver, *The Philosophy of Management*, London and New York: Pitman, 1924, Reprint, 1965.

Sherman, Harvey, *It All Depends*, Univ. Of Alabama: Univ. of Alabama Press, 1966.

Simon, Herbert A., *Administrative Behavior: A Study of Decision-making Processes in Administrative Organization (2nd Ed.)*, New York: Macmillan, 1957.

——. *Models of Man*, New York: John Wiley, 1957.

——. *The New Science of Management Decision*, New York: Harper, 1960.

——. *The Shape of Automation for Men and Management*, New York: Harper & Row, 1965.

Sloan, Alfred P. Jr., *My Years with General Motors*, New York: Doubleday, 1964.

Staw, B. M. and G. R. Salancik, *New Directions in Organizational Behavior*, Chicago, Ill.: St. Clair Press, 1977.

Steiner, George A., *Top Management Planning: Studies of the Modern Corporation*, New York: Macmillan, 1969.

——. *Business and Society*, New York: Random House, 1971.

Stobaugh, Robert and Daniel Yergin, eds., *Energy Future: The Report of the Harvard Business School Energy Project*, New York, Random House, 1979.

Strunk, William S. and E. B. White, *Elements of Style,* New York: Macmillan, 1962.

Taylor, Frederick Winslow, *Scientific Management,* Reprint, Westport, Conn.: Greenwood Press, 1972.

Tead, Ordway, *The Art of Leadership,* New York: McGraw-Hill, 1935.

Thompson, David W., *The Manager: Understanding and Influencing Behavioral Change,* Chicago: Bradford Press, 1974.

Toffler, Alvin, *Future Shock,* New York: Random House, 1970.

Townsend, Robert, *Up the Organization: How to Stop the Corporation from Stifling People and Strangling Profits,* New York: Knopf, 1970.

Train, John, *The Money Masters,* New York: Harper & Row, 1980.

Urwick, Lyndall Fownes and E. F. L. Breck, *The Making of Scientific Management,* 3 Vols., London: Management Publications Trust and Pitman, 1946-48.

Urwick, Lyndall Fownes, *The Elements of Administration,* New York: Harper, 1944.

U. S. President's Committee on Administrative Management (Brownlow Committee). Report with Special Studies, Washington, D. C.: U. S. Government Printing Office, 1937.

Van de Ven, Andrew H. and Diane L. Ferry, *Measuring and Assessing Organizations,* New York: Wiley-Interscience, 1980.

Vogel, David, *Lobbying the Corporation: Citizen Challenges to Business Authority,* New York: Basic Books, 1978.

Waldo, Dwight, *The Administrative State,* New York: Ronald Press, 1948.

Walker, James W. and Harriet L. Lazer, *The End of Mandatory Retirement: Implications for Management,* New York: John Wiley, 1978.

Walton, Clarence (ed.), *The Ethics of Corporate Conduct,* Englewood Cliffs, N. J.: Prentice-Hall, 1977.

Wareham, John, *Secrets of a Corporate Headhunter,* New York: Atheneum, 1980.

Ways, Max (ed.), *The Future of Business: Global Issues in the 80's and 90's,* New York: Pergamon Press, 1979.

Webber, Ross A., *Time and Management,* New York: Van Nostrand, 1972.

Weidenbaum, Murray L., *The Future of Business Regulation: Private Action and Public Demand,* New York: AMACOM, 1979.

Wilson, James Q. (ed.), *The Politics of Regulation,* New York: Basic Books, 1980.

Wright, J. Patrick, *On a Clear Day You Can See General Motors: John Z. DeLorean's Look Inside the Automotive Giant,* Grosse-Point, Mich.: Wright Enterprises, 1979.

Whyte, William, *The Organization Man,* New York: Simon & Schuster, 1956.

Work in America: A Report of a Special Task Force for the Secretary of Health, Education and Welfare, Cambridge, Mass.: MIT Press, 1973.

Zolezwik, A., *Human Dilemmas of Leadership,* New York: Harper & Row, 1966.

The reader may gain some additional insights and value from the investment of time, thought and money in this book by making notes on the forms shown here.

I. CONCEPTS FOR SPECIAL ATTENTION

Page No.	Section/Subject/Concept	Why It Merits Special Attention

II. CONCEPTS/POINTS I CAN APPLY IMMEDIATELY, SHORT RUN, LONG RUN

Page No.	Concept	Apply-Why-Where How-When	Results: Anticipated Actual

III. CONCEPTS/POINTS I WISH TO LEARN ABOUT

Page No.	Concept	Method of Learning	Estimated		Actual	
			Start	Complete	Start	Complete

IV. CONCEPTS/POINTS I WOULD MODIFY
OR DISAGREE WITH

Page No.	Concept	My View—Why

V. APPLICATION OF MY VIEWS

Concept	Apply-Why-Where How-When	Results Anticipated Actual

VI. SPECIFIC GOALS I WOULD LIKE TO
ACCOMPLISH IN THE NEXT 1-5 YEARS

Goal	How It Will Be Accomplished Evaluation Criteria	Implementation Estimated Actual	Result

VII. REACTIONS TO I-VI FROM A LONGER TIME PERSPECTIVE

Six Months Since Completion of the Book

One Year Since Completion of the Book

Two Years Since Completion of the Book

Longer

ABOUT THE AUTHOR

Sigmund G. Ginsburg was appointed Vice President for Finance and Treasurer, University of Cincinnati, September 1, 1978. As the University's chief fiscal planning, control and investments officer, he prepares the budget, accounts for revenues and expenditures, develops the fiscal control systems and the informational base for financial planning and decision-making, coordinates the University's investments portfolio and advises the President and the Board of Trustees of the University's fiscal status. He also coordinates collective bargaining with the faculty. He is the project manager for implementation of a major computer system dealing with personnel records, affirmative action and payroll. He designed the organizational plan and supervises the Payroll and Employee Records Processing Services unit.

From 1972-78, Mr. Ginsburg was Vice President for Administration and Planning and Treasurer of Adelphi University, Garden City, New York. As the University's chief management and fiscal officer, activities reporting to him included: Budget, Controller, Computer Center, Personnel, Affirmative Action, Building and Grounds, Institutional Research and Planning, Purchasing, Financial Aid, Security, Administrative Services and Operations Auditor. He was the University's chief negotiator with unions representing the faculty, maintenance and security staffs.

Prior to joining Adelphi he served in New York City's Office of the Mayor for six years and held the position of Assistant City Administrator from 1967-1972. He was responsible for directing studies concerned with management, organization, policies and planning for the City and its major departments, and for supervising all management analysis activities and personnel in the Office of the Mayor, Office of Administration. He also created, directed and obtained foundation and City funding for the New York City Urban Fellowship Program, the first of its kind in the country. The program conducts a nationwide competition and selects twenty outstanding university students to serve full-time for an academic year at the highest levels of city government. Mr. Ginsburg received the City of New York Merit Award for 1969.

He has held positions as: a Management Analyst, Organization and Procedures Department, and Assistant Manager, Personnel Administrative Services Division, The Port Authority of New York and New Jersey; Assistant to the President, Hudson Institute; First Lieutenant, U. S. Army (awarded Army Commendation Medal); and Management Intern, Office of the Secretary of Defense.

Mr. Ginsburg attended Dartmouth College where he held a Daniel Webster National Scholarship, the highest honor bestowed by the College, and graduated in 1959, Phi Beta Kappa, magna cum laude, Colby Prize in Political Science. He was awarded fellowships for his graduate work in public administration at the London School of Economics and Political Science and at Harvard University where he received the M.P.A. degree in 1961 and held an Administration Fellowship.

He is an Adjunct Professor of Higher Education Administration in the College of Education and an Adjunct Professor of Business Administration in the College of Business Administration at the University of Cincinnati.

He was an Adjunct Associate Professor of Management in the School of Business at Adelphi from 1972-78; and Adjunct Assistant Professor of Government in the graduate division at John Jay College of City University of New York from 1970-1972; and a Lecturer in Management, graduate division, at Baruch College, City University from 1967-1970.

Mr. Ginsburg served on the City Manager's Working Review Committee for the Cincinnati 2000 Plan and on the Citizen's Advisory Committee for the Wyoming, Ohio Board of Education. In 1980, he answered listeners questions about the World of Work, on a weekly program on WGUC, the University of Cincinnati and national public radio station in Cincinnati.

He is co-author of Managing the Higher Education Enterprise, *published in 1980 by John Wiley & Sons, Inc., New York and author of more than fifty articles and chapters in books dealing with management; finance; personnel; university and public administration.*

He is Associate Director of Cicco and Associates, Inc., a national comprehensive consulting firm and has served as a consultant to the New York State Department of Education. He has delivered papers and been a guest speaker at many professional society meetings, is active in a variety of professional organizations, and served on the Editorial Board of the Public Administration Review *and as Assistant Chairman of the 1972 National Conference of the American Society for Public Administration.*

Mr. Ginsburg is married and has two children, and is a resident of Cincinnati, Ohio.

INDEX

454   *Index*